# The Complete Know and Grow Vegetables

# The Complete Know and Grow Vegetables

*J. K. A. Bleasdale, P. J. Salter, and others*

Oxford New York
OXFORD UNIVERSITY PRESS
1991

*Oxford University Press, Walton Street, Oxford* OX2 6DP

*Oxford New York Toronto*
*Delhi Bombay Calcutta Madras Karachi*
*Petaling Jaya Singapore Hong Kong Tokyo*
*Nairobi Dar es Salaam Cape Town*
*Melbourne Auckland*

*and associated companies in*
*Berlin Ibadan*



*First published, in two volumes, 1979 and 1982*
*Revised edition, in one volume, first published 1991*
*as an Oxford University Press paperback*



*British Library Cataloguing in Publication Data*

*Bleasdale, J. K. A. (John Kenneth Anthony) 1928–*
*The complete know and grow vegetables.*
*1. Gardens. Vegetables. Cultivation*
*I. Title II. Salter, P. J. (Peter John) 1928–*
*635*

*ISBN 0–19–286114–X*

*Library of Congress Cataloging in Publication Data*

*Bleasdale, J. K. A.*
*The complete know and grow vegetables / J. K. A. Bleasdale, P. J. Salter, and others.*
*p. cm.*
*Rev. and updated version of: Know & grow vegetables, 1979, and Know and grow vegetables 2, 1982. Includes index.*
*1. Vegetable gardening. 2. Vegetables. I. Salter, P. J. (Peter John) II. Bleasdale, J. K. A. Know and grow vegetables 2. III. Title.*
*635–dc20 SB322.B64 1991 90–7866*

*ISBN 0–19–286114–X*

*Typeset by Colset Private Limited*
*Printed in Great Britain by*
*Clays Ltd.*
*Bungay, Suffolk*

# Preface

All the authors of the contributions to *Know and Grow Vegetables* 1 and 2 have had the opportunity to revise their chapters in preparation for the publication of this *Complete Know and Grow Vegetables*. Some chapters have been considerably revised, notably those on 'Insect pests' and on 'Choosing a variety'; others required no revision, their information and approach having stood the test of time. The response from gardeners to *Know and Grow* 1 and 2 makes us absolutely confident that we have embodied in a readable form a great deal of the scientific information that the vegetable grower will find useful.

Gardening is often considered an art where the skills and the experience of the gardener are paramount. The master artists of the gardening world write books to describe how they create their masterpieces, but their guidance is often of limited value because it lacks the disciplined approach of science. The essence of the scientific observation is that it must be repeatable and that as a scientist you must be able to define the conditions that make it repeatable. Thus there is a very high degree of certainty that the findings in this book will work for you. However, the approach is not to give you rather dry technical instructions but rather to provide you with the understanding that will enable you to make decisions and take actions appropriate to your circumstances.

All the authors are enthusiastic gardeners as well as being scientists, so they know the context in which they want you to use their knowledge. They hope that you enjoy and benefit from the practical results presented here.

# The Contributors

The Editors, who are also contributors, are:

**Professor J. K. A. Bleasdale**, formerly Director, National Vegetable Research Station, Wellesbourne, Warwickshire, which is now part of the Institute of Horticultural Research.

**Dr P. J. Salter**, formerly Deputy Director and Head of Plant Physiology Section, National Vegetable Research Station.

The other contributors are:

**Dr R. T. Burchill,** Deputy Head of the Crop and Environment Protection Division and Head of Field Vegetables Department, Institute of Horticultural Research.

**J. W. Chowings**, Head of Vegetables and Ornamentals Department, National Institute of Agricultural Botany, Huntingdon Rd., Cambridge.

**T. J. Cleaver**, Head of Field and Glasshouse Department, Institute of Horticultural Research.

**M. J. Day**, Head of Vegetable Trials Section, National Institute of Agricultural Botany.

**Dr D. Gray**, Head of Annual Crops Department, Crop Production Division, Institute of Horticultural Research.

**Professor N. L. Innes**, Deputy Director, Scottish Crop Research Institute, formerly Head of Plant Breeding Section, National Vegetable Research Station.

**H. A. Roberts**, formerly Head of the Weeds Section, National Vegetable Research Station.

**D. A. Stone**, Soil Science and Crop Nutrition Section, Institute of Horticultural Research.

**Dr A. R. Thompson**, Head of Entomology Section in the Field Vegetables Department of the Crop and Environment Protection Division, Institute of Horticultural Research.

**Dr W. G. Tucker**, Liaison, Scientific Services, and Information Division, Institute of Horticultural Research.

**G. A. Wheatley**, formerly Head of Entomology Section, National Vegetable Research Station.

## Contents

# 1 Space to grow

Most gardeners are restricted in the area they can devote to vegetables so spacing crops to get maximum yield makes sense. The allotment holder is more fortunate, but even here getting the most from each square metre is a desirable objective because nearly all the chores and costs of vegetable growing are entirely dependent upon the area cultivated. Why dig, fertilize, weed, and water more land than is necessary to produce an adequate supply?

Most gardening books will tell you precisely the distance apart for, say, rows of onions and precisely how far apart along the row to thin the plants once they have emerged. Few of them seem to agree with each other and even fewer explain why they think their spacing is right. But in general they all tend to be overgenerous in the space given to all crops. If you want to get the best return for your efforts, research has now produced results that can help you decide the best spacing for your crops. What gardener could test fifty different spacings for a runner bean crop to find the best? Research *has* done this, and although it has been directed towards commercial requirements the results are equally useful to the gardener and they are discussed later in this chapter. Research has also established the principles of vegetable-crop spacing and has shown how to control not only the yield per unit area but also the size of the individual bulbs, roots, or hearts. For example, spacing alone can determine whether you produce a crop of small pickling onions or more normal-sized ones for casseroles and frying. Indeed, spacing is such a potent tool that it can produce new crops such as leaf-lettuce and mini-cauliflower, both of which are described later.

All gardening is fundamentally an attempt to control the

conditions under which chosen plants grow. Our control of most of the things that matter is at the best only partial – we rarely get rid of all the weeds for all of the time, or have exactly the perfect balance of soil conditions. The beauty of spacing is that we really can have precise control over it. The difficulty is that we need to know what the right spacing is before we can exercise that control. Let us start resolving the difficulty by explaining some of the principles involved.

## Populations and patterns

The population of plants is the number per unit area and the pattern, obviously enough, describes the way in which the population is arranged. Both are of vital importance and affect each other. Common sense will tell us that this is so. For example, it is obvious if we have only one cabbage plant per hectare that the pattern does not matter. As soon as we have two cabbages per hectare we can see that if we planted both of them in the same hole they would not do as well as if they were well separated. We can also see that even if the cabbages grow to a size warranting an entry in the record books the yield per hectare would be pathetic. If we gradually increased the number of cabbages on our hectare and kept them as evenly arranged as we could, the yield would at first increase completely in step with the increase in the number of cabbages. Each cabbage would be more or less the same size and that size would be the maximum that the conditions would allow. If we gradually increased the number still further, but kept them evenly arranged, each cabbage would be smaller because it would gradually have increasing competition from its neighbours. However, the yield per hectare would be greater even though the steps in the increase would no longer be as great for each extra cabbage as they were when there were only a few cabbages. As numbers increase even more the individual cabbages get even smaller and eventually a point is reached where total yield per hectare is at a maximum.

This type of response to increasing plant population happens with all crops and we know from research the populations needed for the maximum yields of most vegetables. However, it is at precisely this point that vegetables begin to differ from each other. Some crops, such as carrots, hold their maximum yield as populations are further increased. This is very convenient as it means we can have maximum yield and can control the size of the individual plants. For example, commercial growers can produce similar yields per acre of medium-sized carrots for shop sales, or of very small carrots for canning whole, simply by using higher populations for the canning crop. However, some other vegetable crops are not so obliging for, although the total amount of vegetation produced per hectare will remain at a maximum as population is increased, the yield of the part we want may begin to decline. With red-beet this decline is quite rapid, with other crops the decline still occurs but is so slight that we can accept it provided increasing the population gives us the control of size we want. An example of this is onions, where the highest populations used to produce small bulbs for pickling give slightly less than maximum yield, but if you want pickling onions this doesn't matter.

Unfortunately, it is also true that the populations giving maximum yield of some vegetable crops give individuals that are too small for normal use. Of course, people differ in the size they would consider normal or acceptable. It is precisely at this point that disagreement between spacings recommended in different gardening books arises and even more acutely between such spacing and those found by research and commercial growers to give the best yields. Most of the professional gardeners who write gardening books have decided, through the influence of shows and a natural tendency, that large is beautiful. Most commercial growers have found that the housewife thinks small is beautiful – although there are obviously limits in both directions. Onions again provide a good example in that at the populations giving maximum yield per unit area the individual bulbs are that awkward in-between size of about 32 mm. (1¼ in.) in diameter – slightly too big for pickling and needing too much peeling to be practical for stews or frying. Consequently, commercial growers use a population somewhat below that giving maximum yield in order to get a better size – mostly above 38 mm. (1½ in.) in diameter. Their loss in total yield is minimal, but if you want to take pride in producing large onions you can only do this by losing even more yield. But let us now turn to the pattern of plant arrangement and again let common sense be our guide.

The soil containing the nutrients and water our crops need is evenly distributed. The solar energy our plants are to convert into food for us is also evenly distributed, so it seems to be reasonable to expect our plants to be able to make the maximum use of these resources if they, too, are evenly distributed. Why then do we grow many crops in rows with the plants crowded within the row (Fig. 1.1) and a relatively large space between the rows? If what our common sense tells us is right, then each plant ought to be in the middle of a circle representing its space and the pattern should be one giving the minimum overlap of these circles (Fig. 1.2) with the maximum amount of the ground covered. Why don't we do this? Is our common sense nonsense? Research has shown that, for all intents and purposes, common sense is right so the mystery deepens.

To find the answer we have to go back to those school history lessons and recall Jethro Tull and Turnip Townsend from the recesses of our minds. They were agriculturalists concerned about the need to fallow land every few years to reduce the weed problem. Jethro Tull invented a seed-drill, the first, so that crops could be sown in rows rather than broadcast. He also invented a hoe pulled by a horse to travel between the rows to kill the weeds. He and others did experiments with rows of wheat 183 cm. (6 ft.) apart and compared the yield with that obtained from broadcast crops. He got better yields from the rows but, we now realize, only because he was controlling devastating weed-growth by horse-hoeing. Instead of leaving the land fallow, turnips were grown in rows for feeding to sheep and agriculture in the eighteenth and nineteenth centuries gradually moved over to row-cropping. Late in the eighteenth century vegetables were grown in market gardens on the edge of towns and the system was to grow crops in strips about 122 cm. (4 ft.) wide separated one from

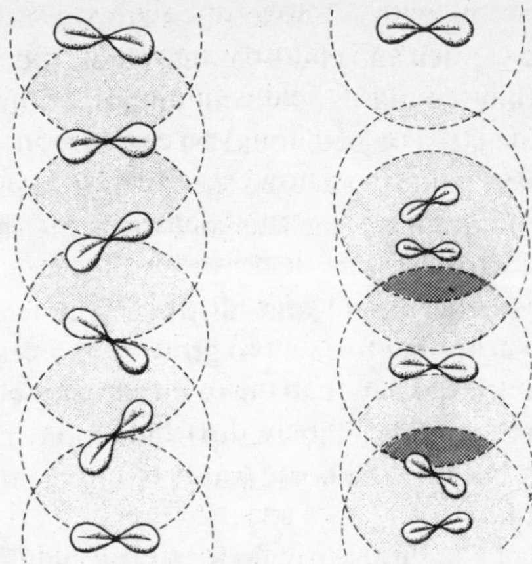

Fig. 1.1. Regularly spaced plants in a row (*left*) all suffer equally from competition represented by the shaded areas where the circles of each plant's domain overlap. When irregularly spaced the competition is also irregular and so the plants become more uneven in size. In both rows the plants are competing, but there is space between the rows not being used.

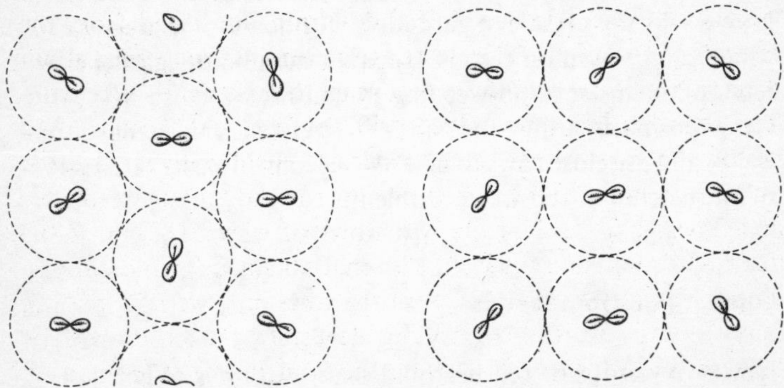

Fig. 1.2. The left-hand arrangement of plants makes fullest use of the land and reduces competition between plants to a minimum. A square arrangement (*right*) is less effective.

the other by narrow paths. The seed for crops was broadcast on these strips and women and children were employed to remove the weeds and to thin the plants to get an even distribution over the strip. The whole strip or bed could be reached from the paths.

The industrial revolution caused the towns to expand, destroying the traditional market gardens and diverting the labour for weeding into factories. The railways enabled vegetables to be brought from further afield and all these factors combined to induce the row-cropping farmers to grow vegetables. They did it in the only way they knew and so row-cropping became established as the method of vegetable-crop production. The rows were very wide apart because the horse-hoe was still the prime method of weed control.

Research has brought us full circle. In the eighteenth century the cheapness of labour made it possible to hand-weed evenly distributed vegetable crops grown in beds. In the twentieth century herbicides control the weeds and beds are again used, the 'paths' being the wheel tracks of a straddling tractor. The modern patterns of crop arrangement are as near-even within the bed as it is practicable to achieve.

Most of the potent selective-herbicides available to commercial growers are not on sale to gardeners, although some are available which can be used on certain crops. Generally, the gardener will rely on hoeing or hand-weeding to control weeds so it is sometimes sensible to adjust the pattern of plant arrangement to some extent and use close rows to make weed control easier. Let us look in more detail at the weed problem.

## Competition from weeds

If we grow crops of red-beet and onions in rows 45 cm. (18 in.) apart we can hoe between the rows and leave an undisturbed band of soil coincident with the row. Thus, between the rows will be weed-free, but within the row there will be a band of weeds. On other plots we grow the crops in an identical manner, but arrange things so that the band of undisturbed soil with the weeds is exactly the same width but is between the rows of crop. Thus, the weeds are the same in both lots of plots, they only differ in their position. On still other plots we assiduously remove all the weeds with the minimum of disturbance to the crop and whilst the weeds are very small. When we harvest the crops we find that the onions with weeds are a write-off regardless of whether the weeds were in the row or between the rows. In experiments with red-beet the relative yields for such a comparison were: weed-free 100 per cent, weeds in-the-row 78 per cent, weeds between-the-rows 64 per cent.

We learn from this that the broad leaves of red-beet can suppress weeds but that the slender tubular leaves of onions have no smothering capacity. We also find, somewhat surprisingly, that weeds nearer to a smothering crop are less damaging than those further away. This is because the nearer weeds are always under some suppressing influence, whereas those further away and between the rows had a non-suppressed start, got above the crop, and so eventually exerted a big effect on the crop rows.

Research of this kind has shown us how to use the crops themselves to help us to control the weeds. For example, if an evenly distributed crop of carrots is kept clean until it has two trueleaves (not the seed leaves but the 'true' or feathery ones), then the crop itself will smother all subsequent growth of annual weeds. Until we had persistent herbicides for commercial carrot crops the biggest problem was not weeds in the beds but weeds growing in the tractor wheelings where there was no competition from the crop.

Generalizing, we can say that crops with broad smothering type leaves can be used to suppress weeds. The essentials are as rapid and complete a shading of the soil surface as is practicable together with diligent weeding up to as near to that time as is possible.

From what has been said previously it follows that as even a distribution of the crop plants as is possible will give the quickest complete smothering of weeds and the quickest and most complete usage of all the sunlight available to the crop. However, this may only be marginally quicker than can be obtained by using fairly close rows and these do have the advantage of allowing us to remove most of the weeds by careful hoeing with a small hoe.

Onions are not going to help us to smother weeds so we may choose to lose some yield by using wider row spacings to make hoeing easier. But even here the closer the rows the better the yield.

Before going on to consider the spacing of some of the most popular vegetable crops we can summarize the principles that will guide us.

The *population* is the number of plants per unit area; ideally we will want to use the population or populations giving maximum yield, but if the individual's size is too small we may have to compromise and use a lower population. With some crops a wide range of populations give maximum yield and with these we can use population to control size without loss of yield, higher populations giving us the smaller sizes.

The *pattern* in which the plants are arranged should be as near even as possible as this ensures maximum yield and will generally help by suppressing weeds. However, some compromise is desirable to make hoeing easier, particularly if the slight unevenness of distribution has only a minimal effect on yield and the crop is one which does not have smothering foliage.

It also needs to be stated that in the later detailing of the spacing for crops, the assumption is made that the soil is fertile and that water will not be seriously limiting. Desert farming is practised successfully in many arid parts of the world and its major characteristic is the sparseness of the planting. To survive every plant must have a large area for the roots to obtain enough water (see Chapter 4). We are not interested in such extremes, although just occasionally our temperate climate can seem more like a desert. Similarly, neither are we catering for situations where the nutrient supply is so deficient that even widely spaced cabbages would give hearts no bigger than tennis balls. However, even in these extreme situations the principles governing the patterns of plant arrangement still apply. An even pattern of plant arrangement ensures the full exploitation of whatever resources of soil and situation exist.

## Transplanted crops

### Cabbage

In experiments with summer cabbage, spacing the plants 35×35 cm. (14×14 in.) gave the highest yield of small heads which were big enough for most families. Wider spacing up to 45×45 cm. (18×18 in.) did not reduce yield but gave bigger heads and slightly earlier hearting. Although this difference in spacing may seem small the closer spacing gives 65 per cent more plants than the wider one, emphasizing the need for a measuring stick when planting. It may be sensible to grow some cabbage at each of the two spacings to meet the varied demand that can exist even within a family. Few research results are available for winter or spring cabbage. With the latter, rows 30 cm. (12 in.) apart with plants 10 cm. (4 in.) apart seems likely to be effective if plants are removed for use to give a final spacing of 30×30 cm. (12×12 in.) for hearted greens. Winter cabbage are probably little different in their space requirements to summer cabbage.

### Cauliflower

A range of cauliflower types needs to be grown if the gardener is to produce throughout the year. As a general guide the later the crops are planted in the year the wider the spacing required. For the early summer cauliflower planted from pots in March, 53×53 cm. (21×21 in.) will be an adequate spacing. For late autumn-maturing types and for winter cauliflowers 68×68 cm. (27×27 in.) or even 76×76 cm. (30×30 in.) will be necessary to produce a large curd because of the mass of foliage produced by these types. With summer and autumn cauliflower, experiments have shown that the spacing for maximum yield is very dependent on water supply. If you are able to water this crop frequently, spacings from as close as 43×43 cm. (17×17 in.) will give similar total yields to wider spacings, but the closer spacing will naturally give small curds. In drier conditions, spacings from 61×61 cm. (24×24 in.) to 86×86 cm. (34×34 in.) are more suitable (see Chapter 4).

## Mini-cauliflower

If certain varieties of cauliflower are grown at very close spacings they produce high yields of miniature curds 38–89 mm. (1½–3½ in.) diameter each suitable as a portion for one person. They are ideal for home freezing, particularly as another consequence of the close spacing is that all the plants tend to produce curds which are ready for harvest within a few days of each other.

A suitable spacing is for the rows to be 23 cm. (9 in.) apart with the plants 10 cm. (4 in.) apart within the row. Ideally, this should be achieved by spaced-sowing rather than transplanting as this gives a more uniformly maturing crop. Several varieties, although not all, of the normal types of early summer cauliflower are suitable, notably No. 110, Garant, and Predominant. Some seedsmen also offer special varieties. Several sowings can be made within a year to provide a succession.

## Calabrese

Plant populations ranging from 5 to 107 per square metre (0.5 to 10 plants per square foot) all give similar yields, but quality tends to be better at higher populations. Twenty-one plants per square metre (two per square foot) will give good-quality spears with about half the yield from terminal shoots and half from side-shoots. The plants are remarkably insensitive to the pattern of arrangement up to a between-row distance of 61 cm. (24 in.). Thus, 8×61 cm. (3×24 in.), or 10×45 cm. (4×18 in.), or 15×30 cm. (6×12 in.), would all be expected to yield equally well.

Wider spacings will give larger spears with more of the yield coming from side-shoots. Very close spacings suppress side-shoots and give smaller terminal spears which tend to be all ready for harvest at the same time. This can be useful if you plan to deep-freeze some for later use.

## Brussels sprouts

Most gardeners treat sprouts as a 'cut-and-come-again' crop, picking off each plant the sprouts as they become ready. If this is what is wanted then a spacing of 91×91 cm. (36×36 in.) is as productive as closer spacings, especially if the aim is to allow the individual sprouts to reach full size before they are picked. This wide spacing is also desirable to allow access for picking.

An alternative approach is to adopt the method used by commercial growers to produce sprouts for freezing. This involves a closer spacing of 50×50 cm. (20×20 in.), removal of the top growing-point and small leaves of the plant when the biggest sprouts are about the size of your little fingernail, and a single harvest taken when the very bottom sprouts are just past their best. This will give you a bulk supply of small sprouts suitable for home freezing and it can be a good tactic where pigeons are expected to eat most of the standing crop in the winter.

### Lettuce

The normal 'butterhead' type of lettuce grown during the summer months is adequately spaced at 30×30 cm. (12×12 in.). Lettuce are almost the perfectly circular crop, corresponding very closely to Fig. 1.2. Some economy of space can be made by a triangular rather than a square pattern of planting. Circles of diameter 30 cm. fit into this pattern if the plants are 30 cm. (12 in.) apart in rows 27 cm. (10½ in.) apart. This pattern of planting is particularly valuable for frame or cloche crops which can be grown as close as 23×20 cm. (9×8 in.) on a triangular pattern.

### Leaf lettuce

This term is generally used to describe lettuce of the Salad Bowl type that never form true hearts, but you can obtain a supply of leaves from normal varieties. These are transformed by growing them at such close spacing that they do not heart and all they produce are leaves. The spacings are so close that the crop is not transplanted, but it is included here with conventional transplanted lettuce for continuity and completeness.

Research has shown that the most suitable varieties are certain cos types, notably Paris White Cos, Lobjoits Cos, and

Valmaine. Other types and varieties can be bitter at the early stage of growth at which this crop is harvested. Seed is sown in rows 13 cm. (5 in.) apart (if you adopt a bed-system it is easier to sow rows across the bed) with the aim of getting 12–15 plants per 30 cm. (12 in.) of row. In mid-season the crop is ready for harvest in 40 days from sowing as compared with 60 days for conventional crops. Early in the season the corresponding figures are 50 and 80 days. After cutting the stumps will regrow to produce a second crop. The equivalent of four or five normal hearted lettuce per week from mid-May to mid-October can be obtained from as little as 4–5 square metres (5–6 square yards) of garden by following the sowing sequence shown in Fig. 1.3. Slightly less than one square metre should be sown on each of ten dates. For the later sowings ground cleared from earlier sowings can be re-used.

Freshly harvested, these leaves are very enjoyable although those who like the crisp heart of conventional lettuce may be disappointed.

## Celery

No spacing experiments have been carried out with trench celery as with this crop the area needed for the trench dominates the crop spacing. Self-blanching celery, the sort grown above ground without earthing-up, has been studied and to produce sticks you will need approximately 760 square cm. (120 square in.) per plant. This can be 30×25 cm. (12×10 in.) or even 33×23 cm. (13×9 in.) or, best of all, 28×28 cm. (11×11 in.). How can we be so precise? If the spacing is wider than this, blanching of the sticks does not occur. Indeed, to get good self-blanching at this spacing you will need high soil-fertility and plenty of water. But if you get everything right so that you obtain rapid growth to give you succulent celery, then it will be a good size and well blanched at 760 square cm. per plant. One can almost say that if you can't produce the conditions that make this spacing precisely right, then you won't be able to grow good celery.

Of course, you can plant closer and you will get higher yields

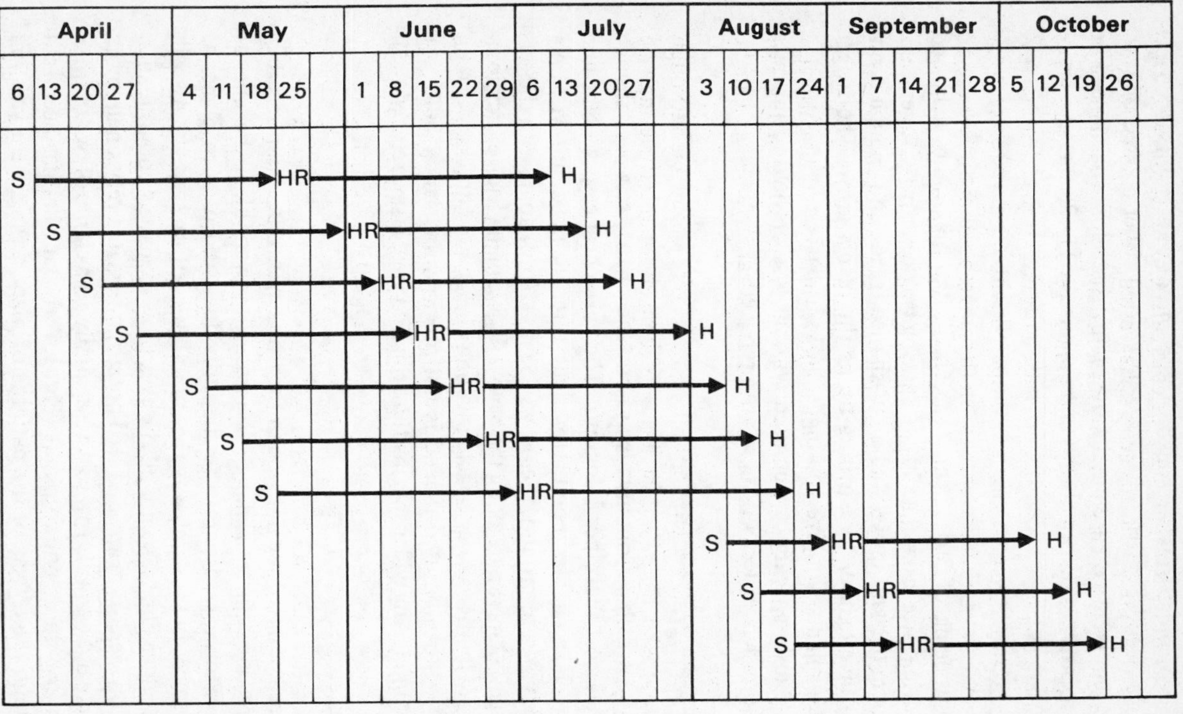


Fig. 1.3. A programme to produce a continuous supply of leaf lettuce.

but of much smaller sticks. A spacing of 15×15 cm. (6×6 in.) gives slender hearts which are very good either cooked or raw. However, if you are buying the plants such close spacing can be expensive. You can always compromise at 23×23 cm. (9×9 in.)!

### Leeks

A spacing of 30×15 cm. (12×6in.) gives maximum yield and normal-size leeks. The 30 cm. spacing between rows gives enough room to plant into a shallow V-shaped trench and enough room to invert the V by earthing up as the plants grow. The bigger transplants will give you bigger leeks at harvest.

Closer spacing can be used without loss of yield to produce more slender leeks if these are preferred.

### Onion sets

As a sensible economy always buy the smaller sets even though they cost more per kilogram. They are cheaper per plant and much less liable to bolt. If you are after the maximum yield per unit area of ground, then rows 25 cm. (10 in.) apart with the sets 5 cm. (2 in.) apart along the rows will give high yields of medium-sized bulbs. Wider spacings along the row up to, say, 10 cm. (4 in.) can be used if land is not precious and larger bulbs are wanted. Any wider spacing than this and yield is severely reduced.

### Potatoes

Seed potatoes are not seed in the true sense. Like onion sets they are dormant transplants. We can, however, liken the bud or 'eye' on a seed potato to the individual seed of such plants as lettuce. In the same way that not all the lettuce seed we sow will produce plants, so not all the eyes grow to give us potato plants. However, from any one seed potato, unless it is very small, more than one eye will grow so we essentially get a clump of two or three or even more potato plants (Fig. 1.4). From what has been said about the effects of the patterns of plant arrangement you will already be alarmed at the prospects of such an uneven pattern of arrangement arising from the clumping.

The effects of this clumping are twofold. It reduces yield somewhat, and it means that a lot of potatoes are crowded together in the soil as the new crop grows. It can be shown that this produces such congestion that some tubers are forced to the surface – they don't grow there, they are forced there by their own growth and that of other tubers.

We can reduce clumping and this overcrowding by using small seed potatoes. If we used very small seed each weighing about 10 g. (⅓ oz.) they will not produce many stems or many tubers each. But if they are planted evenly and moderately closely spaced they will produce a high yield, they will not need any earthing-up at all, and the whole crop can be grown on-the-flat by planting the small seed 10 cm. (4 in.) deep.

Why should moderately close spacing be essential? The answer to this lies in the fact that potato plants behave exactly like all the

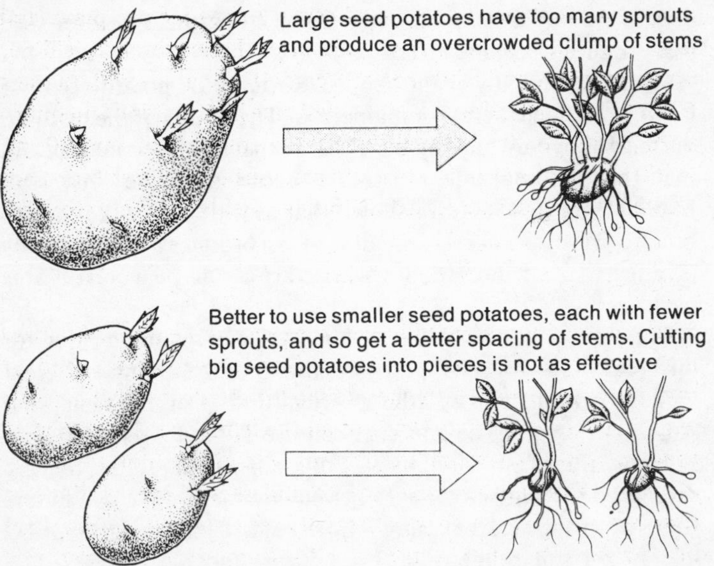


Fig. 1.4. Large seed potatoes give clumps of stems reducing yield.

other plants we have discussed so far. The more space you give them the bigger they get – or, in the case of potatoes, the more space you give a clump the more tubers and the bigger tubers you will harvest per clump. Thus, wide spacing will, even when small seed is used, lead to an overcrowding of the tubers in the ground and some will be forced to the surface and become green in the light.

So far we have arrived at two reasons for using small seed: first, to reduce clumping, and second, to reduce greening. Both these objectives could be achieved by cutting large seed into planting pieces, but this should only be done if you cannot obtain small seed. Those of you who are mathematically inclined will see why, once it is appreciated that the number of eyes on a potato is directly proportional to its surface area and not to its weight. Thus, if we have two tubers one weighing 28 g. (1 oz.) and the other 56 g. (2 oz.) the larger one will have fewer than twice as many eyes as the smaller one. Weight for weight, and remember seed potatoes are sold by weight, we get more of what we want, eyes, if we buy small seed. No amount of cutting of larger seed can produce the same effect.

Farmers generally plant about 2.5 tonnes of potato seed per hectare (1 ton per acre) for maincrops. The results of the research outlined above are making them realize that this is too inexact and that the planting rate must take account of the seed size. Experimental results have shown that as little as 0.75 tonne per hectare (6 cwt. per acre) of small seed can produce a crop virtually identical to one from 5 tonnes per hectare (2 tons per acre) of large seed.

The farmer has available to him tables of planting rates for different sizes of seed potatoes for each of many different varieties produced by the Agricultural Development and Advisory Service. The gardener can use Table 1.1 as a guide or can work things out for himself. For maincrop plantings, the aim should be to plant 20–30 eyes per square metre (2–3 per square foot) of cropped area using whole seed. This will give 21–32 'plants' per square metre (2–3 per square foot).

Early potato crops introduce another dimension and that is the

**Table 1.1**

**A guide to the within-row spacing of potatoes as determined by the size of seed when grown in 76 cm. (30 in.) rows**

| **Seed size:** | **Large** | | **Medium** | **Small** | **Very small** |
|---|---|---|---|---|---|
| Number per 10 kg. | under 120 | | 120–160 | 160–200 | over 200 |
| (Number per 14 lb.) | (under 75) | | (75–100) | (100–125) | (over 125) |
| 'King Edward' | 43 cm. | (17 in.) | 38 (15) | 36 (14) | 30 (12) |
| 'Maris Piper' | 43 | (17) | 38 (15) | 30 (12) | 30 (12) |
| 'Pentland Dell' | 41 | (61) | 30 (12) | 28 (11) | 23 (9) |
| 'Pentland Crown' | 30 | (12) | 28 (11) | 25 (10) | 20 (8) |
| 'Pentland Ivory' | 28 | (11) | 25 (10) | 23 (9) | 20 (8) |
| 'Majestic' | 28 | (11) | 25 (10) | 20 (8) | 20 (8) |
| 'Desirée' | 28 | (11) | 25 (10) | 20 (8) | 18 (7) |

importance of the food reserves in the seed potato for the early growth and yield of the crop. These reserves are also important as an aid to recovery from frost. If the early growth is cut back by frost it is vital that there are adequate reserves for re-growth. The dilemma of wanting a minimum of clumping and a maximum of reserves is resolved by using relatively large seed-tubers which have been stored in conditions that give only one or two sprouts from the 'rose' end of each seed (Fig. 1.5). To do this you have to buy the seed potatoes as early as possible—preferably in September or October—and keep them somewhere warm, about 18 °C (65 °F), until you can see the eyes at the rose-end breaking into growth. The tubers should then be stored cool, around 7 °C (45 °F), until near planting time when warmth and light are used to forward the sprout. The early sprouting of the rose-end eye suppresses the sprouting of the other eyes on the seed-tuber and so gives us what we need for early crops—large reserves and few sprouts.

Of course, it won't be as good if you have many sprouts and reduce them to only one or two by rubbing the others off at planting. If you do this this you will have already dissipated some of the reserves by producing unwanted sprouts. Still, it is better than planting with a lot of sprouts on the seed-tuber.

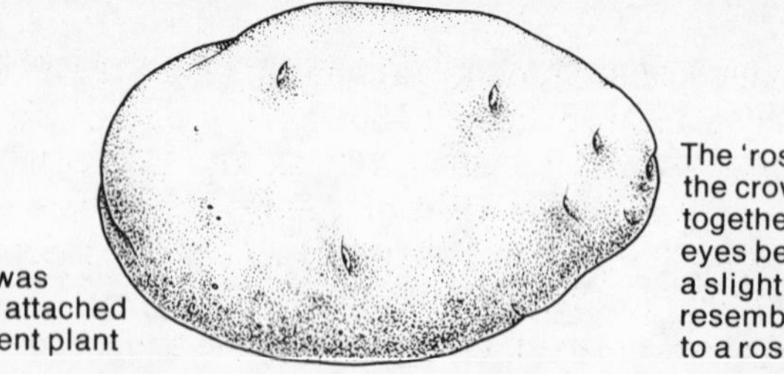


Fig. 1.5. The eyes at the 'rose' end of seed potatoes can be started into growth soon after harvest. If they are then held in cool conditions until put to sprout in the spring, only one or two eyes will produce shoots. This is what is needed for early production. If all sprouting is delayed until the spring more eyes will sprout and this is what is needed when small seed potatoes are used for maincrops.

Having got large but sparsely sprouted seed it can be planted to give much the same *plant* spacing as for maincrops. Namely, 21–32 main-stems per square metre (2–3 per square foot) as counted shortly after the stems come up through the soil. This will mean planting 32–43 sprouts per square metre (3–4 per square foot) as not all sprouts manage to emerge.

Incidentally, with the maincrop seed we want to get as many eyes to grow as possible so the pre-planting treatment is different from that for early seed. Maincrop seed should be stored cool, between 7 and 10 °C (45 and 50 °F) until early spring. You will then find many of the lower eyes as well as those at the rose-end will break into growth.

If you try growing potatoes on the flat you can be really lazy and plant them as you dig. If when they are just through you cover the shoot with plant pots, then a quick spray with a paraquat/diquat mixture (Weedol) will see off the young weeds and by the time the next crop of weeds comes through you will have a good smothering canopy of potato leaves. Of course, you must not forget the other advice in this book about the nutrient and water needs of the crop, and this 'lazy' method of culture is less good on heavy soils. These are best dug in the autumn as then the winter's frosts can help you to produce a good tilth.

## Shallots

Each shallot planted produces a clump of plants. To avoid having too many plants per clump it is better to use sets each weighing about 10 g. (⅓ oz.) (i.e. about 100 per kilo (50 per lb.)). These will give the maximum yield of good-sized shallots given 300 square cm. (48 square in.) of space each. This can conveniently be 15×20 cm. (6×8 in.) or 10×30 cm. (4×12 in.).

If larger sets are used, say of a size giving about 45 per kilo (20 per lb.), then it is better to use a wider spacing of about 15×30 cm. (6×12 in.), otherwise bulb-size at harvest will be reduced. The total yield will be similar to that obtained with the smaller sets which are, therefore, always to be preferred, especially as they are also less prone to bolting.

## Tomatoes

Detailed experiments have shown that when evenly distributed 'on-the-square' outdoor tomato plants each need about ¼ square metre (approximately 2½ square ft.). One of the main advantages of these close spacings is the increase in early yield that is obtained. For example, ½ square metre (5 square ft.) per plant gave only half the early yield of plants with ¼ square metre (2½ square ft.) each, but there was relatively little difference in total yield at the end of the season when a larger-growing, more vigorous variety was used.

Thus, as a general guide, outdoor bush-types such as Amateur or Sleaford Abundance should be planted 48×48 cm. (19×19 in.). If planted in 122 cm. (4 ft.) wide beds, then two rows per bed spaced 38 cm. (15 in.) from the paths and with the plants 38 cm. apart gives convenient arrangement of the required population. This spacing is also suitable for staked varieties, such as Moneymaker.

Plants can be expensive, so it is tempting to use wide spacing. However, it must be remembered that your early yield, obtained when tomatoes are relatively expensive, will be greater with the closer planting and your end-of-season glut correspondingly less. If you have a cold frame you can, with the new techniques described in Chapter 2, easily grow your own transplants.

## Crops grown from seed

Most of the spacings for these crops will involve using rows closer than those you may consider normal. If you use a bed-system as described earlier you will find it easier to use a small hoe between the close rows if you run the rows across the beds rather than along them. A commercial grower runs his rows along the beds which are straddled by his tractor, but this is the only way he can do it. He would also use a tractor-drawn hoe if for any reason his herbicides failed to work. So don't be put off if a 'professional' tells you you've got your rows running the wrong way.

### Carrots

This is the crop on which many of the principles of crop spacing already described were first established. The more recent research has revealed another important and probably general principle. Simply stated, this reveals that *allocating* each plant an even amount of circular space is not enough to ensure an even-sized crop of roots. This is because those plants which emerge first remain ahead of others and, as it were, 'take' more space than they are entitled to. Consequently, they are bigger than they should be on the basis of the area they occupy, and their neighbours are smaller.

Thus, it has become important to get a rapid and even emergence of the seed in order to improve crop uniformity (see Chapter 2). Precise mathematical relationships describing the effects of spacing and the time-spread of emergence have been developed and are being used on behalf of commercial growers who, for example, aim to produce high proportions of their crops in the limited size-ranges required for canning whole or for pre-packing.

In the garden such sophistication is not warranted, but it is important to realize that if you are growing populations which will give maximum yield, quite a *number* of the plants (sometimes as many as 20 per cent) will be too small to use. Their total weight will be small and all the spacings referred to in this chapter take account of this and are those which give maximum usable yield even though some of the total yield will be unusable. Gardeners seem to abhor this seeming waste and this is one of the reasons why gardening books tend to recommend wider spacings than those described in this chapter. These wider spacings give few or no waste plants, but they also give lower usable yields. Commercial growers have no such illusions.

Carrots can be sown from February to July and can be harvested as soon as the roots are big enough to eat. Thus, if the objective is to produce medium-sized carrots they can always be obtained by allowing sufficient time to reach that size and then harvesting them. If the time available is short, as when early crops are wanted or when the land cleared from early potatoes is re-used, then competition between the plants must be minimal to get the most rapid growth of the individual plants. In these situations low populations, 54–75 plants per square metre (5–7 per square foot) are used. The yields obtained will be low, but this is acceptable in view of the short-term nature of the crop.

Higher yields are obtained by allowing a longer period for growth, and for maximum yields February/March sowings are harvested from November onwards. However, such long-term crops are generally of poorer quality, particularly in their shape and skin, than crops sown in early May for harvest from November onwards. For such crops populations of 160–215 plants per square metre (15–20 per square foot) will give the highest yields of medium-sized carrots.

In the garden both short-term and long-term crops should be sown in rows no more than 15 cm. (6 in.) apart. For a reminder on how to use the crop to help you to control the weeds, I refer you back to the part of this chapter on 'Competition from weeds'.

The best place to store carrots for winter and spring use is in the ground where they are grown. They must be protected from frost and this can be done by piling autumn leaves on to them. It is as well to put some slug bait down under the leaves and to be sure to have a settled depth of at least 23 cm. (9 in.) of leaves. Straw 30 cm. (1 ft.) deep is an effective alternative.

## Parsnips

The maximum yield of roots of the larger-rooted varieties such as Offenham is likely to be obtained with 32 plants per square metre (3 per square foot). Somewhat higher populations will give slightly lower total yields. With smaller-rooted varieties, such as the canker-resistant Avonresister, the maximum yield of roots is obtained at 64–75 plants per square metre (6–7 per square foot) but at this population the roots will be small at around 38–50 mm. (1½–2 in.) crown diameter. This size is becoming more favoured by housewives and can also be obtained with the larger-rooted varieties by growing them at 64–75 plants per square metre. If you want most of the roots to be more than 5 cm. in crown diameter the population should not exceed 21 plants per square metre (2 per square foot). It should be noted that Avonresister should only be grown at this population if you expect to be troubled with canker. At this lower population it will yield 25 per cent less than the larger-rooted varieties because of its inherently smaller root-size.

Experimental results indicate that provided the ratio of the between-row spacing to the within-row spacing (the rectangularity) does not exceed 2½:1, yield is not reduced. Thus, for 21 plants per square metre (2 per square foot) the maximum row spacing would be 34 cm. (13.4 in.) with the plants 13.5 cm. (5.5 in.) apart in the row – 30×15 cm. (12×6 in.) giving a rectangularity of two may seem simpler. For 64 plants per square metre (6 per square foot) rows 19 cm. (7½ in.) apart with the plants 8 cm. (3 in.) apart would be suitable.

## Red-beet

With early crops of the Detroit type of red-beet the objective is to minimize competition as much as is consistent with getting a reasonable yield. This is achieved by establishing 54 plants per square metre (5 per square foot) in rows no wider than 18 cm. (7 in.) apart. The within-row spacing can easily be calculated because in each square foot there will be 144÷7=20.6 in. of row. There are to be 5 plants in this length of row so they must be 20.6÷5=4.1 in. apart, so we would aim at a 4 in. spacing in rows 7 in. apart for early beet. For the longer-term maincrop up to 161 and not less than 107 plants per square metre (15 to 10 per square foot) will give the maximum yield of medium-sized roots if the rows are no wider than 30 cm. (12 in.) apart. If you want to produce small beet for pickling whole, don't be tempted to use more than 215 plants per square metre (20 per square foot). Red-beet is one of those crops where total yield is very much depressed at high populations and even at 215 plants per square metre you will lose some yield.

### Onions

We have already dealt with onions from sets under 'Transplanted crops'. Onions from seed may be sown in the early spring or in August provided these latter are of overwintering varieties. The sowing date is critical for the overwintered crop and rapid emergence is also vital. Crops in the north of Britain must be sown no later than the first week in August, whereas those in the south should be delayed until the middle of the month. The reason this is so critical is that if the plants are too small when the winter starts many will be killed and if they are too big many of them will go to seed rather than form bulbs. We have already learnt that spacing also affects plant size so it will be evident that overcrowding of the August-sown crop could reduce plant size and so reduce the chances of winter survival.

The aim should be to have in the spring 65–86 plants per square metre (6–8 per square foot) in rows no more than 30 cm. (12 in.) apart. To allow for some winter losses it is as well to establish 108 plants per square metre (10 per square foot) in the autumn, using any spring thinnings for salads.

The best population for the spring-sown crop is 86 plants per square metre (8 per square foot), again the rows not being wider than 30 cm. (12 in.), and there are some indications that 23 cm. (9 in.) is better. This population will give bulbs mostly more than 38 mm. (1½ in.) in diameter, but there will be a few smaller ones of pickling size. The population giving the maximum yield of onions varies somewhat depending upon the variety but is about 215 plants per square metre (20 per square foot). However, the onions would be too small for normal purposes and somewhat too big for pickling. If you want to grow small onions there is little loss in total yield if the population is increased to 376 plants per square metre (35 per square foot) and this will give you a much better size for pickling.

### Salad onions

Commercially the variety White Lisbon and selections from it are most widely used for the salad crop. Using this variety, experiments have shown that both for the overwintered and summer crops 323 plants per square metre (30 per square foot) in rows 10 cm. (4 in.) apart or in 8 cm. (3 in.) wide bands with 30 cm. (12 in.) between centres gives the best yields. Sowing a band rather than a single row has also been applied commercially to other crops, notably carrots. The aim is to reduce the effects of overcrowding within the row by spreading the row from a single line to a broader strip. It works well, but it can increase the chore of weeding when, as is usually the case with gardeners, herbicides are not used.

### French beans

All the research on the spacing of this crop has been concerned with commercial crops grown for freezing. Such crops are grown to be harvested by machine on one occasion only. In the garden, pods are picked when they are ready and several harvests are made over a period. It seems probable that this difference in harvesting technique will affect the spacing that should be used.

The research for commercial crops has shown that 32–43 plants per square metre (3–4 per square foot) can be expected to give the maximum yield and that an even pattern of plant arrangement is an advantage. Access for hand-picking will, however, tend to dictate using rows about 45 cm. (18 in.) apart. Thus it would seem that the plants should be 5 cm. (2 in.) apart in the row. Certainly they should be no closer than this and it seems that if they are more than 10 cm. (4 in.) apart yield will be lost.

## Runner beans

This is one of the most popular garden crops and research results are available to guide us on its best spacing. In these experiments the crop was supported on canes arranged as in Fig. 1.6, and the following combinations of path width and row width (*a* and *b*, respectively, in the Figure) were tested 91 cm. (3 ft.) and 30 cm. (1 ft.), 91 cm. (3 ft.) and 61 cm. (2 ft.), 122 cm. (4 ft.) and 30 cm. (1 ft.), 122 cm (4 ft.) and 61 cm (2 ft.), and 152 cm. (5 ft.) and 30 cm (1 ft.). At each of these combinations the within-row spacing of canes (*c* in the Figure) used were 15, 30, 45, 61, and 76 cm. (6, 12, 18, 24, and 30 in. respectively). Each of these cane arrangements was studied with either one or two plants growing up each cane. This gave a range of plant populations of from 1.4 to 21 plants per square metre (0.13 to 2.0 per square foot) of field and picking was done every three to four days from early August to mid-October.

The results were startling. As population increased from 0.13 to 2.0 plants per square foot yield increased from 2.2 to 5 kilos per square metre (4 to over 9 lb. per square yard). It was also clear that the more even the plant arrangement the higher was the yield. For example, averaged over the within-row spacing 91 cm. (3 ft.) paths with a 61 cm. (2 ft.) twin-row gave a 12 per cent higher yield than a 122 cm. (4 ft.) path and a 30 cm. (1 ft.) twin-row. Further, two plants at each cane gave lower yields than the same population spaced as single plants at each cane, the differences ranging from about 10 per cent at high populations to 20 per cent at lower populations.

High populations delayed the first pick by about three days and the date by which half the eventual crop was picked by up to six days. These effects are very small as compared with the large effects on total yield. No effect on quality was observed.

Commercially an overriding factor governing the conclusions from this work was the cost of the canes and their erection. When

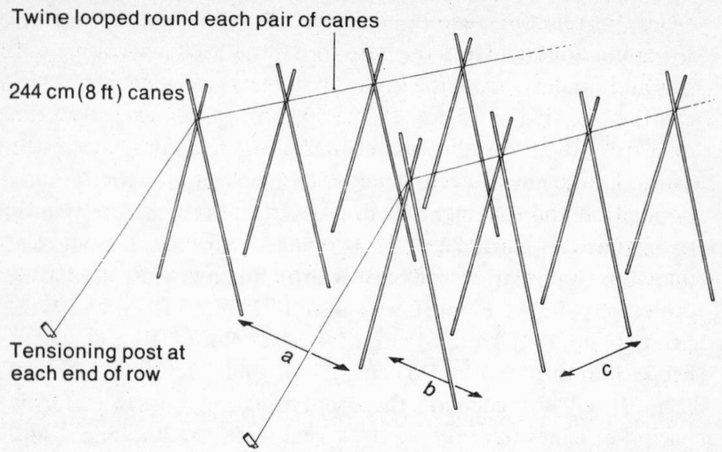


Fig. 1.6. A diagram of the cane system used to support the runner beans grown in the experiments described. ($a$ = path width, $b$ = twin-row spacing, $c$ = within-row spacing.)

this was taken into account the spacing giving maximum profit per unit area was a 91 cm. (3 ft.) path, with twin-rows 61 cm. (2 ft.) apart and canes 30 cm. (12 in.) apart within the row with 2 plants at each cane, giving a population of 10.7 plant per square metre (1.0 per square foot).

In the garden it is unusual to grow more than one twin-row so the path width is somewhat irrelevant. If a system of using 122 cm. (4 ft.) beds with 30 cm. (1 ft.) paths is adopted for the vegetable garden it seems evident that one bed would be devoted to beans using a twin-row spacing of 61 cm. (2 ft.) with each row set in 30 cm. (1 ft.) from the edge of the bed. As canes are expensive some economy can be achieved by using a mixture of canes and strong string. It is more convenient in the garden to use canes to provide a rigid cross member rather than the tensioned wire shown in Fig. 1.6. If 244 cm. (8 ft.) canes are used for this purpose and the row is longer than 8 ft. the canes should be overlapped by at least 45 cm. (18 in.) and lashed together. Each pair of canes must be lashed to the cross member. The within-row canes, for economy, can be spaced at 61 cm. (2 ft.) intervals with string horizontally from the base to base of each cane along each row and similarly from the tip to tip of each cane. Vertical strings can then be tied at 15 cm. (6 in.) spacings along each row running from the top to bottom strings along the same lines as the canes. One plant at each string and cane will give the required population and spacing. It is important to keep on top with the picking as this encourages the production of more pods and so increases total yield. It also ensures you get fewer old and stringy pods.

### Broad beans

Research on the spacing of this crop has established that 22 plants per square metre (2 per square foot) will give maximum yields when a single destructive harvest is used. With tall varieties there seemed to be no advantage in using rows closer than 46 cm. (18 in.), but with the shorter, compact varieties, rows 23 cm. (9 in.) apart gave higher yields. When the crop is to be picked on more than one occasion, as is usually the case in the garden, it would be expected that lower populations would be adequate. Thus, 11 cm. (4½ in.) apart in 46 cm. (18 in.) rows would be likely to give maximum yields of tall varieties with 23×23 cm. (9×9 in.) being more suitable for compact varieties.

### Peas

As with French beans all the spacing research with this crop has been aimed at producing high yields at one destructive harvest. The varieties used are 'determinate' in that each plant tends to stop growth once it has formed pods at the first two or three flowering positions on the stem and this is unlike the majority of garden varieties. Experiments have shown that 64–86 plants per square metre (6–8 per square foot) in rows not more than 18 cm. (7 in.) apart are likely to give the maximum yield. Results have been much more variable and unpredictable than with other crops in that occasionally populations as low as 43 per square metre (4 per square foot) can yield just as well or even slightly better than higher ones. Thus, we can only talk of 64–86 plants per square metre being more often right than wrong.

The population and row spacing used commercially can be adopted in the garden, leaving the peas to support each other, and harvesting the crop as it is cleared on one occasion only. A succession would then have to be achieved by successional sowings and, of course, only the shorter-stemmed varieties should be used.

The evidence from experiments is that peas respond to being regularly and evenly distributed and that a succession of pods, as required when the crop is to be picked more than once, is encouraged by lowering the population. Thus, if you want to pick-over your crops it would seem reasonable to aim at 43 plants per square metre (4 per square foot) and obtain this by sowing in bands of 3 rows each 11 cm. (4½ in.) apart with the plants 11 cm. apart in each row and with the centre rows 61 cm. (2 ft.) apart.

If the rows run across 122 cm. (4 ft.) beds divided by paths you will be able to pick the crop more easily than if the rows run along such a bed.

## Intercropping

With many of the more widely spaced, slower-growing crops it is possible to use the temporarily unneeded space between young plants to grow other quick-maturing crops. This can, with advantage, start ahead of the transplanting of such crops as Brussels sprouts. Thus a catch crop of hearted lettuce can be planted in April, leaving spaces for the sprouts to be planted in mid-May. The lettuce will be cleared by mid-June.

Of course, radishes are the ideal quick-growing crop for exploiting the odd no-man's-land, but if all such opportunities were diligently used to grow this crop the average vegetable garden would produce more radishes than it would be prudent to eat.

The golden rule is to avoid the intercrop interfering with the maincrop. If you imagine the intercrop as weeds competing with the maincrop you will appreciate that if too much enthusiasm is applied to intercropping serious damage can be done to the yield of the maincrop. The evidence is that the maincrop would not fully recover from any competitive check caused by early intercropping.

The safe rule is to attempt to exploit only the very centre part of the wide spaces that separate some crop plants early in their growth. Even then such intercropping should be brief and extra fertilizer and water may have to be given to make up for what the intercrop removes.

Of course, using the right spacings for the maincrops implies that you will be on razor's edge as far as any additional interplant competition is concerned. Thus, not only must you be very careful about intercropping but you must also be alert to prevent nature from intercropping for you with weeds. Getting the better of the weeds in the vegetable garden is one of the keys to success. Remember, it is easier to kill weeds by hoeing when they are very small and that preventing the seeding of weeds is vital. One year's seeding is seven year's weeding!

**Table 1.2**

**A summary guide to spacing your vegetable crops**

| Crop | Row spacing × spacing within row (cm.) (1 cm. = 0.39 in.) | Additional comments |
|---|---|---|
| **Beetroot** | | |
| early crops | 18 × 10 | For early maturity of 'Detroit' type |
| maincrop | 30 × 2.5 | For maximum yield of medium-sized roots |
| **Beans** | | |
| broad | 46 × 11 | For tall varieties |
| | 23 × 23 | For compact varieties |
| dwarf | 45 × 5 | For maximum yield as even a pattern of arrangement as possible |
| runner | 61 × 15 | For cane arrangements see p. 26 |

**Table 1.2** (*cont.*)

| Crop | Row spacing × spacing within row (cm.) (1 cm. = 0.39 in.) | Additional comments |
|---|---|---|
| **Brussels sprouts** | | |
| regular picking | 90 × 90 | To give successional picking as sprouts mature |
| for freezing | 50 × 50 | For single harvest of small sprouts |
| **Cabbage** | | |
| spring types | 30 × 10 | Remove plants for use to give 30 × 30 for late-hearted greens |
| summer | 35 × 35 | For small heads |
| | 45 × 45 | For larger heads |
| winter | 45 × 45 | Similar to summer types |
| **Calabrese** | 30 × 15 | At this spacing both terminal and side spears produced |
| **Carrots** | | |
| early crops | 15 × 10 | To limit competition and get rapid growth |
| maincrops | 15 × 4 | For medium-sized carrots |
| **Cauliflower** | | |
| early summer | 53 × 53 | Those varieties maturing June–July |
| autumn | 68 × 68 | Those varieties maturing August–November |
| winter | 76 × 76 | (Broccoli) Those maturing December–May |
| mini | 23 × 10 | To produce curds 4–9 cm. in diameter |
| **Celery** | | |
| self blanching | 28 × 28 | To give high yields and good blanching of sticks |
| | 15 × 15 | To produce slender hearts |
| **Leeks** | 30 × 15 | Will give maximum yield of normal-sized leeks |

| Crop | Row spacing × spacing within row (cm.) (1 cm. = 0.39 in.) | Additional comments |
|---|---|---|
| **Lettuce** | | |
| early crops | 23 × 20 | Triangular patterns for frames or cloches (p. 11) |
| normal | 30 × 30 | For butterhead, cabbage, or cos types |
| leaf | 13 × 2 | For non-hearted leaf production (pp. 11–12) |
| **Onions** | | |
| bulb | | |
| from seed | 30 × 4 | To give medium-sized bulbs |
| from sets | 25 × 5 | Will give high yields of medium-sized bulbs |
| for pickling | 30 × 1 | To give high yields of small bulbs |
| salad | 10 × 2.5 | Can also be sown in a band |
| **Parsnips** | 30 × 15 | For high yields of larger-rooted varieties, e.g. 'Offenham' |
| | 19 × 8 | For smaller roots |
| **Peas** | | |
| for picking over | 11.5 × 11.5 × 46 | Sow in three-row bands each row 11.5 cm. apart with 46 cm. between each band |
| **Potatoes** | | See Table 1.1 (p. 17) |
| **Shallots** | 20 × 15 | If using small sets |
| | 30 × 15 | If using large sets |
| **Tomatoes** | | |
| bush types | 48 × 48 | This close spacing gives more early yield |

# 2 Sowing and planting

More seeds are wasted and more plants are condemned to produce less than their full potential by poor sowing and planting methods than almost any other cultural practice within the gardener's control. In fact, producing the right conditions to encourage rapid germination and growth of seedlings and transplants is the foundation on which high yields of good-quality vegetables are produced. Although this is easier said than done there are certain principles which can be used as a guide by the gardener. If these are appreciated and if the novel methods of sowing described later are followed, then more predictable plant populations with more efficient use of seeds and plants will be obtained, not to mention the increased satisfaction and rewards for your efforts.

## Getting the right number of plants

Gardeners intuitively appreciate that sowing too many or too few seeds may lead to a crop failure. In fact, getting the right number of plants to grow per square metre for each different vegetable is probably the single most important gardening operation. From seeds this can be very difficult to achieve. For one thing we need to know how many of the seeds will emerge as seedlings. This cannot be done simply by counting the number of seeds we sow because an unknown proportion of them, often as many as half, fail to produce seedlings.

## Getting the plants to grow at the right time

The *number* of plants established is not the only aspect of seedling establishment which is important in ensuring good reliable yields of vegetables. It is also essential to be able to get crops growing at the 'right' time, especially when successional sowings of peas or lettuce are made to provide a continuous supply for the kitchen. A delay in emergence may mean a gap in supply. It is well known that seedlings from one sowing do not all emerge at the same time. Does it matter, then, if it takes a long or short time for all the seedlings to emerge? This will depend on the particular vegetable. For example, with lettuce and cabbage which are spaced widely apart the differences in times of emergence of the individual seedlings, which can be up to ten days, helps to give a continuous supply of heads. This is because the earliest emerging seedlings give the earliest maturing plants and the latest to emerge the latest maturing heads, usually a great advantage to the gardener. However, with other crops which are more closely spaced, such as carrots, onions, or parsnips, a long period of emergence of seedlings can be a disadvantage. This is because the earliest seedlings to emerge, which become the largest, will 'crowd out' the later emerging ones, which then may only produce small worthless roots or bulbs.

## To sow or plant?

It is usually easier to get a high proportion of the seeds emerging rapidly and all at the same time by raising seedlings under glass in seed trays or soil blocks and then, at a later stage of growth, transplanting them into the garden. This has led to the belief among some gardeners that crops can be established more easily in this way than those sown directly into the garden soil and that the resulting crops will be better. This is not invariably so. Some crops do not readily recover from the damage caused by transplanting. For example, research has shown, even with cauliflowers which are relatively easy to establish, that transplanting may give poorer crops than those raised from seeds sown directly into the garden. Furthermore, some crops such as celery, which are traditionally transplanted, are difficult to establish well either from plants or from directly sowing the seeds.

The reasons why some crops are sown directly whilst others are best transplanted will be investigated a little later. First, it is useful to understand how to influence the number of seedlings that emerge and establish themselves as plants.

## Why don't all seeds produce plants?

The successful establishment of healthy seedlings is the end point of a complex process which can be regarded as three separate events. First, the production of 'live' seeds. Secondly, the germination of the seeds which involves the uptake of water to start the growth of the root through the seed coat. Finally, the growth of the root downwards and the growth of the shoot upwards to the soil surface.

## How many seeds are 'live'?

One of the reasons why some seeds fail to germinate is because they do not contain a live embryo. This occurs because fertilization of the flower was incomplete or because the fertilized seed did not develop properly. Most of these 'dead' seeds are removed during the preparation of the seeds for sale.

A much more common reason for seeds failing to germinate is because some seeds have abnormal or underdeveloped embryos. This is common in carrots, parsley, celery, and parsnips, and the seeds need to undergo further development before germination can occur. In these circumstances germination is often delayed and consequently the seed in the soil becomes more vulnerable to disease and pest attack. This is one of the reasons why it is difficult to obtain good emergence from these particular crops and why the seedlings take such a long time to appear. Of course, these particular vegetables are also often sown early in the spring when soil temperatures are low, and this will further delay emergence of the seedlings.

Some seeds fail to germinate, or if they do germinate fail to grow vigorously, because they are diseased. Such seed and seedling diseases are described in Chapter 6.

Some seeds are particularly 'difficult' because they require special conditions before they will germinate. For example, seeds of many celery varieties require light for germination and will not germinate in the dark or if *buried* in the soil. Freshly harvested lettuce seeds will not germinate readily, but good germination can be obtained after a few months of storage. The 'corky' layer around beetroot seeds (which are really fruits) contains compounds which can inhibit germination. This is often rubbed off by the seedsmen to produce a smooth, round 'fruit'. If large amounts of the cork are present the fruits can be soaked in running water for ½–1 hour at a room temperature of about 21 °C (70 °F) to wash out the compounds which delay germination.

Another common cause of poor germination is because the seeds are too 'old'. Generally, seeds kept for some time germinate less well than freshly harvested seeds; even if some seeds do germinate the seedlings often fail to grow properly because they do not produce a normal root or shoot. Such a statement should immediately raise questions in the gardener's mind: is germination reduced by even short periods of storage of the seeds, for example, between buying and sowing them? Is it safe to use seeds which have been kept from previous years?

## Can seeds be used that have been stored for any length of time?

It is not sufficiently appreciated that as soon as seeds are harvested from the seeding plant they start to deteriorate and will eventually die if stored for long enough. However, research has shown that there are differences in how quickly different vegetable seeds deteriorate. For example, onion seeds will lose the ability to germinate more rapidly than tomato seeds; the storage life of some common vegetables is shown in Table 2.1. Most seeds will germinate after two or three years' storage in unsealed containers, but if the seeds are kept in warm and humid conditions then they will often fail to germinate even after a few weeks. So, even when new seeds are bought each year, they will deteriorate if stored in warm, moist conditions before sowing. Often the same packet of seeds is used for a number of successional sowings of, say, lettuce and between sowings the seed packet is left on a shelf in the garden shed. Research has shown that seeds stored under these conditions deteriorate rapidly and this form of storage is often the cause of poor germination and seedling emergence for sowings made later in the season.

The effects of seed deterioration are twofold. The longer seeds are stored the lower the proportion of seeds which are capable of germinating, but long before this occurs the seeds lose their 'vigour'. This means that although the seeds are capable of germinating under *ideal* conditions they do not under poor conditions. For example, in one study 95 per cent of both 'old' and 'new' carrot seeds germinated under ideal conditions of warmth and moisture, but only 35 per cent of the 'old' and 60 per cent of the 'new' seeds germinated under *cold*, *moist* conditions. Research has shown that seedlings from 'old' seeds do not grow as well as seedlings from 'new' seeds so giving, for example, later maturity of lettuce and lower yields of carrots.

**Table 2.1**

**The storage life of some common vegetable seeds kept in unsealed containers in a normally heated room**

| Up to 3 years | Up to 6 years | Up to 9 years | Up to 10 years |
|---|---|---|---|
| Lettuce | Carrot | Cabbage | Tomato |
| Leek | Cauliflower | Swede | Radish |
| Onion | | Turnip | |
| Parsnip | | | |

It is important, therefore, to store seeds properly if they are to be saved from year to year.

## How should seeds be stored?

The loss of the ability to germinate and the loss of vigour can be minimized by proper storage. Remember, high temperature and moist conditions cause rapid deterioration. Therefore, if the seeds are kept dry and stored at low temperatures, they remain alive longer.

In general, for each 5 °C (9 °F) rise in temperature above 0 °C (32 °F) the storage life of the seed is halved. So if it is normally ten years at 5 °C (41 °F) it will be five years at 10 °C (50 °F), and only one year at 21 °C (70 °F) (in your kitchen). Also, for each 1 per cent increase in seed moisture content above 5 per cent up to 14 per cent the life of the seed is reduced by half. So seed with a moisture content of 8 per cent will store for ten years but will only store for five years at 9 per cent moisture content. These two effects can be added together so that if the seeds stored at 5 °C (41 °F) and 8 per cent moisture content remain viable for ten years, then at 10 °C (50 °F) and 9 per cent moisture content they will only remain viable for two and a half years.

What does this mean in practice? When the seed is mature it will take up water from a moist atmosphere or lose it to a dry one. In a maritime climate like Britain's the relative humidity of the air is rarely below 75 per cent and seeds stored in unsealed containers will usually have a moisture content of approximately 10–15 per cent and so will only store satisfactorily for about one year. This is because the seeds are so moist that moulds develop which destroy the tissues of the seed. If seeds are to be stored from one sowing to the next or from one season to the next then they should not be stored in an unsealed packet in the garden shed. This applies equally to seeds in paper packets and to those in tin foil vacuum-packs which have been opened. However, seeds can be stored for at least three to four years in unopened vacuum packs. Store the seeds in a cool place, such as a cellar which is usually at about 10 °C (50 °F) throughout most of the year, and keep them dry. This can be done simply by storing seeds in a glass jar or other *transparent* air-tight container with a small amount of cobalt-chloride-treated silica gel (a teaspoonful per 28 g. (1 oz.) of seeds) placed in a separate open-topped container (see Fig. 2.1). The silica gel (which can be obtained from most chemists) takes up water from the surrounding atmosphere and so dries it. The moist seeds will then lose moisture to the dry air and the seed moisture content can be reduced to about 8 per cent. It will be possible to maintain it at this level provided the silica gel is taken out and dried after it turns from blue to pink. Drying in an oven for two to three hours will drive off the water and when it is dry (indicated by the change from pink to blue) it can be put back in with the seeds. The silica gel will need to be dried frequently to start with, but when the seed moisture content has reached a balance with water in the air in the container less frequent drying will be necessary.

If seeds are stored in this way they should keep in good condi-

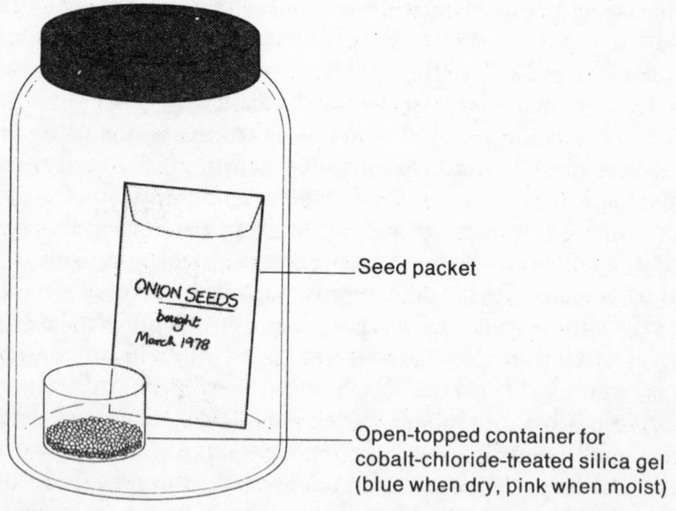


Fig. 2.1. A simple way to store vegetable seeds in a screw-top glass jar.

tion for three or four years. It will then be practical to consider buying larger quantities of seeds of, say, a special variety, which is not always readily available, and keep it for several growing seasons.

Research has shown us how to store seeds to minimize deterioration and much is now known about how the environment during seed growth and harvesting techniques influence seed quality. Nevertheless, it is difficult to produce seeds of a consistently *high* quality which will germinate well under all conditions; some 'seed' years are good and others are bad. Seedsmen can grade out the smaller seeds, which often germinate less well than the larger ones, but this will not guarantee that all of the seeds in a packet will germinate.

**Do seed packets have to contain a certain proportion of 'live' seeds by law?**

It is recognized by all concerned with seed production and marketing that it is difficult to produce consistently good seed and so seeds of nearly all vegetables sold must meet certain *minimum* levels of germination. United Kingdom standards for a number of vegetables are given in Table 2.2. Other countries have similar standards. It is important to realize that these are *minimum* standards and a seed packet will normally contain more 'live' seeds than required by law. The test to determine the number of 'live' seeds is done at the time the seeds are packeted for sale to shops and several months may elapse until the seeds are sown. If the conditions in the shop or home before sowing are poor some of the seeds may die. So, it is best to buy seeds early in the season soon after they are packeted and to store them under good conditions.

The test for determining the number of 'live' seeds is done in a laboratory under *ideal* conditions of light, warmth, and moisture. If these conditions could be reproduced in the garden soil or seedbox all the 'live' seeds should germinate and produce seedlings. However, the soil is hardly ever an ideal medium for

**Table 2.2**

**The UK statutory minimum levels of germination for some vegetable seeds**

| No minimum level required by law | 65% | 70% | 75% | 80% |
|---|---|---|---|---|
| Parsnip | Carrot | Onion | French bean | Broad bean |
| | Leek | Cauliflower | Lettuce | Runner bean |
| | | Calabrese | Cabbage | Pea |
| | | Radish | Brussels sprouts | Turnip |
| | | Celery | Marrow | Cucumber |
| | | Beet* | Spinach | |
| | | | Tomato | |

*Except 'Cheltenham Green Top' which is 50 per cent.

germination and seedling emergence and rarely do all the 'live' seeds emerge.

## Why don't all 'live' seeds produce seedlings?

There are many reasons why 'live' seeds fail to germinate and produce seedlings in the garden. As well as those already mentioned earlier the following are the most important.

### Soil tilth and soil moisture

It is very important to prepare a suitable 'tilth' before sowing so that when the seeds are sown they make good contact with the water held in the pore spaces between the soil particles. The uptake of water into the seed is then rapid and the growth processes begin readily. This uptake of water by the seed is better when a fine rather than a cloddy tilth is prepared. Although a lot of research has been done on the effect of different tilths on water uptake and seedling emergence it is very difficult in practice to produce ideal tilths. The reason is that each soil reacts differently to the various cultivation implements. The same soil will also be affected in different ways, depending on whether it is wet or dry when it is being cultivated. As a general rule, the best tilths for seed sowing are those produced with as little raking of the soil as possible, as this preserves any 'frost mould' on the surface and prevents the loss of capillarity of water. This is the upward movement of water to the soil surface and is facilitated by the close contact of soil crumbs with each other. If the soil is deeply cultivated and seeds are sown into the cultivated layer, capillarity may be so poor that no upward movement of water to the seeds occurs. The upper layers then dry out by evaporation leaving the seeds stranded in dry soil. The most effective procedure is to sow the seeds on to the base of firm soil which has not been raked through and cover the seeds with the 'cultivated tilth'. On loamy, well-structured soils it is relatively easy to produce a good tilth for sowing, but on clays and sandy soils this is more difficult and timely cultivation becomes very important. On clays autumn digging to expose the soil to the natural weathering process will help to produce a good seedbed in the spring. However, some sandy soils dug in the autumn may become compacted by sowing time through the action of rainfall, so making them more difficult to cultivate than those freshly dug. In the long term, tilths on both clays and sands can be greatly improved by incorporating into the soil each year large amounts of compost and other organic matter.

### 'Slumping' of the soil and surface capping

Some poorly structured sandy soils which contain a high proportion of fine sand, silt, or clay particles can 'slump' under the impact of heavy rain or heavy watering. This is because the fine particles in the soils are washed into the spaces between the larger particles. The soil is then said to have slumped. When it is in this condition and wet, all the air is forced out of the soil and the seeds will be starved of oxygen and will eventually rot. Slumped soils are also very compact, which severely restricts the growth of the shoot and root and this can be recognized by the flattening, thickening, and kinking of the roots and shoots when the seedlings are carefully dug up.

Sometimes this slumping is confined only to the top 6 mm. (¼ in.) or so of soil and is referred to as 'capping'. If the soil remains wet under these conditions seedling emergence can occur, but if the soil surface dries this slumped layer forms a hard 'cap' and the seedlings will often fail to emerge. This cap can usually be lifted up from the soil and the seedlings can be found curled round and round underneath (see Fig. 2.2).

The adverse effects of both slumping and capping can be reduced by carrying out the minimum number of cultivations necessary to produce a crumbly tilth and by watering the soil lightly *before* rather than *after* sowing. Some gardeners dribble water into the bottom of the drill before sowing (see Chapter 4). This is a good way of ensuring adequate moisture for germination

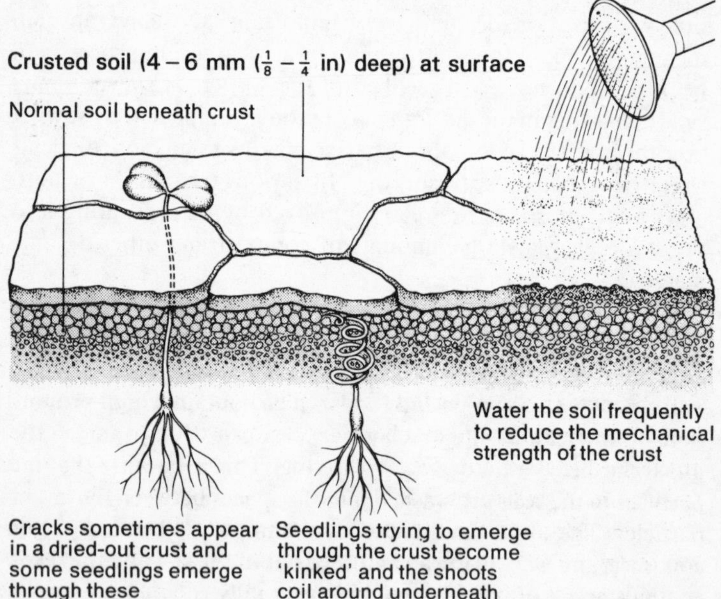


Fig. 2.2. Soil crusting or capping.

without damaging the soil structure. If watering is necessary after sowing then small amounts of water should be applied frequently and with a fine rose. If the soil does form a cap it should be kept wet by frequent waterings to reduce its mechanical strength.

If the sown area is small enough or if widely spaced crops are 'spot' sown on soils prone to capping it is worth considering replacing the soil covering with a non-capping material, such as peat, to encourage rapid seedling growth to the surface.

## Rolling

It is claimed that treading or rolling the seedbed is beneficial for seedling establishment because it improves the tilth and the contact between the seed and the soil water. This will depend on whether it is done before or after sowing and how moist the soil is at the time of consolidation. In cloddy soils rolling the seedbed before sowing will help to produce a good tilth, but only if the soil is at the right moisture content so that the clods crumble. This can only be judged for your soil by experience. Normally rolling should not be necessary. In wet soil its only action will be to compact the soil, which will hinder the growth of the shoot and root. Rolling seedbeds after sowing, particularly if the surface of the soil is moist, can predispose the soil to form a cap if the seedbed dries out rapidly afterwards. Generally, treading or rolling the seedbed is not recommended.

## Sowing depth

To ensure good contact with the soil seeds need to be sown in a drill and covered with soil. However, this can bring other problems because the seedling has to live on its own food reserves until it emerges from the soil and begins to manufacture its own food. If the seed is sown too deeply its reserves may not be sufficient to sustain growth to the soil surface.

Small seeds have small reserves and therefore must not be sown too deeply. For example, the optimum depth of sowing lettuce in moist soil is about 12–19 mm. (½–¾ in.), whereas for beans, which are 500–1000 times heavier, it is about 38–50 mm.

**Table 2.3**

**A guide to the depth of sowing for some common vegetables**

| 38–50 mm. ($1\frac{1}{2}$–2 in.) | 25–38 mm. (1–$1\frac{1}{2}$ in.) | 19–25 mm. ($\frac{3}{4}$–1 in.) | 12–19 mm. ($\frac{1}{2}$–$\frac{3}{4}$ in.) |
|---|---|---|---|
| Broad bean | Peas | Broccoli | Beetroot |
| French bean | Sweet corn | Brussels sprouts | Carrot |
| Runner bean | | Cabbage | Leek |
| | | Cauliflower | Lettuce |
| | | Cucumber | Onions |
| | | Marrow | Parsley |
| | | Radishes | Parsnip |
| | | Swede | Spinach |
| | | Tomato | |
| | | Turnip | |

(1½–2 in.). Suitable sowing depths for other vegetable seeds are shown in Table 2.3.

In practice, it is not easy to draw drills in the soil at the same depth along their length using a rake or hoe, and some seeds will be sown more or less deeply than others. Although the ones sown too deeply germinate they will not emerge and an uneven depth of sowing is a fairly common cause for only a small percentage of the seedlings emerging. Better control of the depth of sowing can be obtained by using a planting board and a simple model is shown in Fig. 2.3. Using this board and a V-shaped scraper, drills can be made at the correct depth along the whole length of row. The board can also be marked off to aid the precise spacing of seeds along the row.

Variation in the depth of sowing is also a major cause of differences in the time of seedlings emerging, because those sown nearer the surface will usually emerge first providing, of course, that the soil is not too dry. Another cause of variation in time of emergence is if the seeds start to absorb water, and therefore start to germinate, at different times. This can occur, for example, if some seeds are sown in a seedbed with a poor, cloddy tilth.

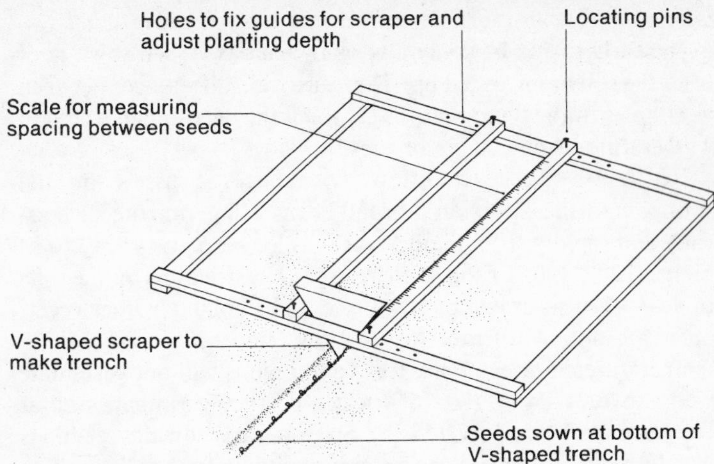


Fig. 2.3. Sowing frame to control the depth of sowing.

## Fertilizer practice

Inorganic fertilizers are usually applied to the seedbed before sowing and forked or raked in, but if large amounts of nitrate fertilizer are applied at this time seedling emergence will be reduced, particularly under dry conditions. This is because the fertilizer prevents germination and reduces growth of the small seedling root. This effect is particularly marked in small-seeded crops such as lettuce and carrots, but it also affects larger-seeded ones such as beans. Provided the soil is kept moist by watering each day the damaging effects of excess fertilizer can be minimized. However, it is probably better to apply a small proportion of the nitrogenous fertilizer required by the crop (up to one-third) to the seedbed before sowing and the rest later when emergence is complete.

## Soil temperatures

In general, seeds take longer to germinate and germinate less well at low than at higher temperatures. For example, emergence may take up to four or more weeks for peas and parsnips when sown in the early spring but only a week or ten days when sown later after the soil has warmed up. There are wide differences between vegetables in the temperatures at which they germinate well and it is useful to know some of these.

Vegetables such as cauliflowers, cabbages, Brussels sprouts, turnips, radishes, peas, and broad beans will germinate successfully and rapidly from temperatures as low as 5 °C (41 °F) to as high as 32 °C (90 °F) and so there are few restrictions on the time of year when seeds can be sown to establish plants. Other vegetables are not so tolerant to very low temperatures or to high temperatures. For example, leeks and onions will not germinate well above 21–24 °C (70–75 °F), nor do they germinate well at temperatures below 7 °C (45 °F). So from early sowings seedlings usually take a long time to emerge. It may also be difficult to establish the new Japanese types of overwintering onions which are sown in August. Often, at this time of the year soil temperatures reach 21–24 °C (70–75 °F), which may reduce seedling emergence. If soil temperatures at seed depth are as high as this it could be prudent to lower the temperature by watering the soil frequently or by covering the soil with a white reflective material such as white polythene or polystyrene.

Another vegetable which will only germinate well within a narrow range of soil temperature is celery, germination being best at temperatures between 10 ° and 19 °C (50 ° and 66 °F). Although lettuce seed germinates well at low temperatures (it will in fact germinate in ice) most varieties of the butterhead (smooth) types will not germinate when soil temperatures are above 25 °C (77 °F). If the soil cools down after a hot spell germination will occur, but only after a considerable delay and when it does occur the seedlings emerge over a long period of time. As soil temperatures above 25 °C occur frequently in late spring and summer, even in England, this is one of the major reasons for poor germination and emergence, resulting in unpredictable supplies of lettuce during the late summer and early autumn. Crisphead varieties of lettuce will germinate well even at 29 °C (85 °F) and so there would be less risk of poor germination if these were used instead. If a crisp variety is not an acceptable alternative then soil temperatures can be reduced by watering or using a white reflective material to cover the soil or seedbox. Alternatively, sowing at a particular time of day will aid germination when soil temperatures are high. Research has shown that sowing between 2 and 4 p.m. gives better emergence than sowing in the morning or early evening. This is because the temperature-sensitive phase of the germination process is completed at night when soil temperatures are lower.

In contrast, carrots, parsnips, and red-beet germinate well at high temperatures but not at temperatures below about 7 °C (45 °F). Germination does occur, but it is very slow and this, in part, accounts for the very long time, often four to six weeks, that it takes for these seeds to emerge from early spring sowings. One of the ways of getting earlier and more rapid emergence is by pre-germinating and fluid sowing the seeds and this will be described later.

Some vegetables, notably sweet corn, tomatoes, cucumbers, courgettes, marrows, peppers, runner beans, and French beans, are particularly sensitive to low soil temperatures. For example, cucumbers and marrows will not germinate satisfactorily below 13 °C (56 °F) whilst peppers require soil temperatures above 15 °C (60 °F) for successful germination. This temperature is not reached on most soils in the United Kingdom until early June, which is too late to sow pepper seeds to get a crop. Other cold-temperature-sensitive crops such as French and runner beans, tomatoes, and sweet corn require soil temperatures above 10–12 °C (50–54 °F) for successful and rapid germination.

It is important to realize with these low-temperature-sensitive crops that if the seeds imbibe water in cold conditions, the growth of the seedlings which eventually emerge is permanently impaired and yields may also be reduced. So the seeds should not be sown until there is little risk of low soil temperatures occurring. This means that for sweet corn and beans sowing should be delayed until soil temperatures reach 10 °C (50 °F). (In the South of England this occurs in about late April to early May and in the North of England a week or two later.) For cucumbers and marrows, sowing should be delayed for a further two weeks. Slightly earlier sowing can be done if the soil temperature is artificially raised by protecting the seedbed and the growing crop with cloches, low plastic tunnels, or clear plastic mulches (see Fig. 2.4). This not only ensures rapid emergence but will advance the time of maturity.

### How can the number of seedlings that eventually emerge be predicted?

Only rarely does the right combination of conditions in the garden seedbed occur so that all the 'live' seeds produce seedlings. These conditions almost always arise by chance and rarely can they be produced to order even though care has been taken with seedbed preparation. Gardeners usually accept philosophically that emergence is unpredictable, nevertheless it is possible to improve on this situation. Sowings can usually be classified into those which give 'poor' or 'good' emergence. If the gardener knew, for example, whether 25, 50, or 75 per cent of the 'live' seeds sown produced plants under particular conditions then, by experience, he could begin to predict how many seedlings would emerge at any one sowing. For example, if 100 'live' seeds were sown and on average only 50 came up for February sowings compared with 75 for April sowings he could sow in future years $100/50 \times 100$ and $100/75 \times 100$ seeds at those sowings, respectively, to obtain 100 seedlings.

It is instructive to see just how many seeds are required to establish, say, 40 lettuce seedlings in a row 152 cm. (5 ft.) long. If the statutory minimum level of germination which is 75 per cent is used as a base for the calculation, and all the live seeds produced seedlings, we would need $(40 \times 100)/75 = 53$ seeds to get 40 seedlings. However, in experiments it is frequently found that only about half of the 'live' seeds emerge and so in order to produce 40 seedlings we would need to sow $(40 \times 100)/75 \times 100/50$ or 106 seeds.

In summary, sowing seeds into soil does not always provide an ideal environment for the germination and growth of the

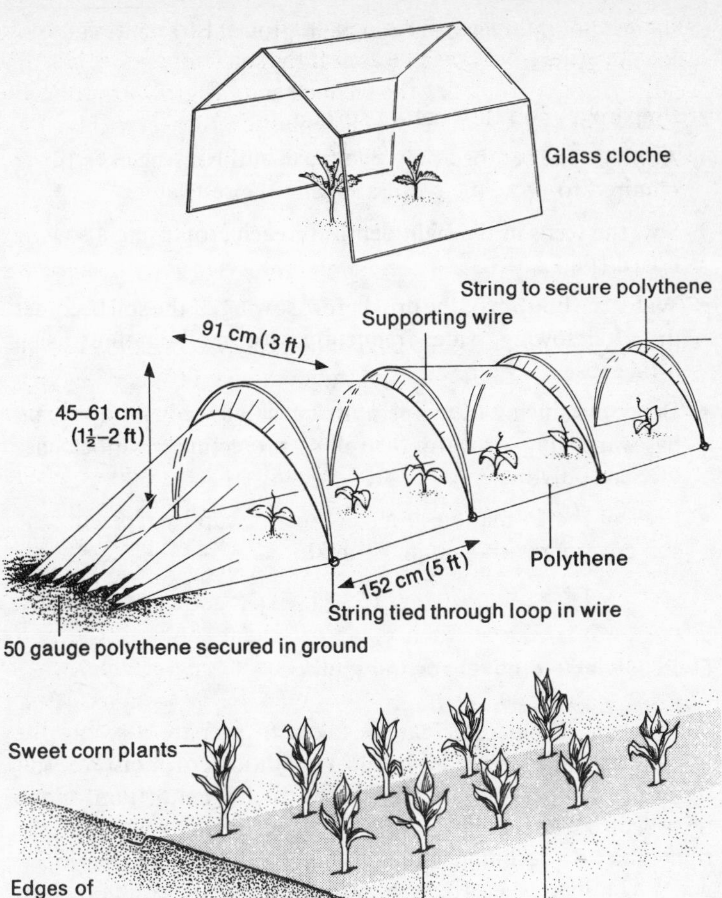


Fig. 2.4. Methods of warming up the soil for cold-sensitive vegetables. Cloches and plastic tunnels are good for French beans, courgettes, cucumbers, and bush tomatoes; clear plastic mulches can also be used for these crops and are also useful for sweet corn.

seedlings, but establishment can be improved by attention to the following points:

- Prepare a good tilth before sowing.
- Apply to the seedbed only one-third of the nitrogen fertilizer required to grow the crop, applying the rest later.
- Sow the seeds at the right depth for each crop using a sowing board (Fig. 2.3).
- Water the bottom of the drill before sowing; if the soil becomes dry after sowing, water frequently with small amounts using a fine rose.
- Delay the sowing of temperature-sensitive seeds until the soil has warmed up or warm the soil by protecting it with cloches or clear polythene.
- Prevent the formation of a soil crust or cap by replacing the soil covering with a compost mixture.

## Fluid sowing—a novel sowing method

Even when considerable care is taken to prepare a seedbed it is still difficult to provide the ideal conditions of moisture, soil tilth, and temperature by traditional garden cultivations alone in order to get the right number of seedlings growing at the right time. So techniques of seed sowing have been developed which eliminate the effects of weather and soil conditions on seed germination and minimize their effects on subsequent growth of the shoot to the soil surface. It is especially useful for getting rapid and uniform emergence of seedlings early in the season when the soil is cold, but it also gives advantages in other circumstances.

This technique is called fluid sowing. The seeds are germinated indoors under *ideal conditions* and the germinated seeds are then sown into the soil in a jelly to protect them from damage. A simple example of how the effects of the soil environment can be eliminated is where soil temperatures greater than 25 °C (77 °F) prevent germination of lettuce seeds sown into the soil during hot sunny weather. However, provided the seeds are *germinated* under ideal conditions (in temperatures below 25 °C) *before sowing* and then fluid sown, seedlings will come up readily even with soil temperatures above 25 °C because such high temperatures do not prevent the subsequent growth of the young shoot.

Fluid sowing of pre-germinated seeds has now been tested experimentally on a wide range of vegetables and for all of them it gives earlier emergence, particularly with those crops such as carrots and parsnips which are normally slow to germinate, or those such as tomatoes which germinate only slowly at low temperatures. In fact, with tomatoes emergence and growth are advanced so much that it is possible to produce ripe crops by sowing directly into the garden soil even where the season has been regarded as being too short to get a satisfactory crop, for example in the United Kingdom.

This method will also give higher and more predictable emergence of seedlings than dry seeds and particularly with 'difficult' seeds like celery. In lettuce it will also give more uniform emergence, all the seedlings coming up at approximately the same time. The advantages found from using this technique with other vegetable crops are listed in Table 2.4. The technique is now starting to be used on a commercial scale in several countries.

The method can be easily adapted for the home gardener, using kitchen containers and utensils. The following steps should be followed:

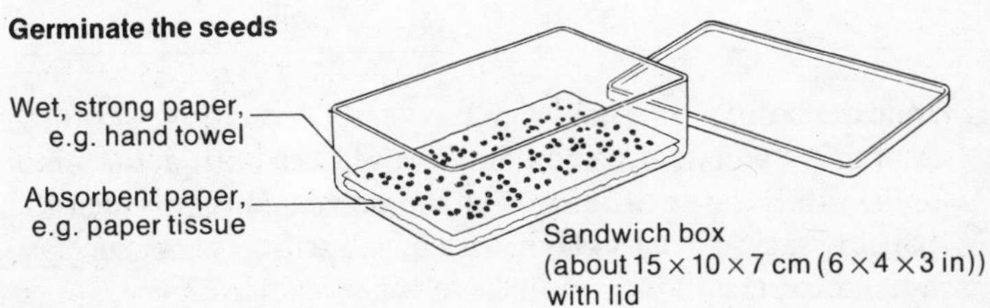

**Table 2.4**

**A summary of likely benefits from fluid-sowing pre-germinated seeds compared with sowing dry seeds**

| | Number of days earlier emergence for fluid-sown pre-germinated seeds compared with dry seeds for | | Other benefits |
|---|---|---|---|
| | early season sowings | late season sowings | |
| **Carrot** | 12 | 5 | Gives higher yields of early carrots |
| **Celery** | 21 | 1 | Better emergence in seedboxes |
| **Lettuce** | 8 | 1 | Better emergence during mid-summer |
| **Onion** (bulb) | 15 | 4 | Higher yields |
| **Onion** (salad) | 15 | 7 | Ready for pulling earlier |
| **Parsley** | 21 | 14 | Better and earlier emergence |
| **Parsnip** | 18 | 4 | Better emergence and ready earlier |
| **Tomato** | 20 | 7 | Mature crops can be produced directly from seeds sown in the garden soil in countries where the season is normally too short |

1. Line the bottom of a sandwich box, empty seed tray, or other container (a margarine container would do) with a 2–3 mm. ($\frac{1}{10}$ in.) thick layer of absorbent, unmedicated paper such as paper tissues; cover this layer with a 'wet-strong' paper such as a hand towel.

2. Sprinkle water on to the paper until it is thoroughly wet and then pour away the excess.

3. Sprinkle the seeds evenly over the paper without completely covering the surface and avoid clumping of the seeds. It is important with celery and parsnips to spread the seeds very thinly—about one seed to every square centimetre (six seeds per square inch).

4. Put the lid on the container and keep the seeds at a temperature of about 21 °C (70 °F) for all the common vegetables. Remember that celery must be kept in the *light* otherwise germination will be poor. Some seeds like lettuce germinate in less than twenty-four hours at 21 °C so it is important to look at the seeds frequently to see if they have germinated. If fluid-sowing of pre-germinated seeds is to be successful the roots should not be allowed to grow too long—up to 5 mm. ($\frac{1}{5}$ in.) for most vegetables, but lettuce should be no longer than 2 mm. ($\frac{1}{10}$ in.). The approximate time needed to produce a root of the right size at the time when the germinated seeds should be sown is shown in Table 2.5 for some common vegetables. These figures should only be used as a guide to the time required because not every lot of seed behaves in the same way.

   Germinating the seeds in this way provides a unique opportunity to see before sowing how many, or how few, of the seeds germinate. If the number of germinated seeds is very much lower than the figures given in Table 2.5 after they have been kept in the box for the required length of time they are probably not worth sowing. However, before a final decision is made whether to discard the seeds or not, wait two or three days longer to see if any more germinate.

5. When most of the seeds are at the right stage they may be sown, but if this is not a convenient time, perhaps because the soil is too wet after rain, the seeds in the container can be placed for a day or two in a domestic refrigerator *but the seeds must not be frozen*. Tomatoes, sweet corn, and beans are an exception to this suggestion and should not be stored at temperatures below 6 °C (42 °F). The seeds can be removed from the box by

**Table 2.5**

**The approximate time required at normal room temperature for the pre-germination of seeds for fluid sowing and the approximate percentage germinated at this time**

| | Time required (days) | Germination (%) |
|---|---|---|
| **Bean** (French and runner) | 3 | 80 |
| **Beetroot** | 6 | 70 |
| **Carrot** | 4 | 50 |
| **Celery** | 10 | 50 |
| **Cucumber/Marrow** | $1\frac{1}{2}$ | 70 |
| **Leek** | 5 | 50 |
| **Lettuce** | 1 | 80 |
| **Onion** | 5 | 50 |
| **Parsley** | 7 | 30 |
| **Parsnip** | 7 | 30–40 |
| **Sweet corn** | $1\frac{1}{2}$ | 80 |
| **Tomato** | 5 | 80 |

washing them into a fine-mesh (preferably plastic mesh) strainer.

**Wash the germinated seeds off the paper**

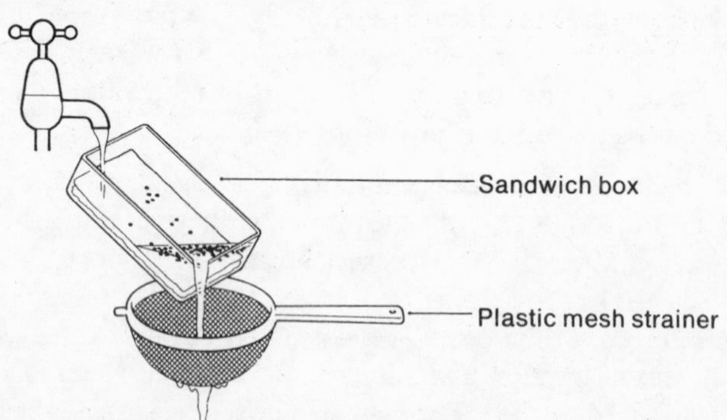

6. The carrier jelly can be made from several compounds, including cellulose-based wallpaper pastes *which do not contain fungicides.* For example, wallpaper paste can be mixed at half normal strength to make a suitable jelly. When the jelly has thickened sprinkle the seeds on to half the required quantity for sowing and stir in using your fingers. Then add the remainder. The seeds should be well mixed in the jelly and should not sink when the mixture is left to stand. If they do the mixture is not thick enough.
7. Fill a wide-nozzled (at least 6 mm. (¼ in.) diameter) cake-icing syringe with the mixture and extrude it into moist soil in the seed drill or into a seedbox containing compost. The mixture should be extruded at a rate of 30 teaspoonfuls to 2.5 metres (10 ft.) of row so this amount of jelly should contain about the right number of germinated seeds. Instead of using a syringe, sowing can be done with a polythene bag. After filling the bag and holding the top closed, cut off a small piece of one corner and extrude the mixture through the hole by squeezing as shown in the figure.

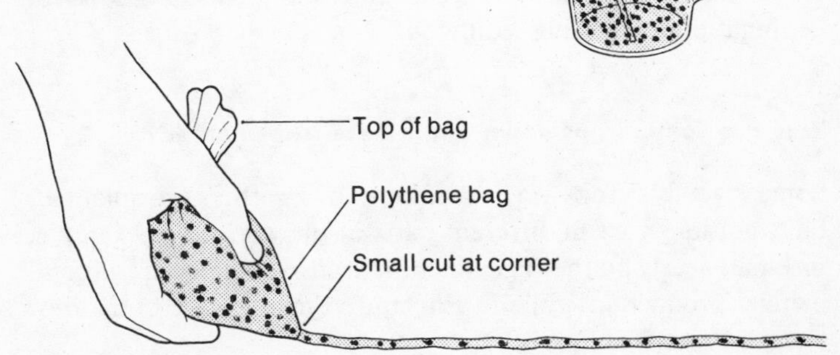

8. After sowing, the jelly containing the seeds needs to be covered in the normal way to prevent it from drying out because the jelly may form a hard film and trap the seeds. Sowing into very dry soil will produce a similar effect and so dry soil should be watered in the seed drill before sowing. For some widely spaced crops it is possible to replace the soil covering by a water-holding material such as vermiculite or a peat compost which does not restrict the growth of shoot to the same extent as soil. Research has shown that higher, more rapid, and predictable emergence can be obtained with these covering materials, but they must be kept moist in drying weather.

### Do 'pelleted' seeds give better emergence than natural seeds?

It is now possible for gardeners to buy pelleted seeds of many vegetables. One of the advantages of using pelleted seeds is that because they are larger than the natural, uncoated seeds accurate placement of the seeds in the soil is easier. However, it should be remembered that 'pelleting' of seeds was originally carried out to make angular-shaped seeds round so that they could be sown at precise spacings with precision drills. There is no experimental evidence which conclusively shows that seedling emergence is any better from pelleted than from natural seeds. Indeed it can often be worse, but great strides have been made in recent years in formulating pelleting materials to reduce the risks of poor establishment from pelleted seeds under marginal conditions for germination and early seedling growth.

### Why are some crops sown and others transplanted?

Some vegetable crops are by tradition sown, others transplanted, but traditions vary in different parts of the world. For example, in Japan nearly all the vegetables are transplanted even for commercial production while in England vegetables are both *sown* and *transplanted*.

One of the advantages of transplanting is that it shortens the growing period in the garden so allowing more crops to be grown on the same land than could be achieved by sowing directly into the soil. For example, the same piece of land could support three or four successive crops of transplanted lettuce in a season but only one or two crops from directly sown crops.

Transplanting can also give higher yields, particularly of heat-loving vegetables such as outdoor tomatoes. Indeed, with tomatoes it is the only sure way in a cool climate of obtaining good *early* yields outdoors. Bulb onions from sown crops do not always mature early enough to be dried easily for storage over the winter and so crops are often raised from sets or plants. More importantly, sets and plants give consistently higher yields than from crops sown directly in the soil in early spring.

Transplanting is also used for crops whose seeds are difficult to germinate in the garden. Celery is a good example because the conditions necessary for good germination are more easily obtained in seedboxes than in the garden soil. It is also used for crops whose seeds are expensive such as $F_1$ hybrid Brussels sprouts.

Transplanting is more common for those plants which are widely spaced such as cabbage and other brassicas because a small plant-raising area will provide plants for a large area of ground, whereas for close-spaced crops, like onions, a very large plant-raising area would be needed relative to the space for growing them to maturity. In addition, it would be tedious to plant out the very large numbers of plants required.

The major disadvantage of transplanting is that the plant is damaged, particularly the roots, in moving it from the seed tray or seedbed to the soil. Because the shoot continues to lose water by transpiration and because the damaged root system is unable to absorb sufficient water from the soil to replenish this loss the plant wilts. When this happens the plant is unable to produce its own food material and growth is temporarily, but severely, reduced. Rapid recovery from this transplanting shock is essential if yields are not to be reduced and maturity delayed. Some vegetables such as cabbage, cauliflower, Brussels sprouts, and tomatoes recover from transplanting more readily than, say, ridge cucumbers or sweet corn and the yielding potential is less affected. The former vegetables can be readily established from plants pulled from a seedbed (so called 'bare-root' transplants which have little or no soil retained around the roots), but the latter vegetables need to be grown in pots or compressed soil or compost 'blocks' and handled carefully in the field. Research has shown that those plants which can prevent excessive loss of water from their tissues and produce new roots readily recover most rapidly.

### What practical steps can be taken to prevent the transplanting check?

When plants are transplanted from seedboxes or a seedbed at least 25–50 per cent of the root system is lost or damaged. Experiments have shown that removing this amount of roots substantially delays recovery from the transplanting shock. So it is important to reduce root damage to a minimum and promote the growth of new roots as quickly as possible.

The amount of damage will obviously be less for plants raised in soil or peat blocks or peat pots than for bare root plants because the intact block of soil can be planted with the minimum of root disturbance. So raising plants in pots or soil blocks is a good way of reducing the transplanting check. Bare root transplants will suffer considerable damage when the plants are pulled for transplanting unless care is taken in the preparation of the seedbed where the plants will be raised. The soil should be well prepared, if possible digging in peat or compost to produce a good friable soil to encourage the growth of a good root system. Sowing too thickly will give too close a spacing and will increase the intertwining of roots which will be damaged when the plants are separated. In the garden 100 plants per square metre (10 plants per square foot) will be a useful population and will reduce root intertwining. Less damage will be done to the plants if they are loosened gently with a fork as they are being lifted. This will also preserve the soil around the roots, so preventing them drying out rapidly. Watering the ground prior to pulling the plants will also help to reduce damage.

During the transplanting of forest trees the roots are often dipped in a water-based gel usually made from sodium alginate to reduce water loss from the roots and to prevent them drying out. This improves re-establishment in trees, but no research work has been carried out on vegetables to demonstrate conclusively its effectiveness.

It is claimed that the degree of transplanting check can be reduced if the plants are 'hardened' prior to lifting. This involves reducing the amount of water to the plants, reducing the growing temperatures, or both during the last week or so of growth before planting out. Hardened tomato plants develop new roots faster probably because 'hardening' increases the sugar content of the leaves and the amount of wax on the leaves. This would aid renewal of root growth after planting and prevent water loss through the leaf surface, but experiments show that 'hardening' does not consistently improve transplant establishment for other vegetables.

Nearly all vegetables can be transplanted at the early seedling stage with little or no check to growth, but the older the plant the greater is the transplanting check. The check is particularly marked in vegetables which are flowering. This is because the plant does not produce new roots as readily at this stage of growth (see p. 96) as younger plants and so recovery from shock and the effects on yield are greater. For example, tomato plants transplanted at the flowering stage give, on average, 20 per cent lower yields than younger plants. Cauliflowers produced from transplants eight to twelve weeks old are delayed in maturity and give smaller and lower quality curds compared with those produced from five- to six-week-old transplants. The ideal growing conditions and length of the growing period for a number of vegetables are shown in Table 2.6.

It is traditional practice to clip off the leaves or parts of the leaves of transplants at, or just after, transplanting. It is generally believed that this prevents water loss, but there is no conclusive

**Table 2.6**

**A guide to the growing periods and conditions for transplant raising**

| | Temp °C(°F) | | Length of growing time |
|---|---|---|---|
| | Day | Night | (weeks) |
| **Cabbage** | 15–20 (60–68) | 10–15 (50–60) | 5–7 |
| **Cauliflower** | 15–20 | 12–15 (54–60) | 5–7 |
| **Broccoli** | 15–20 | 10–15 | 5–7 |
| **Brussels sprouts** | 15–20 | 10–15 | 5–7 |
| **Lettuce** | 15–20 | 10–15 | 6 |
| **Onion** | 15–20 | 7–12 (45–54) | 4–10* |
| **Celery** | 17–22 (63–72) | 12–17 (54–63) | 5–10* |
| **Tomato** | 20–25 (68–77) | 15–17 (60–63) | 6 |
| **Cucumber** | 20–30 (68–88) | 15–20 | 4–5 |
| **Marrow** | 20–25 | 15–17 | 4–5 |
| **Courgette** | 20–25 | 15–17 | 4–5 |
| **Pepper** | 20–25 | 15–17 | 9–10 |

* Shorter period for mid-season crops and longer period for early crops.

experimental evidence to support this practice and it could be detrimental because clipping off part of the leaves will reduce the ability of the plant to make enough food reserves for a new root system. It is common commercial practice in certain parts of the world to clip the leaves off the plants in the seedbeds *prior* to transplanting. This is done to promote a uniform plant size by 'holding back' the larger plants. It is also claimed with celery and tomatoes that this aids recovery of the transplant if the clipping is carried out two to four days before transplanting takes place, but not all the experimental evidence supports this claim.

Water loss can also be reduced by planting out on dull rather than sunny days and also planting out late in the day. Even when this is done it will still be necessary to water the plants frequently until they are 'standing up' and showing no signs of wilting early in the morning. It is not necessary to water all the soil surface, water can be more efficiently used by watering a small area around each plant (see Chapter 4). Although the maintenance of the water status of the plant after transplanting is most important the damaged root system is also less capable of obtaining nutrients from the soil. So for all vegetable transplants, it is beneficial to provide these in a concentrated and readily available form close to the root system. This can be done by applying a 'starter' fertilizer at the rate of 600 ml. (about ½ pint) to the base of each plant. These are commonly made with high analysis soluble fertilizers. A suitable starter can be made by adding 35 g. (1¼ oz.) and 56 g. (2 oz.) of 'Kaynitro' and triple superphosphate, respectively, to 11½ litres (2½ gallons) of water. This should be thoroughly mixed up and left overnight. Any insoluble material left in the bottom of the container can then be discarded.

In summary, transplanting causes damage to the root system. Rapid recovery from this damage can be promoted by attention to the following:

- Prepare the soil carefully and dig in compost or peat where the plants are to be raised.
- Allow adequate growing space for 'bare root' plants to reduce root intertwining.
- Plant young and not old plants.
- Lift the plants carefully from the seedbed.
- Plant out on dull days and water the plants frequently until they are established.
- Apply a 'starter' fertilizer.
- Grow transplants in 'blocks' or peat pots.

# 3 Plant foods and feeding

Discussions between gardeners on the feeding of plants can often become heated because they hold strong views on the subject. Yet for the majority of gardeners these views are based on accumulated experience over the years under particular conditions, and provided acceptable crops are obtained he regards the results as vindication of his feeding policy. Rarely does he have the time, space, or inclination to compare alternative methods or levels of manuring different crops. Although experience is a sound way of learning, the process can be long and difficult. By understanding the principles of feeding crops and by knowing about the general and relative responsiveness of different crops to fertilizers based on the results of many experiments, this process can be made shorter and easier for the gardener.

## Plant nutrition

All plants require a number of 'foods' to be able to grow, some of these being obtained from the atmosphere and others from the soil. Carbon is obtained from carbon dioxide in the air and water is absorbed through the roots. The carbon, hydrogen, and oxygen are combined in a series of complex processes in the plant to produce the carbohydrates which form the necessary basic building materials for plant tissue. The carbohydrates, in turn, are converted into more complex substances such as proteins and fats by combination with mineral nutrients such as nitrogen, phosphorus, and sulphur which are taken up by the roots.

So, as well as ensuring that essential sunlight is not excluded from plants by heavy shading and that there is sufficient moisture available for the plants to grow, the gardener must also ensure that the mineral nutrients necessary for rapid growth are available in the soil. Usually nutrients are added to the soil in the form of fertilizers, composts, or other manures, and in this chapter the nutrients required by various plants are discussed and indications are given of how to decide on the amount of fertilizer or manure to apply to obtain good yields of the different vegetables grown in the garden.

## The essential nutrients

Besides carbon, hydrogen, and oxygen which make up about 95 per cent of plant tissue, there are certain nutrient elements which are essential for growth. Some are required in relatively large quantities, such as nitrogen needed for producing proteins and magnesium which is a constituent of the green pigment chlorophyll. Other nutrients are required in much smaller amounts but are nevertheless just as vital for growth.

It is generally considered that there are twelve essential nutrients taken up from the soil. Six are referred to as major elements and six as minor or trace elements. These are listed below:

| **Major elements** | | **Minor elements** | |
|---|---|---|---|
| Nitrogen | (N) | Iron | (Fe) |
| Phosphorus | (P) | Manganese | (Mn) |
| Potassium | (K) | Boron | (B) |
| Calcium | (Ca) | Zinc | (Zn) |
| Magnesium | (Mg) | Copper | (Cu) |
| Sulphur | (S) | Molybdenum | (Mo) |

The elements required for plant growth occur naturally in most soils, being derived from the weathering of minerals or the atmosphere in rainwater (nitrogen), or by the decay of plant material.

Soil micro-organisms help to decompose slowly organic matter or humus and produce the simplest forms of nitrogen and other nutrients which can be absorbed by the roots of plants. At the same time, nutrients are lost from the soil by leaching, this being a particularly large source of the loss of nitrogen in coarse or sandy soils.

Crops take up the nutrients from the soil in considerable quantities and the natural cycle of the return of decaying plant waste to the soil is broken if the crop is removed for consumption. It is therefore necessary to supply extra nutrients as manure or fertilizers to make up for these losses and to ensure good growth of succeeding crops.

## The soil as a nutrient source

As well as acting as a base for the plant roots to grow, the soil provides the main source of the plant's nutrients, the majority of which are dissolved in the soil water. A good soil structure is, therefore, vitally important for the plant to be able to develop a good root system to obtain the water and nutrients it needs and so to grow satisfactorily. Some methods of obtaining good soil-structure are briefly discussed in Chapter 4 (p. 91).

The roots of some vegetables have been shown to grow far deeper in the soil than many gardeners realize. For example, in well-drained porous soils, roots of some crops such as parsnips and broad beans have penetrated 122 cm. (4 ft.) or more. However, feeding of most crops is done by applying fertilizers or digging composts in the top 30 cm. (12 in.) of soil. This produces more favourable conditions for root growth in this top layer, but deeper rooting enables the plant to obtain nutrients from the lower layers of soil containing moisture, especially in drought periods. For this reason, it is worthwhile digging in compost or manures as deeply as possible.

## Soil acidity and the use of lime

Too often it is evident that some gardeners are under the impression that a good dressing of lime all over their vegetable patch each autumn is an essential for good cropping. At the other extreme, there are those who never consider liming their gardens.

Depending principally on its content of calcium, a soil can be acid, neutral, or alkaline, the former condition indicating that alkaline materials such as calcium salts are in short supply and the latter that abundant alkaline salts are present (for example, in a calcareous or chalky soil). It is well known that some plants prefer acid soils whilst others prefer more alkaline conditions. Two things are therefore important for the gardener to know—first, whether his soil is acid or alkaline, and secondly, the preferred level of acidity or alkalinity of the crops he intends to grow.

### Soil pH

The acidity-alkalinity of a soil is usually measured on the pH scale. The theory and basis of this scale is beyond the scope of this book, but a value of 7 indicates the neutral mid-point of the scale, which is the pH of chemically pure water. The pH of soils usually ranges from about 3 in acid moorlands to about 8 or 9 in soils containing high proportions of chalk or limestone (calcium carbonate). The majority of soils have a pH in the range 4.5–7.5.

A satisfactory estimate of soil pH can be obtained with an indicator dye which changes colour with the degree of acidity or alkalinity of soil solution. This method forms the basis of several soil test-kits which are on the market. Usually a small amount of soil is shaken with distilled water and the indicator added; after settling, the colour of the clear solution is compared with a standard colour chart.

The acidity or alkalinity of a soil influences the availability of some nutrient elements to plants. A deficiency of calcium can occur at low pH values, but it is difficult to distinguish the symptoms from those of high concentrations of aluminium and manganese which become soluble in acid conditions.

Fig. 3.1. Young cauliflower plant showing symptoms of molybdenum deficiency. (Note that the main growing point has not developed; the young leaves are characteristically stunted.)

Molybdenum deficiency is more prevalent when the soil is acid and is best known for producing 'whiptail' in cauliflower, with a characteristic deformation of the leaves and death of the growing point (see Fig. 3.1). At high pH values, deficiencies of iron, manganese, and boron are common, since these trace elements are rendered insoluble in the soil and therefore become unavailable to plants. The symptoms of these deficiencies are described later in this chapter.

It is impossible to give a precise guide as to the soil pH required by each of the different vegetables. Crops grown on organic soils (such as the peats) will grow perfectly well at lower pH values than the same crops grown on mineral soils. There is considerable variation depending on soil type, but it is generally accepted that vegetable crops are best grown on mineral soils with pH values between 6.0 and 6.5. On a peaty soil, plant growth will generally be satisfactory with a pH value of 5.5–6.0.

## Plant sensitivity to pH and lime

The various species of plant grown in the garden differ in the range of pH values within which they will grow successfully; an attempt is made to indicate these ranges below:

**Soil pH values preferred by vegetable species**

| pH 5.0–6.0 | pH 5.5–7.0 | | pH 6.5–7.5 |
|---|---|---|---|
| Potato | Broad bean | Parsnip | Asparagus |
| Rhubarb | Brussels sprouts | Pea | Beetroot |
| | Cabbage | Radish | Carrot |
| | Cucumber | Swede | Cauliflower |
| | French bean | Sweet corn | Celery |
| | Marrow | Tomato | Leek |
| | Parsley | Turnip | Lettuce |
| | | | Onion |
| | | | Spinach |

## How much lime?

Adjustment of the soil pH for individual crops is impossible as it often takes several seasons to correct soil acidity by liming. The best policy is to adjust garden soils to about 6.5 (5.8 if a peat soil) at which all vegetables should grow successfully.

A simple pH test will indicate whether a soil needs liming but the amounts required are dependent on the soil type. A sandy soil with a course texture requires about 270 g., a loam 540 g., and a clay or organic soil 810 g. per square metre (½ lb., 1 lb., and 1½ lb. per square yard respectively) of ground limestone to raise the soil pH one unit, i.e. from pH 6.0 to 7.0. It is preferable to use several annual dressings of smaller quantities rather than to use a large amount on one occasion. Hydrated lime can also be used, the effects being similar except that hydrated lime reacts more quickly with soil but is less pleasant to handle.

### When to apply lime

The purpose of liming is to neutralize the acidity in the soil, but this is a process that is not completed quickly. In the case of hydrated lime, damage to crops can be caused if it is applied just before sowing or planting. The best time to apply lime is prior to autumn digging so that crop damage is avoided and the full effect of the liming achieved. It should be applied in the rotational sequence before the lime-loving crops.

In most situations, the natural trend is for soil to become acid so liming is normally required, but there are a few soils where it may be desirable to make them more acid and this presents greater difficulty. However, the incorporation of acid peat into the soil can assist the process. Sulphur and ferrous sulphate are also used with success on some soils (135 g. per square metre; 4 oz. per square yard). If a gardener has a very alkaline soil, he is perhaps best advised to avoid plants which require acid conditions and to avoid using fertilizers such as 'Nitrochalk', which contain calcium.

## Fertilizers and manures

Fertilizers and manures are applied to the soil to ensure that the plant has sufficient nutrients to enable it to grow satisfactorily. On visiting a local garden shop, a gardener is often faced with a wide variety of types and proprietary brands of fertilizer and this can be confusing. A knowledge of the basic forms of fertilizer can often help in making the correct choice for the vegetables to be grown.

Most 'artificial' or inorganic chemical fertilizers contain one or more of the three major nutrients: nitrogen, phosphorus, and potassium. These nutrients occur widely, but plants can only absorb them in specific chemical forms. Thus, the value of a fertilizer is measured by how much of its nitrogen, phosphorus, or potassium is actually available to plants. The contents of major nutrients have to be given on the label or bag of inorganic fertilizer as '%N' for nitrogen, '%$P_2O_5$' for phosphorus, and '%$K_2O$' for potassium. The higher the percentage of a particular nutrient, the greater is the amount of that nutrient in a given weight of a fertilizer. For example, a fertilizer containing 20 per cent $P_2O_5$ has twice the concentration of phosphorus as one with 10 per cent $P_2O_5$.

### Nitrogen fertilizers

Nitrogen fertilizers are generally in the form of ammonium salts, nitrate, or urea. The common forms include:

| | %N |
|---|---|
| Sulphate of ammonia | 21 |
| 'Nitrochalk' | 21 |
| Ammonium nitrate | 34.5 |
| Urea | 45 |
| Nitrate of soda | 15.5 |
| Calcium nitrate | 15.5 |

Sulphate of ammonia is a common and easily obtainable nitrogen fertilizer which is not readily leached from the soil since the nitrogen in the form of ammonium is held on the clay particles. The ammonium nitrogen displaces calcium from the clay and forms soluble calcium sulphate which is leached from the soil. Since calcium is lost, the effect is to make the soil more acid and, whilst this may be an advantage for acid-loving plants and in calcareous soils, it is generally considered to be undesirable in the vegetable garden. In very sandy soils, which do not contain many clay particles, the ammonium nitrogen will not be retained in the soil and will be leached more quickly. Sulphate of ammonia is a quick-acting fertilizer but not as quick-acting as those containing the nitrate form of nitrogen. It should be applied to moist soil and watered-in if at all possible. The effect of watering-in is to overcome its tendency to scorch leaves and roots, which can cause a check to growth before beneficial effects can be obtained. It is a cheap and easily stored material and its best use is to give a quick boost to growth for leafy crops such as spinach and cabbages.

'Nitrochalk' and ammonium nitrate both contain ammonium and nitrate forms of nitrogen. 'Nitrochalk' also contains chalk which counteracts the acidifying effects of ammonium nitrogen. Both are rapid in their action due to their nitrate content. They are incorporated in the soil prior to sowing or planting as a base dressing and used later as a side dressing for boosting crop growth when extra nitrogen is required. Both of these fertilizers take up moisture, which leads to deterioration and difficulty in handling. It is therefore important that they are stored in sealed plastic bags.

Urea contains a high proportion of nitrogen which is converted to ammonium carbonate in the soil. Gaseous ammonia is formed and can be lost if it has not been well mixed into the soil. Nitrate of soda (Chilean nitrate) and calcium nitrate (nitrate of lime) are rapidly acting nitrogen fertilizers. The fact that plants respond more quickly to nitrogen in the nitrate form make them very useful for side dressings on growing crops. Beet and celery also respond to sodium and it is with these crops that nitrate of soda has its main use. Again, these nitrates absorb moisture and must be kept in airtight containers.

### Phosphorus fertilizers

The main forms of inorganic phosphorus fertilizers are superphosphate (20 per cent $P_2O_5$) and triple superphosphate (44 per cent $P_2O_5$). These consist mainly of calcium phosphates which are to a large extent soluble in water but, in the soil, are quickly rendered relatively insoluble and, therefore, unavailable. The phosphate is subsequently slowly released into the soil solution and so becomes available to the plant.

### Potassium fertilizers

The two main potassium fertilizers are potassium chloride (muriate of potash, 60 per cent $K_2O$) and potassium sulphate (sulphate of potash, 49 per cent $K_2O$). The sulphate is more expensive but is easier to store and is probably the safest to use in the garden as damage can arise from the use of the chloride, particularly in the early stages of growth.

### Compound fertilizers

Ready-mixed or compound fertilizers contain varying proportions of nitrogen, phosphorus, and potassium. These are often convenient to use as they are time-saving and are often in a granular form which makes handling easier. A method of abbreviation is often used to describe how much of each available nutrient is in any fertilizer. For example, if a fertilizer contains 20 per cent N, 10 per cent $P_2O_5$, and 10 per cent $K_2O$, it is referred to as a 20:10:10 fertilizer. There are a wide range of compound fertilizers available to gardeners, probably the most common being one which contains equal amounts of N, $P_2O_5$, and $K_2O$, for example 'National Growmore' (7:7:7).

Although the more concentrated fertilizers need less storage space for a given amount of nutrients, they are more likely to cause damage to young seedlings unless carefully applied. With care, however, they can be used successfully and often the gardener can obtain surprisingly good value for money by choosing according to the nutrient contents of the various compound fertilizers available to him.

### Organic manures and composts

High prices are often paid by gardeners for organic fertilizers in the belief that they have properties which provide better sources of nutrients than the so-called 'artificial' fertilizers. Whilst the bulky manures do contribute substantially to improving the physical condition of poorly structured soils, so giving better growth, it is equally true that organic manures such as blood, bone or fish meal, composts, farmyard manure, seaweed, and the like depend for nutrient value on their content of nitrogen, phosphorus, and potassium in exactly the same way as chemical fertilizers.

Research has shown that organic sources of nitrogen such as blood and bone or fish meal produce no greater yields than the equivalent amounts of inorganic fertilizers. The claim that they can be used more safely, without damage or scorch to crops, because the nitrogen is released more slowly is open to question since, when finely ground, these fertilizers can release inorganic nitrogen rapidly.

Nevertheless, these materials may be readily available to the gardener and an indication of their nitrogen, phosphorus, and potassium contents are as follows, though it should be noted that they vary according to source and processing:

| | %N | %$P_2O_5$ | %$K_2O$ |
|---|---|---|---|
| Dried blood | 12–14 | 2.5 | 1 |
| Hoof and horn | 14 | 2.5 | – |
| Bone meal | 4 | 7 | – |
| Fish meal | 9 | 2.5 | – |
| Seaweed (dried) | 1.5 | 0.5 | 5 |
| Wood ashes | – | 2.5 | 5 |

Farmyard manure varies widely in nutrient content but on average somewhat less than ¼ per cent N, ¼ per cent $P_2O_5$, and ½ per cent $K_2O$ may be expected to be available. Thus large amounts are required to supply the plants' nutrient needs and much of the benefit achieved is from the improvement of soil structure. Sewage sludges can provide useful quantities of nitrogen and phosphorus but often contain high amounts of metals, particularly when they come from industrial areas. These metals can be toxic to plants so sludge should be used with the utmost caution.

One of the most common and deep-rooted beliefs among certain gardeners and consumers is that crops grown with organic manures are in some way more nutritious than crops grown with chemical fertilizers. There is no scientific evidence to support this view. The plant uses nutrients from the soil in their simplest form and there is no evidence to show that it makes any difference where they come from.

### Liquid fertilizers

There are many brands of liquid fertilizer on the market containing varying proportions of the three major nutrient elements and often minor elements. Usually they are sold in solid form which needs dissolving in water or as concentrates which need diluting. Liquid feeding is particularly useful in glasshouses but can also be useful in the vegetable garden when individual plants can be treated for deficiency of a particular nutrient. As the nutrients used for this form of feeding are already in solution, they clearly act more quickly than those applied as solid fertilizers. The instructions on the label of the product being used must be followed to get the best results, since over-use can lead to damage to plants.

Plants also have the ability to absorb nutrients in solution through the leaf as well as through the root so that foliar feeding is possible. The amounts of nutrients that plants are able to absorb in this way are relatively small and invariably it is more worth while to concentrate on feeding through the soil. However, the problem of a soil with a low magnesium content will often take several years to correct by incorporating magnesium-containing fertilizers into the soil, whereas spraying with a 2 per cent solution of Epsom salts (magnesium sulphate) on two or three occasions during the growth of a crop is invariably successful. The minor elements boron, molybdenum, manganese, zinc, and copper can all be applied as foliar sprays to supply these nutrients to plants or, in some cases, to correct disorders.

## Fertilizing vegetables

If all soil was ideally fertile and contained sufficient quantities of all the nutrients to supply the needs for plant growth, there would be no need to apply additional nutrients in the form of fertilizers or manures. Of course this is rarely the case, although some soils have adequate supplies of some nutrients so they do not require further additions. The majority do require regular dressings of fertilizers to ensure optimum yields.

### Response to fertilizers

The way in which a plant responds to applications of a fertilizer depends principally on the nutrient content of the soil and the type of crop. Even when no fertilizer is applied, a yield is obtained which represents the effect of the nutrient that is already in the soil. An application of fertilizer may increase the yield substantially, but the application of twice the amount will not necessarily double the increase in yield. The return in extra yield becomes progressively less with each additional portion of fertilizer applied and a point is reached where the cost of applying a larger amount would not be justified for the small return that would be obtained. This type of response is considered to follow 'the law of diminishing returns'.

Obviously less fertilizer will be required for optimum yield if the soil contains large amounts of a given nutrient than if it contains relatively low quantities. So in order to get an idea of how much fertilizer to apply a commercial grower submits samples of his soil to a laboratory and obtains a chemical analysis. By shaking the soil with sodium bicarbonate and ammonium nitrate solutions, the laboratory is able to determine the amounts of phosphorus and potassium in the soil which are 'available' for plants and which the roots can extract. It is not possible to get a measure of nitrogen availability from laboratory tests and the grower uses his knowledge of past cropping on a particular site to help him estimate the amount of nitrogen likely to be available in the soil. Account is also taken of the rainfall, the soil texture, and previous applications of organic manures.

Research over many years has provided much information on the responsiveness of crops to fertilizers and has shown that the response varies depending on the levels of nutrient in the soil and the different vegetables. For example, Brussels sprouts can be grown satisfactorily on a soil containing relatively low amounts of available phosphorus and so require only small additions of this nutrient, whereas lettuce require larger amounts of phosphate fertilizer in order to produce high yields. This provides a good example to dispel the myth that a heavier crop removing more nutrient from the soil must require a larger quantity of nutrient applied as fertilizer, for Brussels sprouts take up far more phosphorus than lettuce but obtain it by more efficiently extracting it from the soil.

Having obtained an analysis of his soil for phosphorus and potassium and having assessed the likely nitrogen status of the soil, the commercial grower will consult tables of responses and get guidance as to the amount of these three nutrients that are necessary for the crop that he is growing. Unfortunately the gardener is not in a position to obtain a chemical analysis of his soil and, unlike the soil test-kits for pH measurement, test-kits for phosphorus and potassium on the market at the time of writing are not altogether reliable. However, 'rapid-tests' have been developed recently at the National Vegetable Research Station and it is hoped that these will be on the market in the near future. The gardener will then be in a position to assess his requirements more accurately. In the meantime, it is possible for gardeners to use the information available on vegetable fertilizer requirements by making certain assumptions which are described later.

## Injury to plants by fertilizers

Sometimes the responses to fertilizers are less than expected, particularly when nitrogen is applied. These are invariably caused by an adverse effect of applying fertilizer which offsets the yield-increasing effect. As the amount of fertilizer applied is increased the beneficial effect is dominant at first, producing increases in yield, but as the amounts increase, the adverse effect becomes important and with high levels of fertilizer yields are actually reduced. The effect can be such that with some crops too much fertilizer can produce lower yields than applying no fertilizer at all.

The injurious effects of applying fertilizer are caused by too high a concentration of salts in the soil solution, particularly when nitrates and chlorides are used, causing damage to young roots. Broadcast applications of nitrogen fertilizers before sowing can severely depress the numbers of seedlings emerging as well as causing reduced growth of those that do survive. The effect is most marked in the early stages of growth and, although well-established plants can tolerate the conditions, the potential yield of the crop is hardly ever achieved. Similar effects can be obtained with potassium, especially if muriate of potash is used, but phosphate fertilizers do not produce such a serious problem.

## How to apply fertilizers

The adverse effects of applying nitrogen and potassium fertilizer before sowing or transplanting young plants may be overcome in several ways:

- Use only part of the required amount of nitrogen fertilizer before sowing and side-dress the remainder after the crop is established.
- Spread the nitrogen fertilizer between the rows so that the

young roots do not come into contact with high salt concentrations.

- Keep the soil moist until seedling emergence is complete or a transplanted crop is established.
- Apply potassium fertilizers in the autumn before digging.
- Use sulphate of potash which causes less damage than muriate of potash.

Whilst it is generally inadvisable to have nitrogen and potassium fertilizers concentrated near the seeds or young roots, there can be a distinct advantage in placing phosphate fertilizers in this position. Young plants can benefit considerably from extra phosphate supplies, and as phosphate fertilizers tend to become rapidly unavailable to plants in the soil, this provides a ready source of supply in the region which the roots quickly penetrate. Putting the required amount of superphosphate in a band about 5 cm. (2 in.) to the side and 5–7.5 cm. (2–3 in.) below the seed is often found to be more beneficial than broadcast applications since the fertilizer in the band is in less contact with the soil and is not absorbed, so remaining available to the roots for a longer time. Crops responsive to the placement of phosphate fertilizer include onions, lettuces, carrots, and French beans.

### When to apply fertilizer

Different crops have varying lengths of growing season and common sense tells us that crops which have a short duration of growth, such as radishes and lettuces, need ample nutrients from the start of their growth. In contrast, crops such as Brussels sprouts and leeks, which have a long period of growth, require their nutrients over a considerably longer period of time. Phosphate and potassium can be applied at almost any time prior to sowing or planting, but if a fertilizer containing nitrogen is being used it should be applied just before sowing and/or during the growth of the crop, especially on light soils.

The timing of nitrogen applications is the key to successful growing of many crops. The best advice that can be given is to make sure by top dressing that a crop has ample nitrogen when it is growing most rapidly. If heavy rainfall occurs at any time, it is more than likely that a considerable proportion of the applied nitrogen has been lost from the top-soil.

### Interaction between nutrients

The balance of nutrients available to the plant is important and chemical reaction in the soil and at the plant roots can lead to one nutrient element affecting the uptake of another either by increasing (enhancement) or reducing (antagonism) the amount taken up by the plant. The use of a nitrate fertilizer tends to enhance the uptake of potassium from the soil and so it is preferable to use a nitrogen fertilizer containing nitrate when growing a crop which requires a high level of potassium for good growth. Antagonistic effects are far better known, one of the most common being the reduction in uptake of calcium and magnesium by the use of potassium fertilizers. Leaves showing magnesium deficiency are probably those most commonly brought to the scientist or adviser for diagnosis. It probably occurs more on tomatoes than any other crop since they are invariably given high potassium feeds in glasshouses. For this reason, magnesium sulphate (Epsom salts) is often included in feeds for tomatoes.

Many antagonistic interactions between both major and minor nutrients have been demonstrated and a few of the important ones are as follows:

- Potassium reduces the uptake of manganese, copper, zinc, and magnesium.
- Magnesium reduces the uptake of potassium and calcium.
- Nitrate nitrogen reduces the uptake of phosphorus.
- Calcium reduces the uptake of potassium and magnesium.

Fortunately, most plants can grow satisfactorily in soils containing widely varying amounts of most nutrients without the risk of serious effects from interactions. Nevertheless, when a deficiency of a particular nutrient occurs (p. 80) it is often helpful to consider whether the problem has been caused by excessive manuring with fertilizers containing antagonistic nutrients.

## A system for the garden

We have seen how different crops vary greatly in their need for nitrogen, phosphate, and potassium fertilizer, and how soils also vary in their nutrient content. The amount of each nutrient required can be predicted accurately only if the amount already in the soil has been measured by chemical analysis. As the gardener is unlikely to be able to get his soil analysed readily, a method of forecasting fertilizer needs without soil analysis can be used. Although it can only be approximate as it depends on a number of assumptions (in particular, that most plant waste is returned to the soil as compost) it is nevertheless a good guide.

Nitrogen fertilizers behave differently from either potassium or phosphate in soil because nitrogen is readily leached out of the soil by heavy rainfall and fresh applications are necessary for each crop. Furthermore, quite large amounts of nitrogen are required for high yields of many vegetables. On the other hand, the benefits from phosphate and potassium fertilizer usually last for several years and so, in the garden, it does not matter greatly how or when they are applied, or if the amounts vary from year to year. However, the average application over a number of years must be sufficient to maintain levels in the soil above the minimum for good growth of all crops and to replace that taken out of the system by the vegetables we eat. It follows then, that the best plan for using fertilizers in the garden is to adjust the nitrogen application for each crop and to maintain phosphate and potassium at roughly the same levels in the soil for all crops.

### Nitrogen

Fertilizers containing nitrogen are usually worked into the soil immediately before sowing, or applied partly at this time and partly as a mid-season top-dressing between the plants. The total amounts of a range of nitrogen fertilizers which can be applied to meet the needs of various vegetables are given in Table 3.1. To find how much fertilizer to apply, first look on the bag and check the percentage N in the fertilizer. Then find, in Table 3.1, the percentage N which is closest to it and apply the amount appropriate for the crop you intend to grow. For example, broad beans will need 136 g. per square metre (4 oz. per square yard) of a fertilizer containing 5 per cent N but only 51 g. per square metre (1½ oz. per square yard) of one containing 15 per cent N.

### Phosphate and potassium

If your nitrogen fertilizer also contains about the same percentage of phosphate ($P_2O_5$) and potassium ($K_2O$) as of N (e.g. 7:7:7 or 15:15:15) you will automatically apply enough phosphate and potassium along with the nitrogen. If your nitrogen fertilizer does not contain phosphate or potassium, you must apply these two nutrients separately. This can be done, for example, with 68 g. per square metre (2 oz. per square yard) of superphosphate and 34 g. per square metre (1 oz. per square yard) of sulphate of potash either in the autumn or before sowing, but other phosphate or potassium fertilizers could also be used with amounts adjusted according to the percentage $P_2O_5$ or percentage $K_2O$. It can also be done by applying farmyard manure at about 5.4 kg. per square metre (10 lb. per square yard).

## If things go wrong!

If plants have an insufficient supply of a major or minor nutrient, they invariably show visual symptoms of the deficiency. However, it is often possible to correct a deficiency by treatment of the plants or the surrounding soil. Some of the more common symptoms are now tabulated together with possible remedies. These will aid you in making your own diagnoses and cure.

**Table 3.1**

**Amount of fertilizer (grams per square metre) required to meet the nitrogen demands of vegetable crops**

| | **Percentage nitrogen in fertilizer (quoted on bag or packet)** | | | | | | |
|---|---|---|---|---|---|---|---|
| | **5** | **10** | **15** | **20** | **25** | **30** | **35** |
| Pea | 0 | 0 | 0 | 0 | 0 | 0 | 0 |
| Carrot; radish | 51 | 25.5 | 17 | 17 | 8.5 | 8.5 | 8.5 |
| Broad bean; parsnip; swede | 136 | 68 | 51 | 34 | 34 | 25.5 | 25.5 |
| Lettuce; onion | 187 | 102 | 68 | 51 | 42.5 | 34 | 34 |
| Calabrese; French bean; turnip | 221 | 119 | 68 | 59.5 | 51 | 42.5 | 34 |
| Leek; potato (early) | 306* | 153* | 102* | 76.5* | 59.5* | 51* | 42.5* |
| Potato (main crop); red-beet; spinach; summer cauliflower | 374* | 187* | 136* | 102* | 76.5* | 68* | 42.5* |
| Brussels sprouts; summer cabbage; winter cabbage | 510* | 255* | 170* | 136* | 102* | 85* | 76.5* |

* For drilled crops, the amount of fertilizer quoted for lettuces should be applied prior to sowing and the remainder after the crop is established.

**Major element deficiencies**

| | Symptoms | Treatment |
|---|---|---|
| **Nitrogen** | Usually the first symptoms are pale yellow leaves at the base of the plant where leaves also die prematurely. These leaves have reddish and orange tints in the case of brassicas. Growth is poor | Apply a top-dressing of nitrogen fertilizer around the plants and water in |
| **Phosphorus** | In some plants no symptoms appear but growth is poor and slow (lettuce). Lower leaves can exhibit a dull, blue-green coloration | Cure is difficult with the current crop as phosphate fertilizer cannot be watered in. Try placing some superphosphate under the surface of the soil close to the roots |
| **Potassium** | Older leaves develop chlorosis (loss of green) colour) followed by scorch around the leaf margins (see Fig. 3.2). Brown spots can occur on leaves | Apply muriate of potash around the plants and water thoroughly |
| **Magnesium** | Symptoms begin on the older leaves; chlorosis between the veins gives a mottled or 'marbled' effect. The veins remain green and leaves fall from the plant. In tomatoes 'green back' occurs on the fruit (a green shoulder surrounding the calyx) | Apply Epsom salts (magnesium sulphate) as a foliar spray (20 g. dissolved in a litre of water (3 oz. per gallon)) every two weeks. May also be watered on to the soil |

| | Symptoms | Treatment |
|---|---|---|
| **Calcium** | Young leaves 'cup' or curl inwards and the growing point is often deformed or blackened. Calcium deficiency causes 'tip-burn' in lettuces, 'blackheart' in celery, 'blossom-end rot' in tomatoes, and 'internal browning' in Brusseels sprouts | Spray fortnightly with a calcium nitrate solution (3 g. per litre) ($\frac{1}{2}$ oz. per gallon) |

## Minor element deficiencies

| | Symptoms | Treatment |
|---|---|---|
| **Zinc** | Leaves develop a yellow mottling and young terminal leaflets rosette | Spray with a solution of zinc sulphate ($1\frac{1}{2}$ g. per litre) ($\frac{1}{2}$ oz. per 2 gallons) |
| **Iron** | Young leaves turn pale and chlorotic—almost bleached in severe cases. Veins remain dark green. Occurs mostly on chalky soils | Spray or water with sequestered iron (obtainable at garden shops) |
| **Manganese** | Interveinal chlorosis of older leaves giving a mottled appearance. Spots of dead tissue on the leaf ('marsh spot' in peas and beans) | Spray with manganese sulphate solution ($1\frac{1}{2}$ g. per litre) ($\frac{1}{2}$ oz. per 2 gallons) |
| **Boron** | Very similar to calcium deficiency. Terminal buds die. Blackening of crown of beetroot. Hollow or split stems in brassicas | Spray with borax solution (6 g. per litre) (1 oz. per gallon) |

| | Symptoms | Treatment |
|---|---|---|
| **Copper** | Symptoms vary according to crop. Youngest leaf tips of onions turn yellow/ white, wilt, and twist. Young leaves of beans and peas turn greyish green. Only common on peaty soils | Spray with Bordeaux powder or cuprous oxide ($1\frac{1}{2}$ g. per litre) ($\frac{1}{2}$ oz. per 2 gallons) |
| **Molybdenum** | Leaf lamina fails to develop, resulting in a strap-like leaf. Interveinal yellow-green mottling of older leaves, 'Whiptail' of cauliflower and broccoli – growing point stunted or blind (see Fig. 3.1) | It is too late when symptoms develop! (Water the seedbed with a solution containing 6 g. ammonium or sodium molybdate per litre (1 oz. per gallon) next time this crop is grown) |

The symptoms given for the various nutrients are given only as a guide. It should be emphasized that variations occur between crops. Other factors which may give symptoms can resemble or be associated with nutrient disorders. Damage caused by weed-killers and root damage by pests which can cause reduction of nutrient uptake (for example, mild cabbage root fly damage can give the appearance of nitrogen deficiency) and some virus infection symptoms can be very similar to nutrient disorders. Lettuce mosaic virus symptoms are similar to those of magnesium deficiency, both giving a distinct 'marbling' or mottled effect to the leaves.

The remedies outlined are 'last resort' actions but do not exceed the amounts stated. Prevention is of course better than cure and tell-tale symptoms one year should be remembered and noted to ensure that action is taken to prevent a recurrence in future years. Fertilizers are readily obtainable which contain several or all of the various trace elements and can be used if deficiency symptoms regularly appear.

Fig. 3.2. Leaves of turnip showing chlorosis around the edges of leaves caused by potassium deficiency.

# 4 Watering vegetable crops

Gardeners are well aware that watering their vegetable crops gives better growth, better quality, and higher yields. This has led to the belief that all vegetables will always benefit from watering, and the more water that is given the better. *This is not so*. It is very easy to give too much water too often.

Apart from the waste of water, time, and effort, watering unnecessarily may merely increase the growth of the plant without increasing the size of the edible part. It may discourage root growth (making the plants more drought-susceptible), it may wash nitrogenous fertilizers out of reach of the roots, and it may reduce flavour. So it is worth understanding how vegetable crops respond to watering. It is also worth knowing how to water different vegetables effectively and efficiently.

How do we decide when water should be given and how much to apply? Fortunately a lot of research has been done on this subject and these questions can be answered for many crops.

However, before dealing with individual crops an understanding of why plants require water, and of the many factors which affect the plants' needs and response to watering, will give a better appreciation of the water requirements of different crops.

## Why plants require water

Plants take up water from the soil through their roots and it is lost from their leaves into the surrounding atmosphere through small pores or stomata. The loss of water from the plant into the atmosphere is a physical process which is determined by the amount of sunshine, temperature, relative humidity of the air, and also the amount of wind experienced, and, as such, can be calculated or measured. However, the plant is able to restrict its water loss when there is a shortage of soil moisture or when the rate of loss is extremely high – a necessary survival mechanism.

So, during long, hot, sunny days in summer any vegetable crop where leaves fully cover the ground, and which has a plentiful supply of soil moisture, will lose by evapotranspiration more than 5.4 litres of water per square metre (1 gallon per square yard) of crop per day. Conversely, under cloudier, cooler conditions and with shorter days in spring and autumn the water loss may be as little as 0.7–1.4 litres per square metre per day (1–2 pints per square yard).

Whatever the conditions large quantities of water pass through the plant during the course of its growth, but only a small proportion becomes incorporated into the cell tissue. This large throughput gives several benefits: the stomata remain open and all parts

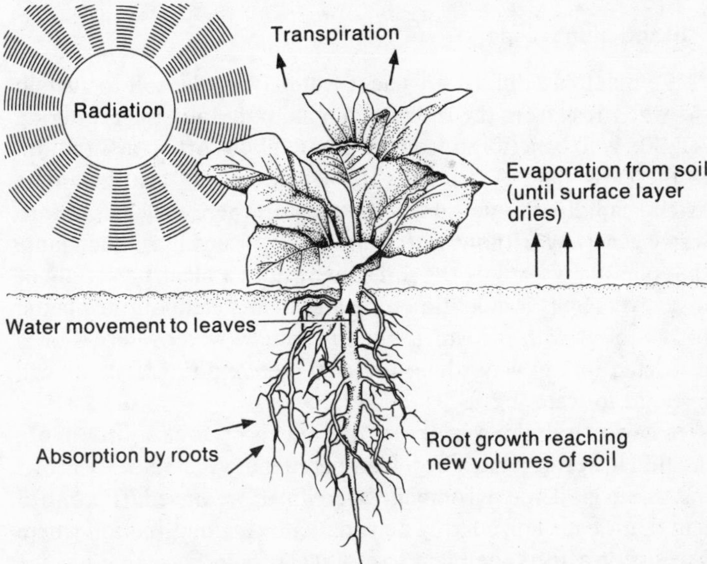


Fig. 4.1. Water loss from the plant and soil.

of the plant tend to be in a fully turgid condition. This enables photosynthesis, respiration, and other essential processes to take place efficiently. It helps the absorption of nutrients by the roots and their movement within the plant. In addition, the loss of large quantities of water by evaporation from the leaf surface has a beneficial cooling effect under hot conditions.

## Plant response to watering

Very few gardeners are curious enough to leave a few plants unwatered to see what difference watering will bring about. But there are often situations when watering will not produce any effect at all and, in some instances, where it will cause unwanted effects. So it is useful to outline the circumstances and factors which cause a plant to respond or be unresponsive to watering and the nature of any response.

### Will the plant respond?

If the plant can obtain sufficient water from the soil to sustain the water loss from the leaves at a maximum rate, then watering is unlikely to benefit the growing plant. This is often the situation in the early part of a plant's life when actively growing roots extend rapidly into new areas of wet soil where they can absorb water generally without restriction. But if rainfall is inadequate to replenish dry soil, if the soil cannot hold a plentiful supply of water, if there is competition for water from neighbouring plants, or if root growth is insufficient to tap new water reserves or is restricted in any way, then, under these conditions, plants will respond to watering.

It is worth looking at these different aspects in a little more detail. However, it must be remembered that vegetables are growing in the garden environment over which we have little control and that we are considering a dynamic, changing situation where one factor affects the plant's response to another.

## The soil water reservoir

The amount of water held in the soil reservoir is obviously a crucial factor affecting any plant's response to watering. Water is retained in the soil both in the pore spaces and as a thin film over the surface of the particles (see Fig. 4.2). When soil is holding the maximum amount of water under freely draining conditions it is at 'field capacity'. As the soil gradually dries out by evaporation from the surface or by extraction by plant roots, the water is held by the soil with greater and greater surface-tension forces. As a result the plant has greater and greater difficulty in absorbing the water until a stage is reached when the roots cannot take up the water fast enough and the plant starts to wilt. When the plant does not regain its turgid state even overnight then the soil moisture content has reached the 'wilting point' and the plant will eventually die if it is not watered. The

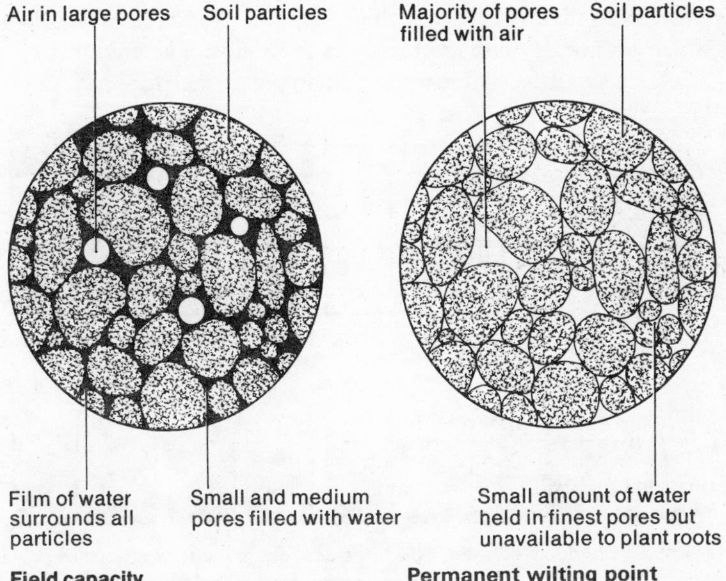


Fig. 4.2. Representation of the soil moisture status at the condition of field capacity and permanent wilting point.

water held by the soil between these two conditions of field capacity and the wilting point is 'available water' for plants.

Obviously the soils which contain the most available water will sustain the plants for the longest time before wilting occurs. Even at the wilting point there is still water in the soil, but it is held in the smallest pores with such force that the plants cannot absorb it and so is called 'unavailable water'.

The amount of available water held in a soil will depend on the size of the individual particles present, which gives differences in soil *texture*, and on the way the particles are grouped together, which alters the *structure* of the soil.

*Soil-texture effects.* Observant gardeners know only too well that if the soil contains a high proportion of coarse sand particles then water drains freely through it and very little is retained. On these soils plants need to be watered frequently. But if there is a good mixture of coarse and fine sand together with some smaller particles of silt and clay then these loams are good retentive soils which do not dry out so quickly as the sands. The amounts of available and unavailable water held in the surface foot of repre-

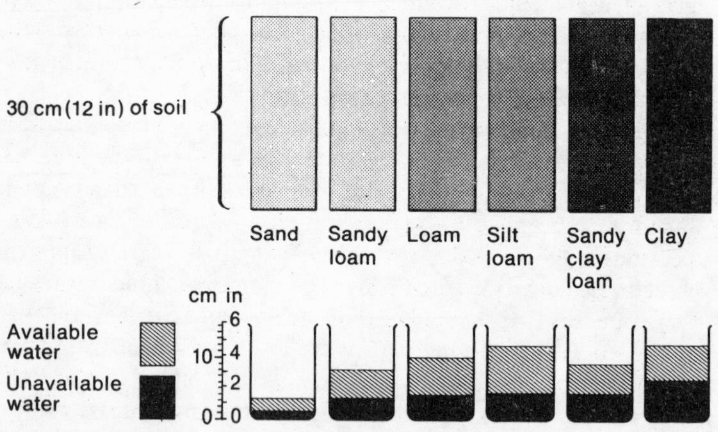


Fig. 4.3. Comparative amounts of available and unavailable water held by soils of different texture at field capacity.

sentative soils of different textures are shown in Fig. 4.3. It can be seen that a plant growing in the silt loam would have four times the amount of water available to it than a comparable plant growing in the coarse-sand soil; it would therefore not require watering so frequently.

There is not much that even the gardener can do about altering the *texture* of his soil to make it more retentive of water. In days gone by clay was often spread on coarse sandy soils to help water retention, but this is no longer done even on a small scale. However, the gardener can influence the *structure* of his soil quite considerably.

*Soil-structure effects.* A well-structured soil can hold considerably more available water than a poorly structured soil of the same texture. This is because the structure gives more pores of the right size to hold water which is readily absorbed by plant roots. In a well-structured soil the mineral particles are grouped together with colloidal and organic material to form stable soil crumbs which give a good tilth. Such soils do not get too compact and give an ideal medium in which an optimum combination of water and air and an adequate pore space is provided for root growth. These conditions allow greater and more thorough root penetration and more efficient extraction of the water.

The most effective way of improving soil structure and thus increasing the available water capacity of a soil is to dig in farmyard manure, home-made compost, peat, or other bulky organic manures. These should be added in large amounts, at least 5.4 kg. per square metre (10 lb. per square yard) per year, on poorly structured, coarse-textured soils. The manures should always be well rotted and they should be thoroughly mixed with the soil over the full depth of rooting if they are to be most effective. They should not be buried in a solid mass at the bottom of a trench. The benefits are likely to be substantial. For example, studies showed that after applying 10 lb. per square yard of farmyard manure before each crop over a six-year period, the amount of available water held in the top 45 cm. (18 in.) of a sandy loam soil had been increased by over 25 per cent and in the surface 15 cm.

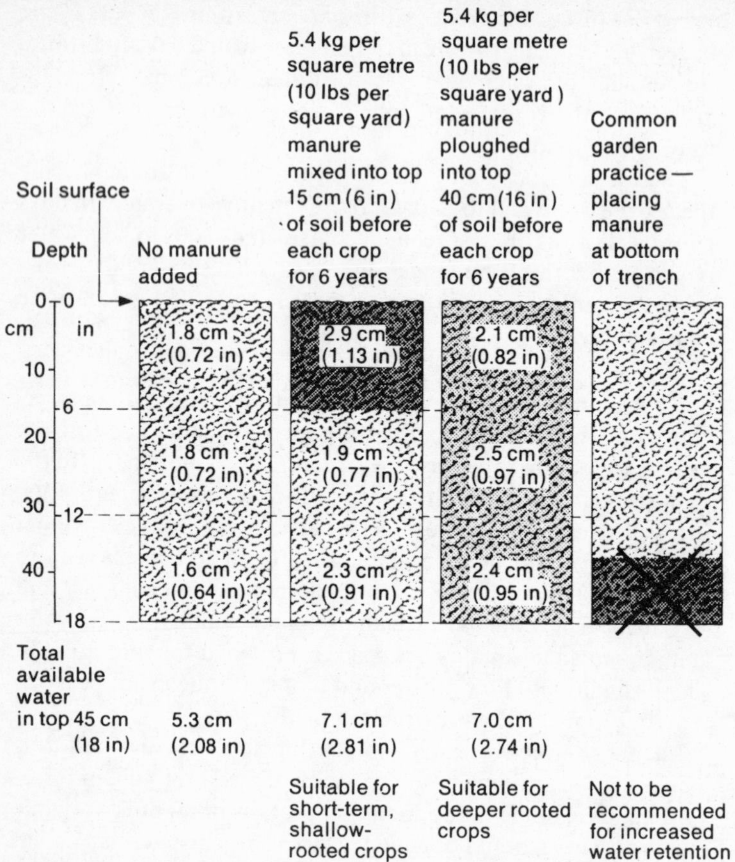


Fig. 4.4. An example of bulky organic manures increasing the amount of available water retained in a sandy loam soil.

(6 in.) of soil by over 70 per cent (see Fig. 4.4). This is one sure way in which the need for watering of crops in the garden can be reduced.

## Drying out of the soil

As the soil dries out through plant roots extracting water and evaporation from the surface, a soil moisture deficit will arise. This is normally measured in terms of the depth of water, in inches, which would be required to rewet the soil to the condition of field capacity. So during a settled period of dry, sunny weather, a well-grown crop which completely covers the ground could remove from the soil each day up to 5.4 litres of water per square metre (1 gallon per square yard), increasing the soil moisture deficit by about 0.5 cm. (0.2 in.). Conversely, during unsettled weather with frequent showers and some heavier periods of rain, the soil reservoir is 'topped up' by rain water. The amount may completely replace or exceed the water lost by evapotranspiration over the period and in these latter circumstances the soil moisture deficit would be reduced. Commercially, the average soil moisture deficit can be calculated for any part of the country from meteorological data in order to work out the need for irrigation of different crops.

The gardener knows that, normally, the wetter the soil the better will his crops (and weeds) grow. However, as the soil dries out there may not be much change in the appearance of his plants until the wilting point is reached, but long before this stage plant growth will have been affected as water absorption becomes more difficult for the plants. So, in deciding when to water vegetables in dry periods we have to strike the right balance between waiting until the plants wilt, with a consequent small or big loss of yield, or watering frequently with all the time and effort that that involves. Fortunately definite guidance can be given for the majority of vegetable crops and will be found later in this chapter.

## Competition for water

During the early phases of plant growth the roots will grow rapidly, continually working into fresh areas of soil to absorb water and nutrients. This phase will continue either until root growth is reduced because of limiting factors within the plant often correlated with flowering and fruiting, or because the volume of soil available to the plant has been fully occupied. This volume of soil can be limited in depth by poor soil conditions preventing penetration by the roots or, laterally, by the presence of other plant roots. So if plants are spaced widely apart the roots of each plant have a greater volume of soil from which to extract the available water and, therefore, the larger the plants can grow without the need for watering. Conversely, when plants are grown closely together the volume of water which can be extracted by each plant is restricted. Consequently, the more frequently do they need to be watered if growth is not to be adversely affected.

To illustrate this effect the results of experiments have shown that if plants of early summer cauliflower, which are very sensitive to water shortage, were grown at normal commercial spacings of 61 × 61 cm. (24 × 24 in.) or closer, they responded to irrigation by producing larger heads. If, however, they were grown at a wide spacing of 86 × 86 cm. (34 × 34 in.) the plants did not respond to watering by growing better or producing larger curds, even under drying conditions. Obviously, the root systems of the widely spaced plants had been able to exploit fully the extra water held in the bigger volume of soil. So for certain plants watering may be unnecessary if wider spacings are used. This is another way in which the need to water can be reduced, providing space is not at a premium in the garden.

It must be remembered that weeds strongly compete for the limited quantity of available water held in the soil. They should be removed therefore as soon as they appear or can be handled. In this way all the soil water reserves can be used by the crop plants.

Mulching crops with compost, leaves, or peat is a useful way of preventing water loss from the soil surface. To get the maximum effect the materials should be put around the plants after watering or following rainfall.

## Root growth

It has been mentioned that root growth may not be maintained

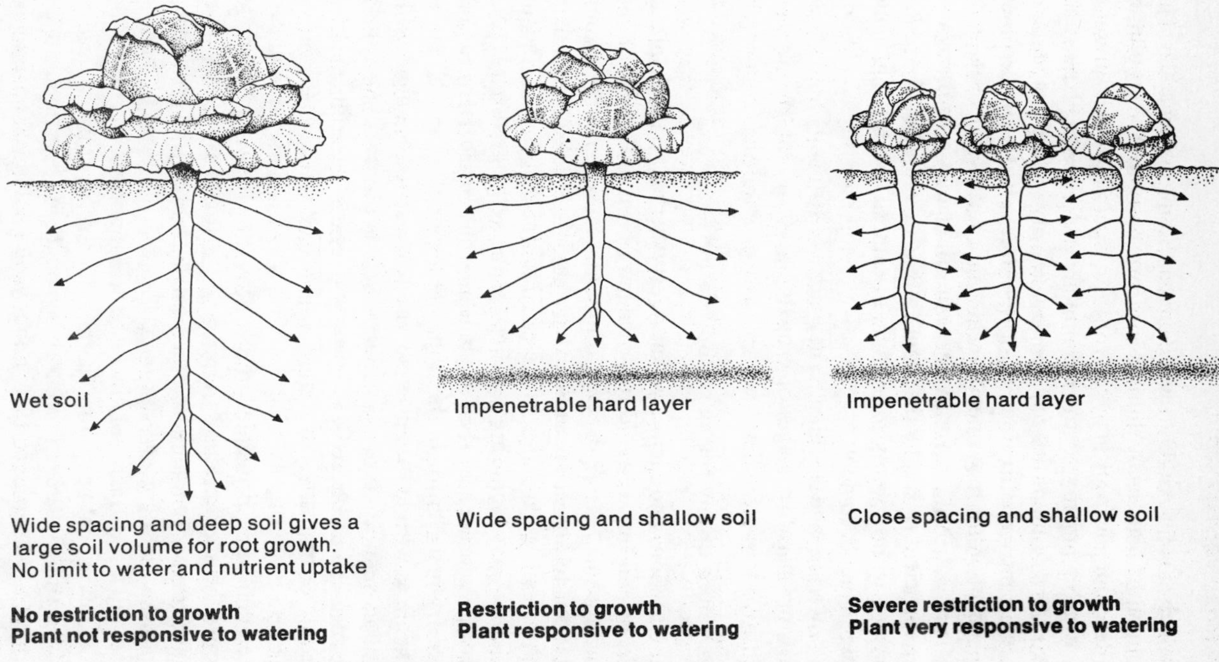


Fig. 4.5. Rooting factors affecting the plants' response to watering.

at a high rate throughout the life of some crops. In general whenever annual plants pass through the flowering and fruiting phases of development root growth is very much reduced because the plant gives priority to the development of flowers, fruit, and seeds. As a result of this reduced root activity instead of the roots growing into new regions of soil, water absorption becomes dependent on the movement of water through the soil to the root surface. But this water movement in soil cannot take place at a rate sufficient to supply the plant's needs except when the soil is very wet within twenty-four hours of rainfall or watering. Thus these plants become very responsive to soil moisture conditions at flowering and fruiting. They are consequently known as 'moisture-sensitive' stages of growth.

## The nature of any response to watering

The situations and factors which affect whether vegetable plants will, or will not, respond to water have been outlined. We can conclude that, except in certain circumstances, whenever the soil dries out to any appreciable extent, say after seven to ten days without rain, then plants will respond to watering in a number of different ways. Some are beneficial as far as the gardener is concerned; some are not. It all depends on what we are trying to produce from the crop. Is the object to produce as much leaf as possible as with lettuce or cabbage? Is it to produce high yields of roots such as carrots, or tubers such as potatoes? Or is it to produce the edible seeds of peas and beans, or fruits such as tomato or marrow? Watering will affect the growth of the different plant organs in different ways and it is useful to understand the basic principles of the growth response in order to choose the appropriate watering strategy for each type of crop.

The nature of the plant response will depend on the type of crop and the stage of growth at which watering is done. Watering generally results in a rapid increase in leaf and shoot growth. So with summer cabbage, for example, increases in size of head at harvest time have been found to be roughly proportional to the amount of water given throughout growth. This effect is to be welcomed because the whole of the cabbage head is edible and what is required.

Root crops such as carrots or red-beet may also respond to frequent watering by increased leaf growth. However, this is not necessarily accompanied by a proportional increase in the edible part of the plant, which in these crops is the root. So with these crops a more judicious use of the watering can is required.

Similarly, too much water available to pea, broad bean, and dwarf French bean plants early in their growth will result in excessive vegetative growth without any beneficial effects, and even adverse effects, on the yields of peas or beans produced. When these crops start to flower and produce pods, however, then watering becomes very beneficial. The reason for the change lies in the nature of the plant's response. At flowering time a plentiful supply of water will increase the number of flowers which form pods and, in the case of peas and broad beans, will increase the numbers of seeds which set in each pod. Watering these crops as the pods are swelling will tend to increase the size of the peas and beans and the number of pods. So with these legume crops the effects of watering will vary at the different stages of development.

Apart from the effects on the weight and size of the edible parts of the plants watering can affect the time of maturity of the produce. Watering during dry periods can so enhance the growth of crops such as early potatoes that earlier lifting can take place. On the other hand watering of bulb onions late in growth may delay the natural ripening of the bulb. So it is not possible to generalize on this aspect.

Watering can also affect the quality and flavour of vegetables. In very general terms the more water that is given to crops the less flavour they have. It then becomes a matter of personal taste whether, for example, a strong or weak flavoured turnip is preferred. As a general guiding rule the conditions which give high yields, large-sized vegetables, and good visual appeal are not usually the same conditions which result in highly flavoured vegetables.

### Reducing the need for watering

Points from previous pages of ways in which the summer chore of watering can be reduced may be summarized as follows:

- By improving the soil water reserves
  add bulky organic manures and mix thoroughly with the soil.
- By encouraging greater ramification of the plant roots
  increase the rooting depth by deeper digging
  space transplanted crops wider apart.
- By conserving water in the soil
  mulch the soil surface
  remove all weeds.

### How to water crops most effectively

When watering cannot be avoided but water supplies or the time to water are limited then the 'art' of watering needs to become a science so as to become as efficient as possible. The aim should be to obtain the maximum possible yield response from a given quantity of water applied. Research on this subject has indicated three major ways in which water may be more efficiently used in commercial irrigation practice. They are: watering at moisture-sensitive stages of growth, limiting the frequency of watering, and limiting the amount of water given, either singly or in combination. These findings can be equally applied to the garden situation.

### Water at moisture-sensitive growth stages

One obvious way of making the most efficient use of limited amounts of water is to irrigate only at those stages of growth when the most beneficial response is obtained and to withhold water at the other growth stages when increases in the yield of the edible parts are not obtained. The example of the moisture-sensitive stages of growth of peas and beans, those of flowering and podding, have already been noted and the reasons for the increases in the yield already outlined.

A similar pattern of response is shown by other vegetable crops grown for their seeds and fruits, such as tomato, marrow, and sweet corn. In these crops, too, there is a reduction in root activity during flowering and as the fruits are developing and so the plants become particularly responsive to watering at these times.

With maincrop potatoes nearly all varieties respond with an increase in tuber yields when the crop is watered after the tubers have been formed. A plentiful supply of water during the growth of the tubers gives higher yields and larger potatoes at lifting time.

## Limiting the frequency of watering

Some crops do not have moisture-sensitive stages of development and to obtain *maximum* growth and yield it is often necessary to water them as frequently as possible. However, with many of these crops the response to more frequent watering shows that the law of diminishing returns is operating. For example, four waterings may have given a much smaller increase in yield for each watering than a single watering. In these circumstances, therefore, reducing the number of waterings should be a more efficient way of watering.

To illustrate this point the results of experiments with summer cabbage grown on a sandy loam soil may be quoted. This crop is very sensitive to water shortage at all stages of growth so that to get the maximum rate of growth and the maximum size of head the plants must be watered frequently. It was found that when the crop was watered eleven times between planting and harvest the head weight was increased by 100 per cent compared with plants receiving only rainfall. However, if only two waterings were given the weight was increased by 80 per cent whilst a single watering, given about two weeks before the cabbage was ready to cut, increased the head weight by 65 per cent. Obviously, in terms of the effort put into applying the water, the most efficient strategy was to water once only, a fortnight before they were ready for cutting.

This general strategy of watering on fewer occasions if water or time is short can be applied to most of the crops where the leaves and shoots are eaten, for example the brassicas, lettuce, and celery. The most effective time to give a single watering to all these crops is between ten to twenty days before they are expected to mature. In a similar way if watering of potatoes has to be limited a single application should be given just after the tubers have formed when they are at the 'marble' stage (see p. 108).

It should be emphasized that this limited watering policy will not produce maximum growth and yields of these crops but will be one of the most efficient methods of watering.

## Limiting the quantity of water applied

The third method of maximizing the desired response for the minimum of effort is to give smaller quantities of water to the crops than is necessary to rewet the whole depth of the soil. This is *not* saying: give a little and often. It is indicating that if watering is done less frequently, following the advice given in the last section, then it is generally unnecessary to thoroughly soak the soil below a depth of 30 cm. For example, it may be decided that a summer cabbage crop should not be watered until two weeks before cutting. Depending on the weather the soil may have dried out to such an extent that it would require up to 65 litres per square metre (12 gallons per square yard) to rewet it down to the full rooting depth of the crop. By only applying 22 litres per square metre (4 gallons per square yard) and, therefore, only wetting perhaps the surface foot of soil, a maximum response to this quantity of water will be obtained.

With the exception of watering seedlings and tranplants it is not really worth while giving less than 11 litres per square metre (2 gallons per square yard) at any one time, especially in hot weather. This is especially so if the water is applied evenly over the soil surface because a significant proportion of that quantity would be evaporated from the wet soil surface and be of no use to the plants.

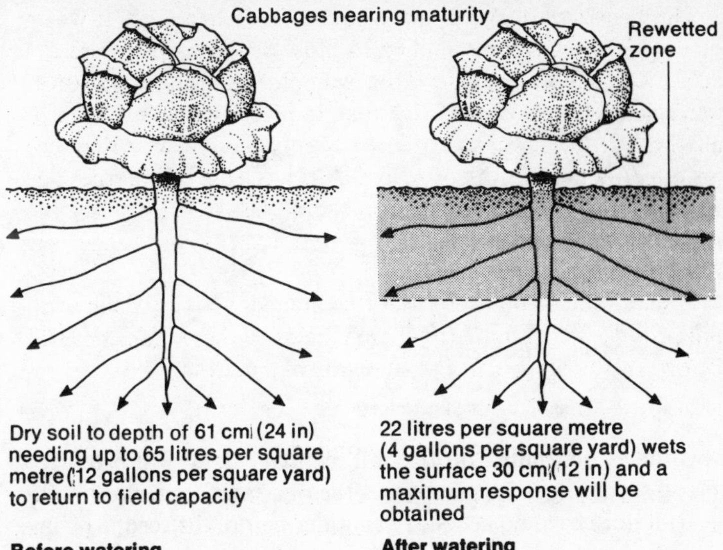


Fig. 4.6. Efficient watering: limiting the quantity of water given to the crop.

## Recommendations for watering the different crops

### All vegetable crops

*To aid seed germination.* Adequate soil moisture is essential for the establishment of all crops, whether grown from seed or transplants. For crops which are not to be transplanted, but are to be grown to maturity where they are sown, it is essential that soil moisture is adequate to ensure good, uniform, seed germination. The best policy is to try to avoid having to water the soil after sowing as, on some soils, a surface 'cap' or crust will form and prevent the seedlings from emerging (Chapter 2). So, if the soil is dry, dribble water along the bottom of the seed drill immediately before sowing the seed using about 1 litre of water to 1.3 metres (1 gallon to 20 ft.) of row (see Fig. 4.7). Alternatively, if the soil is too dry to produce a good tilth, water the whole area just before making the final seedbed preparations. After one to

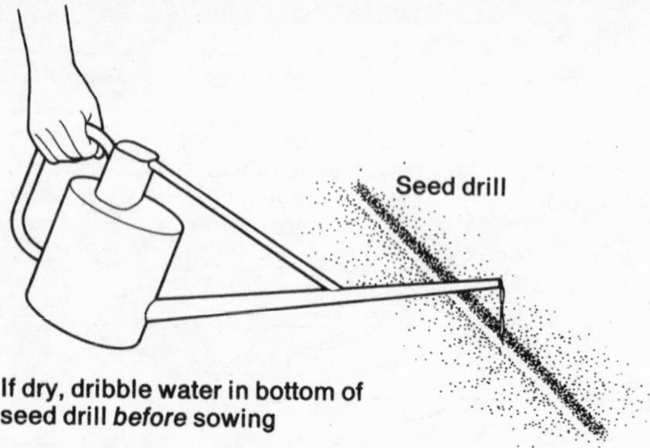


Fig. 4.7. Watering to aid seed germination.

two days, depending on the soil, a final raking will produce a good seedbed and the seeds can then be sown into moist soil.

If it does become necessary to water before the seedlings have emerged and also when watering small seedlings, use a fine rose on the watering can or hose to give small droplets. This will do less damage to the plants or to the soil structure. Should a 'cap' form on the surface following heavy rain before the seedlings emerge, keep the soil surface wet by frequent light waterings and the seedlings will be able to push their way through it.

*To establish transplants.* Transplanting is a traumatic shock for all plants; roots are damaged and the plant cannot replace water lost from its leaves fast enough and wilting occurs. It is, therefore, of crucial importance to water the transplants frequently, daily if possible, with not more than 142 ml. (¼ pint) per plant on each occasion. There is no point in applying more if the water is directed around the base of the plant; do not spread it all over the soil surface (see Fig. 4.8). During the recovery period if the weather is sunny the plants can be covered with newspapers to reduce the water loss from their leaves.

*To water-in fertilizer.* For all crops, small quantities of water can be used to wash top-dressings of fertilizers into the soil during dry periods, so making the nutrients available to the plants. It can

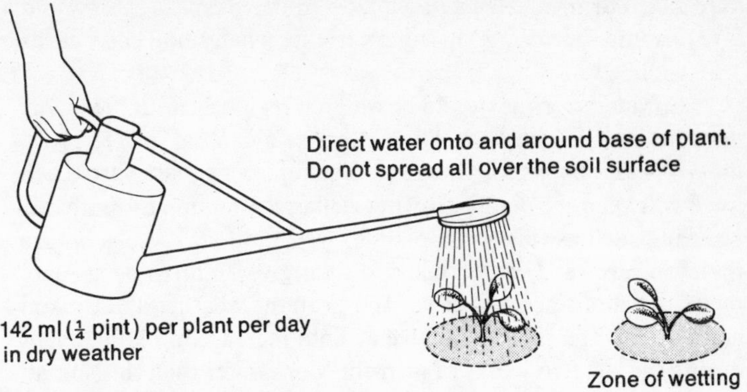


Fig. 4.8. Watering after transplanting.

also be beneficial in the early spring when there is no shortage of water. In these circumstances it is done to make available top-dressings of nitrogenous fertilizers to crops such as spring cabbage which may be short of nitrogen if it has been leached out by winter rains.

### Leafy vegetable crops

Those crops where the leaves or the shoots are eaten – for example, cabbage, cauliflower, sprouting broccoli, kale, calabrese, lettuce, celery, and spinach – should be watered frequently to obtain maximum yields. The most tender, succulent crops are produced when the plants have never been checked in their growth either by shortage of water or nutrients. Especially with these crops it should be remembered that the maximum response to watering can only be obtained if there are sufficient nutrients available, and especially nitrogen, to maintain rapid growth.

With celery, daily waterings can be very beneficial under dry conditions. From sowing in the seedbed the aim should be to encourage a fast rate of growth by frequently watering, at least weekly, during dry weather. With 'difficult' crops such as cauliflower, checks to growth due to water shortage at this early stage may have harmful effects much later in life, resulting in premature heading (buttoning) in some varieties when small early curds are produced.

Transplanted crops should be watered regularly until the plants have become established. Thereafter, as a general guide, 11–16 litres of water per square metre (2–3 gallons per square yard) each week will keep the plants growing well in dry summer months. If watering such as this is impossible, wait until two weeks before the crops are ready to be cut and then give 22 litres per square metre (4 gallons per square yard) if both the weather and the soil are dry; this treatment will give a rapid increase in plant weight during the last two weeks of growth. More water than this should not be given to crops such as cabbage and lettuce, otherwise bursting of the heads may occur.

With Brussels sprouts the plants should be watered-in after planting. Thereafter it is unlikely that watering is worthwhile with this widely spaced crop except possibly in extremely dry conditions such as those experienced in 1976 and 1990.

## Fruiting vegetable crops

*Legumes—peas and beans.* Crops of peas, broad beans, and French and runner beans give big increases in yield of the edible seeds and pods if they are watered during flowering and as the pods are growing. Once the seedlings have emerged through the soil they should not be watered, unless severe wilting occurs in very dry weather, until the plants start to flower, otherwise too much stem and leaf growth will be made. Then, throughout the flowering and pod-growing periods, water should be given twice a week at the rate of 5–11 litres per square metre (1–2 gallons to the square yard). The water should be directed to the base of the plants.

If watering of these crops has to be limited for any reason, 5–11 litres per square metre should be given as the first flowers start to open. This should be followed by a watering as the pods are swelling. Both waterings will be very beneficial in dry weather.

As we have seen, watering at flowering time will tend to

increase the number of peas and broad beans which set within the pods. In addition a plentiful supply of water to the roots as the pods are swelling will increase the size of the individual peas and beans and will delay the time when they go overmature and become tough and 'starchy'. With French and runner beans frequent watering (and frequent picking of the beans) will increase pod-set and yield and will also improve the quality of the pods by delaying the onset of 'stringiness' and maturity.

It is a long-held belief that the problem of pod-setting in runner beans is associated with dryness of the atmosphere around the flowers during flowering. The traditional remedy has been to create humid conditions around the flowers by syringing or spraying the plants once or twice a day during dry weather. In fact, experimental work over several years, including very dry ones, has shown that syringing never had a beneficial effect and often has tended to *decrease* the number of pods which set. It is possible that the yield increases claimed for this practice are the result of actually applying sufficient water so that it ran down the plant to the soil and acted as a light irrigation. Indeed, there is some experimental evidence that small quantities of water applied to the soil during flowering will give better pod-set than syringing the plants.

*Other fruiting vegetables.* Crops such as tomatoes, marrows, cucumbers, and sweet corn also require plenty of water at flowering time and as the fruits are setting and growing. With these crops the plants should have top priority for any limited quantities of water after transplanting in order to get rapid establishment.

With outdoor tomatoes once growth has re-started after planting watering will not normally be required until flowering starts. This treatment will encourage the growth of the root system. (If plants are grown in bags of peat or compost regular watering will be required throughout growth because of the restricted volume available to the roots.) From flowering-time onwards plenty of water will enable fruits to set and grow but at the same time allow shoot growth to continue, which is essential if high yields are to be obtained. Shortage of water during fruiting results in smaller fruit and smaller total yields. It can also make worse certain disorders such as blossom-end rot which gives a typically black shrunken area at the end of the fruit.

There is some evidence with this crop that fruits produced under dry conditions, although smaller, have much more flavour than those grown under wet conditions. It therefore becomes a matter of judgement for the gardener. If maximum yields of large fruit are required plants should be watered daily in hot sunny weather. If lower yields and smaller, more highly flavoured fruits are wanted the plants should be watered about twice a week, but the fruit should be examined regularly to make sure that the tell-tale symptoms of blossom-end rot are not appearing.

With sweet corn, also, once the plants have got established watering is not normally needed until flowering (tasselling) starts. Then watering at this stage will increase the number of seeds formed on each cob and a plentiful supply as the seeds are filling will increase the size and improve the quality of the cob.

When growing marrows and courgettes plenty of water should be given throughout their life. In the early stages it is necessary to get rapid growth in order to build up a big framework with a large leaf area to sustain the fruits when they form. Once fruiting has started copious amounts of water are needed at frequent intervals as these fruits are nearly all water.

With widely spaced plants such as outdoor tomatoes and marrows, water is conserved if a small pot is sunk into the ground close to the plant and water is poured only into the pot and not on to the surface of the soil.

## Root vegetable crops

With such crops as carrot, parsnip, beetroot, and radish too frequent watering will result in unbalanced, lush, foliage growth. The aim should be to keep the plants growing steadily by watering every two to three weeks if necessary, before the soil gets very dry. In this way root quality will be improved. When watering every fortnight in dry weather 16–22 litres of water per square metre

(3–4 gallons per square yard) should be given on each occasion to a crop when the storage roots are actively growing. For a crop at an early stage of growth 5 litres of water for each metre (1 gallon per yard) of row may be sufficient.

Watering (or rain) after a prolonged dry spell will often cause the roots of carrots and parsnips to split; that is why the soil should not be allowed to become too dry.

#### Potatoes

With this crop different watering policies will be required depending on whether early harvests or high yields are wanted and also which varieties are grown.

*Earlies.* If a high yield of an early variety is the objective then the crop should be watered throughout the growing period at ten to fourteen day intervals, giving 16–22 litres of water per square metre (3–4 gallons per square yard) on each occasion. In this way rapid growth is encouraged and if the plants are not lifted until the foliage starts to die back high yields will be obtained.

However, if earliness is of overriding importance, water should not be given until the tubers have reached the size of a marble (the 'marble' stage, as illustrated in Fig. 4.9). Then one good watering should be given, applying about 22 litres per square metre (4 gallons per square yard).

From the limited experimental evidence at present available on the response of early potato varieties to different soil moisture conditions it would appear that Vanessa, Arran Pilot, and Home Guard are fairly tolerant of drought conditions. In contrast, Maris Peer and Ulster Sceptre appear to be susceptible to dry conditions and under such conditions yields can be much affected. On this evidence Maris Peer and Ulster Sceptre would respond much more to watering than the other varieties named.

*Maincrop.* For maincrop potatoes water should not normally be given until the tubers start to form. This stage coincides approximately with that of flowering and for most varieties a single, heavy watering of 22–27 litres per square metre (4–5 gallons per

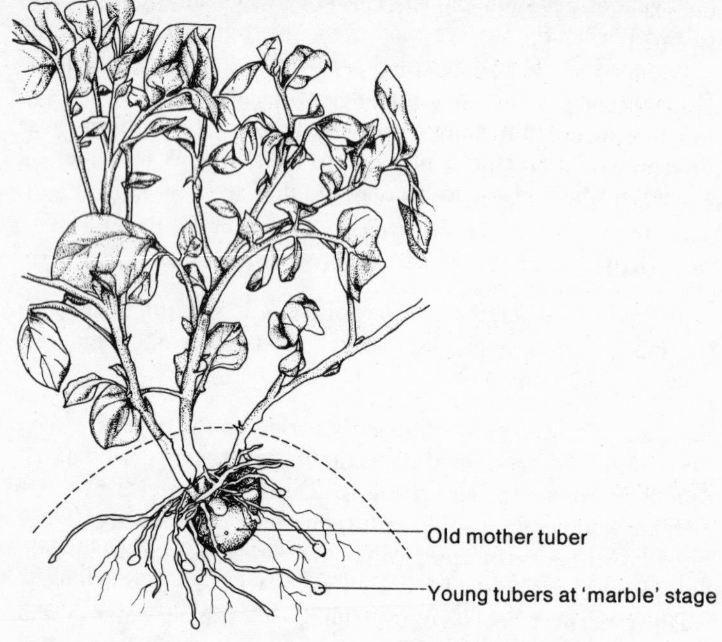


Fig. 4.9. 'Marble' stage of growth when potatoes should be watered.

square yard) when the tubers are at the marble stage can be very beneficial. The effect is to increase the size of the tubers and this can be very welcome if the variety tends to produce a large number of small- to medium-sized potatoes. Examples of such varieties are King Edward and Ulster Torch. However, if the variety characteristically produces only a small number of potatoes, for example Majestic, then watering should be given ten to fourteen days before the tubers start to form. This will stimulate the production of more tubers per plant. If this is followed by a watering at the marble stage, yields of these varieties will be improved both by an increase in the number and the size of the potatoes.

It is important to try to keep the tubers growing steadily so as to reduce the number of misshapen tubers and those with cracks and secondary growth which result from stop–go conditions for growth.

Again, from limited experimental evidence, it would appear that Pentland Crown shows tolerance to drought conditions and, therefore, would be a suitable variety to grow where watering of the crop would be impossible. On the other hand King Edward and Maris Piper appear to be susceptible to dry conditions, and would be expected to respond well to watering at the marble stage; the variety Majestic appears to be intermediate in its response to soil moisture conditions.

There is evidence that watering reduces the number of tubers affected by common scab.

## Onions

*Bulb onions.* Little experimental work has been done on the water requirements of this crop. As it has sparse foliage, is normally grown at wide spacing in the garden (to get large bulbs), and generally develops a deep root system, it is not considered to respond well to watering. Furthermore, wet conditions at a late stage of bulb growth delay maturity and are believed to affect adversely the storage characteristics of the bulbs. Undoubtedly, under very dry conditions such as those experienced in 1976, onion plants will benefit from frequent watering, especially in the early stages of growth before the plants have developed a good, deep, root system. It would be prudent not to water after the middle of July for the late, keeping varieties.

For the very early, overwintered, Japanese varieties which mature in June and July such reservations are not so important. The bulbs of these varieties will not keep for more than two to three months and so are grown for immediate consumption. Therefore they can be watered right up to harvest time under drought conditions. However, under moderately dry conditions it is unlikely that this overwintered crop will respond to late watering for, by this time, the plants have developed a deep root system.

For this crop it is essential for successful overwintering that the seeds are sown at the correct time in August for the area and that germination is immediate and rapid. At this time of the year the soil is quite likely to be too dry for successful germination of the seed and so watering of the drills before sowing, or the seedbed after sowing, may be essential to get satisfactory establishment.

*Salad onions.* This crop is sown at intervals throughout the spring and summer to provide a continuous supply of produce. Watering of the seedbed may become essential at certain times during the summer to get satisfactory seed germination. Thereafter plenty of moisture in the soil will encourage rapid growth of this crop.

## Seed crops

Many keen gardeners save their own seed from particularly good vegetables they have grown. It is known that root growth of many crops is considerably reduced at flowering time and as the fruits and seeds are forming so water absorption is often adversely affected. The quality and size of seeds produced can also be greatly affected by the weather conditions prevailing at this crucial stage of development. It is, therefore, very beneficial to water at frequent intervals any seed-producing plants at their moisture-sensitive stages. The water should be directed only to the base of the plants.

**Table 4.1**

**A summary guide to watering your vegetable crops**

| Crop | Category* (see footnote) | Time to water | Amount of water to give in litres per square metre (gallons per square yard) | Additional comments |
|---|---|---|---|---|
| **Beetroot** | C | Before soil becomes too dry and growth is checked | 11 (2) (along row in early stages) | Improves the size and quality of the roots |
| **Bean** | | | | |
| broad | B | At the start of flowering and throughout the pod-forming and picking period | 22 (4) per week depending on rainfall and weather conditions | Improves pod-set and quality. Syringing of runner beans is not helpful (see p. 105) |
| dwarf French | B | | | |
| runner | B | | | |
| **Broccoli** | | | | |
| (winter cauliflower) | C | For three to four weeks after transplanting in July to get established | Up to 142 ml. ($\frac{1}{4}$ pint) per plant per day in dry warm weather | Further waterings may be required in August and September if weather dry |
| sprouting | C | | | |

Table 4.1 (*cont.*)

| Crop | Category* (see footnote) | Time to water | Amount of water to give in litres per square metre (gallons per square yard) | Additional comments |
|---|---|---|---|---|
| **Brussels sprouts** | C | For three to four weeks after transplanting to get established | Up to 142 ml. ($\frac{1}{4}$ pint) per plant per day in dry warm weather | Watering not normally required after plants are established. |
| **Cabbage** (all types) | A | As frequently as is practicable in dry weather | Up to 22 (4) per week | If water is short give single watering two to three weeks before harvest is expected |
| **Calabrese** | A | | | |
| **Carrot** | C | Before soil becomes too dry and growth is checked | 11 (2) (along row in early stages) | Watering at later stages after soil has got too dry may cause splitting |
| **Cauliflower** | A | As frequently as is practical throughout growth | Up to 22 (4) per week | If water is short give single watering two to three weeks before harvest is expected |

| | | | | |
|---|---|---|---|---|
| **Celery** | | | | |
| self blanching | A | As frequently as is practical throughout growth | Up to 22 (4) per week | Improves the size of stick and its quality |
| trench | A | | | |
| **Leek** | C | Water after transplanting to get established | 70 ml. ($\frac{1}{8}$ pint) per plant per day in dry warm weather | Additional waterings can be given if large leeks are required |
| **Lettuce** | A | As frequently as is practical throughout growth | Up to 22 (4) per week | Improves size and quality. When water is short give application seven to ten days before harvest |
| **Marrow** (and courgette) | A | As frequently as is practical throughout growth | May need 11 (2) twice per week | Water copiously as soon as fruits form |
| **Onion** | | | | |
| bulb | C | Water if necessary to get plants established | Up to 70 ml. ($\frac{1}{8}$ pint.) per day if dry | Do not water in later stages of bulb growth |
| salad | C | Water before sowing to get seed germination if dry | 1 litre to approx. 1.3 metres of row (1 gallon to 20 ft. of row) | Can be watered at any stage if soil very dry |

Table 4.1 (*cont.*)

| Crop | Category* (see footnote) | Time to water | Amount of water to give in litres per square metre (gallons per square yard) | Additional comments |
|---|---|---|---|---|
| **Parsnip** | C | Before soil becomes too dry and growth is checked | 11 (2) (along row in early stages) | Improves size and quality of roots |
| **Pea** | B | At start of flowering and throughout the pod-forming and picking period | 22 (4) per week depending on weather conditions | Improves pod-set and quality |
| **Potato** | | | | |
| early | B | For earliest crops water at 'marble' stage | 22 (4) | Response depends on variety (see p. 107) |
| early | A | For high yields water throughout growth every ten to fourteen days | 16–22 (3–4) on each occasion | Response depends on variety (see p. 107) |
| maincrop | B | For most varieties water at 'marble' stage and thereafter | 22 (4) | Response depends on variety (see pp. 108–9) |

| | | | | |
|---|---|---|---|---|
| **Radish** | C | Water to get germination and weekly thereafter | 11 (2) (along rows) | Frequent watering will give too much leaf growth |
| **Shallot** | C | Water if necessary to get established | Up to 70 ml. ($\frac{1}{8}$ pint.) per plant per day | Rarely requires watering after establishment |
| **Spinach** | A | As frequently as is practical throughout growth | Up to 22 (4) per week | Improves quality |
| **Swede and turnip** | C | Before soil becomes too dry and growth is checked | 11 (2) (along row in early stages) | Improves size and quality but reduces flavour |
| **Sweet corn** | B | At tasselling and cob-swelling stages | 22 (4) on each occasion | Improves size and quality |
| **Tomato** | B | To get plants established and at flowering and fruiting stages | 11 (2) twice per week or more | Very frequent watering increases yield but reduces flavour |

* A Crops which respond beneficially to frequently waterings; B Crops which give maximum responses of edible part when watered at the moisture sensitive stages; C Crops which are not so responsive as the others and which should be watered prudently.

# 5 Insect pests

Protection of vegetables from damage by insect pests is important in the vegetable garden if a lot of effort is not to be wasted. In gardens, more often than not, insects find a favourable environment where they can multiply very rapidly.

It does not take many insects per square metre to do a lot of damage to a crop such as potato. A single female turnip moth, the parent of the cutworm caterpillar, can lay more than 1,000 eggs. As only one or two caterpillars per square metre can seriously damage potatoes, the offspring from one female moth have the potential to seriously damage 300–500 square metres of crop.

Of course, nature does not usually allow this to happen; most of the offspring fail to survive the early larval stages after leaving the eggs. Only two survivors, one of each sex, are needed to maintain the population of the moth at the same level from one generation to the next. If two of each sex survive, the population would tend to double, as would damage to a crop.

Changes that favour an insect pest, for example an increase locally in its food supply or elimination of some of its natural enemies (parasites and predators), can cause it to increase in numbers alarmingly, and crop damage to become more severe. Conversely, however, if conditions become *less* favourable to the pest then it will decline in numbers. It is this principle of making the environment less favourable to pests that we try to exploit in the vegetable garden, by one method or another, to avoid the worst impacts of pest damage. Complete elimination of pests is neither necessary nor desirable.

Not all vegetables suffer severely from pest attacks and some types of pest do more serious damage than others. It is therefore helpful to know which crops are most at risk, which pests are worth controlling by direct effort, and how best to deal with each type of problem.

Commercial methods for protecting field-grown vegetables are not often suitable for the garden but the methods, evolved after a century-and-a-half of observation and research, incorporate the essential background information on pests' habits, life-cycles, and ecology. This information is the basis of present-day techniques of pest control in both field and garden. Much is known about what to do and, equally important, what not to do, to protect vegetables against insect and other pests.

Pest life-cycles and remedies are described in many books and leaflets available to the gardener, but few accounts outline the principles which underlie the selection of available methods, or make known their limitations.

## The main pests

Birds and various small mammals such as rats, mice, voles, rabbits, and hares as well as the insects and nematodes (eelworms) which concern us here can damage vegetables. The main pests are listed in Table 5.1, indicating when damage occurs (in Britain), the most obvious symptoms, methods for avoiding or preventing damage and the expected effectiveness of insecticide treatments.

Some pests feed out of sight on or in seeds or roots in the soil. Others feed on the stems, leaves, or fruits of plants where their damage is easily seen – if you know what to look for. Many pests are single insect species which have to be considered individually, for example the cabbage root fly or the carrot fly. Others, for example aphids, comprise many different species with similar, if not identical, forms and remedies. Known variously as blackfly, greenfly, plant lice, dolphins, blight, or merely as 'fly', aphids are perhaps the most familiar of pests to gardeners.

There are many different species of aphids with different host-plants but all have one feature in common – they feed by piercing

**Table 5.1**

**Common vegetable pests and their control**

| Crop | Pest | Times of damage and symptoms | Control measures: Avoidance | Control measures: Chemical effectiveness (see p. 158) |
|---|---|---|---|---|
| All | Cutworms | May–September. Plant stems eaten away at soil level; holes and cavities in root crops and potatoes in late summer. | Destroy caterpillars. Search soil near a damaged plant; at night, inspect plants and soil with a hand-lamp. Cover plants with NWHS–mesh. | ** |
| | Leatherjackets | March–July. Stems bitten through at soil surface; ragged feeding on lower leaves. | Ensure soil well drained. Clear land and dig before end of September, especially if previously grass. | * |
| | Wireworms | March–September. Stems bitten below soil level. Potato tubers with small deep holes. | No root crops or potatoes for two years after digging up grass. | * |
| | Chafer grubs | July–October. Roots gnawed 5 cm. (2 in.) or more below soil surface. | Keep garden clean and weed free. | * |

| | | | | |
|---|---|---|---|---|
| | Millipedes | April–July. Seed, stems of young plants, roots, tubers eaten (not foliage), and millipedes nearby. | Search soil near damaged seedlings and remove the millipedes. | * |
| | Slugs | January–December. Lower leaves, stems, roots, tubers holed, mainly in damp sites or during and after wet weather. Slime trails present. | Trap with beer in shallow dishes. Good drainage. | ** |
| **Asparagus** | Asparagus beetle | June–October. Foliage stripped and stems damaged. Beetles and greyish–green larvae present. | Remove beetles and larvae | *** |
| **Beans** | Bean seed fly | April–October. Seeds do not germinate, or seedlings weak and distorted. | Sow into a good, 'stale' seedbed. Cover with NWHS-mesh. | ** |
| | Black bean aphid | June–July. Colonies of blackfly on stems near top of plant. | Pinch out tips of plants when flowered and small colonies formed. Transfer ladybirds to plants. Cover with NWHS-mesh. | *** |
| | Red spider mite | Mid- to late-summer. Dwarf or runner beans, rarely on broad beans. | | ** |

**Table 5.1** (*cont.*)

| Crop | Pest | Times of damage and symptoms | Control measures: Avoidance | Control measures: Chemical effectiveness (see p. 158) |
|---|---|---|---|---|
| | Pea and bean weevils | April–July. Leaves notched around margins. White grubs may be damaging root nodules. | | *** |
| **Beetroot, spinach** | Pygmy beetle Springtails, etc. | April–July. Poor seedling emergence, young seedlings breaking off at soil surface, or falling over. | | * |
| | Mangold fly | Yellowish blisters and mines on leaves. | Late sowing (mid-May) | *** |
| **Brassicas** | Cabbage root fly | May–October. Seedling and transplants dying, stunted, or wilting. White maggots on and in roots, few side roots remaining, swedes and turnips scalloped (Fig. 5.1(*c*)). | Discs around transplants (Fig. 5.2). Cover with NWHS-mesh until plants about 20–25 cm. (8–10 in.) high. | ** |
| | Cabbage aphid | May–November. Mealy grey aphid on leaves and stems. | Destroy overwintered brassica plants by May. Transfer | ** |

| | | | | |
|---|---|---|---|---|
| | | Leaves puckering. | ladybirds to lightly infested plants. Cover with NWHS-mesh until plants about 20–25 cm. (8–10 in.) high. | |
| | Caterpillars | May–October. Holes in leaves, plants 'skeletonized'. Frass in or collecting at base of leaves (Fig. 5.1 (*b*)). | Inspect plants twice weekly and destroy eggs and caterpillars. Cover with NWHS-mesh while adults actively egg-laying. | ** |
| | Flea beetles | March–September. 'Shot-holes' in leaves (Fig. 5.1 (*a*)). | Sow early (March) or late (June). Cover seedlings with NWHS-mesh until well established. | ** |
| | Turnip gall weevil | August–April. Large nodules on main tap-root, with white grub (or cavity) inside. Not usually important. | | |
| **Carrots** | Carrot fly | June–July. Seedlings die. Plants stunted with reddish leaves. Base of tap root of young plants damaged. October–March. Carrot with mines, some with thin whitish maggots inside. | Use a partially resistant variety. Sow well away from shelter or tall plants, thinly and early (mid-March) or late (mid-June) to avoid eggs of first brood. During mid-May to mid-June, cover with NWHS-mesh. Lift early carrots before September and all carrots by November. | ** |

Table 5.1 (*cont.*)

| | | | Control measures | |
|---|---|---|---|---|
| **Crop** | **Pest** | **Times of damage and symptoms** | **Avoidance** | **Chemical effectiveness (see p. 158)** |
| | Willow-carrot aphid | Late May–July. Small pale green aphids on foliage, with white cast skins readily seen. Seedlings soon wilt, become very stunted and die. | Inspect seedlings daily late May–mid-June. Cover with NWHS-mesh. | *** |
| | Springtails | April–June. Seedlings dying. Bitten at soil level. Small jumping insects on soil. Not readily seen. | Water. | ** |
| **Celery, celeriac** | Celery fly | May–September. Large blister mines in leaves. | Reject seedlings with blistered leaves. Pinch out and destroy blistered leaves. | ** |
| | Carrot fly | July–October. Reddish-brown small holes and mines in stems and crown at or below soil surface. | Cover plants with NWHS-mesh during August–early September. | * |

| | | | | |
|---|---|---|---|---|
| **Cucumber, marrow, pumpkin** | Aphids<br>Whitefly | June–September. Stunting with leaves mottled, puckered, and brittle. Colonies of aphids on undersides of leaves. | Destroy virus-infected (mottled) plants promptly to prevent spread of infection. Brush off and destroy colonies while small. Cover with NWHS-mesh while aphids are migrating. | ** – Aphids<br>* – Whitefly |
| | Red spider mite | June–September. Minute orange-red mites and eggs on undersides of leaves. Leaves pale, brownish, brittle. | | ** |
| **Leeks** | Stem nematode | April–June. Young plants distorted, stunted, and some dying. Later, plant stems swollen, thickened and readily rot. | Crop rotation. | None |
| | Leek moth | April–May. Centre and growing point of young plants damaged by caterpillar. | | * |
| **Lettuce** | Foliage aphids | June–October. Colonies on undersides of leaves and in centre of plants. | Use resistant variety. Aluminium-foil mulch may deter winged aphids from alighting. Cover with NWHS-mesh. | ** |

**Table 5.1** (*cont.*)

| **Crop** | **Pest** | **Times of damage and symptoms** | **Control measures** | |
|---|---|---|---|---|
| | | | **Avoidance** | **Chemical effectiveness (see p. 158)** |
| | Lettuce root aphid | June–August. Plants wilting and dying. White waxy colonies on roots. | Use resistant variety (Table 5.2). Cover with NWHS-mesh. Do not grow lettuce continuously on same land. | * |
| **Onions, shallots** | Onion fly, Bean seed fly | May–September. Seedlings dying, often in groups. | Sow into 'stale' seedbed especially for August sowings. Cover with NWHS-mesh after sowing or planting out. Remove and burn infested plants. | ** |
| | Stem nematode | April–June. Seedlings stunted, later plants thick-necked. | Rotation of crops. Good weed control. Remove and destroy infested plants. No other susceptible crops for two or three years. | None |
| | Thrips | June–August (hot weather). Leaves silvery and shine in sun. Many minute blackish thrips present. | | ** |

| | | | | |
|---|---|---|---|---|
| **Parsley** | Carrot fly | July–December. Reddish-brown mines in crown of plant, with small, whitish maggots. | Lift and burn badly affected plants. | * |
| | Aphids | June–August. Small pale green aphids and whitish cast skins present. | Cover with NWHS-mesh in mid-summer. | ** |
| **Parsnip** | Carrot fly | June–July. Mining on surface of swelling root. September–February. Reddish-brown mining penetrating root, often with small, whitish maggots. | Cover with NWHS-mesh May–mid-June. Lift crop and clamp before November to miss worst damage. | * |
| **Peas** | Bean seed fly | April–June. Poor seedling emergence, seedlings distorted. | Sow into a good, 'stale' seedbed. Cover immediately with NWHS-mesh. | ** |
| | Birds | February–July. Seedlings pulled out or severely damaged. Pods ripped open. | Net; NWHS-mesh or black thread strung over rows. | None |
| | Pea and bean weevil | March–July. Margins of leaves with U-shaped notches. | | *** |
| | Pea aphid | May–July. Large green (occasionally pink) aphid, mainly on young leaves or growing point. | If only a few, remove by hand. Cover with NWHS-mesh during June. | *** |

**Table 5.1** (*cont.*)

| **Crop** | **Pest** | **Times of damage and symptoms** | **Control measures** | |
|---|---|---|---|---|
| | | | **Avoidance** | **Chemical effectiveness (see p. 158)** |
| | Pea thrips | June–August. Flowers fail to develop. Pods silvery and distorted. Black or yellow thrips numerous on flowers and pods. | | ** |
| | Pea moth | June–August. Small white caterpillars in pods eating developing peas. | Sow early for crop to flower before early June. Cover with NWHS-mesh. | * |
| **Potato** | Potato cyst nematodes | April–September. Foliage stunted, weak, and grows slowly. Roots poorly developed. Tubers small. Minute white or yellow-brown cysts, numerous on roots in July. | Rotation of crops and sow resistant varieties (eg. Maris Piper). Do not grow potatoes on infected land for at least six years. | None |
| | Wireworms, Cutworms | July–August. Holes in tubers. | Do not grow potatoes for two years after grass. Heavy rain or watering in June–July reduces cutworm | * |

| | | | | |
|---|---|---|---|---|
| | | | damage, and some varieties may be less susceptible than others. | |
| **Radish** | Flea beetle | March–September. Numerous small round holes in leaves (Fig. 5.1 (*a*)). | Sow very early (March). Inspect regularly for damage. Cover with NWHS-mesh. | ** |
| | Cabbage root fly | May–September. Whitish maggots scoring and mining the developing bulb. | Sow early (March) or late (June) to miss damage by the first brood of maggots. Cover later sowings with NWHS-mesh. | ** |
| **Sweet corn** | Frit fly | May–June. Growing point wilts and may die. Small white maggot in central shoot. | Sow late or transplant after plants have 5–6 leaves. Cover with NWHS-mesh after sowing. | * |
| **Tomato** | Potato cyst nematode | May–August. Plants stunted, grow slowly and yield small fruit. | Crop rotation. | None |
| **Turnip, swede** | Flea beetle | March–September. Numerous small round holes in leaves (Fig. 5.1. (*a*)). Small white grubs on roots of young seedlings. | Sow early (March) or late (June) to miss severest damage. Cover in spring with NWHS–mesh. | ** |

Table 5.1 (*cont.*)

| Crop | Pest | Times of damage and symptoms | Control measures: Avoidance | Control measures: Chemical effectiveness (see p. 158) |
|---|---|---|---|---|
| | Cabbage root fly | June–September. White maggots scoring and mining on and in the swelling main root. | Sow after May to miss severe spring attack. Cover with NWHS-mesh during May and July–early August. | * |
| | Turnip gall weevil | April–May. Seedling with round galls on tap root at or just below soil level. August–September. Round galls on swelling roots contain small, white grub. | | ** |

the plant tissues, sucking the sap, and thereby reducing the vigour of the plant (see also Chapter 6, p. 171) which, to plants such as lettuce, is often more important than the feeding damage. Their method of feeding makes them especially vulnerable to so-called 'systemic' insecticides which are absorbed by the plants and move with the sap mainly upwards and laterally to the growing points and to leaf tips and edges. The aphids' mouthparts pierce the plant's vascular tissues and the insects acquire lethal doses of insecticide as they suck up and concentrate the sap. Modern-day insecticides soon degrade within the plants and, when used correctly, will have vanished by harvest time.

Several soil-inhabiting pests feed on a wide range of crops (Table 5.1) but the severity of damage often varies locally from year to year and is notoriously patchy on a field scale, often associated with nearby shelter. The 'patches' are often about 'garden-size' so adjacent gardens or allotments can differ in the levels of pest infestation they experience. Examples of pests which tend to have a patchy distribution are cutworms (caterpillars of noctuid moths), leatherjackets (larvae of the daddy-long-legs flies), wireworms (larvae of click beetles), cockchafer grubs, millipedes (not centipedes), and slugs. Slugs are not insects, of course, but they do seriously damage many types of vegetables.

Most other pests damage only a few types of vegetable and usually confine their attentions to one botanical genus or family. Thus the cabbage root fly only attacks cruciferous plants which include brassicas and radish; the carrot fly is confined to umbelliferous crops such as carrots, parsnips, celery, parsley, celeriac, and so on. Many aphids are even more specific, each species attacking only a very restricted range of host-plants. The peach-potato aphid is a notable exception and will live on many different garden plants. It is also a very efficient transmitter of many plant viruses.

Understanding the reasons why pests are tackled in different ways not only begins to make sense of a complex subject but often also suggests combinations of methods that are suited to particular circumstances. Recognition of the different stages of the life-cycles of pests, each characteristic type of damage and the time when it occurs can therefore be very rewarding. If you know where to look and what to look for, the pests that visibly affect the leaves, stems, or fruits of vegetables can be detected and dealt with before they cause serious damage.

### Are pests more troublesome in gardens than in fields?

The answer is very often 'Yes', because of the favourable, sheltered environment of most gardens. The garden environment will also usually contain a wide range of suitable host-plants, cultivated and uncultivated, and is often flanked by other gardens in different states of care and neglect.

A garden hedge or fence, of course, is no barrier to insects so isolation is not a remedy often available to the gardener. The relatively small scale of operations also affords little scope for avoiding pest attack by crop rotation. Host crops are likely to be in the ground most of the year, providing the opportunity for pests to survive from season to season. Where feasible, a break in a sequence of brassica crops, for example, is desirable, even to the extent of occasionally missing a year.

Arithmetic also has a place in seeking to understand why plants may be more vulnerable to attack in gardens than in fields. The number of host plants is usually small compared to the number of offspring that a single insect can produce. Thus there will usually be more insects per plant in a garden than in a field. Various combinations of these factors make gardens an ecological paradise for many pests and they respond accordingly.

### Types of pest damage

Not all pest damage is equally important, so how can we decide when action is needed or when some damage can be accepted? Let us consider three main categories of pest damage. First, there are pests which kill the plant before harvest; secondly, there are those which damage a part of the plant that is not to be eaten; and, thirdly, there are others that damage the edible part. In each case the acceptable level of damage will be different.

Loss of plants when seed, seedlings, or young plants are severely damaged and die results in an uneven gappy stand. The surviving plants then have more room to grow and quite often will become larger than they otherwise would. The total yield per unit area may not be much affected but the plants will vary in time of maturity and size at harvest. This can be commercially detrimental but in a garden, when only a few plants are lost, the spread of time-of-maturity among the survivors can be an advantage. Crops to which this can apply are those growing fairly thickly in rows, for instance carrots, radishes, onions, or peas. Seedling losses of 10–20 per cent are not then very important, would hardly be noticed, and more often than not, would be dismissed as poor germination. On the other hand a 10–20 per cent loss of widely spaced brassica transplants such as cabbage or Brussels sprouts would be very obvious though it may still be just about acceptable.

Cutworm caterpillars can spectacularly kill plants of several crops, including lettuce and young brassicas. They chew through the stems near soil level, either cutting them off or weakening them so much that they snap off when it is windy. Quite large plants can be killed in this way. Again, a little of this type of damage can be tolerated, but not too much. Death of 20 per cent or more generally calls for action in the form of a search for the caterpillars, after dark by torchlight, when they are feeding.

It is essential to watch young seedlings closely to detect damage at an early stage when action is still possible. Many small soil-inhabiting insects such as springtails (*Collembola*) and flea beetles can damage seedlings just before or after they emerge. The attacks often occur suddenly during an occasional warm day in spring. Flea beetles can quickly wipe out a sowing of radishes, swedes, or turnips and a sudden infestation of the willow-carrot aphid can similarly kill or seriously check young carrots.

If, on the other hand, carrots become severely infested with the larvae of the carrot fly, even well-established young plants can be killed. Once affected, little or nothing can be done to save that crop. Another sowing may still be feasible but it should be delayed, for example until mid-June in central England, until the peak egg-laying period of the first generation of flies has usually passed.

Provided plants are not killed, considerable amounts of damage to non-edible parts can often be tolerated. For example, it is not necessary to achieve complete protection from damage by cabbage root fly maggots on the roots of Brussels sprouts, cabbages or cauliflowers during spring and summer. Other examples are light infestations of caterpillars on brassicas, flea beetles eating small holes in the leaves of radish (Fig. 5.1(*a*)), swedes, or turnips, and weevils notching pea or bean leaves. The effects of these pests are generally minimal, especially if the plants are growing well. Damage to roots often escapes notice until it becomes so severe that plants wilt or become stunted or die.

(*a*)

(*b*)

(*c*)

Fig. 5.1. Examples of pest damage that is unsightly but not very important in the garden. (*a*) Slight flea beetle damage on a leaf of a maturing radish plant; (*b*) young caterpillars of the small cabbage white butterfly, which can be picked off, and a little frass that can readily be washed off the undamaged cauliflower curd; (*c*) ugly but largely superficial damage to swedes by maggots of the cabbage root fly.

With leaf-feeding pests of root crops, you can watch how the damage develops and treat only if the attack is becoming severe. It is not advisable, however, to allow aphid infestations to persist. Aphids not only transmit viruses but most also form large colonies very rapidly and severely stunt plants. An example is the black aphid attacking broad beans. The peach-potato aphid is unusual in this respect for it does not often develop large colonies and is hardly ever serious in itself outdoors. Its importance arises from the several viruses it can transmit. These can greatly reduce the vigour of its many host-plants and yields can suffer.

Even small amounts of damage are not nowadays acceptable when pests affect the edible parts of plants, though a little can sometimes be tolerated if it is superficial and there is no intention to store the produce. Quite apart from the actual damage, contamination of produce for the kitchen by the presence of the pest or its debris (frass, cast-skins, or honey-dew) can make it repulsive and unsuitable to eat (Fig. 5.1(*b*)). Yield may not be much affected so it is mainly the poor cosmetic quality of the produce, or difficulty of cleaning it, which makes it unacceptable in the kitchen.

The superficial damage to swedes (Fig. 5.1(*c*)) caused by cabbage root fly maggots is an example where some damage can be tolerated. With low infestations, the damage will generally be superficial and easily removed when the roots are peeled but in severe attacks the maggots burrow deeply, making the roots virtually unusable.

Similarly, carrot fly damage to carrots, parsnips, or celery tends to be very shallow until early autumn when the maggots begin to penetrate deeply, making the produce worthless. Even lightly attacked carrots or parsnips will not store well because the wounds provide entry for the bacteria and fungi which cause rots. There will usually be increased wastage if damaged roots are mixed with undamaged roots during storage.

To summarize, therefore, severe pest damage can only be tolerated if only a few plants are affected, or if the damage is to parts of the plant that are not to be eaten. If edible parts are affected, then good protection will usually be needed.

## Knowing the pests and recognizing their damage

There are stages in the life histories of most pests when it is difficult or impossible to deal with them. At other times they may be very vulnerable. It is therefore important to know their weak points and when to deal with them.

Several different types of caterpillar feed on vegetable brassicas – cauliflowers, cabbage, and Brussels sprouts – and their habits differ. The large cabbage white butterfly lays its eggs in groups of ten to twenty. Its dark caterpillars have gold and green markings and remain gregarious. They can demolish a plant within a few days but, fortunately for the gardener, often affect only a few plants.

In marked contrast, the small cabbage white butterfly lays eggs singly on the undersides of the outer leaves of brassicas and few plants escape its attack. On hatching from the eggs, the pale green caterpillars feed first on the outer leaves where the eggs were laid and then, as they grow older, move towards the centre of the plant where they can be difficult to see. There may only be one or two per plant at any one time, droppings, or frass, near the hearts of the plants marking their presence. Both species of caterpillar tend to feed mostly during the day. This is the time to look for them during mid- and late summer.

The grey–green caterpillars of the cabbage moth, however, and also cutworms and leatherjackets, feed mainly at night and hide during the day. They are easiest to find after dark, using a hand-lamp in mid- to late summer and autumn.

Frequent inspections, often referred to as 'monitoring', are important to detect early signs of attack and to note not just whether the plants are being damaged but whether the damage is, or is not, increasing. If damage is not getting worse the attack is probably largely over, but the weather plays an important role here.

Insects are cold-blooded animals which feed and grow quicker and are generally more active when it is warm rather than when it is cold. Few are active at temperatures below about 6 °C (42 °F) and most reach a peak of activity between 15 ° and 30 °C (60 ° and 85 °F).

In changeable, unpredictable climates there may be seasonal differences of three weeks or more in the times when the pests appear. Calendar dates are therefore not very reliable guides to the appearance of pests and their damage, nor are they for timing control measures. For example, in the past thirty-five years in central England the first cabbage root fly eggs have been found on dates ranging from 20 April to 8 May. Research has shown that the fly begins to lay eggs when the common hedge parsley (*Anthriscus sylvestris*) is just beginning to flower, with about one in twenty of its flower heads showing white. This is not just coincidence. The cabbage root fly needs to feed before it lays eggs and the nectar of these flowers is often virtually their only source of food in the spring. Brassica plants just being planted or not well established by this time will almost always need protection against this pest, using either an insecticide or a physical barrier (p. 144) within three days of planting-out.

Aphid attacks often take gardeners by surprise because vast numbers of the insects can migrate long distances when the weather is suitable, particularly on calm, warm evenings in early summer. They settle out of the air more or less at random and, after landing on a plant, probe with their mouthparts to determine whether it is suitable as a host before starting to feed and reproduce. Aphids multiply very rapidly indeed at temperatures above about 18 °C (64 °F), but their colonies can be wiped out even more quickly by heavy rain or fungal diseases.

Parasites and predators such as ladybirds, hover fly larvae, and ground beetles can prevent rapid growth of aphid colonies, but they cannot be relied upon. The natural enemies are often too late to prevent serious damage to the crop.

The mealy cabbage aphid first appears on brassicas in early summer, but it does not usually produce very large colonies at this time. Soon, parasites, predators, and fungal diseases begin to have an impact on the aphid population which dwindles and may almost disappear for a few weeks in mid-summer. Do not be lulled into a false sense of security, however!

The worst attacks by the cabbage aphid usually occur from late July to November. Brussels sprouts infested at this time are difficult to get clean. The honey-dew secreted by the aphids encourages black moulds to grow on the leaves and the developing sprout buttons. Even if the aphids are killed, they cannot be easily removed from within the enfolding leaflets of the sprout buttons. Sprouts badly affected in this way are not very acceptable for eating and are quite unsuitable for freezing.

### Pest warning services

Prompted by articles in magazines, radio, and television programmes, the gardener still has to rely largely on his own local knowledge of the times of appearance of the various pests and the methods available for controlling them. Viewdata and teletext services have been developed to provide more detailed up-to-the-minute information and warnings of the onset and development of attacks by pests (and diseases). After a bold start in the UK, but poor support, the services have had to be largely curtailed. Various financial constraints coupled with a reluctance by potential users to pay directly for the services brought to an abrupt end what had seemed a promising development.

To be widely useful, information for warning services has to be obtained by regular 'scouting' of adequate samples of crops in all regions. An extensive co-ordinating organization is therefore needed and is inevitably expensive to run. An important source of free guidance in the UK has been the Agricultural Development and Advisory Service of the Ministry of Agriculture, Fisheries and Food. However, changes in policy and financial constraints in recent years have severely trimmed the free services in favour of a commercial outlook on the advisory activities. This is especially frustrating as up-to-the-minute independent advice, with accurate forecasting and monitoring of pest attacks, is more than ever essential for field crops if chemical treatments are to be minimized without undue risk to crops. An alternative organization is needed to co-ordinate and sustain a network of voluntary 'scouts'. If growers and gardeners could join forces and create a sufficient demand, modern 'high-tech' methods of communication are available to disseminate the information swiftly and widely.

## Avoiding pest damage

### Garden hygiene

Good gardening practices have always aimed to keep the garden clean and tidy. Waste plant material, plant debris such as rotting cabbage or lettuce leaves and stumps, thinnings, and unwanted produce all harbour pests and should be promptly removed, buried, or preferably properly composted. This helps to deny pests the essential continuity of host-plants, destroys remaining insects and avoids attracting pests from elsewhere.

Research into the factors attracting insects to their host-plants is showing how plants are recognized as suitable for egg-laying or feeding. Even intact plants release volatile chemicals in minute concentrations into the atmosphere and these can act as an attractant for their particular pests. Bruising or cutting plants releases even higher concentrations which is why carrot thinnings left lying on the ground can attract carrot fly from considerable distances downwind of the source of odour. It does not take the flies long to find the remaining plants in the row, lay eggs around them and cause more severe damage to the carefully singled plants than would have occurred had they not been singled. Hence the general recommendation is to sow carrots *thinly* so that singling is unnecessary.

Many weeds also harbour pests of vegetables, a good reason for keeping down weeds in the vegetable garden, even on uncropped parts. For example, wild radish supports cabbage root fly maggots. Chickweed is a host of the peach-potato aphid and also a reservoir of viruses affecting lettuce which this aphid readily transmits. Certain species of thistles (*Sonchus*) support colonies of the lettuce root aphid on their roots, providing the pest with a continuity of host-plants from year to year.

## Resistant varieties

Growing resistant plant varieties would solve many pest problems. In the past, the availabilty of resistant varieties has depended on the plant breeder finding suitable genetic material among existing stocks, or in the wild, to incorporate into commercial varieties. The lettuces Avoncrisp and Avondefiance were bred at the Institute of Horticultural Research, Wellesbourne during the 1960s. They are so resistant to attack by the lettuce root aphid that, for practical purposes, they are immune.

The need to reduce pesticide usage has since encouraged plant breeders to develop other resistant lettuce varieties. Some are only partially (incompletely) resistant to the foliage-feeding aphids but are none the less useful against light infestations and to integrate with other methods. Aphid-resistant and partially resistant lettuce varieties are listed in Table 5.2. Some varieties of carrot are also now known to be partially resistant to damage by carrot fly larvae.

Immunity to pests has been hard to find but even partially resistant varieties are helpful to the integrated programmes of pest (and disease) control now being evolved. Gene-transplant techniques are, however, opening up new possibilities for developing pest-resistant plants much more rapidly than has been possible in the past. Pest (and disease) organisms will inevitably still adapt themselves to the altered characteristics of the plants so it is still problematical whether an endpoint of entirely durable resistance can ever be achieved.

There are three main types of resistance to pests. Plants can be tolerant and support large numbers of insects without being severely affected. This is not very satisfactory for vegetables because it permits the insects to do damage and helps to breed larger populations, making them even harder to control. Some varieties are less attractive to pests than others but this is not easy to sustain or even demonstrate.

The most important type of resistance is where the pest cannot survive as well on one variety as on another. At its most extreme, this type of resistance makes the plants immune to attack, as with the lettuce varieties mentioned above. A few established varieties of carrot are partially resistant to the carrot fly maggots but several more resistant varieties are already emerging from recent advanced breeding programmes. When available, they will greatly help gardeners to overcome this hitherto intractable problem.

So, looking ahead, new varieties of many vegetables, including carrots, lettuce, and some brassicas, can be expected to be less susceptible to pests, though few will be entirely immune.

### Crop rotation

On a garden scale, merely moving crops a few metres one way or the other has little or no effect on attacks by most pests. Only soil-inhabiting forms capable of little movement are likely to be affected, for example nematodes (eelworms) causing crop 'sicknesses' and, of course, soil-borne fungi (Chapter 6) such as *Pythium* spp.

To counter nematodes, a three-year crop cycle is worth practising. Potatoes and tomatoes (hosts of potato cyst nematodes) can be followed by brassicas and radishes (liable to clubroot disease and the brassica cyst nematode). In turn, other crops which can follow and benefit by rotation are carrots, celery, parsnips, onions, lettuce, and legumes which can all suffer from soil-borne pests or diseases. If one part of a garden becomes infested, extreme cleanliness will also be needed to avoid movement of soil to uninfested areas. More elaborate systems are possible, of course, but they can be difficult to sustain and are unlikely to affect the incidence of freely moving insect pests on a garden scale.

### Intercropping

The desire to limit use of insecticides has re-awakened the interest in the potential of intercropping. This practice – growing two or more different crops intermingled on the same land – has been widely used for centuries in the less-developed forms of agriculture, particularly in the tropics and subtropics. In developed agriculture, however, the dependence on mechanical methods of harvesting has, until recently, inhibited exploration of intercropping practices on a field scale. This is not, of course, an impediment in the vegetable garden, nor are any slight reductions in yield which sometimes result from intercropping.

Evidence of reduced pest damage in interplanted as compared with single-planted vegetables is mainly subjective; there are few facts. Claims are often made among gardeners that interplanting carrots and onions, in particular, reduces attacks by both the carrot fly and the onion fly respectively. A deterrent effect of the onions to the carrot fly was found to occur only while the onion leaves were expanding. It ceased once the plants began to bulb.

The operative word is 'reduces'. Although the plants are usually less damaged when rows of the two crops alternate than when grown apart, the level of protection is neither certain nor very great. Research has not so far found ways of making intercropping more effective but the advent of even partially resistant varieties of carrot to carrot fly, for example, offers new scope. An integrated approach, intercropping with partially resistant varieties, may often suffice in gardens. The effects are likely to be proportionally additive; if intercropping reduces damage by 50 per cent and a further 50 per cent reduction can be achieved by using a partially resistant variety (p. 139), the combined effect would be about 75 per cent protection.

Undersowing Brussels sprouts with clover, though not very practical, has also been observed to reduce infestations of several pests including cabbage root fly, cabbage aphid, and caterpillars. The clover provided cover encouraging predatory beetles to feed on the pests, so helping to reduce, but not entirely prevent, damage.

There seem to be two main ways that intercropping reduces pest damage. The ground is better covered and provides more shelter for beneficial predatory beetles, and the pests are less attracted when odours of the host plant are intermixed with those of non-host plants.

## Plant density

The present trend towards producing smaller vegetables is largely achieved by growing plants closer together at higher density (Chapter 1). Does this affect pest damage? The answer has to be 'Yes, very much so'. For the immediate crop, it will generally be beneficial in terms of less pest damage per plant, but there is a trade-off. Although a given number of insects immigrating to attack more plants than usual should cause rather less damage to each plant, *more* insects are likely to survive so the next generation will probably be larger. Where a pest such as the carrot fly can normally maintain a large local population, the end result may not be as favourable as at first envisaged. The converse is, of course, also likely to occur. A reduction in the number of plants of a crop between one season and the next can result temporarily in more severe damage than previously experienced, though perhaps only for one or two seasons.

We see, therefore, that the pest responds to the increase or decrease in its food supply, though on a garden scale the effects may not always be great and may pass unnoticed.

## Sowing and planting dates

Adjusting sowing or planting dates can avoid the worst periods of attack by some pests. Peas sown early or very late avoid much of the damage caused by pea moth maggots in the pods because the crops will not be flowering from mid-June to early July when the moth is laying its eggs.

Very early sowings or transplantings of brassicas pass the most vulnerable stage before severe attacks of the flea beetle occur. Late sowings or plantings will also miss most of the attacks.

Carrots sown early will have an extensive root system by the time the carrot fly maggots are feeding on them in June and July and few plants will therefore be killed. Early sowing, however, will not prevent the large third-stage maggots mining in the roots, often killing the taproot and stunting the plants. If sowing of carrots is delayed until June, they miss the period of peak egg-laying by the first generation of carrot fly but are liable to be damaged in late autumn and winter by the later broods.

The carrot fly also attacks parsnips, celery, and several perennial herbs which can act as 'bridges' between one year's crop and the next. Growing these alongside successive sowings of carrots virtually guarantees a substantial build-up of the pest and serious damage each year.

### Cultivations

Autumn digging has been found to be more effective than spring cultivations for reducing the numbers of overwintering pupae of the cabbage root fly.

Sometimes it is desirable not to sow seeds into freshly cultivated land. For example, the maggots of the bean seed fly feed on organic matter in the soil as well as on seeds and seedlings of peas, beans, or onions. The fly lays eggs freely in freshly disturbed soil and a sowing delayed for about 10 days after cultivating the seedbed has often been found to prevent attacks on, for example, autumn-sown onions. This may also be applicable to spring-sown peas and beans, which are frequently attacked by bean seed fly maggots.

## Preventing pest damage

Methods for preventing pest damage fall into three categories: physical, biological, or chemical. The examples discussed here are intended to illustrate principles.

There are many old remedies, some with little foundation and even in conflict with known facts. The copious use of 'soot and lime' against carrot fly, or a disinfectant to prevent cabbage root fly damage to brassica plants are examples where research has been unable to support claims made for the treatments. Use of a disinfectant on cauliflowers actually reduced plant growth. Without doing rigorous scientific tests, it is easy to become wrongly convinced that particular practices are beneficial.

## Physical Methods

The removal by hand of foliage-feeding pests can be very effective when not many plants are involved, as in a garden. Brassicas can be kept free from serious caterpillar damage in this way. It is best to look first at the undersides of the outer leaves where the youngest caterpillars feed. Then examine the centres for signs of their droppings and, if you see any, search the heart, leaf by leaf, until the culprit is found. The caterpillars are often well camouflaged so you will have to look carefully. Pick them off and destroy them.

It does not take long and you should be able to check twenty or thirty plants in 10 minutes, much quicker than preparing a spray and cleaning the equipment afterwards. Furthermore, you will not have to delay eating the plants to allow the insecticide residues to disappear. By examining the plants twice a week in summer, you can avoid the need for any further treatment.

Occasional aphids can also be crushed by hand to delay the start of an infestation, but it is obviously impracticable to deal with large numbers in this way. An interesting outcome of research into the flight habits of aphids is the use of aluminium foil laid on soil with the shiny side upwards alongside rows of tomatoes or potatoes. The sky is reflected from the foil, discouraging winged aphids from settling on the plants. They are apparently fooled into flying upwards to find the plant instead of towards the ground.

Easy-to-make physical barriers can protect individual brassica plants from the cabbage root fly. The barriers can be either discs of a flexible material placed on the soil surface (Fig. 5.2 (*a*)), or plastic drinking cups from which the bottoms have been removed so that they can be slipped over the plants and lightly pressed into the soil. Both types of barrier reduce the numbers of cabbage root fly eggs laid around the brassica transplants and, if carefully fitted, can eliminate up to 70 per cent of the root damage, sufficient for most purposes and equivalent in performance to an insecticide (Fig. 5.2 (*b*) ).

The discs should be about 15 cm. (6 in.) in diameter with a small

Fig. 5.2. Methods for preventing damage by cabbage root fly maggots to transplanted cabbage, cauliflowers, or Brussels sprouts. (*a*) A 15 cm. (6 in.) disc of carpet foam underlay fitted snugly around the stem immediately after transplanting; (*b*) the maggot damage to the roots stunts the plants (*centre*) and is prevented as well by a carefully fitted disc (*left*) as by an insecticide treatment (*right*).

3 mm. (⅛ in.) central hole and a slit to the outer edge of the disc so that they can easily be placed around the young plant stems and lie neatly on the soil surface. A foam carpet underlay makes suitable discs and will expand as the plant stem grows, so eliminating an unsatisfactory feature of the stiff tarred-felt discs first recommended over a century ago. These barriers also act as a soil mulch, reducing loss of moisture, and they provide a haven for beneficial predatory beetles that feed on cabbage root fly eggs and maggots. This is, of course, why the discs can be so effective.

Recently, a new type of covering has been devised for seedbeds and young plants. It is a very lightweight fine-meshed, non-woven sheet made from heat-sealed fibres (abbreviated in Table 5.1 to NWHS – Non-Woven Heat-Sealed mesh) which can keep out many small airborne insects including aphids, flea beetles, and root flies provided it is put in place *before* the plants become infested. Laid loosely over the soil shortly after sowing, or over plants after transplanting, the fine mesh-like material also creates a favourable micro-climate for seed germination and plant growth and helps the plants to mature early. The material is quite tough and is supported entirely by the plants without needing additional ribs to form a tunnel along the rows, the edges being dug into the soil to hold them down. It must be in place *before* any attacks occur. There is little experience to guide its use so any suggestions are speculative at present.

Vegetables for which the non-woven sheet has been used successfully include lettuce, various brassicas, leeks, potatoes, and certain herbs. Apparently it can be reused and so promises to be an environmentally friendly method for protecting plants from many types of pest, including birds.

Various monitoring devices, usually traps of one kind or another, can be used to detect some pests. They are either coloured (usually bright or fluorescent yellow) sticky traps or devices baited with a potent attractant. An example of successful commercial use of a pheromone is for traps used to monitor the appearance of the pea moth as a guide to the timing of large-scale spraying operations on commercial pea crops. While these are rather expensive for most gardeners to buy individually, the use of traps to reduce moths on an allotment site may well be worthwhile as a collective investment where pea moth is frequently a problem.

## Biological Methods

The use of biological agents to control pests seems at first sight to be very attractive. However, like the pests themselves, parasites, predators, and diseases caused by fungi, bacteria, and viruses are affected by temperature and therefore are likely to be unreliable where the climate is variable and unpredictable as in Britain.

The principal organisms are often already present in the garden; the problem is how to adjust conditions to favour the natural enemies rather than the pest. In glasshouses this is possible, but reliable procedures for using natural enemies outdoors on a field or garden scale have not yet been developed.

Specific bacterial toxins that kill caterpillars are used commercially in some countries with success. To be useful in the vegetable garden, strains or preparations of pathogenic organisms are needed which act rapidly to prevent undue damage continuing while the treatment is taking effect. The ideal in this respect has yet to be achieved.

Are predators and parasites of use? Undoubtedly they are. They play an important stabilizing role and without them pest populations would be much larger and the damage to vegetables much greater, although the gardener may not be easily convinced that this is so. The realization of the importance of predators and parasites is the basis for all sound pest control practices. We may not be able to do much to increase the natural enemies of pests, but we can certainly take care not to destroy any more of them than is essential, if only by being most careful not to use pesticides unnecessarily and never in excess of immediate needs.

Ladybirds have been abundant in Europe and have overwintered in large numbers in recent years. As they emerge from hibernation sites they can be collected whenever seen and transferred to fruit trees, blackcurrants, and other garden plants where they can find overwintering stages of insects such as aphids. Later, putting them on to beans and brassicas when aphids are migrating, or just starting colonies, can be very effective in delaying the multiplication of the pest.

Unfortunately there is no guarantee of success. Only by examining the plants regularly can we decide, for instance, whether natural enemies are holding aphid infestations in check, whether a local thunderstorm has, or has not, dealt effectively with an aphid infestation, or whether a chemical treatment will, after all, have to be used. Observations and routine monitoring of the plants are vital to successful pest control.

## Chemical Methods

There are many old chemical remedies for protecting vegetables from pests, usually aimed at repelling them or attracting them into traps. Some of the chemicals are decidely toxic to man and animals and would never be approved if they were being introduced as new chemicals today. For example, soot and 'whizzed naphthalene' contain carcinogens; sodium fluoride and mercury compounds are acute poisons in their own right. On the other hand, beer is such an effective attractant for slugs that research workers use it as a bait when studying them.

Several well-known insecticides are obtained from plants, for instance derris, nicotine, and pyrethrum. Indeed many plants contain chemicals with insecticidal properties. This may partly account for the fact that most plants resist most insects and is the basis of many present research programmes to find new insecticides. Turnips and swedes, for instance, contain certain insecticidal isothiocyanates, while rhubarb leaves contain high concentrations of oxalic acid, which is very toxic to man.

Man and the environment have had centuries to adapt to naturally occurring chemicals, so it is often argued that they are safer than newly synthesized compounds. The point is debatable and certainly does not apply to acute toxicities. Nicotine, for instance, is highly toxic to man, and pyrethrum to fish.

Since 1940 chemists have produced many very potent insecticides but most have not been suitable for small-scale use in gardens and many have now ceased to be used because they are hazardous to the user or the environment, or leave excessive residues in produce. When used exactly as recommended, those available to the gardener are unlikely to leave residues in plants or soil, or affect other animals in the environment. The gardener cannot, however, expect to achieve the levels of protection available to a commercial producer.

A visit to any local garden store shows how much reliance is now placed on chemicals to control garden pests. We need pesticides to garden effectively, but we also need to know how to choose and use them wisely.

The words pesticides, chemicals, or poisons conjure up emotions ranging from suspicion and distrust of the unknown to fear bred largely from tales of fiction. It is impossible to prove that a particular chemical is harmless. All that can be said is that, after extensive testing, harmful effects arising from its correct use have not been detected. There thus has to be a value-judgement that the remote risk of possible, as yet undetected, harmful effects is acceptably small relative to the benefits to be gained from using the pesticide. This, of course, applies universally to all chemical products used, or generated, by man for whatever purpose.

There are a few important points of principle to bear in mind. Virtually all chemicals, whether common salt, detergents, therapeutic drugs, plastics, or pesticides (insecticides, fungicides, herbicides, etc. are all classed broadly as pesticides) are toxic to animals or plants if they are present in excess. Some, of course, are very much more toxic than others and these we tend to think of as poisons. However, it is wrong to refer to less toxic chemicals as being non-poisonous.

Two important rules are that, first, it is the amount of chemical reaching an organism that determines whether or not it will be toxic and, secondly, organisms can tolerate more of some chemicals than they can of others. Hence, pesticides which are toxic to certain plants or animals may not be comparably toxic to others.

A third important rule concerns the duration of exposure to a chemical. The amount reaching the organism multiplied by the time of the exposure determines the toxic dose. Whereas a large dose can act very quickly, a small dose may take a long time to be effective and very small doses may act so slowly that they do not seem to be toxic at all. The organism can break down and excrete the chemical quicker than it is absorbed so the chemical is ineffective, but that does not mean that it is entirely harmless.

Most countries now have regulatory authorities to scrutinize and approve new pesticides to ensure that they will not create undue hazards when used as directed (see also Chapter 6, p. 186). Official procedures ensure that products will not persist unnecessarily long in the soil or in plants, so protecting the environment from long-term effects, and that they satisfactorily control the pest or disease as claimed. An immense amount of research and development goes into modern pesticides to make quite sure of these points. Pesticides still offer the surest means of protecting garden vegetables from pests (and diseases).

If vegetables are being grown for show, and must be absolutely unblemished, then some chemical protection against pest and disease damage is usually essential. However, this is by no means the case if they are being grown to be eaten. The quest for absolutely blemish-free produce for the kitchen is not only a waste of time and money but it can lead to excessive use of pesticides, now illegal in many countries. The result can be attractive vegetables that carry residues of the chemicals in excess of those considered desirable in food for human consumption.

After using chemicals in the garden you have no way of knowing what levels of residues remain in the produce at harvest. However, a product's 'Directions for Use' will embody the results of the extensive testing done before the product is approved and take fully into account the need for residues to dissipate before harvest. If for no other reason than this, it is most important to follow carefully the instructions for using pesticides—and NEVER over-use them.

How can we know whether a treatment is needed? How is the use of chemical treatments kept to a minimum? Whenever possible we try to make use of all available methods for protecting our crops and avoid relying entirely on one. This is called 'integrated control'. For each crop consider your past experiences to identify the most serious problems likely to arise and then think of other problems relative to these.

For example, if birds or slugs regularly take most of your peas then it is most important to protect against these pests first before dealing with the minor damage done by the pea and bean weevil. Similarly, if every year cabbage root fly maggots kill many brassica plants in the seedbed, prevent this before being concerned about minor flea beetle damage. Damage occurring on the part of the crop you eat will of course be less acceptable than damage affecting other parts of the plant.

You will need to think ahead (Fig. 5.3). For many soil pests, preventive measures are the most satisfactory and only your past experience with crops in *your* garden can guide you as to whether they may be necessary. Pests such as the cabbage root fly, carrot fly and bean seed fly can severely damage plants but in some circumstances rarely seem to cause serious problems. You are fortunate if this applies to you.

## Pesticide products

A bewildering array of pesticide products is available and, in many countries, the use of pesticides in both field and garden is now subject to statutory regulations.

In the UK, for example, the Control of Pesticides Regulations (1986) followed from the Food and Environment Protection Act of 1985 (commonly referred to as FEPA). By statute all pesticide products, and the ways they are used, must be approved. It is an offence therefore to use non-approved products OR to use approved products in ways which differ from the specific conditions of use on which approval was granted.

The range of products approved for any particular purpose will, of course, be continually changing as new products appear and old ones become no longer available. Accordingly, in a book such as this it is not now feasible to list products or active ingredients in relation to particular uses. Any listing would soon become

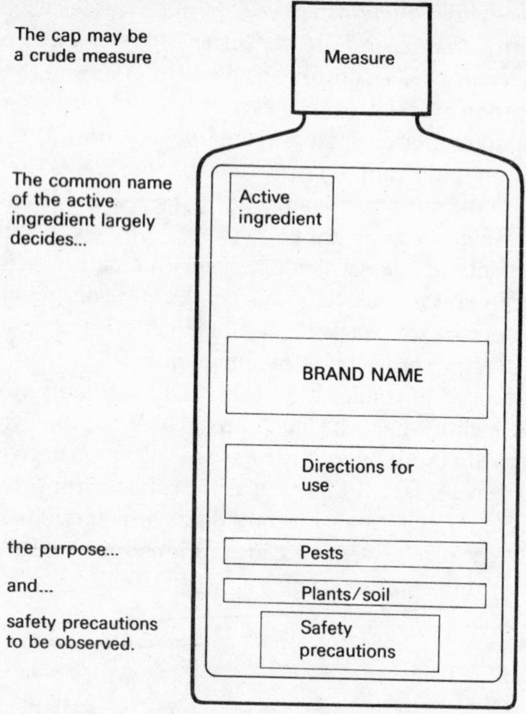


Fig. 5.3. What to look for on the label of a pesticide product. Reputable products and all those officially approved are well labelled and the wording is carefully chosen to mean precisely what it says. Additional brochures giving more information may also be available for some products.

invalid and seem to be recommending illegal uses of products.

The gardener therefore needs continually to refer to the specific instructions accompanying each product in the range on sale in a shop or garden centre to find those which can be used for particular purposes. Lists of products are periodically published but contain little detail about uses and are unlikely to be authoritative much beyond the date of publication.

If you already know the chemical required, you need only locate a supplier. However, if it is a long-established remedy, you should also determine whether it is still approved for the purpose and whether more effective alternatives have become available. Technology is advancing year by year and more suitable products may now be available. Shop assistants may be able to guide you in your choice, but reliable advice is not easy to find.

As already implied, the manufacturer's recommendations on the label of the product contain very important information which is often updated (Fig. 5.3). Even if you have used the product before, carefully read the label again. Note the nature of the contents, the 'Directions for Use' and any safety precautions. More detailed information is sometimes given in associated brochures which may be available on request.

## Pesticide Names

There is often confusion about the names of garden chemicals because each product has two types of name and both are important. The brand name, usually a registered trade-mark, identifies the manufacturer and often, by reputation, the quality of the product. It may also be a continuity name for a series of allied products and is usually a guide to reliability. The active ingredient, however, may be changed from time to time even though the brand name is retained, and more than one active ingredient may be present. You will have to search the label well to find out what you are buying.

Labels on all approved products in the UK state the internationally agreed common name or names of the active ingredient(s). Usually this will be in small print, for example 'contains dimethoate'. This common name is the main clue to the *purpose* and *use* of a product. Each active ingredient has particular characteristics that determine how it will behave when it is used and the pests that it can control. It may move systemically through a plant, or it may be particularly suited to use in soil.

More than one manufacturer may sell products containing the same active ingredient. The brand names will be different as will the detailed directions for use because these relate to the formulated product (the brand name), rather than to the active ingredient.

Some products are available in several different formulations, such as dusts, powders, granules, or liquids, each with particular uses. Dusts are mainly adopted for older materials and few modern products are formulated in this way. They are very difficult to apply precisely without overdosing both the plant and the soil. Dusts are, however, one of the simplest ways of incorporating insecticides into soil and will probably continue to be used for certain products. Granular formulations are intended primarily for application to soil. Again, they are not easy to apply precisely but they are less hazardous to use than dusts. Garden products are often available as liquid or wettable powder formulations which can be used to make sprays or drenches.

Sometimes liquid formulations can damage plants so it is important to note any cautionary statements on the label indicating types of plant which are susceptible to particular formulations.

Brands containing more than one active ingredient may be able to deal with several pests. Mixtures for general use, adopting the blunderbuss principle, are convenient but unfortunately they conflict with sound practice in the vegetable garden; one or other of the ingredients will almost always be applied unnecessarily.

### Directions for use

The labels on containers are precisely worded to provide reliable information obtained after extensive research and development. It is most unlikely that you can improve a product's effectiveness safely by using your own initiative and ignoring the instructions; and it may even be illegal to do so. You might put at risk your crops, animals, and even people, including yourself, your family, and pets.

As well as telling you what to do, the instructions also state what you must *not* do, and this is just as important.

Directions for use may indicate when to use the product but will always state a recommended dose and how to apply it. This is usually critical and the dose must NEVER be exceeded in any circumstances. Sometimes a slightly smaller dose, perhaps half that recommended, would be sufficiently effective for your purposes, because the approval system and the manufacturer have to cater for the worst circumstances and these may not be yours. You will have to judge whether the performance of the reduced dose is still adequate, but do not blame the manufacturer if it is not.

It is essential to wear eye protectors and rubber gloves when handling concentrated pesticides. If there is any risk of getting your everyday clothes contaminated, wear a light overall which can be laundered separately from other clothes. Whatever you do, do not allow either concentrated or diluted liquid to fall on your skin or get into your eyes or mouth. If it does, rinse it off immediately.

A common difficulty arises when very small amounts of dilute sprays or drenches are needed, as in the average garden. Instructions may be given on the amounts of a product to use in 5 or 10 litres (approximately 1 or 2 gallons) when often only a litre or so is needed at any one time for a small hand-sprayer. After all, plants do not have to be drowned in spray; in fact most is adhering to the plants just before the liquid begins to run off the leaves.

Small volumes of concentrated liquid products are much more readily measured in metric units (1 millilitre = 1/1000 litre) than in Imperial units (fluid ounces and gallons). To convert from Imperial units use 28 ml. for 1 fluid ounce; 1.1 litres for 2 pints; and 4.5 litres for 1 gallon. A safe and accurate method for measuring a few ml. (millilitres) is to use a 10 ml. capacity measuring cylinder, obtainable from pharmacists, or a calibrated hypodermic syringe, marked indelibly with a few spots of paint to identify it for garden use only. The needle should be destroyed and replaced by about 10 cm. (4 in.) of narrow-bore (1–2 mm.) (*c.* $\frac{1}{16}$ in.) flexible plastic tube. This will reach into the narrow-necked containers used for pesticides and you can accurately measure out small volumes of even rather viscous preparations.

If two or more mixes have to be prepared in quick succession, do not wash out the syringe after each one but be very careful to do so thoroughly when the job is finished.

Products in powder or granular form are even more difficult to measure accurately for small-scale use. One method is to weigh out a larger amount (but not on the kitchen scales), and from this to get smaller amounts by carefully heaping it into a cone, and halving and quartering the cone until the desired fraction remains. If you can then find a small tube or other container that will hold this quantity, mark it at the right level so that it can be used to measure out further amounts by volume.

The amount of granular products to be applied to the soil is often quite critical and is often much less than is generally realized. Sometimes doses of granular and powder formulations are not very clearly stated and you should then determine how little you can use rather than how much, and record the information for future reference.

## Safety

Changing attitudes to pesticides have led to a decision process which should always precede their use, as follows. First, is it necessary to use a pesticide at all? Secondly, if it is necessary, which is the safest product to use by the safest application method? Thirdly, when the safest product has been identified, what additional precautions are needed to protect oneself, other people, animals, and plants, and the local environment? Specific precautions are likely to include:

- Buy no more pesticides than you will use within a season.
- Never keep or use products more than three years old.
- Store pesticides on a high shelf, preferably in a locked cupboard well away from children and pets.
- Wear eye protection and unlined plastic or synthetic rubber gloves when handling a concentrated material, washing them thoroughly inside and outside after use.
- Promptly wash off any pesticide falling on your skin.
- Never suck up concentrates by mouth into tubes or pipettes.

- Do not remain exposed to pesticide vapours for more than a few minutes at a time and then only when unavoidable.
- Follow instructions on the label meticulously.
- Do not spray plants in flower when bees are active.
- Do not eat sprayed crops until the minimum interval as stated on the label has lapsed since the treatment.
- Keep concentrated pesticides out of streams, rivers, and ponds. Most of them are very toxic to fish and other aquatic life.
- Never, never put pesticides in containers normally associated with food or drink, such as screw-capped soft-drink or medicine bottles.

Pesticides are a boon to the gardener when they are used wisely and judiciously as intended but to avoid destroying populations of beneficial insects, it is important not to overtreat. A garden which is sterile of beneficial insects is ecologically very unstable. In such situations the gardener may become entirely dependent on chemicals and may well find that their effectiveness fluctuates. This is because they are no longer backed up by the natural parasites and predators which play a hidden, but nevertheless important, part in keeping pest populations within bounds.

World-wide, more than 450 pests of crops and of man have become resistant to many different pesticides. We cannot, therefore, rely on any one insecticide to be effective indefinitely and we know that intensive exposure of insects to chemicals almost guarantees that they will become resistant sooner rather than later. The more sparingly pesticides are used, the more durable will be their usefulness to the community.

## Crops and pests

Methods for dealing with some of the more frequent pests of vegetables in gardens are only briefly discussed here and are summarized in Table 5.1. For reasons already stated, the column referring to 'Chemical' control measures shows the likely effectiveness of recommended treatments against *severe* attacks by the pests. As a guide only, in Table 5.1 the asterisks (*) indicate that chemical methods can be expected to be *** very effective, ** moderately effective or *, for one reason or another, only partially effective. The gardener can therefore judge whether it is likely to be worthwhile in the garden to resort to chemical treatments to protect particular crops.

The form of calendar illustrated in Fig. 5.4 can be adapted to suit the gardener's pest control requirements. It can act as an aid to memory so that important operations are not overlooked.

## General soil pests

Cutworms, chafer grubs, leatherjackets, millipedes, wireworms, and slugs can attack most vegetable crops. They mainly occur in large numbers under grass or in neglected gardens and usually become less of a problem after the ground has been cultivated for a few years. The effectiveness of soil treatments depends very much on the type of soil, crops on peaty or heavy soils being more difficult to protect against these and other soil-inhabiting pests than those growing on light sandy soils. It is always difficult to incorporate chemicals evenly, whether as liquids or powders, into heavy or wet soils. The pesticide is imperfectly distributed and so is less effective.

## Asparagus

The principle pests are asparagus beetle and slugs. The beetles are brightly coloured, with a reddish thorax and yellow rectangular markings on black wing cases. They appear in early summer and feed on the foliage and stems of the asparagus plant. Damage can be readily prevented by using an appropriate insecticide when the pest first appears.

Slugs characteristically leave shiny slime-trails and can be controlled adequately by baited traps or a molluscicide.

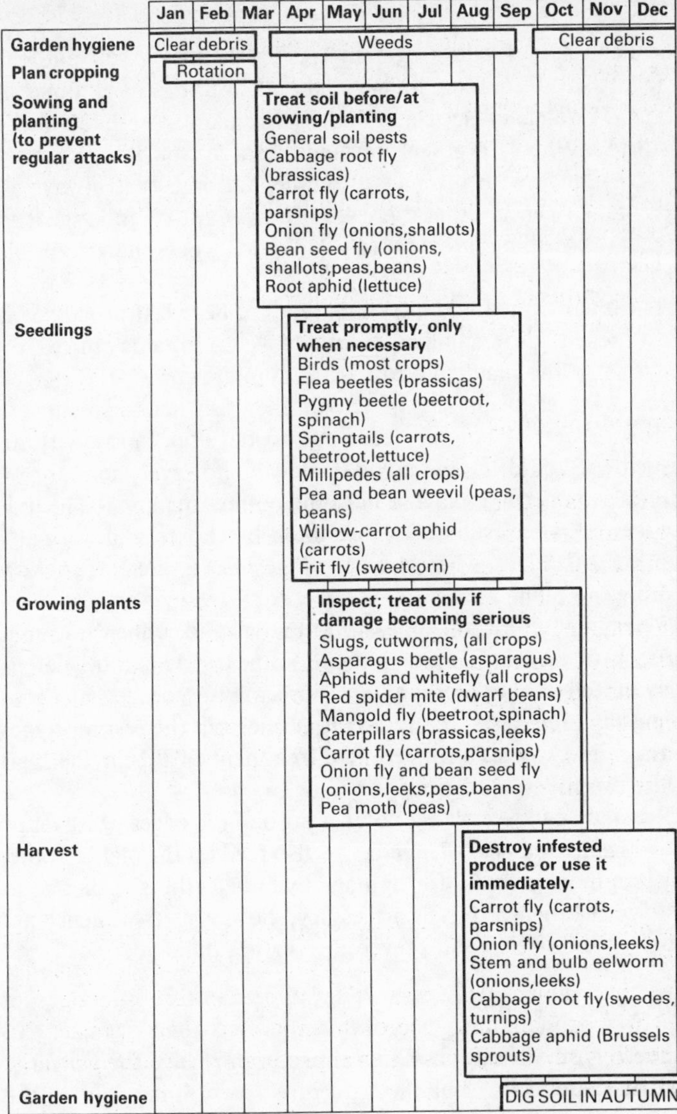


Fig. 5.4. A simple pest control calendar to adapt to requirements.

## Beans

The bean seed fly lays eggs in freshly disturbed soil and the maggots will feed and damage seed and seedlings of all types of beans. If damaged seed germinates, the plants are likely to be distorted. Where the pest is prevalent, treat the soil along the rows in accordance with product recommendations. It is always an advantage to ensure that the seeds are sown into a good seedbed so that the seedlings grow rapidly and quickly pass the susceptible stage.

The black bean aphid infests all types of beans. If broad beans are attacked, allow small colonies to develop for a day or two on the tops of the plant to ensure that immigration of the winged forms is largely over. Then pinch out the tips when the plants are in full flower. If colonies continue to develop, spray with an aphicide. Should the plants be in flower, however, special precautions are needed to avoid harming pollinating insects, including bees. A selective insecticide should be chosen and normally applied after dark when the beneficial insects are not actively visiting the plants.

Red spider mites sometimes infest French and runner beans but rarely broad beans. Treatment with an acaricide can be moderately effective but several applications may be needed at about seven-day intervals if the acaricide cannot kill the resting stages of the mite. Any need for repeated treatments will be made clear in the product's 'Directions for Use'.

Pea and bean weevils eat notches around the edges of leaves of broad beans and peas. Their larvae also feed on the plants' roots, but it is most unusual for damage by either adults or larvae to justify treatment. If it is necessary, however, treatments are usually very effective in preventing further damage.

## Beetroot and spinach

Numerous small soil-inhabiting insects can reduce the germination of these crops, but they are rarely very important in the garden. The maggots of the mangold fly mine inside the leaves leaving yellowish blisters, but very severe attacks of this pest are necessary before there is any significant effect on yield. Badly infested leaves can be picked off and destroyed, only very heavy infestations requiring treatment with an insecticide.

### Brassicas and radish

Many different pests attack these crops but treatments are not always necessary. Summer brassicas such as cabbage and cauliflower are most affected. Seedlings can be killed and badly checked by the attacks of the cabbage root fly. These attacks can be largely prevented by using physical barriers such as discs placed around the plants (Fig. 5.2(*a*); p. 145) or non-woven fine-mesh material. Alternatively, the soil can be treated with a suitable insecticide at sowing time or immediately after transplants are set out. If established plants become infested, the damage can sometimes be limited by drenching the soil, although this is generally a less effective method. During the summer period, insecticide treatments should be applied to transplanted brassicas within three days of planting out, before any previously laid root fly eggs have had time to hatch.

Cauliflowers are most affected by damage, cabbage rather less so and Brussels sprouts are relatively tolerant of this pest. Damage to radishes can be partly prevented by treating the soil with an insecticide at sowing time. As a rule, sprays have generally been found to be more effective than dusts or granules for this purpose. On swedes and turnips, late-season attacks by cabbage root fly are difficult to prevent entirely and usually some superficial damage may have to be accepted.

On young plants, the cabbage aphid is readily controlled by systemic insecticides. In mid- and late summer, maturing cabbage, cauliflowers, and especially Brussels sprouts are particularly liable to become severely infested and become more difficult to protect. A careful watch must be kept to ensure that they do not become too severely infested before treatment. Systemic insecticides are usually employed against aphids. These are absorbed by the plant and tend to move upwards so it is important to treat the lower leaves even though the infestations often appear mainly on the upper leaves.

Cabbage caterpillars belong to several species of butterfly and moth which can all infest brassica crops. The most important are the large and small cabbage white butterflies, the cabbage moth and, occasionally, the diamond back moth. If plants are inspected regularly during the summer, caterpillars or eggs can be removed by hand. When attacks are severe, an insecticide may have to be applied. Treatments are most effective when the caterpillars are small. Of the several different types of insecticide available for use against caterpillars, certain pyrethroids are especially effective. With further development, however, highly effective preparations of insect pathogenic bacteria and viruses can be expected eventually to provide alternative forms of treatment.

Flea beetles can also seriously damage swedes and turnips in the seedling stage, not only by eating small holes in the leaves, but also because their very small larvae feed on the roots. Excessive damage can be prevented by using an insecticide treatment.

The turnip gall weevil produces galls on the roots of brassicas. The galls may superficially resemble those of the disease clubroot except that, when cut open, they will be seen to contain a small white grub, or if late in the season just a cavity from which the adult beetle has already escaped through a small exit hole. This damage is not usually sufficiently important to warrant an insecticide treatment.

## Carrots, parsnips, and parsley

Numerous small soil-inhabiting insects can affect the establishment of carrots, but the main pests are carrot fly larvae and willow-carrot aphid. For effective control of carrot fly it is necessary to sow at carefully controlled rates (Chapter 1, pp. 20–1) to avoid the need for thinning, to lift early carrots by the end of August and not to sow late carrots until the end of May or in June.

Several varieties of carrots are now known to suffer only about half the amount of damage found on other types. They are referred to as being partially resistant to carrot fly damage. The partially resistant varieties at present available are all Nantes types and include Fancy, Ideal, James Intermediate, Early Scarlet Horn, Flakkee, Nandor, Nantucket, and Tip Top. Development of further resistant varieties is now well advanced so both gardeners and growers should be on the lookout for new varieties which will limit the amount of damage caused by this pest.

Although an insecticide applied along the row at sowing time can usually protect seedlings adequately, those now available are not sufficiently persistent to protect crops against the more severe attacks that occur in late autumn and winter. If recommended, a second treatment about mid-August may help against these late attacks. None of the insecticides currently available to the gardener is, however, the complete answer to this pest. An insecticide treatment used in conjunction with a resistant variety, an example of 'integrated control', is the most effective way of combating this pest.

The willow-carrot aphid is readily controlled by a spray with a systemic insecticide but in mid-summer the plants, particularly young seedlings, need examining every two or three days to detect whether they are becoming infested. It can happen very suddenly. On parsnips, a different aphid sometimes appears but rarely causes serious problems.

### Celery and celeriac

The maggots of the celery fly can leave unsightly mines in the leaves of celery, but they can easily be dealt with by pinching out the affected leaflets. Severe attacks can be controlled by an insecticide.

Slugs also damage celery, but these can be kept in check using a molluscicide, usually distributed along the row. The carrot fly is not easy to control on either crop with the chemicals available to the gardener, though treatments applied in late summer may be partially effective.

### Cucumber and marrow

The most important pests affecting these crops are aphids and whitefly. Although aphid infestations can be effectively dealt with using any of several types of insecticide, the whitefly is much more difficult to control. Incidentally, the species of whitefly commonly encountered outdoors is not the same as that which is often found in glasshouses or on house plants. Some of its immature stages are not easily killed so most recommendations stress the need to repeat the treatment after a stated interval. The tissues of cucumbers and marrows are particularly prone to damage by some insecticides and care should be taken when treating them.

### Leeks

Leeks are generally free of serious problems but can be affected by stem nematode, onion fly, thrips and, occasionally, the leek moth. Treatments are not usually needed, but if stem nematode becomes a problem, a sound rotation (p. 140) will have to be practised.

### Lettuce

The several species of aphids which infest the foliage of lettuce can be fairly readily suppressed on young plants by using an appropriate insecticide. They become difficult to kill once the lettuce has started to heart and the aphids have penetrated into the centres of the plants.

An even more difficult problem is to protect lettuce from the root aphid. This can colonize the root systems in mid- to late summer producing distinctive white cotton-wool-like excretions which mark its presence. Insecticides applied at sowing or shortly afterwards tend not to be very effective in seasons when the root aphid is prevalent and attacks are severe.

Fortunately, there are now available many varieties of lettuce which are either partially or fully resistant to the foliage aphids or the root aphid, and some even resist both (Table 5.2). Growing aphid-resistant varieties greatly reduces the need to rely on insecticide treatments.

Lettuce crops can be badly affected by cutworms. The attacks

**Table 5.2**

**Some lettuce varieties resistant or tolerant to the lettuce root aphid or partially resistant to the three common species of aphid found on the foliage.**

| | |
|---|---|
| **Lettuce root aphid** (*Pemphigus bursarius*): | |
| Fully resistant: | Avoncrisp, Avondefiance, Continuity, Grand Rapids, Lakeland, Little Gem (=Sucrine), Sabine, Sigmaball, Sigmahead, Wallop. |
| Tolerant: | Debby, Musette. |
| **Peach-potato aphid** (*Myzus persicae*): | |
| Partial resistance: | Cindy, Crispino, Kellys, Marbèllo, Mondian Norden, Ravel, Reskia, Salina. |
| **Lettuce aphid** (*Nasonovia ribisnigri*): | |
| Partial resistance: | Batavia Blonde de Paris, Batavia de Pierre Bénite, Brioso, Calmar, Iceberg, Imperial, Ithaca, Larganda, Vera, Wenda. |
| **Potato aphid** (*Macrosiphum euphorbiae*): | |
| Partial resistance: | Arctic King, Batavia Blonde de Paris, Batavia de Pierre Bénite, Brioso, Butter Crunch, Calmar, Charan, Great Lakes 366, Ithaca, Larganda, Marbello. |

tend to be sporadic but relatively few of these caterpillars can cause a serious loss of plants. An insecticide applied at planting can give some protection but, if only a few dead plants are seen to have been cut off at soil level, it is often sufficient to search carefully in the soil around damaged plants to find the caterpillars and remove them before they do more damage.

As with many other vegetables, covering lettuce with NWHS-mesh sheet would probably prevent severe attacks by all these pests.

## Onions and shallots

Where attacks by the onion fly occur frequently, seed pre-treated with an appropriate insecticide should be used if available. Alternatively, the soil can be treated at sowing or planting time with an approved insecticide. A later treatment is sometimes advised, applied along the rows when the plants become established. Badly affected onions should be removed and burned.

Plants infected by the minute stem nematode typically become bull-necked, swollen and eventually rot prematurely. The pest can persist from year to year in the soil. Unfortunately there are no chemicals for the gardener to use against this pest. Affected plants should be promptly destroyed (not composted) and other susceptible plants, members of the onion family, beans, peas, rhubarb, and strawberries, should not be grown on the same land for at least three years to allow the nematode population in the soil to decline. Weeds such as chickweed, black bindweed, and mayweed are also hosts of this eelworm and should not be allowed to flourish. Lettuce, or brassicas (if clubroot is not a problem; Chapter 6, p. 180), can be grown on the land instead.

Thrips occasionally attack onions in hot dry weather. Serious damage to young plants can be prevented only if an insecticide is applied at a early stage in the attack.

## Peas

Insects are not always the most damaging pest of peas at the seedling stage, though bean seed fly maggots sometimes cause serious loss of plants. Bird damage, especially, can be acute, birds mutilating or pulling out the seedlings before they become established. Remedies involve either stretching black thread along the rows or covering the crop with a net. The recently available NWHS-mesh is likely to be very effective.

Pea thrips can also be damaging and are likely to be serious if an attack develops in hot dry weather when the pods are forming. An insecticide treatment should only be applied if damage is obviously increasing.

The pea moth is the most disconcerting pest of peas. It lays its eggs on the plant and the minute young caterpillars bore into the pods to feed on the developing peas. In areas where attacks occur frequently, during the period June to mid-August, an insecticide treatment will need to be applied seven to ten days after the first flowers appear in the crop. This will help to reduce damage, but protection is unlikely to be complete.

### Potato

Slugs, wireworms, and cutworms can be among the most damaging of pests in the garden. Slug damage will usually be worst in wet cold conditions. It can be limited by using an approved molluscicide.

Damage by wireworms is most likely to occur when using land which has recently been under grass. It may then be desirable to treat the soil before planting potatoes, consideration being given to any stated risk of affecting the flavour of the produce, especially on lighter types of soil. Once wireworm damage has started it cannot be stopped because further treatment is impractical.

Poor yields of potatoes in gardens are often attributable to potato cyst nematodes which can build up large populations in the soil. There are two important species, one with white cysts and the other with yellow cysts which turn brownish as they age. In the UK, there are four distinct biological races, or pathotypes, of the white-cysted species but only one race, RO1, of the yellow-cysted species. Varieties of potato resistant to race RO1 of the yellow potato cyst nematode include Cara, Maris Piper, Pentland Javelin, and Ukama. Already in trials are some candidate varieties which are partially resistant to the white potato cyst nematode. Relief from damage by this nematode should soon be available.

Even if resistant cultivars are grown, a strict rotation of crops on at least a three-year cycle is necessary to prevent damaging populations of the nematode from building up in the soil.

### Sweet corn

The larvae of the frit fly can damage the growing point of the young sweet corn plants and those sown before the end of May are particularly susceptible to attack. Treatment with an insecticide applied when the shoots emerge can give substantial, if not complete, protection until the plants have developed five or six leaves. After this they become immune.

## Tomato

There are few pests of outdoor tomatoes in the UK, other than the two species of potato cyst nematode, which might present problems to the gardener. To avoid large populations of nematodes building up in the soil, tomatoes should not be grown frequently on the same land. A rotation should be used similar to that needed for potatoes.

## Acknowledgements

The authors are indebted to Dr P.R. Ellis for information on pest-resistant varieties and to Dr S. Finch for guidance on the value of inter-cropping as a means of reducing pest damage.

# 6 Diseases of vegetables

In some years as much as half or more of the vegetables planted in gardens either fail to grow or, if they do grow, produce a yield well below the true potential. Some of the reasons for these losses have been discussed elsewhere, but undoubtedly one of the major contributors is the group known collectively as the '*plant diseases*'.

## What are plant diseases?

Plant diseases are caused by *fungi, bacteria*, and *viruses*. They all live on or inside the plant, drawing nourishment from tissues whether they be roots, stems, leaves, or fruits. Like the common cold, these diseases are infectious and in suitable conditions they spread rapidly.

### Fungi

The fungi are characterized by the production of fine cotton-like threads, one cell thick and usually divided into segments by partitions at regular intervals. Sometimes many threads intertwine to produce solid structures such as the familiar mushroom. Each segment contains essential living material but never the green pigment chlorophyll. Because they lack this they cannot use carbon dioxide in the air as green plants do and therefore they rely entirely upon the host plant for their supply of food.

Many fungi such as grey mould (*Botrytis*) produce chemicals which dissolve the host tissues while others, for example, the powdery mildews, have special sucking organs which they insert into the host and withdraw nutrients.

Most fungi reproduce by producing spores, not unlike minute seeds, which are spread by wind, rain, and other agencies. Others, for example white rot in onions and clubroot in brassicas, produce resting bodies which can lie dormant in the soil until stimulated to grow by the presence of a susceptible host-plant.

## Bacteria

These are often regarded as the most primitive form of plant life. They are a varied group of organisms consisting of minute cells which increase in number by dividing into two. Each half then forms a separate plant, grows, divides again, and continues to do this as long as conditions are favourable. Like the fungi, they contain no chlorophyll and rely mainly upon other organisms to provide them with food.

Some bacteria are beneficial and help in breaking down dead matter, while others absorb or fix nitrogen present in the air, so increasing the nitrogen content of the soil. Another group fix nitrogen within the root nodules of members of the pea family.

Bacteria move in the soil water and can also be scattered by rain and wind. The presence of moisture is essential for bacteria to infect plants; this they do by entering the plant through wounds or through pores on the surface of the leaves. Once established, the symptoms are often distinctive and are easily recognized by the production of mucilage which is associated with a softening of the plant tissues and a strong odour.

Most bacterial diseases of vegetables occur as secondary infections following damage caused by other primary agents. Some, for example halo-blight of beans, are primary parasites and are present within the seed where they infect the plant directly and grow with the emerging leaves (Fig. 6.1).

## Viruses

Viruses are composed of simple particles, often in the shape of rods or spheres, which are so small that they can only be seen with

Fig. 6.1. Halo-blight of beans. Leaf infection.

a special instrument, the electron microscope. This microscope is capable of magnifying the particles by 200 000 times or more. Mosaics and mottles of dark and light green or yellow areas of the leaves are common symptoms of virus infections such as lettuce mosaic and cauliflower mosaic (Fig. 6.2). Most infections cause some stunting of growth, but others can cause excessive growth either of the whole plant or of particular tissues.

Viruses are responsible for some of the most destructive plant diseases and once a plant is infected, it is almost impossible to cure it. They are spread by a variety of means, some by contact on knives and fingers, by leaf hoppers, mites, white fly, eel-worms, and probably most important of all, by greenfly (aphids, Chapter 5, p. 117). Consequently, apart from the need to prevent the direct damage caused by greenfly, it is also important to eliminate this pest as it helps to limit the spread of many virus diseases. In some cases, the virus may be spread by a fungus, for example, big-vein of lettuce, which is carried by a soil-borne fungus. Other viruses such as bean common mosaic and lettuce mosaic are seed-borne.

Fig. 6.2. Cauliflower mosaic virus present in Brussels sprouts.

## Where do diseases come from?

A gardener having decided on the vegetables to be planted for the current season may ask, 'What is the likelihood of my crops becoming infected by some or all of the main plant diseases?' If his garden plot is situated miles from other vegetables then the chances are very small. However, if the plot is close to a neighbour's vegetables, then the risks become greater.

There are possibly five main sources of infection that all gardeners should consider when attempting to raise disease-free vegetables; these are: wind-blown and splash-dispersed spores carried in from neighbouring infected plots or vegetable fields, transplants carrying infection either on the plants or in the soil attached to the roots, soil brought in from infected plots, infected debris either introduced or already present on the plot, and finally seeds infected in previous years.

### Infection from neighbouring plots

Most wind-blown spores, particularly those produced by the powdery mildews, are released in warm, dry conditions and can be carried long distances by the wind. It is almost impossible, therefore, to exclude this source of infection and the gardener anxious to protect his brassicas or his rose bushes from this group of diseases may have to rely upon the regular application of fungicide sprays.

Those spores which are splash-dispersed and carried in rain droplets have a more restricted range of spread. Diseases such as leaf spot of celery (Fig. 6.3) and black spot of roses tend therefore to be confined to the individual gardens.

### Infection from transplants

Plants introduced into new areas will serve as a source of infection if the foliage, stem, or roots are infected. Downy and powdery mildews present on the leaves and clubroot present on the roots of brassicas once established in an area can quickly spread given ideal conditions for growth and multiplication.

### Infection from diseased soil

As with infected soil present on the roots of transplants, similarly, soil carried into a garden on boots, garden tools, wheelbarrows, etc., can serve to contaminate an otherwise disease-free area with fungi such as clubroot and onion white rot (Fig. 6.4).

Fig. 6.3. Leaf spot of celery.

### Infection from debris

Imperfectly rotted compost often carries grey mould (*Botrytis*) and many of the other diseases previously mentioned. Plants infected in the previous season and thrown on to the compost heap may also carry resting spores of the fungus which are activated in the presence of the new crop. In addition, debris remaining on the ground from the previous year may also be a source of infection.

### Infection from seeds

Some diseases such as brassica canker, neck rot of onion, lettuce mosaic virus and halo-blight of beans are able to infect and survive within the seed. When this seed is planted, the disease organism grows with the developing plant to infect the emerging tissues (Fig. 6.1). It is therefore important to try to obtain seed containing either nil or an extremely low level of infection. For example, with lettuce it is possible to obtain seed containing less than 0.1 or 0.01 per cent mosaic infection. In the event of some of the emerging plants appearing infected, these should be

Fig. 6.4. White rot of onion. Healthy and infected onions.

removed as soon as possible to prevent the disease spreading to adjoining healthy plants.

## What determines the presence and severity of a disease?

Although a disease may be introduced into a clean area, climatic and soil conditions (in the case of soil-borne fungi) and the growth stage of the plant must be such that they favour the establishment and growth of the disease organism.

## Soil conditions

Vegetables grown in a fertile, well-drained soil with plenty of organic matter, a balanced supply of nutrients, and adequate moisture stand an excellent chance of withstanding attacks by most diseases. However, seeds that are slow to germinate because the soil conditions are unsuitable develop an inadequate root system and, as the plants take longer to establish, they may become infected by the damping-off fungi.

In the case of clubroot of brassicas, every effort should be made to avoid growing plants in badly drained areas of the garden as these conditions are thought to favour infection by the motile spores. Furthermore, as an acid soil favours the disease it is important to prevent this by applying lime. A pH in excess of 7 helps to suppress clubroot activity. This can be checked with pH kits available from garden suppliers.

## Climate

Although soil temperatures can influence the growth of soil-borne fungi, the main effect of the climate is on those diseases developing above ground level. In general a warm, dry summer favours the establishment and growth of the powdery mildew fungi whereas a wet summer favours the downy mildews (Fig. 6.5), grey mould fungi , and the leaf-spot diseases. At very low temperatures, most fungi and bacteria make poor growth and greenfly do not multiply or fly.

## Irrigation

Overhead systems of irrigation often influence the spread of some of the downy mildews and grey mould fungi. If water is applied late in the day the leaves may remain wet throughout the night thereby enabling the spores to germinate and infect. However,

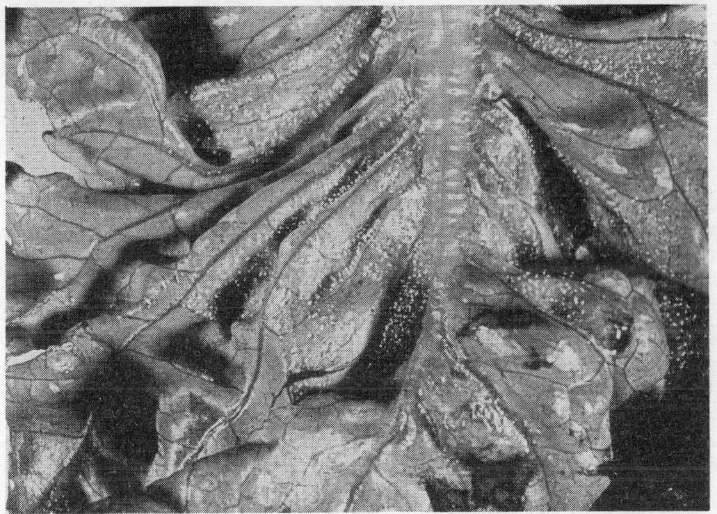

Fig. 6.5. Lettuce downy mildew. Infected leaf.

overhead irrigation can check the development of powdery mildews.

### Planting distance

Densely planted crops can create conditions of high humidity and little wind movement which encourage the growth of many diseases. Close planting can favour disease spread from plant to plant both above and below the ground.

The wider the spacing the less conducive are the conditions for disease establishment and spread. Adequate ventilation at all times restricts most diseases. However, the closer than usual spacings described in Chapter 1 have not unduly increased the risk of disease.

### Planting time

In early sowings out of doors, the soil may still be very cold and, as a consequence, seeds germinate slowly and may be quickly infected by fungi and bacteria able to tolerate such conditions.

This frequently happens with pea seedlings from early sowings. Had the sowing been delayed until the soil was warmer, the more rapid germination of the seedling would have enabled the plant to escape infection.

If it is necessary to sow early in the spring, then cloches placed over the soil a few days before planting help to raise the soil temperature.

A firm seedbed with a good tilth favours quick germination, which in turn helps to reduce the chances of infection.

## How do diseases survive in the garden?

Most diseases are inactive during the resting period of the host-plant. Many fungi survive this period as specialized resting bodies in the soil or on plant debris; others survive as infections in the seed or as fine strands on the surface of the host or in the soil. Most diseases can survive at least one winter, and some, for example onion white rot, have been known to survive for up to twenty winters.

Because viruses spread to all parts of the infected plant, over-wintering presents no problems in the case of perennial hosts. Potato viruses can survive in tubers, whereas viruses with a wide host range may pass the interval between crops by infecting susceptible weeds.

Information on these survival patterns is important for it helps to determine when it is safe to replant a particular crop on land known to be previously infected.

## Are all fungi and bacteria harmful?

Not all fungi and bacteria cause problems as there are some that live entirely on dead and decomposing organic matter. Such organisms are extremely beneficial in that they help to break down waste plant material and so assist in the recycling of nutrients. The rapid removal of plant material, particularly if it is infected with a damaging fungus, can be of great benefit to the control of many diseases. For example, diseases such as grey mould (*Botrytis*) that are able to survive the winter on plant debris would be quickly eradicated if their food source was eliminated. The mildews and moulds on gooseberries, blackcurrants, and strawberries which survive the winter on fallen leaves are quickly eliminated by fungi, bacteria, and components of the soil fauna which help in the rapid decomposition of the leaf.

Apart from those organisms that live entirely on dead plant material there are others, such as grey mould (*Botrytis*), which can live on decaying matter and on healthy plants; others live mainly on healthy plants but spend a short time in the soil or on plant debris; and finally, there are those fungi, such as the rusts and powdery mildews, which survive the winter in their host-plant without causing appreciable damage.

The latter group, once favourable conditions return, rapidly colonize the host-plant, although usually the degree of infection is insufficient to kill the plant.

## Control by avoidance methods

Some of the precautions that the gardener may take to lessen the chances of infection by diseases have already been discussed in the sections dealing with the source of infections and the factors affecting the severity of attack.

Few gardeners can afford the time or expense of regular applications of chemicals to protect their vegetables. Therefore it is important to consider further, alternative, relatively inexpensive 'avoidance' methods of control which, if properly applied, are very effective.

Time spent in considering points such as the lay-out of the garden (planning crop rotations so that wherever possible 'like crops' do not follow 'like crops'), the careful preparation of the soil, ensuring that the ground is free of infected debris, and checking that planting material is healthy, can all help in excluding many troublesome diseases.

## Hygiene

The fungi which cause grey mould overwinter on plant debris; one of the virus diseases, cucumber mosaic virus, that attacks lettuce, vegetable marrow, and cucumber, survives the winter in weed seeds, particularly chickweed. Clubroot survives in the living and dead roots of many brassica weed species. It is important therefore that weeds, plant debris, and roots should be removed and thoroughly composted. In some cases, for example those infected with clubroot, the plants should be burnt. Where material is slow to rot, it should be covered with soil to prevent the release of aerial spores. Plant pots, boxes, and similar containers should be cleaned; water tanks, which may harbour some fungi, should be periodically cleaned. Store rooms, particularly the shelves, should be kept clean and soil and plant debris removed.

## Rotation

Rotation of crops is a valuable aid to disease control in that most diseases attack only one crop or group of related plants and become more prevalent when these crops are grown continuously in the same place.

When a particular soil-borne disease such as clubroot (Fig. 6.6) occurs the gardener should not replant that land with brassicas and related crops such as radishes, but with alternative non-susceptible crops such as onions or lettuce.

In some areas repeatedly cropped with a particular vegetable, a condition known as soil-sickness is encountered. In these situations, despite attempts to apply corrective measures, the yield continues to fall. This does not happen with all crops, neither is it always due to the same cause. The decline in pea yields may be due to eelworm presence or to various soil-borne fungi or a combination of both. In other crops, the available nutrients in the soil may have been exhausted.

On a commercial scale the disorder can often be alleviated by fumigating the soil before replanting. Such treatments are believed to be beneficial in that they destroy the injurious organ-

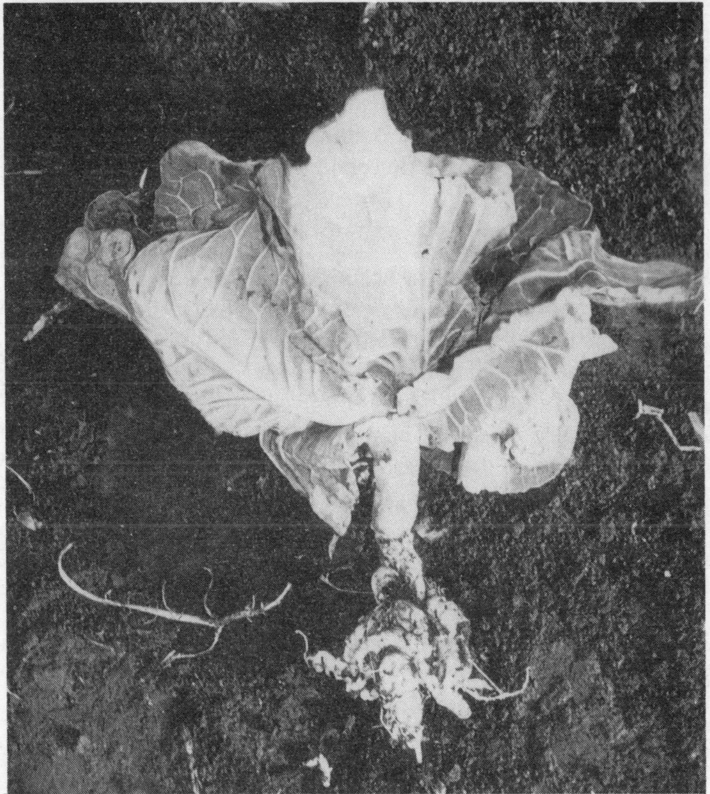

Fig. 6.6 Clubroot of brassica.

isms that build up over the years and they may also help in releasing nutrients into the soil.

For the amateur a possible remedy is to replace the diseased soil with fresh healthy soil. While this is a common practice, particularly in glasshouses, in the garden the magnitude of the task, in that it involves the movement of large quantities of soil, is such that it often makes this approach impracticable.

Where the disease is known to persist for many years in the soil, for example clubroot of brassicas and white rot of onions, rotation can be of little help to the gardener who has little possibility of moving to an alternative disease-free area. In such circumstances, if these vegetables must be planted, then it is important to apply other control measures (see pp. 192 and 195).

With neck rot of onion, which persists on debris for up to two years, a four-year rotation is an adequate means of avoiding infection of freshly planted crops.

### Planning the layout of the vegetable garden

When planning the planting schedule, the adjacent crops should always be considered. Where potato blight is a problem, early potatoes should not be planted close to late potatoes, or tomatoes, neither should virus-free seed potatoes be planted alongside old stock infected with mosaic or leaf roll virus.

Seed crops of biennial plants, such as brassicas, should be separated from first-year crops of the same plant or they will probably infect the seedlings with diseases like dark leaf spot, canker, or virus diseases.

### Healthy planting material

At all times, it is desirable to start with a 'clean slate'. Having 'cleaned' the land of debris and likely sources of infection, it is sensible to follow by planting material free from viruses, fungi, bacteria, and insect pests. Although it may be difficult to obtain such guarantees, the gardener should attempt to obtain seeds from a reputable supplier who gives some assurance of freedom from disease. But remember, despite these assurances, there is always a danger that some seed may be infected, therefore regular inspection of the emerging crops is advisable followed by prompt removal and destruction of any infected plants.

In the case of transplants, these should be raised in a disease-free area or better still in sterilized soil. If clubroot is suspected in the soil to be used for plant raising, then small amounts may be sterilized by heating for about one hour at 150 °C (300 °F). This will also kill many other pests and diseases present. Where the number of plants to be grown is limited, raise each plant in an individual pot of sterilized soil and plant out the entire ball. This provides a disease-free base from which the brassica roots can develop. Once the plant is off to a good start, it is more likely to survive subsequent infection by clubroot spores present in the garden soil.

If the garden is free of clubroot then it is a wise policy to obtain brassica plants only from those areas guaranteed free of the disease.

### Keeping plants healthy

The use of fungicides applied as seed treatments, dips, or sprays will be discussed in the next section; however, there is much the gardener can do to keep his plants free of disease without necessarily having to resort to the use of chemicals.

The application of a balanced manurial programme (see p. 62), planting at the correct time and depth, and avoidance of overcrowding all assist in creating good growing conditions, so that the plants are strong and more able to withstand infection.

The removal of weeds and of diseased leaves, fruits, or plants as soon as the infection is diagnosed keeps the disease at a very low level and so lessens the chances of an epidemic developing, with the inevitable catastrophic consequences.

The time of the year when the disease first appears is also important. An outbreak of powdery mildew close to harvest time often causes little damage and can, therefore, be ignored, but an outbreak early in the life of the plant can have damaging consequences.

## Control by chemicals

Chemicals should only be used in a small garden when it is considered essential. Chemicals are expensive and, furthermore, with some fungicides the fungus can develop resistance. For example, in certain areas the fungus causing grey mould (*Botrytis*) has developed strains which are tolerant to benomyl, carbendazim, and thiophanate-methyl. In such areas, the disease is not controlled by this group of fungicides. Therefore, the less the chemical is used, the longer is its effective life. A detailed description relating to pesticide products which is relevant not only to insecticides but also fungicides and herbicides dealing with aspects such as 'products', 'names', 'directions for use', and 'safety' is given in Chapter 5, pp. 151–7. Nevertheless, there are a number of general points relating specifically to the use of fungicides which warrant repeating here.

## How safe are fungicides?

Although some may be harmful if misused, many are suitable for use in the garden if handled properly and the manufacturer's instructions are *strictly observed* (see also Fig. 5.3, p. 152).

Chemicals are made up in a number of preparations and sold for specific purposes under a variety of trade names. Some compounds are used by seed merchants for treating seeds to eradicate certain seed-borne diseases, for example neck rot of onions, or to give protection against soil-borne damping-off diseases. In this context, it is worth studying seed merchants' catalogues to take advantage of any new developments. Some are used as solutions for dipping roots in before planting out. For example, brassica transplants treated with certain chemicals are able to withstand infection from clubroot spores. However, by far the greatest quantity of fungicide is sold for the purpose of spraying plants during the growing season.

With all chemicals there are golden rules which should be observed at all times:

- Handle with care and only use when necessary.
- Keep chemicals and containers away from children and pets.
- Always follow the instructions (never exceed the recommended amount).
- Note the recommended time intervals which must elapse between the last treatment and harvesting; this will avoid harmful deposits remaining on the vegetables.
- Do not spray when bees are active.

- Do not spray when it is windy, as the chemical may drift on to other crops or into your neighbour's garden.
- *Never* transfer chemicals to containers such as beer or soft-drink bottles.
- Wash out sprayers thoroughly after use and further dilute the unwanted fungicide and dispose of on spare land in the garden.
- Do not apply fungicides with apparatus which has been used for weed killers.
- Wash hands thoroughly on completion of spraying.

## How do fungicides act?

They act either as 'protectants' in that infectious spores landing on the plant surface come into contact with the chemical and are killed, or as 'systemics' which are 'taken up' by the plant. The advantage of the latter group is that there is little danger of them being washed away in rain and, therefore, they remain effective over a long period. Owing to their mode of action, it is often necessary to apply 'protectant' fungicides more frequently than systemic fungicides.

Often a systemic fungicide will help to check a fungus disease that has already become established within the host tissues.

Some fungicides, but not all, can be mixed with other fungicides, insecticides, and foliar feeds; however, *it is always wise to check first with the supplier before using a mixture*, as the combination may be damaging to the plant.

## When should fungicides be applied?

Once a disease is established, it is difficult to destroy it although systemic fungicides may check the growth of some diseases. Generally, however, it is best to anticipate the problem and apply the chemical in the early part of the season. Diseases such as blight, leaf spots, powdery mildews, and downy mildews are best prevented by spraying at an early stage of growth before infections have had time to develop.

The choice of chemical is dependent on how it is to be applied, its persistence, will it damage the plant, and whether it will affect the flavour of the vegetables. In the past, a fungicide would control only one disease, but some chemicals, for example benomyl, carbendazim, and thiophanate-methyl give control of a number of diseases.

It is important, however, to be always on the watch for the first signs of a disease outbreak, *therefore regular inspection of plants is vital.*

The level of control is dependent upon the thoroughness of cover of the plant to be protected. Sprays should only be applied to dry leaves and every effort should be made to wet both the upper and lower leaf surfaces.

### Will fungicides damage plants?

The fact that many fungicides persist for relatively short periods does have certain advantages in that there is unlikely to be a build-up of residues on the plant or in the soil which could be harmful to plants, beneficial insects, and wild life.

Some plants may be damaged by certain fungicides. Seedlings and young plants grown under forcing conditions or in poor light are particularly sensitive. Never spray plants that are wilting because of drought. *In particular, when using a fungicide for the first time on a new variety or unusual plant, check that it is safe by treating a few plants before using the product on a large scale.*

Never hold the spray nozzle close to the plant as the force of the liquid striking it may be sufficient to cause some mechanical injury which is made worse by the presence of the chemical.

Spraying in hot sun should be avoided as damage due to scorching may occur, particularly on young leaves.

### What is the best fungicide to use?

Under the Control of Pesticides Regulations 1986, made under the Food and Environment Protection Act (FEPA) 1985, approval of the use of pesticides is now a legal requirement. It is an offence to use non-approved products or to use approved products in a manner which does not comply with the specific conditions of approval. In buying approved products, the gardener can be certain that the chemicals are of the right kind and in the correct amount for the job they have to do and that the claims for control are fair.

These products contain chemicals which have been considered by the Advisory Committee on Pesticides and Other Toxic Chemicals for possible danger to humans, farm and domestic animals, and wild life, and should not, when used as directed on labels, cause harmful effects.

Gardeners, other than those in the UK, should determine if similar schemes are in operation in their countries. Methods for controlling some of the more frequent diseases of vegetables are summarized in Table 6.1. As a guide, fungicides expected to provide effective control are indicated by ***; moderately effective by **; and those where control is likely to be only partially effective by *. The gardener can therefore judge whether it is worthwhile applying these treatments.

## Resistant varieties

The stage of development or age of the plant often decides whether or not it will be attacked by a disease. The frequently occurring group of fungi responsible for damping-off, attack in the main, young seedlings and rarely older well-established plants; once the tissues become mature they are usually resistant to infection.

The production of vegetables resistant to all diseases is clearly the ultimate solution to the problems discussed so far. At the present time, there are varieties available that have some if not full resistance to certain diseases. However, there is no guarantee that the resistance is permanent as some diseases are capable of producing new forms that will overcome this resistance. This is seen in lettuces where new cultivars resistant to downy mildew in time become infected with the disease. However, there are many vegetables which have been successfully bred for resistance to specific diseases and included in these is the parsnip Avonresister which is highly resistant to canker.

Even partial resistance is helpful, particularly in localities where the disease is not severe.

## Biological control

The control of plant diseases using other non-damaging fungi, bacteria, and viruses has so far received little attention. It is clear, however, that there are situations where some control is given by these beneficial organisms. For example, many of the powdery mildew fungi are attacked by another fungus and, as a result, the former disease is reduced in severity.

One of the most effective 'biological control mechanisms' is the one whereby earthworms are encouraged to remove plant debris and in so doing remove the host tissue for the overwintering fungus.

Urea applied to fallen apple leaves has been most effective in encouraging a fungal and bacterial population which decomposes the leaf to a stage where it is readily digested by the earthworm. In doing so, the apple-scab fungus which was present on these leaves has been eradicated. Doubtless, similar mechanisms can be introduced into the control of vegetable diseases; the rapid decay of plant material infected with grey mould could be a valuable asset in the control of this fungus.

## Common diseases, symptoms, and control

The following list of some of the more common diseases of vegetables and their symptoms has been prepared as a guide to the gardener in the identification of his problem. In all cases, every effort should be made to prevent the occurrence of the disease by taking 'avoidance' precautions, but where these are impossible or have failed, then the application of suitable fungicides should do much to reduce the severity of the infection.

Although there is a large range of chemicals available for the commercial grower, the amateur gardener's choice is limited.

## Where can the gardener seek advice?

Gardeners, like the professional grower, often encounter problems which they cannot solve. In these instances, organizations in the UK such as the Royal Horticultural Society, the Agricultural Development and Advisory Service, County Council and Local Authority Advisers, state-financed research stations, and many of the commercial companies supplying chemicals for use in the garden are able to offer advice on identification and the necessary measures for control of the disease. (The British Agrochemicals Association, 4 Lincoln Court, Lincoln Road, Peterborough PE1 2RP annually produces a Directory of Garden Chemicals.) In other countries, such advice may be obtained from similar organizations.

## Conclusion

Gardeners tend to grow a great variety of crops, each of which may at some time or another suffer from attack by fungi, bacteria, or viruses. Although the number of possible diseases is high, in reality the number likely to be troublesome in any one season is often small. Much of this danger can be further reduced by attention to good management practices and sensible cultivation such as rotation of crops and keeping the ground free from weeds, the reservoir for many of the diseases.

As a general guide to the production of disease-free crops, observation of the following points will go a long way to reaching this desirable 'state of affairs':

- Make sure the soil is well prepared and that the surface is free from old decaying plant material.
- Plant high-quality seeds preferably containing full or some

resistance to infection. Use certified potato seed; use transplants raised in healthy soil or treated with a fungicide dip; if the disease is one that is known to infect seeds, try to obtain disease-free seed or seed that has been treated.

- Plant at the correct time, i.e. when conditions are most favourable for the germination and establishment of the plants. Soils should be warm, moist, but not too wet. A quick and healthy establishment of the seedling will help to protect it from damping-off diseases.
- Once the seeds have germinated, this promptly as overcrowding can lead to stagnant conditions favouring disease outbreaks.
- Feed and water correctly.
- If disease outbreaks are suspected, apply the relevant fungicides, keeping strictly to the recommendations as laid down by the manufacturers.
- Diseased material should be removed and destroyed as soon as possible. If allowed to remain, it will serve to infect the remaining healthy plants.
- Non-storable crops, such as lettuce, should be sown little and often. This helps to avoid an excess of overmature plants remaining in the ground. Always remove these plants as they often become diseased and can serve as a source of infection for newly sown plants.
- Where possible, rotate the crops as this helps to prevent the build-up of certain soil-borne diseases such as clubroot.

Adherence to these principles, should ensure the production of high quality, disease-free vegetables.

**Table 6.1**

**Common vegetable diseases and their control**

| Crop | Disease | Symptoms | Control measures | |
|---|---|---|---|---|
| | | | Avoidance | Chemical effectiveness (see p. 187) |
| **Beans** French and runner | Anthracnose (Fig. 6.7) | Cankers on stems, brownish lesions associated with leaf veins. Lesions on pods | Remove infected plants. Plant healthy seed, Rotate crops | *** |
| | Chocolate spot | Brown spots on leaves | Remove infected plants | *** |
| | Grey mould (*Botrytis*) | Grey mould on pods and stems. Prevalent in wet weather | Remove diseased parts. Ensure good ventilation | *** |
| | Halo-blight (Figs. 6.1 and 6.13) | Small spots on leaves surrounded by a yellow halo. Water-soaked spots on pods | Remove and burn diseased plants | * |
| | Mosaic virus | Yellow leaf veins and mottles | Virus is seed-borne. Remove infected young plants early in season and burn | * |
| | Root rot | Leaves yellow, shrivelled. Roots, stem base—brown/black | Remove and burn diseased plants. Rotate crops | ** |

**Table 6.1** (*cont.*)

| Crop | Disease | Symptoms | Control measures | |
|---|---|---|---|---|
| | | | Avoidance | Chemical effectiveness (see p. 187) |
| **Cabbage, cauliflower, Brussels sprouts** | Cauliflower mosaic virus (Fig. 6.2) | Mosaic with dark green vein banding | Remove and destroy | * |
| | Clubroot (Fig. 6.6) | Discoloured leaves; wilting in warm weather. Swollen roots | Raise plants in sterile soil; keep soil well drained and alkaline | ** |
| | Damping-off | Plants fail to emerge or seedlings fall over | Raise plants for transplanting in clean soil. Avoid sowing in cold, wet soil | ** |
| | Downy mildew | Usually on young plants. Leaves yellow, white areas on under-surface. Often troublesome on cauliflower seedlings | Avoid overcrowding. Raise plants in clean soil | ** |
| | Powdery mildew | Powdery white spots on leaves | Remove infected leaves | ** |
| | Wire stem | Base of stem black and shrunken. Seedlings often die but may survive as stunted plants | Avoid sowing in cold wet soil. Avoid overcrowding | * |

| | | | | |
|---|---|---|---|---|
| **Carrots** | Damping-off | Plants fail to emerge | Avoid sowing in cold wet soil | ** |
| | Motley dwarf virus | Centre leaves yellow mottled, outer leaves turn red, yellow, or purple | Remove and burn | * |
| | *Sclerotinia* rot | White mould on stored carrots | Avoid growing on land infected in the previous season | ** |
| | Violet root-rot (Fig. 6.8) | Slight yellowing of leaves. Roots covered in purplish threads | Destroy diseased roots. Avoid growing root crops on land for at least one year | * |
| **Celery** | Leaf spot (Fig. 6.3) | Brown rusty spots on leaves and stems | | *** |
| **Cucumber family** | Cucumber mosaic virus | Mottled and yellowed leaves, surface distorted. Stunted plants may die | Remove and destroy infected plants | * |
| | Damping-off | Plants fail to emerge or soon die | Do not sow in cold wet soil | ** |
| | Grey mould (*Botrytis*) | Grey furry mould on fruit. Attacks stems | Remove and destroy infected parts | *** |
| | Powdery mildew | Powdery spots or patches on leaves | Maintain good ventilation | ** |

**Table 6.1** (*cont.*)

| Crop | Disease | Symptoms | Control measures: Avoidance | Control measures: Chemical effectiveness (see p. 187) |
|---|---|---|---|---|
| **Lettuce** | Beet western yellows virus (Fig. 6.9) | Interveinal yellowing of outer leaves | Remove and burn. Common in groundsel and Shepherd's purse, therefore keep ground free of these weeds | * |
| | Damping-off | Plants fail to emerge or soon die | Do not sow in cold wet soil | ** |
| | Downy mildew (Fig.6.5) | Pale green or yellow angular areas on the older leaves; these may bear white spores, especially on lower surface. Infected areas die and become brown. Occurs mainly in autumn | Remove diseased leaves. Avoid overcrowding. Use resistant varieties | ** |
| | Grey mould (*Botrytis*) | Serious in cool damp weather. Often causes a basal stem rot followed by collapse of the plant. Produces many grey spores on decaying leaves | Destroy affected plants. Remove infected debris. Maintain good ventilation | *** |

| | | | | |
|---|---|---|---|---|
| **Lettuce** (*cont.*) | Mosaic virus (Fig. 6.11) | Yellow mottling on leaves, growth stunted | Use only seed containing less than 0.1 per cent mosaic infection as stated on packet. Remove young infected plants and burn. Grow resistant varieties if available | * |
| **Onions, leeks** | Damping-off | Plants fail to emerge | Do not sow in cold wet soil | ** |
| | Downy mildew | Pale oval areas on leaves, tips of leaves become pale and die back. Leaves often fold downwards at infected area | Avoid contaminated and badly drained soils. Ensure adequate ventilation | ** |
| | Neck rot (Fig. 6.10) | No symptoms visible in the field, occurs as a grey mould on the neck in store | Remove diseased bulbs from store. Store only undamaged bulbs | *** |
| | White rot (Fig. 6.4) | Plants stunted, foliage turns yellow and wilts. White mould on onion base | Remove and burn. Avoid growing in infected land. Do not delay thinning seedlings | ** |
| **Parsnip** | Canker | Roots blackened and cracked; roots rot | Lime soil, grow resistant variety, such as Avonresister. Later sowings are often less badly affected | * |

**Table 6.1** (*cont.*)

| Crop | Disease | Symptoms | Control measures | |
|---|---|---|---|---|
| | | | Avoidance | Chemical effectiveness (see p. 187) |
| **Parsnip** (*cont.*) | Damping-off | Plants fail to emerge | Avoid sowing in cold wet soil | ** |
| **Peas** | Damping-off | Peas fail to grow | Prepare the soil well. Sow when soil warm and not too wet | ** |
| | Downy mildew | Yellow blotches on leaves, brown mould on under-surface | Rotate crops. Remove and burn affected plants | ** |
| | Leaf and pod spot (Fig. 6.12) | Sunken brown cankers on stems of plants, tan-coloured lesions on leaves | Remove and destroy diseased plants | ** |
| | Powdery mildew | White powdery spots on leaves. Prevalent in dry seasons | Remove affected leaves | ** |
| **Potatoes** | Blight | Appears late in season. Brown patches on leaves. On underside, blighted areas have a white fringe | Avoid planting near discarded potatoes from previous year. Plant healthy seed | ** |
| | Common scab | Scab areas on tubers. Edges of lesions ragged | Severe on light, dry soils. Dig in compost but do not lime. Use healthy seed | * |

| | | | | |
|---|---|---|---|---|
| **Potatoes (*cont.*)** | Leaf-roll virus | Leaflets roll upwards and become hard and brittle. Plants stunted | Remove and burn infected plants. Plant certified seed | * |
| | Mosaic virus | Yellow mottling of leaves | Remove and burn. Plant certified seed | |
| | Powdery scab | Less frequent than common scab. Lesions are powdery on the surface | Severe on heavy wet soils. Follow a crop rotation | * |
| **Tomatoes** | Blight (outdoor plants) | Grey/brown edges to leaves; russet-brown 'marbled' areas on fruits. Disease may come from infected potatoes | | ** |
| | Grey mould (*Botrytis*) | Usually occurs on damaged areas. Grey fluffy area | Remove diseased tissues | *** |
| | Mosaic virus | Light and green leaf areas. Leaf distortion. Stunting or poor growth | Remove infected plants as soon as possible and burn | * |
| | Stem rot | On mature plants. Leaves yellow, brown canker on stem base. Black dots in cankered area | Destroy infected plants. Use sterile soil | ** |
| **Turnip, swede** | Turnip mosaic virus | Leaf mosaics and/or death of leaf and growing point | Remove and destroy diseased plants | * |

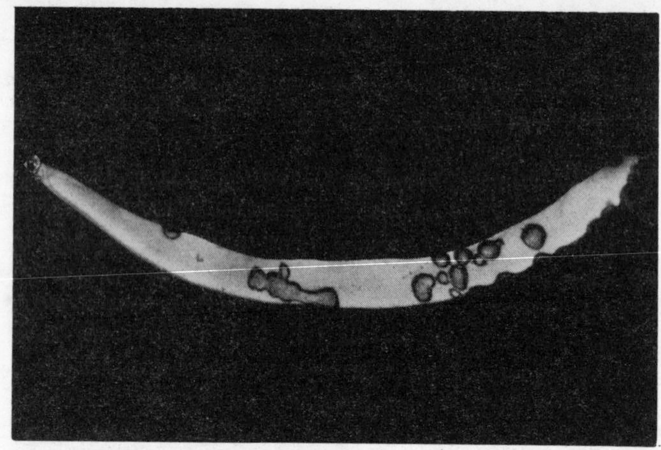

Fig. 6.7. Anthracnose of bean. Pod lesions.

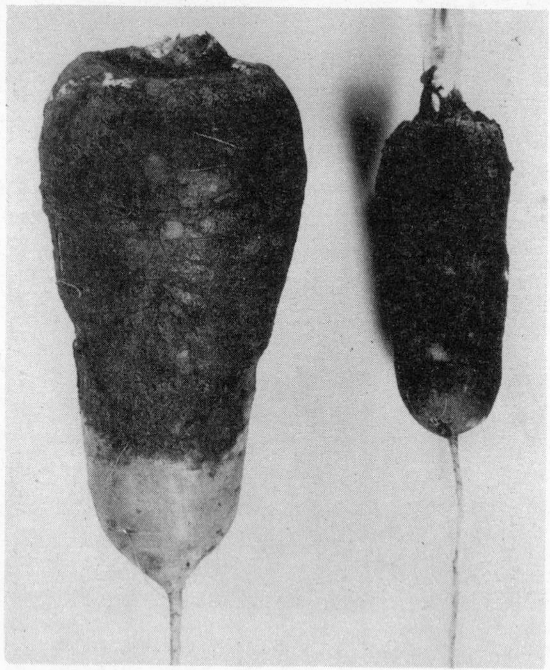

Fig. 6.8. Violet root-rot of carrot.

Fig. 6.9. Beet western yellows virus on lettuce. Infected and healthy plants.

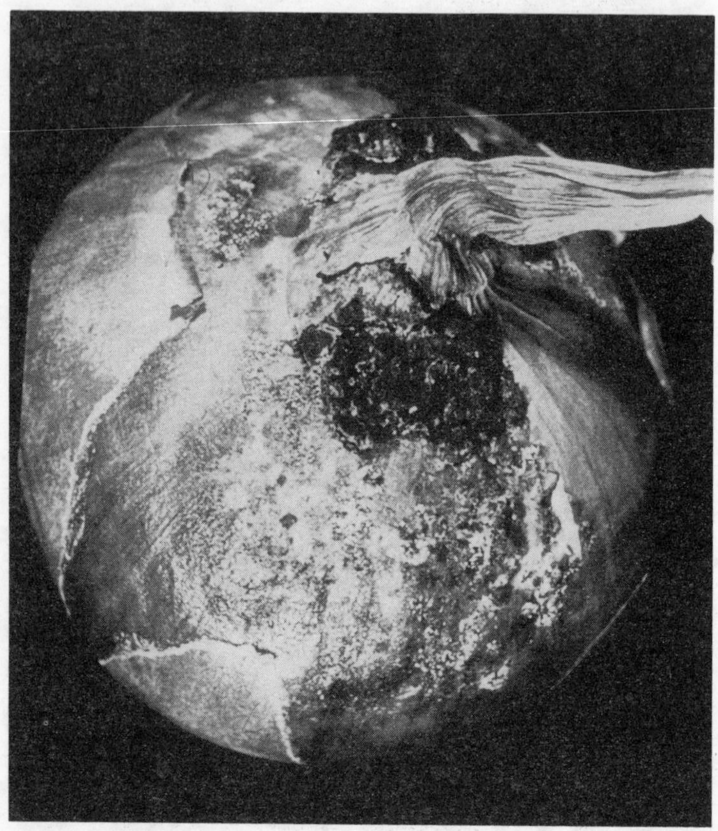

Fig. 6.10. Neck rot of onion.

Fig. 6.11. Lettuce mosaic virus. Healthy (C) and infected (1–5) plants.

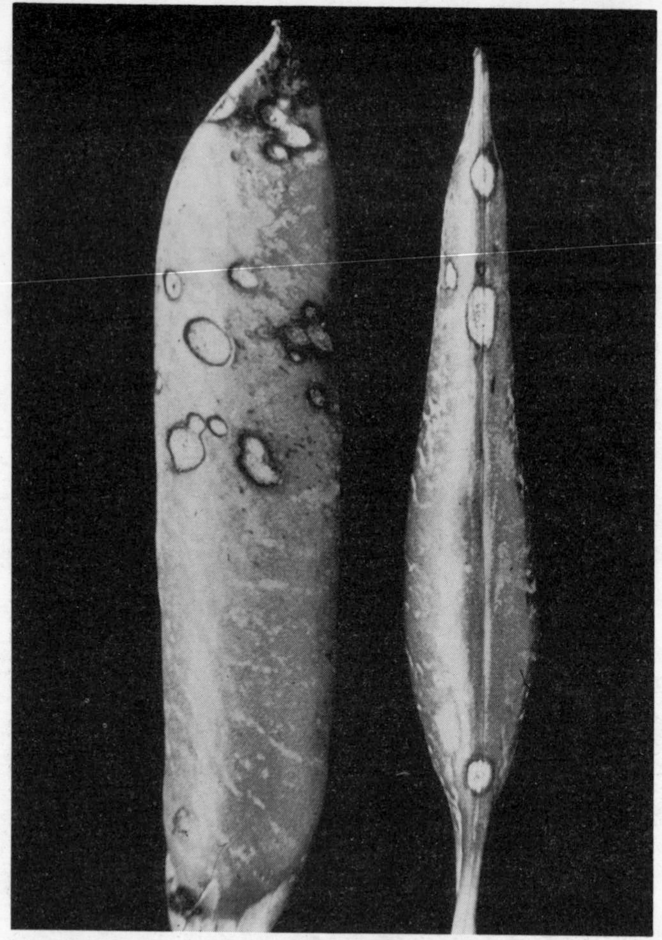

Fig. 6.12. Pod spot of peas.

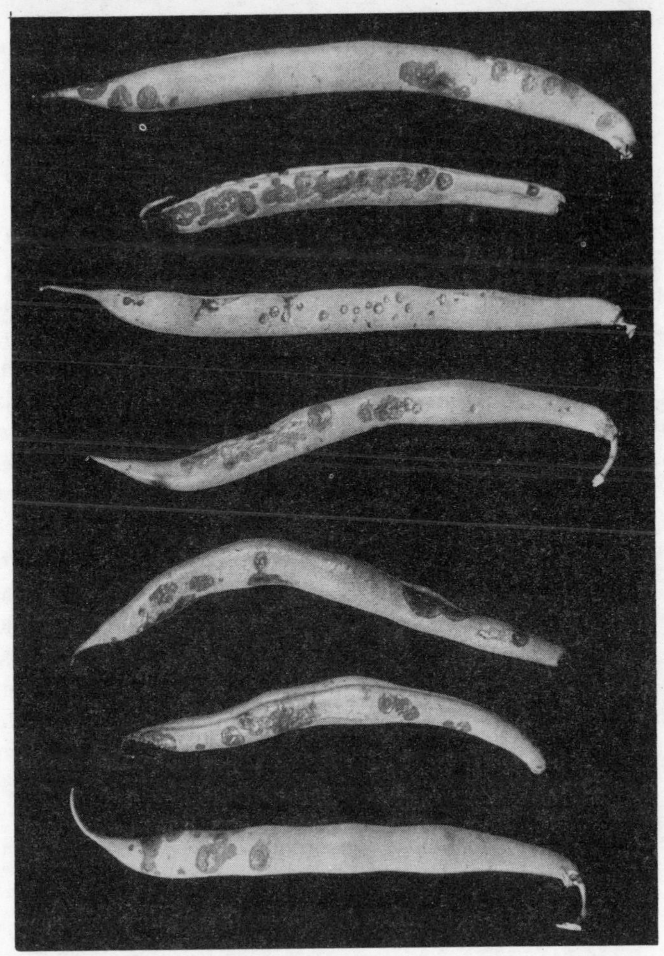

Fig. 6.13. Halo-blight of beans. Pod infection.

# 7 Choosing a variety

How do *you* choose vegetable varieties for growing in your garden? Do you choose the variety you have grown for the past few years with satisfactory results, or pick one almost at random from the range offered in a catalogue or on a seedsman's display stand? Or do you wisely seek as much information and advice on the subject as possible, including asking neighbouring gardeners who are likely to have similar growing conditions?

Choosing a variety best suited to your particular needs can be difficult, as there is a wealth of varieties for each vegetable crop and there are about thirty different vegetables! Seedsmen generally assess their varieties in special field trials where each variety is subjected to almost identical growing conditions. In this way they are able to build up a picture of the performance and characteristics of each variety. This enables them to decide when to eliminate varieties with faults and also to give a brief description of the main characteristics of the best varieties in their seed catalogues and on seed packets. Generally speaking, however, the seedsmen do not attempt to make detailed comparisons of varieties in their catalogues, but draw special attention to their varieties with new or 'novel' features.

It is impossible to recommend the current varieties that are 'best' for every situation, for these may well differ for different soils, different regions and for different purposes. We shall, however, discuss the characteristics of groups of varieties of most outdoor vegetable crops, and suggest a number that you should try in your garden in comparison with your old favourites. Before doing so, however, we shall indicate sources of information to help you make your choice and describe legislation and official testing that is necessary before a new variety reaches the seedsmen's catalogues.

## Vegetable trials

Many seed catalogues mention awards made by the Royal Horticultural Society (RHS) who have conducted vegetable trials since 1818. The Society invites breeders and seedsmen from all parts of the world to submit new or improved varieties for testing in their trial grounds, now at Wisley Gardens in Surrey. Each year seven or eight types of vegetables are selected; the frequency of trials for any particular crop depends on the popularity of that crop and the rate of introduction of new varieties.

Wisley is a favourable location but does experience severe frosts. The trials are simple, unreplicated comparisons, and a high standard of cultivation and horticultural skill ensures good plant stands, ample nutrition and moisture on all plots. In each trial at least one currently-recognized variety is included for comparison. Assessments are made by a panel of experts who make awards based on uniformity, growth habit, yield and quality, disease resistance and colour. Only outstanding varieties are awarded a First Class Certificate, whilst Awards of Merit and Highly Commended are made to good varieties in descending order of performance.

These trials have proved to be very valuable to gardeners and growers in indicating the nature and merits of the varieties tested. However, as the number of trials are limited, each crop is tested only every few years, so that it is possible to have excellent new varieties on sale that have not as yet been assessed by the RHS.

Although the RHS is the only organization to undertake variety 'trials' for gardeners, there are official Government-sponsored trials by the National Institute of Agricultural Botany (NIAB), Cambridge, of a number of vegetable crops to provide guidance for commercial growers. Based on the results of these trials NIAB regularly publish Vegetable Growers' Leaflets on the major commercial vegetables, Brussels sprouts, cabbages, carrots, cauliflowers, butterhead and crisphead lettuce, bulb onions (spring- and autumn-sown) and a Recommended List of potato varieties. These leaflets contain a great deal of information about the more important characteristics of varieties that have been included in NIAB vegetable variety performance trials. Such trials have been grown at a number of different sites each year, often at Experimental Horticulture Stations (EHSs) or Farms (EHFs) of the Agricultural Development Advisory Service (ADAS) of the Ministry of Agriculture, Fisheries and Food (MAFF). The value of the NIAB trials lies in their being done at several sites over three years, and in each trial, each variety is tested in three randomized plots so that a statistical test may be used to compare the different varieties in the trial and give a reliable result. For the so-called minor vegetable crops there are relatively fewer trials organized by NIAB. In recent years they have had trials of beetroot, calabrese, courgettes, parsnips, salad onions, celery, sweet corn, leeks, chinese cabbage, and swedes whilst MAFF have done trials on such crops as rhubarb and runner beans at EHSs so that information in their annual reports is often useful in identifying good new varieties.

A leaflet written by NIAB staff entitled *Vegetable Varieties for the Gardener* and published in the Wisley Handbook series by the Royal Horticultural Society makes use of the results of NIAB trials to suggest varieties for the crops that they have tested.

## How do new varieties get on to the market?

Nowadays a breeder or seedsman looks to commercial vegetable growers to take up a new variety first, in the knowledge that the sale of seed in small packets to the general public is likely to follow. However, before seed of new varieties can be sold to anyone it must undergo certain official tests, so that buyers are protected from purchasing the same variety under different names. Varieties which pass the criteria of the 'Distinctness, Uniformity and Stability' (DUS) tests are accepted for entry on the National

List of Vegetables. They can then be marketed. DUS tests are conducted by NIAB for the MAFF or by the Agricultural Scientific Services of the Department of Agriculture and Fisheries for Scotland (DAFS). These tests assess the uniqueness of a new variety by ensuring that it is different from other varieties, and that it is sufficiently uniform within the crop and stable from year to year. When a variety has been accepted for inclusion in the National List it is also acceptable for the EC Common Catalogue so that it can be lawfully marketed in EC member countries. A variety may be marketed in the UK, therefore, even if it is not on the UK National List, provided it is included in the Common Catalogue and has therefore been tested in one of the EC member countries.

It is illegal to sell seed of varieties under the wrong name or which is not on the National List or Common Catalogue. This regulation has undoubtedly done much to rationalize the great number of different names attributed to the same varieties. However, it has to be recognized that varieties will only remain on the official lists for as long as a seed firm is prepared to maintain them. Some old varieties are lost because there is insufficient demand for them to be economically worthwhile for a seedsman to multiply seed stocks. Fortunately steps have been taken at the Institute of Horticultural Research, Wellesbourne (IHR), to safeguard against the loss of valuable breeding material by collecting and storing old, displaced varieties of vegetables in a vegetable Gene Bank.

In addition to National Lists, there is an increasing trend to encourage investment in the breeding of improved varieties by plant variety rights schemes, which are equivalent to 'plant patents'. Varieties entered for Plant Variety Rights are subjected to the same sort of DUS tests as apply to National Lists. Where a variety is accorded rights, the holder of the rights is entitled to a royalty payment on the sale of all seed of that variety for the period that his rights remain in being, subject to a maximum period of 20 years for vegetables and 25 years for potatoes.

## Varieties bred at Government-sponsored institutes

We are often asked, particularly at IHR Wellesbourne Open Days, to provide lists of suppliers of seed of varieties bred at the IHR and other Government-sponsored research institutes, for example, our butterhead lettuce Avondefiance or the cabbage Celtic from the Scottish, Crop Research Institute. It is appropriate, therefore, to explain how such varieties usually reach the gardener as the research institute which breeds them does not market the seed.

At the same time as a vegetable variety undergoes official DUS tests, the breeder (whether private or public) is usually concerned with building up seed stocks. The breeder produces small quantities of élite seed, officially known as 'pre-basic'. In the case of varieties bred at Government-sponsored institutes, this is sold to commercial seed companies who multiply the pre-basic seed to produce basic and commercial seed. Great care is taken in the production of both pre-basic and basic seed, and multiplications are frequently made in glasshouses or polythene tunnels where strict control over pollination is possible.

The multiplication to commercial seed is often done in countries where a hot, dry climate is more suitable for seed production. This final generation of seed is sold to the general public. There are variations of this scheme but in general the same overall pattern is followed. Seed of Government-bred varieties is available from most, though not all, seed companies.

## Breeding for improved quality

A commonly held opinion, particularly among older gardeners, is that new varieties of vegetables have been bred only to increase yield and this has been achieved at the expense of quality, especially flavour. Quality characteristics such as colour, texture and flavour have received considerable attention from vegetable breeders, and in recent years, beetroot, carrots and sweet corn have all been improved for sweetness. New celery varieties are less pithy, green French bean varieties are now stringless and improvements in this direction are also being made in runner beans. Indeed the last five years have seen the development of supersweet sweet corn which is many times sweeter than older varieties. These new varieties also retain their sweetness longer.

Flavour is extremely difficult to define and characterize, and tastes vary. As growing conditions affect the flavour of a variety, the breeder has not found it easy to quantify flavour differences, though more and more breeders are turning their attention to flavour components in vegetables and major successes have been achieved, such as the elimination of the bitterness in cucumbers. Until techniques are developed to quantify flavour components the plant breeder must still rely on subjective assessments, usually by taste panels. We remain unconvinced that there has been as serious a loss in flavour in new varieties as is sometimes claimed, and would argue that only the individual, by trying a number of old and new varieties grown side by side, under the same conditions, is best placed to judge which flavour pleases him or her most.

The appearance of produce of new varieties has shown considerable improvement over old varieties. For example, modern Brussels sprout varieties produce smooth solid sprouts, compared with the loose and wingy sprouts of the older open pollinated varieties. Modern cauliflower varieties have solid, deep, white curds with no bracts and riciness. New carrot varieties are available with smooth skins and even colour throughout the root with no sign of yellow cores. In addition, disease resistance bred into new varieties has resulted in blemish-free sprouts, cabbage, parsnips, and carrots.

### Self-pollinated varieties

When a plant sets seed with its own pollen this is called self-fertilization, and where this is the normal method of reproduction the plant is called an inbreeder. In inbreeding crops self-fertilization usually takes place without the assistance of insect-pollinators, although there are exceptions. For example, visits by bumble- or honey-bees to the flowers of runner beans are necessary to get pods to set. Runner beans are perfectly capable of setting pods containing seeds by self-fertilization but their flower structure is such that it needs a bee to 'trip' the flower so that pollen grains land on the surface of the stigma and penetrate to the ovules. Dwarf French beans have no such problems and set their own seed quite readily without pollination by insects, because pollen is deposited directly onto the stigma surface within the flower.

Among inbreeders are lettuce, peas and tomatoes. Lettuce is so strongly self-fertile that breeders have difficulty in making their crosses, while French beans, peas and tomatoes can cross-fertilize if cross-pollen is present, usually having been carried there by bees, when the female parts of the flowers are receptive. Because of this ability to set cross-seed, seedsmen usually grow their seed of these crops in isolation.

When breeding new self-pollinated varieties the breeder usually starts with a variable population, often created by crossing together different varieties. After repeatedly selecting large numbers of single plants and testing their offspring for seven or eight generations, seed of each of the most promising offspring is bulked for testing as potential new varieties.

## Cross-pollinated varieties

A number of vegetable crops, particularly brassicas, onions and carrots, are either cross-pollinating or set much more seed of better quality when cross-pollinated. Such crops can and do set varying quantities of self-fertilized seed but usually these seeds produce plants that are weaker than those from crossed seed. Cross-pollinating plants have special biological mechanisms in their flower parts that encourage cross-mating and usually insect pollinators are involved in moving pollen between plants. As usual, there are exceptions and both sweet corn and beetroot are wind-pollinated. Until recently, varieties of cross-pollinated crops were maintained by growing a large population of each variety in isolation so that crossing took place between plants within the variety but there was no contamination from other varieties. The advantage of crossed, or hybrid, seed in cross-pollinating crops has been exploited by plant breeders to breed hybrid varieties which are superior to open-pollinated varieties.

## Hybrid varieties

Hybrid breeding is highly specialized and much more costly than older, more traditional methods (see Fig. 7.1). In the first place, the breeder has to devise and use special techniques to force a plant that is usually cross-fertilized to set self-fertilized seed. Inevitably the amount of seed that is set is much less than that

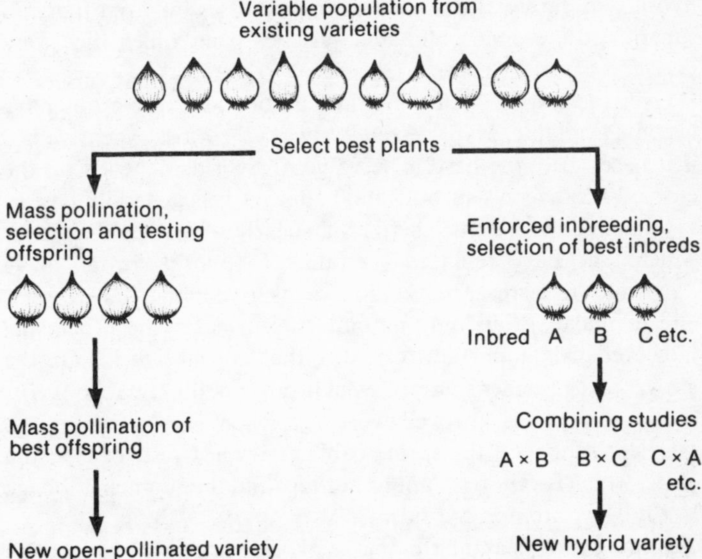


Fig. 7.1. Simplified version of breeding open-pollinated and hybrid varieties in cross-pollinated vegetables.

obtained from cross-fertilization, and the offspring from the self-fertilized plant is much less vigorous, or suffers from 'inbreeding depression'. Forced inbreeding over several generations, accompanied by rigorous selection and elimination of any plants that show defects, provides extremely uniform, though somewhat weak inbreds. Intercrossing of pairs of uniform inbreds gives hybrids which are of better quality and higher yielding than the inbred parents from which they were derived, and are equally uniform. Unfortunately not all pairs of inbreds combine well and it is usually necessary to judge the performance of hybrids by trial crosses, thus increasing the cost of the breeding programme. As inbred seed is costly to produce, and yields of hybrid seed (which sets on, and is harvested from weak inbred parents) are relatively low, the cost of hybrid seed is high. Breeders have tried various methods to increase hybrid seed production and more use is being made of double-cross hybrids, where hybrid from (A×B) is crossed with hybrid (C×D). Unfortunately these double-cross hybrids are rarely as uniform as single crosses but are often still superior to the open-pollinated varieties from which they were derived.

Over the last ten years hybrid varieties of many crops have become available. Hybrid seed is always the most expensive but is it necessarily the best? The value of hybrids depends on the crop. With Brussels sprouts and cabbages it is generally true to say that hybrids are much better than nearly all of the old varieties which they have replaced—certainly $F_1$ hybrid sprouts have done much to increase marketable yields for commercial growers, and to make sprout buttons more uniform for the processor. However, it is important to realize that not all hybrids are the answer to a gardener's prayer, even in cross-pollinating crops, for some non-hybrids are well worth growing. For example, two excellent cabbages, the spring cabbage Avon Crest, bred at the IHR, which is very resistant to bolting, and the summer cabbage Derby Day, are non-hybrids.

Among carrots and bulb onions hybrid varieties have recently established themselves as offering higher potential quality and, in the case of onions, better storage potential than non-hybrids.

Because inbreeding depression is extremely severe in onions and carrots, the parents used to make hybrids have only been inbred for two or three generations and are not completely uniform so that their hybrids are still somewhat variable. In the self-pollinating crops, such as lettuce, French beans and peas, hybrids are extremely difficult to breed and usually their advantage over self-pollinated varieties is so small that it is not economically worthwhile to embark on hybrid breeding programmes. However, there is always the exception and although tomatoes readily self-pollinate, $F_1$ hybrid tomatoes do generally outyield self-bred varieties and often have resistance to several diseases. As it is relatively simple to produce large numbers of hybrid seed by hand-pollination of tomatoes $F_1$ hybrids have understandably become popular, and among outdoor bush tomatoes, Sleaford Abundance and Alfresco are both hybrids that give excellent yields. With a renewal of commercial interest in outdoor tomatoes some of the non-$F_1$ hybrid bush selections from Canadian and Russian material seem likely to do well.

## How is seed produced?

Most of the vegetable seed sold in the UK is produced overseas, although some seed production, particularly of brassicas, is still done in Essex. A seedsman usually hedges his bets by placing contracts with two or more seed producers, as inevitably there are crop losses from pests and disease attacks, flooding, and invasion by unwanted livestock or rabbits and hares. With partial seed crop failure, demand can outstrip supply, particularly if a variety has a major outlet among commercial growers. It is not surprising therefore to find occasionally that a seedsman is 'out of stock'.

As a generalization, all seed production is best left to the specialist, especially as seed-borne diseases such as halo-blight in runner beans, mosaic virus in lettuce, *Alternaria* disease in brassicas, and neck-rot in onions, can cause serious problems to the amateur. In addition, with cross-pollinated crops, and even those that are largely self-pollinating, there may be contamination because of inadequate isolation of seeding crops, so that unwanted crosses from other varieties or even from wild species occur. Apart from disease problems, the seed obtained in our extremely variable climate may be of poor quality and low germination.

Among the cross-pollinated crops the low frequency of pollinators such as honey-bees and low temperatures at flowering can lead to problems with seed-set. With biennial crops there is the added difficulty of crops occupying land for two years, thus increasing the possibility of the build-up of pests and diseases. With such biennials there is inevitably a tendency for the amateur to harvest seed from plants that most readily 'run to seed', or 'bolt' (see page 382). When this happens you can unwittingly make your next crop much more susceptible to bolting.

Temptation to produce and keep seed from a hybrid variety should be avoided, as plants raised from such seed will not provide replicas of the hybrid parent from which they derive, but will be a highly variable population containing both good and bad types known to the scientist as segregants.

In view of the difficulties in multiplying your own seed, and with the possible exception of the 'easier' crops such as peas and beans (and even these have their problems), seed production is best left to the specialist.

To minimize expenditure on seed it is best to store any you don't use employing the method described in Chapter 2.

## Varieties

In their leaflets, NIAB specify the average number of days to maturity of different varieties of vegetables. These figures can vary from year to year and place to place and should be taken as no more than a guide; the important aspect of the information is the relative order in which varieties mature as this does not usually vary. All such information has been taken into account here. Where continuity of production is sought (see Chapter 8) an attempt is made to include at least two varieties for a particular harvest period. In the varieties listed here emphasis is given to 'all-purpose' rather than the specialized varieties often sought by the commercial grower. Sometimes the commercial grower will see defects in a variety that are unlikely to affect a variety's attractiveness to a gardener. For example, for several years the butterhead lettuce variety Avondefiance has been the standard against which new varieties have been judged in NIAB's trials. This variety, which is resistant to lettuce root aphid, to tipburn disease and to several races of downy mildew, gives excellent crops from June to October. Unfortunately, from a commercial viewpoint, it has a somewhat pointed base, which makes it difficult to pack into boxes for market, and if exposed upside down on a supermarket shelf, its 'butt' turns brown. Both these 'defects', which are unlikely to be of any importance to the gardener, are leading to it being replaced with other varieties by the commercial grower.

Occasionally a variety gives outstanding yields and quality under very fertile conditions but suffers more adversely, relative to other varieties, under poor growing conditions. Some hybrid varieties of Brussels sprouts certainly behave in this way; such varieties have not been included in our lists. It is recognized that some companies and individuals specialize in seed to produce mammoth plants of, for example, onions, for horticultural shows. No attempt has been made to include such strains or varieties, although the listed varieties should give a high quality product.

The cultural notes that are usually to be found on a packet of seed of a particular variety should be taken as guidelines to ensure that a variety is not sown at the wrong time or for the wrong purpose. For example, there is no point in attempting to grow the glasshouse lettuce variety Dandie as a summer garden lettuce or to attempt to grow Roscoff broccolis (winter cauliflower) in the north of England, as they only do well in the milder parts of southern Britain. Varieties will only be at their best if sown at the correct time and at the optimum spacing, and fertile conditions are required to ensure best results. Gardeners raising plants for agricultural shows may deviate from the sowing dates indicated in this chapter by raising seedlings earlier than specified under heated glass or indoors. In listing a number of varieties in the following pages, we have taken into account the likely availability of seed to gardeners, as quite often seed of a new variety may be available in bulk to commercial growers but not in small packets. All the varieties listed are advertised by at least two seedsmen selling seed to gardeners.

As there is little information from comparative trials on asparagus, kohl-rabi and shallots, no attempt is made to list varieties for these crops. Asparagus crowns are often available from local growers, who have selected and maintained their own strains. Over the next few years new French hybrids are likely to become available.

Kohl-rabi, a brassica grown for its swollen, bulbous stem which develops just above ground level, has a flavour between cabbage and turnip. It should be harvested when young and tender. Both purple- and white-skinned varieties have white flesh.

Shallots are a hardy, perennial onion whose bulb splits and divides to form six to twenty new shallots which are excellent for pickling. Particularly popular in more northern regions, red and yellow varieties are available as bulbs, often as virus-free stocks, from a number of suppliers. Many gardeners maintain their own stocks but it is advisable to replace these from time to time if the proportion of stunted or diseased plants builds up.

Where necessary, sowing times have been given for particular varieties; for a full description of sowing and harvest dates, see Chapter 8.

The different shapes that are obtainable in carrots, onions, parsnips, and red beet are illustrated in Fig. 7.2.

## Beetroot

The breeding of bolting-resistant, globe-shaped varieties has made possible earlier sowings to produce deep-red, small, tender roots which are excellent hot, as well as cold for salads. Other selections are available for main cropping but the early, bolting-resistant varieties are also suitable. Beetroot 'seed' is a dried flower head or cluster which can contain as many as three

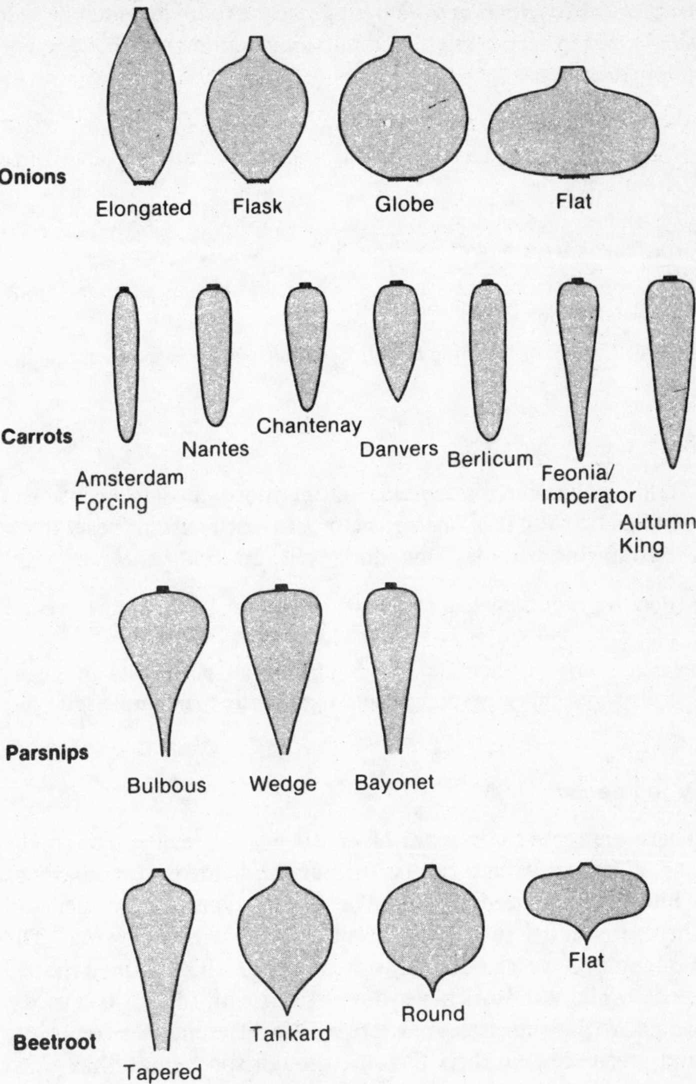


Fig. 7.2. Key to shapes of bulb and root crops.

true seeds. Monogerm varieties are now available which have a single seed in each cluster, thus allowing better control over plant population.

**Avonearly, Boltardy** Both are early, globe-shaped (Detroit-type) varieties with resistance to bolting and red flesh that is almost free from white rings.

**Cheltenham Mono** A monogerm, broad-shouldered, long-rooted, medium-size variety of good quality, suitable for slicing.

**Monopoly** A monogerm variety with globe-shaped roots and good internal colour.

**Detroit Little Ball** Suitable for May sowing, produces excellent quality roots.

## Borecole or Curly kale

In this crop, which is popular among more northerly gardeners perhaps because it is one of the most frost-resistant vegetables, the following varieties have done well in recent years.

**Fribor** A hybrid of medium height with fine, curly, deep-green leaves for harvesting November to February.

**Pentland Brig** A vigorous kale producing an abundance of young leafy shoots in early spring; more frost-hardy than purple-sprouting broccoli.

## Broad beans

There are three main types of broad beans, Seville, Longpods, and Windsors, which can be further subdivided on the basis of white or green seed colour. The Seville types are hardier and therefore more suitable for autumn or winter sowing. The Longpods have slender pods with up to eight kidney-shaped seeds, while Windsors have shorter pods with four or five seeds, which are flat and circular. There is little difference between white and green seeds in their flavour, though some think that green seeds are more tender.

A fourth type, the Dwarf or Fan-podded, are bushier, dwarf plants which mature quickly, carrying many small pods, each with three seeds, and varieties of this type are particularly useful for the small garden.

The varieties that are listed according to their sowing period have given good results over many years.

*Seville*

**Aquadulce Claudia** A tall white-seeded variety for sowing in late October/November; has a good flavour.

*Longpods*

**Imperial Green Longpod** A tall, very long-podded, green-seeded variety for February to April sowing; good for freezing.

**Exhibition Longpod** The traditional synonym of the variety Conqueror, it is a heavy cropping white-seeded bean with good flavour for spring sowing.

**Hylon** Late-maturing with an average of seven white seeds per pod.

*Windsors*

**White Windsor** Produces late yields from sowings during March–May.

**Express** Early-maturing with four white seeds.

**Jubilee Hysor** Late-maturing, producing six white seeds per pod.

*Dwarf (Fan-podded)*

**The Sutton** A white-seeded variety for sowing under cloches in November/December or in the open from February to July.

## French beans

The listed varieties have done well in trials done by the NIAB, the Processors and Growers Research Organization, Peterborough, and the Campden Food Preservation Research Organization.

**Aramis** Produces thin stringless long pods.

**Delinel** A variety with very long thin stringless pods.

**Kinghorn Wax** A waxy-podded type with fleshy, stringless pods.

**Pros** A stringless variety with slightly curved, medium-green pods that are oval in cross-section. Very good for cooking or freezing as whole pods.

**Tendergreen** A popular heavy cropper with fleshy, stringless, round pods which freeze well.

## Runner beans

Most gardeners grow runner beans as a climber with supports, thus ensuring a heavier yield of cleaner pods than is obtained from 'pinching-out' the crop by removal of the growing point. The dwarf variety Hammonds-Dwarf Scarlet is available but has the disadvantage that many of its pods are damaged through contact with the soil; 'pinched-out' Kelvedon Marvel has given good results as a dwarf crop.

Some white-flowered varieties are simply white-flowered variants of scarlet-flowered varieties (for example White Achievement), but others (for example Desiree) are quite distinct from scarlet forms. Several relatively stringless varieties have been introduced recently, including Desiree and Red Knight. Among the varieties listed here are those that have done well in trials at ADAS EHSs, or in trials at the IHR.

**Achievement, Enorma, Crusader, Prizewinner, Scarlet Emperor, Streamline** All good maincrop varieties with long, straight, green pods.

**Desiree** White-flowered and white-seeded, it produces long stringless pods.

**Liberty** Red-flowered with very long pods.

**Kelvedon Marvel** An early variety with shortish pods. Suitable for 'pinching-out' under cloches and also as a 'pinched' outdoor crop.

**Pickwick** A dwarf variety with red flowers and short stringless pods.

**Red Knight** A red flowered variety with medium-length pods which are stringless.

## Broccoli, sprouting

There are as yet no named varieties of this excellent garden crop, which provides a welcome fresh vegetable during March/May. Seed is usually sold as either purple- or white-sprouting broccoli, both of which are subdivided into early- or late-. There is not a marked difference between early- and late-purple-sprouting in terms of maturity which together provide spears in March and April. However, within white-sprouting the early strains are distinctly different from late, giving spears in March/April while the late crop provides spears or small, cauliflower-like heads in May.

Nine-star perennial broccoli has a central head surrounded by several smaller heads and may be a form of late-white-sprouting broccoli. Although plants may, with care, last several years, their yields are not maintained and there is a danger of their acting as foci for the carry-over of pests and diseases.

### Brussels sprouts

As the NIAB do annual trials at three or four sites on Brussels sprout varieties, and trials were also done at the IHR, there is a lot of information on which to base decisions about which varieties to grow.

The efforts of plant breeders have produced a crop that is 'in-season' over a period extending from September to March. With the exception of early hybrids, most $F_1$s now 'hold' their buttons well and produce sprouts of much better quality than open-pollinated varieties, so only hybrids are recommended here. Although a harvest period for maximum yield is given, most varieties will continue to produce some harvestable sprouts beyond that period. The varieties listed according to their maturity, or harvest period, all give high yields.

*Early (September/November)*

**Oliver** Medium to short plants giving high yields of large smooth pale sprouts.

**Peer Gynt** Short to medium plants with medium-sized, smooth, solid sprouts. Lower sprouts may open out if not picked as they mature.

**Mallard** Medium to short plants producing a high yield of medium to large sprouts of good quality. Plants stand erect.

**Roger** Tall plants with very high yield of large good quality sprouts which are fairly slow to deteriorate.

*Mid-season (November/January)*

**Citadel** A medium-tall variety with good quality round sprouts.

**Widgeon** A British-bred variety with heavy yields of excellent quality.

**Rampart** A tall, high-yielding variety producing medium to large sprouts of good quality. Although cropping starts in the mid-season period, it holds its buttons well.

*Late (December/March)*

**Achilles** A British-bred variety with small- to medium-sized, mid- to dark-green sprouts of excellent quality which hold well. A tendency to fall over in some localities.

**Fortress** Short plants producing round solid sprouts. Plants show very good winter hardiness.

## Cabbages

By careful planning in the medium-sized to large garden or allotment, it should be possible to meet a household's needs all the year round by growing different types of cabbage. Varieties are listed according to maturity, or harvest period, and most have done well in NIAB trials.

Spring *(March/May)*

**Avon Crest** A pointed-head cabbage of good uniformity that can be used as spring greens or as a late-maturing headed cabbage with medium to large, firm hearts. It is extremely resistant to bolting and can also be sown in early July to produce an autumn cabbage.

**Durham Early** Another dark-green variety of good uniformity, best used as greens. It produces conical, medium-sized heads.

**Dorado** Very good quality heads with good colour at maturity, although slightly blue in young stages. Useful for greens or small solid hearts. Needs good ground conditions.

**Offenham 1-Myatts Offenham Compacta** A medium- to dark-green variety for April/May maturity, it has medium to large heads and is of good uniformity and bolting resistance. Suitable for greens and hearts.

*Summer (June/July)*

**Derby Day** A round cabbage which can be brought to maturity early by sowing under glass in February. Of moderate to good uniformity it has small, blue-green heads. Suitable for greens and hearts.

**Hispi** A popular early-maturing hybrid with good, uniform, dark-green pointed heads.

**Golden Cross** Hybrid producing the earliest round dark green cabbage; has short internal stalks.

**Spitfire** Hybrid with pointed heads maturing later and standing longer than Hispi. It is very uniform with an attractive dark green colour.

**Marner Allfruh** An early-maturing variety with medium mid-green, round to oval heads of good uniformity. Dense head with low percentage of internal stalk. Also suitable for late sowing to harvest in August.

*August/September*

**Castello** Hybrid with dense uniform round heads with very long standing ability.

**Minicole** A popular hybrid with small, oval, solid heads that stand for up to three months without serious deterioration.

**Stonehead** A hybrid producing uniform, solid, round, small heads that will stand for about a month without deteriorating.

*Autumn (September/November)*

**Hawke** Hybrid produced by crossing Christmas Drumhead and white cabbage. Heads dark green and rather oval with good standing ability.

**Rapier** Hybrid similar to Hawke but heads more round.

*Winter (November/February)*

*White*

**Jupiter** Hybrid with round, uniform heads with dark-green outer foliage and good standing ability. Suitable for use as fresh cabbage, for coleslaw, or for storage until March in frost-free, cool conditions when cut before frost damages the heads.

**Hidena** Another hybrid with round to oval heads that have dark, grey-green outer leaves; it has good standing ability. Also suitable for use as fresh cabbage, coleslaw or storage.

*January King*

**Aquarius** A hybrid with pale, grey-green, small heads which will stand up to two months without serious deterioration.

**January King – Hardy Late Stock 3** Medium sized heads, dark green, tinged with deep purple.

*December/February*

*Savoy × White Cabbage Hybrids*

**Celtic** An outstanding hybrid with uniform, round, medium-green heads which have solid, dense, white hearts; it will usually stand up to two months without deteriorating.

**Tundra** Hybrid similar to Celtic with more of a Savoy appearance and later-maturing. It will stand in the garden until February or March.

*Savoys*

**Ice Queen** Hybrid with flat, round, medium-green, uniform heads with fine blisters; standing ability up to two months.

**Wirosa** Hybrid maturing in December with good quality and standing ability.

**Wivoy** Hybrid, late-maturing, with small heads which can stand in the garden until March or April.

## Calabrese (or green-sprouting broccoli)

The harvest season for calabrese, often known as poor man's asparagus, is summer and autumn. When the central head has been harvested, the later development of side-shoots gives extra crop. Although hybrids have almost replaced open-pollinated varieties, for a greater spread of harvest, older varieties such as Green Sprouting or Italian Sprouting may attract some gardeners.

The varieties listed have done well in trials at the NIAB.

**Corvet** A medium-early hybrid with uniform heads having small buds, medium to pale green in colour. More suitable for cultivation in the northern half of England, and in Scotland.

**Green Comet** An early hybrid producing a high yield of medium-sized heads with uniform buds. After cutting the primary head, secondary heads are freely produced.

**Mercedes** Early hybrid producing large heads having medium-sized dark buds. Plants short.

## Carrots

Modern varieties of carrots have been selected for deeper orange colour, better texture and elimination of quality defects such as green-topped, split and forked roots.

There are a number of different types, the shapes of which are illustrated in Fig. 7.2; those that are available to gardeners are described briefly in the order of their maturity or harvest period. New shapes are now being derived from selections made in crosses of the main types, and further improvements are being made in colour and root quality. Among older varieties of carrots, St Valery, which is also known as New Red Intermediate, has a long, tapered root of good colour and texture and is still used by gardeners for exhibition purposes.

Seedsmen have traditionally made their own selections and until recently there was a proliferation of different names, many of which were synonyms for the same variety. The National List and Common Catalogue for carrots now contain far fewer names, but there are still a number of approved selections that have been made by different breeders and seedsmen from recognized varieties. Several seedsmen market very good selections under group names, for example, Armsterdam Forcing, Nantes and Chantenay Red-Cored, so that a useful experiment would be to compare some of the selections listed here with your traditional source of seed. The varieties listed are those that have done well in NIAB trials.

*Amsterdam Forcing*. This stump-rooted (rounded tips) group has small- to medium-size, slender, cylindrical roots and is most suitable for early forcing under glass or plastic. It has relatively little foliage and yields are lower than those of maincrop carrots.

**Amsterdam Forcing – Sweetheart and Amsterdam Forcing – Amstel** are useful selections with slender roots and good internal colour, but sometimes show greening within the root.

*Nantes*. The roots are of medium size and have a cylindrical stump shape, usually with a slight shoulder and sometimes tending to taper. They are intermediate in size and foliage between

Amsterdam Forcing and Berlicum. Like Amsterdam Forcing they can be used for forcing.

**Nantes–Express** and **Nantes–Tiptop** Selections with medium-length cylindrical roots and good internal colour.

**Nanco** Hybrid with uniform smooth cylindrical roots.

**Nandor** Hybrid with uniform short cylindrical roots.

**Narman** Hybrid late maturity with cylindrical roots and deep flesh colour.

*Chantenay*. This group is widely grown by British growers for canning, dehydrating, and the fresh market. The roots are of medium size and have a conical, stump shape. The foliage size is between that of Berlicum and Autumn King.

**Chantenay Red-Cored/Supreme** A selection with good internal colour.

*Berlicum*. Large, cylindrical or slightly tapering roots have rounded tips (stump-rooted).

**Berlicum–Berjo** A good yielder that has produced roots with a good flesh colour, and a low level of splitting but has a tendency to internal greening.

**Camberly** Berlicum type with slightly tapered roots. Deep flesh and core colour and little internal greening.

**Cardinal** Hybrid with uniform, long, cylindrical roots.

*Autumn King*. This group has rough-skinned roots which are very large, and have a tapering stump-rooted shape, usually with bold shoulders. Varieties have large, vigorous foliage, mature late and give heavy yields of roots with inferior quality to that of the Chantenays.

**Autumn King–Vita Longa** Gives high yields of good core and flesh colour.

### Cauliflowers

Cauliflowers were developed in northern Europe to give summer-maturing types, and in maritime regions of north-western Europe including England, to give winter and spring types. The introduction of cauliflowers to Australia in the nineteenth century resulted in further types being developed from which has recently been bred a series of varieties maturing in the autumn.

A 'broccoli' variety currently sold as a novelty is Romanesco, which is really a primitive form of pale-green cauliflower originating in Italy. Somewhat variable, this variety has a texture and taste different to other broccolis and cauliflowers.

Among cauliflowers there is a wide range of maturity types and it is possible to produce cauliflowers commercially throughout the year in the UK. However, the curd of the cauliflower is extremely susceptible to frost and winter-maturing forms can only be grown successfully in relatively frost-free areas, such as Cornwall and Pembrokeshire. These winter cauliflowers should not be confused with the winter-hardy or spring-maturing cauliflowers which are ready from March to early May, and can be grown in a much wider range of conditions.

New varieties are fast replacing the older traditional ones such as the Autumn Giant Veitch's Self-Protecting. New varieties selected from old traditional English varieties have a place in the garden, for example, Asmer Pinnacle and Vilna. However, many new varieties developed by crossing a wide range of summer and autumn types now provide the higher quality sought by gardeners. Hybrids offering better uniformity are also available.

A number of new varieties have done very well in NIAB trials where yield, curd size, and quality of curd (which includes freedom from defects such as looseness, bracts, riciness, and discolouration) have all been taken into account. The best of these varieties are listed according to their harvest period.

*Early Summer (June/July)*

**Montano** Hybrid maturing in early June; has very good quality, although rather knobbly heads.

**Alpha-Paloma** Matures in mid-June, produces well-protected heads of good depth and quality.

**White Summer** Maturing during the latter half of June, has good quality deep curds which are slightly ivory in colour.

**Dominant** Matures in late June producing acceptable quality.

*Choosing a variety*

*Summer and Autumn (August/November)*

**Plana** Hybrid suitable for planting to mature between early August and mid-September.

**Dok Elgon** This variety gives best results when grown for maturity in late August and September and during this period produces deep well-protected heads.

**White Rock** Suitable for maturing from mid-August to the end of September. This variety produces very deep well-protected heads when grown under good conditions with adequate moisture.

**Wallaby** An Australian-bred variety suitable for maturing during the latter half of September. It is a vigorous variety producing good quality heads.

**Canberra** Very late Australian variety with very well-protected heads which are medium-sized and white, but tending to be loose.

**Barrier Reef** Matures in October. Produces vigorous plants with well-protected but not very solid heads.

*Winter (December/April)*

Often known as Roscoff broccoli these are only suitable for south-west Britain. No varieties are listed in current catalogues, but where varieties are available they will be described as Roscoffs.

*Spring (March/May)*

**Asmer Snowcap March** Very early English Winter type which can produce heads of moderate quality in a mild early Spring.

**Walcheren Winter – Armado April** Matures in April.

**Walcheren Winter – Markanta** Matures in late April/early May.

**Walcheren Winter – Birchington** Matures in late April/early May.

**Walcheren Winter – Maystar** Matures in May.

**Asmer Pinnacle** Late English Winter type producing heads which tend to be loose and yellow in late May.

**Vilna** Very late maturing. Heads tend to be loose, yellow and bracted when produced in June.

## Celery

Self-blanching and green varieties of celery should be used when summer cropping is required, but if sown too early they tend to bolt. They are also rapidly replacing the traditional 'trenching' types for cropping later in the year, but do not survive frosts. Thus for winter cropping a 'trench' variety is essential.

*Traditional or trench*

**Fenlander** A traditional trench celery which will blanch to produce medium-length succulent sticks which are free from stringiness, and of good flavour.

*Self-blanching*

**Celebrity** A Lathom self-blanching type but with slightly longer sticks.

**Lathom Self-Blanching** An early, crisp variety, with a good flavour and very good bolting resistance.

*Green*

**Greensleeves** Produces attractive pale green sticks of good flavour.

## Chinese cabbage

The barrel type is the most popular form of this crop and is like cos lettuce in shape, having a mild flavour mid-way between cabbage and celery. Other types include the tall or Michilli which is three times as tall as broad, and Pak Choi with broad fleshy petioles. They can be eaten like a lettuce or cooked as a cabbage. The crop requires a combination of shortening days and fairly high temperatures to avoid bolting and ensure good growth, therefore sowing is best done in July. Like calabrese, it is best sown *in situ*, as it does not transplant too well from the soil but can be raised in pots or peat blocks for transplanting. It is very useful as a catch crop to follow, say, early potatoes. New varieties from Japan have become more readily available as there is increasing commercial interest in this crop especially for varieties with bolting resistance.

**Kasumi** Barrel-shaped heads tending to be loose with a short internal stalk, but very good bolting resistance.

**Tip Top $F_1$** A quick-maturing variety with barrel shaped heads. Moderate bolting resistance.

**Jade Pagoda** Large medium green, rather loose heads of the Michilli type with moderate bolting resistance.

**Mei Quing Choi** A Pak Choi which is green-stemmed with moderate bolting resistance.

## Leeks

For many years, particularly in southern England, this excellent winter-hardy vegetable was regarded as merely a flavouring for soups but has now become much more popular in its own right.

The listed varieties have done well in NIAB trials.

**Autumn Mammoth – Argenta** Although maturing in late autumn this attractive leek, which has a non-bulbous shank about 12.5 cm. (5 in.) long, is suitable for harvesting in winter.

**Autumn Mammoth – Goliath** Is similar in maturity and type to **Autumn Mammoth – Argenta.**

**King Richard** Matures in the early autumn and has a long shank 25.5–30.5 cm. (10–12 in.) and pale flag. It is not winter hardy.

**Swiss Giant – Albinstar** Maturing in the autumn and early winter. It has a long shank with some bulbing and medium to pale green flag.

**Blauwgroene Winter – Alaska** For spring harvesting. Leeks are short and very bulby but with a dark green flag.

## Lettuce

Within this crop there are three main types: butterheads (which have soft delicate leaves), crispheads (which are usually larger with crisp, wrinkled, succulent leaves), and cos (which have longer leaves that are crisp and sweet). Butterheads and crispheads are sometimes referred to collectively as cabbage types. There are also some loose-leaved types from which the leaves can be regularly picked.

Varieties suitable for glasshouses have usually been bred for short-day (winter) conditions and are liable to bolt if grown outdoors in summer.

A number of varieties are promoted on the basis of their resistance to downy mildew. There are a great number of different races or strains of the fungus that cause this disease, so that resistance of a particular variety may 'break down' if the fungal strains in a locality are of the type to overcome a variety's resistance. Lettuce mosaic virus resistance, and resistance to root aphids have also been bred into a number of new varieties.

The listed varieties have done well in NIAB trials and in experiments at the IHR.

*Butterhead*

**Avondefiance** An extremely reliable variety for cropping from June to August which withstands dry conditions and high temperatures, it produces a heavy yield of good quality heads, medium to dark green in colour. Its hearts tend to be open and bases pointed. Resistant to root aphid and to some races of downy mildew.

**Dolly** For cropping from June to October. Fairly large well-formed heads with good resistance to downy mildew and lettuce mosaic virus.

**Musette** Medium to dark green heads with leaves slightly thicker than average. Good resistance to downy mildew and resistance to lettuce mosaic virus and root aphids.

*Crisphead*

Breeding effort has been increased on this type of lettuce in recent years, but major improvements are awaited. Webbs Wonderful is an old favourite. The following varieties will produce solid 'Iceberg' heads which have become popular.

**Avoncrisp** A variety resistant to root aphid and to some races of mildew, it can suffer badly from tipburn. More suitable for the looser 'Webbs' type of head production.

**Malika** For cropping in June and September/October. Fast growing so can quickly become over-mature. Suitable for 'Webbs' heads and medium-sized 'Iceberg' heads.

**Saladin** For July to September. Large dark green heads which hold well. Suitable for 'Webbs' heads and large 'Iceberg' heads.

*Cos*

**Lobjoits Green Cos** A dark-green variety with medium to large high-quality heads with well-turned-in hearts. Heads subject to tip-burn, so they should be harvested before becoming too dense.

*Choosing a variety*

**Little Gem** A small, quick-maturing, sweet variety half-way between cabbage lettuce and cos in shape.

**Valmaine** Not as attractive as Lobjoits Green Cos but less susceptible to tip-burn.

*Special purpose*

**Salad Bowl** A bolting-resistant, loose-head variety with endive-like yellow/green leaves that can be picked as required without cutting the whole plant.

**Lollo Rossa** Non-hearting variety with red tinged leaves waved and serrated at the edges.

**Winter Density** Suitable for autumn sowing, this dark-green variety is intermediate in appearance between cos and cabbage lettuce.

**Valdor** Suitable for autumn sowing (do not sow in spring or summer), this winter variety has large heads and tolerates cold, wet conditions.

## Marrows and Courgettes

Although some varieties are suitable for both courgette and marrow production, $F_1$ hybrids, which are often earlier and higher yielding, are usually better for courgettes. When grown as marrows, current $F_1$ hybrids have a tendency to reach a large size before attaining the thick skin that is desirable for storing marrows. In addition, the shape of current $F_1$ hybrids is not as cylindrical as that of the popular open-pollinated All Green Bush types, which are best grown as marrows. The following varieties have done well in NIAB trials.

*Open-pollinated bush type*

**All Green Bush** Bush type with green cylindrical fruits.

**Brimmer** Attractive cylindrical green fruits, a variety suitable for courgette production.

*Open-pollinated trailing type*

**Long Green Trailing** A variety with long, cylindrical-shaped, pale and dark green striped fruit that sometimes thickens at the blossom end.

*$F_1$ hybrid bush type*

**Ambassador** Produces many cylindrical green courgettes, and may also be grown on to produce marrows.

**Early Gem** A high yielder with dark green fruits with pale flecking, that are good as courgettes, but may also be grown on to produce marrows.

**Gold Rush** Cylindrical, golden yellow fruits which are suitable for courgettes, although these are not as popular as green fruits.

## Onions

The introduction of Japanese varieties of onions to the UK for autumn sowing has increased the versatility of the bulb onion crop. Although the bulb shape and skin quality of varieties of the autumn-sown crop fall short of that of the spring-sown, newer varieties are considerably improved. The food values of the two types are no different, and the early harvest period (June/July) of the autumn-sown crop fills a niche in which home-grown bulb onions were not formerly possible. Whereas the autumn-sown crop is best grown by direct sowing, the spring-sown crop may either be raised by direct sowing and thinning, by the use of onion sets, or by plant raising in peat-blocks or modules then transplanting.

The listed varieties for autumn-sown and spring-sown bulbs and for salad onions, are based mainly on results from annual trials by NIAB at several sites.

### Bulb onions

*Spring-sown*

All varieties have globe-shaped bulbs and are listed in order of maturity.

**Caribo** Hybrid. Thick-skinned, dark straw-coloured bulbs. Bulbs store very well.

**Hygro** Hybrid. Vigorous variety with thick straw-coloured skins. Stores well.

**Rijnsburger – Balstora** Thick dark straw-coloured skins. Stores well.

**Rijnsburger – Robusta** Late maturing and producing onions with dark straw-coloured skins. Stores well.

*Sets*

Several varieties are sold as sets for planting in late March or April; they should not be planted earlier (see Chapter 12).

**Sturon** A good-yielding variety with round bulbs that keep moderately well.

**Stuttgarter Giant** A variety with large, flat onions that store moderately well.

*Pickling onions*

**Paris Silver Skin**, **Barletta**, and **The Queen** are all good silverskin onions suitable for pickling. It is also possible to use brown-skinned varieties normally grown for large bulbs by growing them at close spacing; **Giant Zittau** is suitable for pickling.

*Autumn-sown (not suitable for storing)*

**Buffalo** Hybrid, producing a very high yield of flattened globe-shaped bulbs with thin stems.

**Express Yellow O-X** One of the earliest maturing (early June) hybrids, with pale, semi-flat, thin-skinned bulbs, it has lower yields than later-maturing varieties.

**Imai Early Yellow** A mid-season (mid-June harvest) variety with high yields of flat-shaped bulbs with yellow skins of moderate thickness.

**Senshyu Semi-Globe Yellow** Matures about ten days later than Imai Early Yellow, it has high yields of globe-shaped bulbs with fairly thick stems.

*Salad onions*

**White Lisbon** The traditional salad onion used for pulling young in the spring. Quick growing with silvery skin and mild flavour.

**White Lisbon-Winter Hardy** This variety is the hardiest of salad onions for harvesting in spring but tends to bulb faster and blanch better than White Lisbon.

The traditional salad onion belongs to the species *Allium cepa* while so-called Welsh or Japanese bunching onions are *Allium fistulosum*. These bunching onions are usually sold under a Japanese name, for example **Hikari**. They are not winter hardy and they do bolt very readily, but the flower stalks are hollow and they are virtually free from bulbing.

## Parsley

Strictly speaking, parsley is a biennial herb, but because it is so popular and, unlike most herbs, there are a number of different varieties, it has been included here.

The varieties that are listed have done well in trials at IHR and NIAB.

**Bravour** A variety with dark-green, curled foliage on longish stalks. Good winter hardiness.

**Moss Curled** A reliable, dark-green variety of long standing with finely-curled foliage.

**Curlina** A modem moss curled type.

## Parsnip

On soils where canker is a problem (usually on rich organic soils), canker-resistant varieties should be grown.

The listed varieties have done well in NIAB trials.

*Varieties with good resistance to canker*

**Avonresister** Small bulbous, cream-fleshed roots, that are sweeter than other varieties.

**White Gem** Large roots that are wedge-shaped to bulbous. Smooth skin with white flesh.

**Cobham Improved Marrow** Medium-sized mainly wedge-shaped roots with smooth skin and white flesh.

**Gladiator** Hybrid. Medium to large uniform wedge-shaped roots with smooth skins and white flesh.

*Susceptible to canker*

**Offenham** Medium to large, bulbous- to wedge-shaped roots.

## Peas

The success of pea breeders in producing dwarf 30–90 cm. (12–36 in.) high, modern varieties has made this crop much easier to grow. Heights will vary considerably, depending on soil fertility and growing conditions and a variety sold as '60–75 cm. in height' may reach 90 cm. (36 in.) under favourable circumstances.

Round-seeded (marrowfat) varieties are much hardier than wrinkle seeded varieties and are used for November or early spring sowings. Those varieties with wrinkled seeds should not be sown before the beginning of March, even in sheltered areas. Because of the higher sugar content and better flavour, wrinkle seeded varieties are of better quality than those with round seeds.

Varieties are usually categorized as first earlies, second earlies and main crop on the basis of the time that they take from sowing to reach maturity. As a guideline, early varieties usually take 11–12 weeks, second earlies from 12–14 weeks and main crop 14–16 weeks. Because of the overlap that may occur between the different maturity types, you may find occasionally that one seedsman lists a variety as a second early, while another advertises it as main crop. The time to maturity will vary to some extent with growing conditions. Maincrop varieties, even modern ones, tend to be taller than earlies.

Sugar or mangetout peas are eaten in the pod, just before the peas swell. The so-called asparagus or winged pea (it has four-winged pods) are not peas at all, although they belong to the same family (legumes) as peas. They too are eaten when young, and when cooked the young pods have a flavour that resembles that of asparagus. As the asparagus pea is extremely susceptible to frost it should only be sown when the danger from frosts is past.

Most of the official trials that are done with peas deal with the highly specialized vining pea crop for commercial growers. In addition, however, experience in growing different varieties by gardeners has identified a number of reliable varieties. The varieties that are listed therefore include those that have proved to be highly satisfactory over a number of years, as well as those that have done well in vining pea crop trials.

*First earlies*

**Feltham First** A round-seeded variety, with short- to medium-length stems, suitable for early sowing, particularly under cloches; it has only moderate quality.

**Early Onward** A wrinkled pea, with medium-length stems, suitable for sowing from March onwards, this variety gives high yields of good quality and freezes well.

**Hurst Beagle** A wrinkle-seeded variety, with short stems, suitable for sowing from March onwards, it produces good quality, sweet peas which freeze well. Susceptible to race 1 of pea wilt.

**Kelvedon Wonder** A wrinkled pea, with short- to medium-length stems, giving high yields. Suitable for sowing after March, its tolerance to mildew makes it suitable for autumn-cropping where this disease is a problem.

**Little Marvel** One of the older, wrinkle-seeded varieties, with short stems, which does well under cloches, producing peas of very good flavour.

**Meteor** A hardy, round-seeded variety, with short stems, for early sowing.

*Second earlies*

All varieties listed here have wrinkled seeds and should not be sown before March.

**Hurst Green Shaft** A very good variety, with medium to long stems, that gives high yields of good quality peas suitable for freezing. Resistant to race 1 of pea wilt.

**Onward** An established favourite, with short- to medium-length stems, which gives high yields of good quality peas that are suitable for freezing.

**Poppet** Semi-leafless variety producing dark green medium-sized peas. Variety resistant to race 1 of pea wilt.

*Main crop*

The variety listed has wrinkled seeds and should not be sown before March.

**Senator** A tallish variety, giving high yields of peas with good flavour.

## Potatoes

Quality in a potato variety is difficult to define, as tuber appearance, dry matter content, flavour, texture and cooking characteristics all play a part. Also, varieties behave differently in different regions and personal and regional tastes differ. For example, among maincrop potatoes, Kerr's Pink, a floury potato, is popular in Scotland, whereas Majestic, a good keeper with a slight tendency to discolour after cooking but which makes excellent chips and sauté potatoes, has greater consumer appeal in England. Both these old varieties are being replaced by more modern ones, as are the first earlies Home Guard and Arran Pilot.

For the individual gardener it is advisable to grow a number of different varieties so as to determine which variety or varieties has greatest appeal. The NIAB publishes a booklet describing a large number of potato varieties, which is available from the Institute.

Early potatoes are usually grouped into first and second earlies. In sheltered, more southerly areas, first earlies can be ready for harvest in late May but generally speaking are ready for digging in June/July, while second earlies are available in July/August. With earlies it is best to use them when fresh and they are best served boiled, though larger ones make good chips and can also be used to make sauté potatoes.

Maincrop potatoes are usually harvested from September to October, and can be stored over winter.

Potato-cyst eelworms (potato 'sickness') can be troublesome in gardens, particularly on land which has repeatedly grown potatoes. As there are no practical curative measures, varieties with resistance to any of the strains of this pathogen are at an advantage over susceptible varieties on infested soil.

The majority of varieties which are listed in order of maturity have done well in NIAB trials and should be readily available.

### *First earlies*

**Arran Pilot** Sprouts early and rapidly, produces high yield if left later. Waxy texture and good flavour. Long oval tubers with white skin and flesh.

**Maris Bard** A very early, high yielder with white, short, oval tubers with white flesh. Sprout development is fairly late for a first early variety, so preliminary sprouting of tubers will result in an earlier crop.

**Epicure** Old early variety producing moderate yields of deep-eyed tubers with a very floury cooked texture. Good frost recovery. Shape round, skin and flesh white.

**Foremost** Moderate yields of white-skinned, oval-shaped tubers that cook well and have a good flavour.

**Pentland Javelin** One of the later first earlies, this variety is slow to sprout but bulks later than some early varieties, giving high yields of uniform, roundish, white tubers with white flesh. Is resistant to one race of potato-cyst eelworm ($RO_1$) and can therefore yield well when susceptible varieties fail.

*Second earlies*

**Estima** A high-yielding early bulking variety with attractive oval, yellow-skinned tubers with pale-yellow flesh. Good drought and blight resistance.

**Marfona** New, very high-yielding and tending to produce large tubers, but bulks up fairly early. Shape short oval to oval, skin light yellow, flesh cream to light yellow. Susceptible to slug damage. Suitable for boiling and baking.

**Red Craigs Royal** A red mutant-form of Craigs Royal, this variety bulks quickly and gives a moderate yield of oval, white-fleshed tubers that cook well.

**Wilja** A high-yielding Dutch variety with very uniform, long-oval tubers of uniform size. Skin and flesh light yellow. Produces large number of tubers per plant near the surface, so needs to be well drilled up. Susceptible to drought. Waxy texture with good cooking qualities.

*Main crop*

**Desiree** An early maincrop with high yields of red-skinned, attractive long-oval tubers with light yellow flesh of good cooking quality with little disintegration on boiling. Scab and slugs can be troublesome.

**Cara** High-yielding late maincrop. Tubers round with white skins and pink eyes, flesh cream. Haulm is late to mature and sprouted seed will ensure an earlier crop.

*Choosing a variety*

**King Edward** Gives moderate yields of oval, white-skinned tubers with red splashes. Yields vary with conditions as it is susceptible to drought. The cream-fleshed tubers are of very good cooking quality. Red King Edward is a fully red-skinned variant.

**Maris Piper** A consistently high-yielding early-maincrop variety with attractive, medium-sized tubers that are short-oval, have white skin and cream flesh, and are of good cooking quality. Although it is susceptible to drought, common scab and slug damage, it is resistant to one strain of potato-cyst nematode ($RO_1$).

**Pentland Squire** A very high-yielding early maincrop variety with large, attractively shaped oval white tubers with white flesh. Closer spacing will help to reduce tuber size, as large tubers can develop hollow hearts. Drought-resistant and some resistance to slugs.

**Romano** High-yielding early maincrop of uniform red, round to short oval tubers with cream flesh. Susceptible to drought.

## Radish

This quick-growing salad crop has varieties with a wide range of shapes and colours. Japanese varieties, usually with long white roots, are likely to become available over the next few years.

The varieties recommended here have done well in trials at the IHR and NIAB.

*Summer*

**Cherry Belle** A popular red-globe variety with crisp, white flesh.

**French Breakfast** A variety with red short cylindrical roots with a white tip.

**Long White Icicle** A long-rooted, white-skinned variety with a pleasant, mild flavour.

**Sparkler** Traditional round red radish but with a white tip at the root end. Slow to become pithy.

*Winter*

**Black Spanish Round** A globe-shaped winter variety with a black skin and white flesh.

**China Rose** A rose-coloured, cylindrical variety with white flesh.

**Mino Early** A long white variety with deeply cut grey-green leaves. Roots 30.5 cm. (12 in.) long.

### Rhubarb

Although seed of some varieties can be purchased, it is advisable to purchase rhubarb crowns to establish this crop. Such crowns should be available in garden centres and from local specialist rhubarb growers.

A number of varieties have done well in trials at Stockbridge House EHS, Yorkshire, and include the early variety **Timperley Early**, which is suitable for early forcing. **Victoria** and **Hawkes Champagne** are good mid-season types while **Cawood Delight** is a high quality, red-fleshed, late variety that is not readily available.

### Spinach

Although an easy crop to grow, if a spinach variety is sown at the wrong time of year, plants will bolt to seed, particularly in dry weather. Although some varieties are described as prickly, the seeds, and not the leaves, are prickly.

Few official trials have been done in this crop, so that the listed varieties are those generally reported to have given good results over a number of years.

**Broad-leaved Prickly** A very winter-hardy variety with thick, fleshy, dark-green leaves.

**Viking** A variety with dark green leaves suitable for sowing from March to July.

### Swedes

Swedes are hardier and usually larger than turnips with a flavour that many prefer to turnips. The availability of varieties resistant to mildew is helping to increase the popularity of this vegetable.

Varieties that have done well in NIAB trials are:

**Marian** A high-yielding variety with good resistance to clubroot on most sites and to powdery mildew. It is globe-shaped with a purple skin and has attractive yellow flesh with a good flavour.

**Acme** Round roots with light purple skin. Small tops susceptible to powdery mildew.

## Sweet corn

Although still a marginal crop in the UK, the breeding of earlier-maturing $F_1$ hybrid varieties makes it possible for gardeners in the south and east of England to obtain reasonable success with 'corn on the cob'. The $F_1$ varieties recommended here should mature about 120–130 days from sowing.

A recent innovation in this crop has been the introduction of varieties with sweeter corn, called supersweets. Most of these varieties are less vigorous than normal varieties and should be sown later when soil conditions and the weather are warmer. They should not be grown alongside normal varieties as excess pollination reduces the sweetness.

The listed varieties have done well in trials done by the NIAB.

**Earliking** Early-maturing with about half of the cobs producing at least 15 cm. (6 in.) of grain.

**Earlibelle** Slightly later than Earliking and producing well-filled cobs.

**Candle; Sweet Nugget** Similar maturity to Earlibelle. Supersweet varieties with very long cobs which may not always fill to the tips, but cobs quite heavy.

**Sundance** Maturing later than Earlibelle. Broad cobs with 18–22 rows of grain. Tips often poorly filled.

**Sweet 77** Later maturing than Sundance. A supersweet variety with moderate yield of very large cobs. Vigour of early growth can be poor.

## Tomatoes, outdoor bush or dwarf

Most tomatoes are grown in greenhouses or under cloches and usually require staking, stopping by pinching-out the growing tip once three or four trusses have formed, and pinching-out of side-shoots. The breeding of bush, or determinate, varieties that require no staking or pinching, together with new methods for raising seedlings (see Chapter 8), has made possible the growing of true 'outdoor' tomatoes, particularly in the south. Although these determinate varieties require no stopping or staking, black plastic can be used to keep fruit off the ground and helps control weeds; straw bedding may help to spread disease.

Results from trials done by IHR show that good results should be obtained from the following varieties:

**Sleaford Abundance** An $F_1$ hybrid bush variety, with little leaf and a heavy crop of small- to medium-sized fruit of good quality, shape and flavour.

**Alfresco** A more vigorous, new $F_1$ hybrid bush variety from the breeder of Sleaford Abundance; about 7 days later maturing than Sleaford Abundance. Small fruits of good quality and flavour.

**Red Alert** Hybrid bush variety having small fruit of good quality and flavour.

**Gardener's Delight** Small fruits of excellent flavour.

**Sweet 100** Hybrid small-fruited variety similar to Gardener's Delight.

## Turnips

A fast-growing brassica crop, turnip roots are of many shapes, sizes and colours. The white-fleshed varieties are best used when young, otherwise they become hot and stringy.

The varieties listed are reported to have given good results over many years.

**Golden Ball** Small, yellow globe-shaped roots with yellow flesh. Fairly hardy, it also keeps well.

**Manchester Market** A green-topped, globe-shaped root with green skin and white flesh, with a mild flavour. Fairly hardy, it also keeps well.

**Purple Top Milan** A very early variety with flat roots with purple tops and white flesh.

**Snowball** A very early, white globe variety with mild-flavoured white flesh.

**Tokyo Cross** Hybrid producing small to medium, very uniform globe-shaped roots with white skin and flesh. May bolt if sown before June.

# 8 Planning continuity of supply

Most gardeners aim to produce a continuous supply of good quality vegetables for the kitchen for as long a period as possible, but even the expert has to put up with either gluts or shortages at times during the year. Of course with crops such as peas, beans, tomatoes, and beetroot, a glut of produce can be preserved by freezing, canning, bottling, or pickling, but not everyone is in a position to make use of surplus produce in this way. Furthermore, with salad crops such as lettuce even the practice of sowing seed every few days to maintain a succession can lead to two or three sowings being ready together. The surplus cannot easily be disposed of or preserved and often finds its way onto the compost heap. Successional sowings can have many pitfalls and the aim of producing a regular supply of fresh quality vegetables is far easier stated than achieved.

Problems of irregular supply can be directly attributable to the unpredictability of the weather. Its variability results in seeds germinating sooner, or later, than expected depending on the soil temperature and moisture content. The seeds may germinate but fail to push up through a hard 'cap' on the soil surface which may be brought about by heavy rain breaking down the soil crumbs and cementing the surface layer. Even when the seedlings have finally emerged, they may experience weather which is fine and warm, enabling the plants to grow very rapidly, or cold, dry and windy which will seriously check growth and retard development.

This unpredictability of the weather and its effects makes the faint-hearted accept fatalistically that nothing can be done to improve the situation. On the contrary, it will be shown that with a knowledge of the way in which weather factors such as temperature affect the growth and development of different vegetable plants (see Chapter 12), the effects of varying weather-conditions can be minimized considerably. The problems of getting predictable supplies of each of the common vegetable crops will then be discussed in some detail in relation to recent research results. Finally, proposals are given for sowing and planting programmes including the production of earlier and later crops by protection and other cultural methods, and for extending the season by storage. Detailed information on the storage of individual vegetable crops is given in Chapter 9.

The choice of crops, the proportion grown of each, and their season for harvesting are matters decided according to individual taste and opportunity (which will include the size and physical advantages and disadvantages of each vegetable plot). Similarly, the productivity of a plot measured in terms of the total weight of vegetables produced per unit area in a year will also depend to a large extent on the amount of time and effort put in by the individual gardener, and also the intensity of cropping practised through growing two or three different crops on the same piece of ground simultaneously, or in succession. These particular aspects will not be dealt with here as there are several sources of reliable information to guide the reader, such as that produced by the RHS in *The Vegetable Garden Displayed*. Rather, the aim of this chapter is to outline principles and the different ways in which supplies of vegetables can be maintained over long periods by minimizing as far as possible the unpredictable effects of the weather.

## Weather and the growth of vegetables

The growth of all plants is greatly affected by weather conditions and especially by temperature, sunshine, and rainfall. These three factors in particular will not only affect the *growth rate* of plants but consequently the yield and the time of maturity. In addition, temperature can influence the *development* of certain vegetable crops especially those whose buds, fruits or seeds are harvested.

Above a certain minimum temperature, which varies for different crops, seeds will germinate and seedlings and plants will grow rapidly if the temperature is, say, in the range of 18–24 °C (65–75 °F) providing moisture supplies are adequate. Under these conditions the plants will develop more or less normally and will produce *sooner or later* the root, shoot, leaf, bud, flower, pod, fruit or seed – whichever part of the plant we actually eat. 'Sooner or later' is the operative phrase, for it is not generally realized that to maximize the growth and development of a particular vegetable plant, the optimum conditions of temperature, radiation, and rainfall may change with the different phases of development. Obviously, problems can be caused if adverse weather conditions coincide with a particularly sensitive stage of growth.

For example, the seeds of butterhead varieties of lettuce will not germinate if the soil temperature exceeds 25 °C (77 °F) – a temperature which is frequently reached in the surface layers of soil during hot periods in summer. The seeds experiencing these temperatures become 'thermo-dormant' and will not germinate until the soil becomes cooler and even then only after some delay. So with this crop a planned successional sowing programme may fail because in spells of hot weather seed germination will not take place on time, even when the soil is moist, and gaps in the succession of crops will inevitably result. This problem has been discussed in some detail in Chapter 8 and readers will know that there are ways of overcoming it which will be briefly described again later.

In general, assuming that this difficulty of thermo-dormancy is overcome, with a vegetative crop such as lettuce where we are only interested in leaf growth, the higher the temperature the faster the leaves grow. As a rule, the growth rate of plants doubles with every 10 °C rise in temperature, hence the spurt in growth during warm periods in spring.

For many crops, however, the plants' response to the weather is not quite so straightforward, for special combinations of environmental conditions may be essential at particular stages of growth in order to 'switch' their pattern of growth to produce flowers, pods or bulbs (see Chapter 12). For example, the majority of cauliflower varieties require periods of relatively cool temperature below 21 °C (70 °F) to 'trigger off' the formation of the cauliflower curd. After the plants have passed through their early stage of puberty, when they are *developmentally* unreceptive to temperature, the accumulated effects of lower temperatures cause the plant to stop producing leaves and instead it initiates the curd. By a process of evolution, and more recently of breeding, we have evolved a series of cauliflower varieties each of which requires a different amount of exposure to relatively low temperatures before the plants will form curds. As a result the earliest varieties of summer cauliflowers, such as Montano, need little in the way of cold stimulus to form curds (and may frequently produce premature 'buttons'). Progressively later-maturing varieties require more and more exposure to low temperature and some of the winter-maturing group may require the equivalent of twelve weeks at a temperature less than 15 °C (60 °F).

So, depending on the prevailing temperatures during the growth of a crop, the curds of a variety will be formed earlier (if the weather is cooler) or later (if warmer) than average, and so the time the curd is ready for cutting will be affected in the same way. We will see later how the different 'cold' requirements of the various varieties can be used to advantage in ensuring continuity.

More information on the precise effects of weather factors on the growth and development of vegetables is given in Chapter 12, whilst the effects of rainfall and watering have been described in Chapter 4.

## How can planned production be made more reliable?

Whether we want to produce a reliable supply of a vegetable over as long a period as possible to supply the kitchen, or whether one particular crop has to be timed precisely for entry at a local show, the nature of the problem is the same: how can we minimize, or even eliminate, the unpredictable effects of weather, especially those of temperature on our crops' growth.

There are five main approaches we can adopt depending on the type of crop and the degree of reliability required; if necessary two or more can be combined in practice:

- by the use of average dates for sowing and planting,
- by taking into account prevailing temperatures in successional sowings,
- by sowing different varieties at the same time to obtain a succession,
- by modifying the environment around the plants, and
- by developing new ways of growing crops.

## Use average dates for sowing and planting

For certain vegetables calendar dates can be a useful guide for timing sowing or transplanting. Although weather conditions can be very different in, for example, the first week of April from year to year, the timing of the harvest of some crops is not critical, or, with others, can be very little altered by the time of sowing. For example the roots of crops such as carrot, parsnip or beetroot may get larger the longer they are left in the ground but do not, in general, deteriorate in quality. Within reason, therefore, sowings can be made at fairly wide intervals of time and the plants can be pulled as required. These crops can also be stored for long periods after growth has finished.

Other crops, such as certain varieties of cabbage, can remain in a mature state for up to two months without being harvested and without deterioration, whilst runner beans can provide a succession of beans from the same plant.

Yet other crops such as onion form bulbs and ripen predictably year after year because bulb formation and maturity are controlled almost entirely by the *length* of the day (see Chapter 12); small variations in the time of sowing may modify the bulb size rather than the time when it ripens. Furthermore, the bulbs can be stored for many months.

Thus with all these types of crop there are no great problems in maintaining supplies over long periods of time and there is not the same need to time sowings precisely to obtain continuity of supply.

With other crops such as lettuce, which have a short harvest period and do not keep, individual sowings are often made on predetermined dates to provide a succession. The gardener soon realizes from experience that the intervals between sowings need to be longer in the spring than in the summer. This is because as the average daily temperature rises throughout the spring to a maximum in mid-summer and then falls in the late summer and autumn (see Fig. 8.1), the time to produce a hearted lettuce will become progressively shorter with later sowings from April until June. Obviously, then, the intervals between sowings need to take this seasonal trend into account and unequal time intervals can be quite successful in regulating the time of cutting of successive crops.

## Make successive sowings dependent on prevailing temperatures

With crops such as peas and French beans a continuous supply of fresh produce can be obtained by making successional sowings

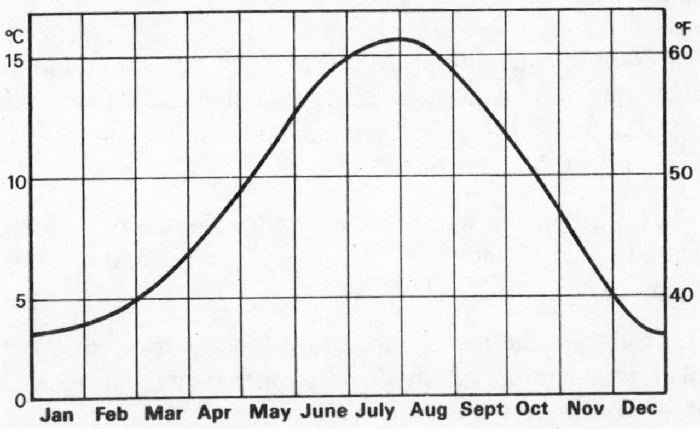


Fig. 8.1. Seasonal trend in mean daily temperature at Wellesbourne, Warwickshire averaged over the years 1952–79.

at intervals. The problem, as with that of lettuce just described, is to decide on the length of the intervals between sowings. If sowings are too frequent then crops from successive sowings may mature together; if the intervals are too long then there will be temporary periods of shortage. Fortunately, a system has been devised for processing crops such as peas.

The basis of the method is that, as plant growth rates are related to temperature, the intervals between successive sowings should be varied depending on the *actual* temperatures since the last sowing, rather than intervals based on average seasonal trends (see Fig. 8.1).

How can this be put into practice?

The unit of measurement used to combine the temperature with its duration is the 'day-degree', 1 day-degree being the equivalent of a rise of 1 °C (or 1 °F depending on the scale being used) from the base temperature for growth for a period of 24 hours. For most crops the assumption is made that plant growth will start when the temperature reaches 5.6 °C (42 °F), although for some crops such as French beans and sweet corn the minimum is 10 °C (50 °F), and for cucumbers as high as 14 °C (58 °F). Growth will then be proportional to the number of day-degrees accumulated over a period of time. The gardener can calculate these accumulated day-degrees approximately as follows:

(1) Record each day at 0900 GMT the maximum and minimum temperatures shown on a 'max and min' thermometer (Fig. 8.2); let us take as an example, a maximum temperature of 20 °C and a minimum of 6 °C.

(2) Calculate the average daily temperature by adding the maximum and minimum temperatures together and dividing by 2, thus $20+6=26\div2=13$.

(3) Subtract the base temperature for growth (5.6 °C). This will give the number of day-degrees for that day, in this example 7.4, to which growth is related. Running totals of accumulated day-degrees can then be recorded from any starting date using either a Celsius or Fahrenheit scale.

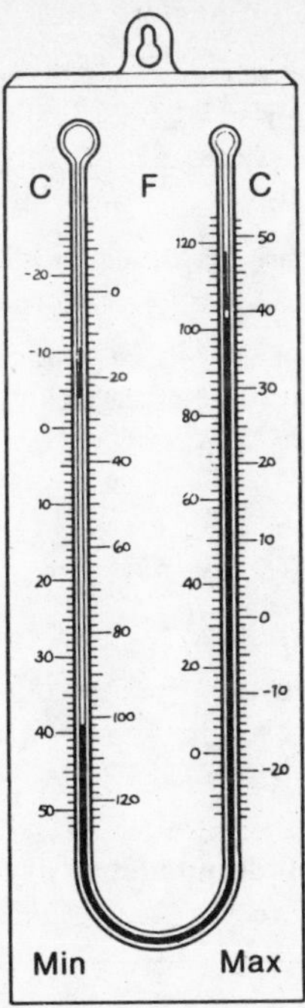


Fig. 8.2. Maximum–minimum thermometer suitable for garden use.

How can this method be used to plan a sequence of successional sowings of a crop? If we know the average number of accumulated day-degrees required for a given variety of vegetables to reach maturity from sowing, and if we also know the long-term seasonal trends of day-degrees for our particular site (see Table 8.1), we can predict fairly accurately when the crop from a particular sowing will be ready to pick. We then decide how rapidly we want our successional crops to follow each other in time of maturity. For example, we may want them to be ready at weekly intervals in July, which at Wellesbourne (Table 8.1) is equivalent to intervals of about 72 day-degrees C (130 day-degrees F). The individual sowings in May will then have to be separated by intervals of 72 (130) *actual* day-degrees accumulated

**Table 8.1(*a*)**

**Average weekly totals of accumulated day-degrees above 5.6 °C at Wellesbourne, Warwickshire**

| Week number | Jan. | Feb. | Mar. | Apr. | May | June | July | Aug. | Sept. | Oct. | Nov. | Dec. |
|---|---|---|---|---|---|---|---|---|---|---|---|---|
| 1 | 3 | 4 | 7 | 14 | 27 | 56 | 68 | 70 | 60 | 45 | 15 | 7 |
| 2 | 3 | 4 | 8 | 17 | 30 | 59 | 69 | 69 | 55 | 39 | 13 | 7 |
| 3 | 3 | 5 | 10 | 23 | 34 | 60 | 71 | 69 | 50 | 30 | 10 | 5 |
| 4 | 3 | 6 | 12 | 24 | 40 | 63 | 70 | 68 | 48 | 29 | 9 | 5 |
| 5 | 3 | 6 | | | 79 | | | 64 | | 23 | | |
| Totals | 15 | 25 | 37 | 78 | 210 | 238 | 278 | 340 | 213 | 166 | 47 | 24 |
| Running totals | 15 | 40 | 77 | 155 | 365 | 603 | 881 | 1221 | 1434 | 1600 | 1647 | 1671 |

**Table 8.1(*b*)**

**Average weekly totals of accumulated day-degrees above 42 °F at Wellesbourne, Warwickshire**

| Week number | Jan. | Feb. | Mar. | Apr. | May | June | July | Aug. | Sept. | Oct. | Nov. | Dec. |
|---|---|---|---|---|---|---|---|---|---|---|---|---|
| 1 | 6 | 7 | 12 | 26 | 48 | 101 | 122 | 127 | 109 | 81 | 28 | 13 |
| 2 | 6 | 7 | 15 | 30 | 54 | 106 | 124 | 125 | 100 | 71 | 23 | 13 |
| 3 | 6 | 8 | 18 | 41 | 62 | 109 | 128 | 125 | 90 | 54 | 19 | 10 |
| 4 | 6 | 10 | 21 | 44 | 72 | 114 | 126 | 122 | 87 | 52 | 16 | 10 |
| 5 | | 10 | | | 79 | | | 115 | | 42 | | |
| Totals | 24 | 42 | 66 | 141 | 315 | 430 | 500 | 614 | 386 | 300 | 86 | 46 |
| Running totals | 24 | 66 | 132 | 273 | 588 | 1018 | 1518 | 2132 | 2518 | 2818 | 2904 | 2950 |

from the previous sowing, rather than by a number of days. In this way we take into account the seasonal trends and vagaries of the weather and a more reliable succession of crops can be obtained.

At present this method is successfully used for programming commercial production of peas, French beans, sweet corn and outdoor tomatoes, and experimentally for predicting the harvest times of lettuce, carrot and mini-cauliflower. Because the necessary information is not yet available it cannot, at present, be used for other vegetable crops. However, the enterprising gardener is recommended to experiment with the method on a range of crops in order to collect quantitative information for his site which will become increasingly valuable to him when planning his vegetable programme in future years.

## Use different varieties

For some vegetables a simple method of getting a continuous succession of produce is to grow a number of varieties which take different lengths of time to reach maturity from the same sowing date. We have already seen that different cauliflower varieties have different 'cold' requirements before curds are formed, and this affects the times when the heads are ready for cutting. Different varieties of other vegetables also respond differently, but consistently, *relative to each other*, to various aspects of the weather, such as temperature thresholds for cold tolerance in beans and day-length effects on bulbing in onions.

The subject has important implications for planning continuity of production. For example, if a number of varieties which take different lengths of time to mature are taken of, say, Brussels sprouts, French beans, cauliflower, and onion and are sown on a single date over a number of years, the varieties of each crop will always mature in the same relative order despite the different weather conditions in each year. The relative order of maturity of varieties used for commercial production has been shown to be so consistent by the NIAB in their official trials (see Chapter 7) that leaflets specify the average order of earliness (or lateness) in numbers of days of the best varieties of the major vegetable crops.

Many of the garden varieties, however, have not been included in this type of trial because they do not have the necessary characteristics essential for today's commercial production systems. Thus, there may only be a more general type of information on the relative maturity of such varieties obtainable from seedsmen and their catalogues. However, for the gardener, general descriptions of 'early' or 'mid-season' could be sufficiently precise as there is often sufficient variability between individual plants of the same variety to supply the kitchen until the next variety is ready.

So depending on the type of crop and the length of the period over which fresh produce is wanted, as few as 2 or 3, or as many as 6–10 different varieties may be needed in order to ensure continuity. Here, perhaps, lies the main disadvantage of this method for the gardener – the cost of buying more packets of seed than normal. But unused seeds can be stored from one year to the next under the correct conditions (see Chapter 2), or fewer varieties can be grown with more times of sowing.

This general approach of using varieties to provide continuity has a lot to commend it, not the least being the simplicity of putting it into practice. It also has the advantage that it is easier to choose the time when seedbed conditions are ideal for sowing because the timing of seed sowing is not so critical as with some of the other methods previously described.

### Modify the plants' environment

When the various aspects of the environment are precisely controlled in air-conditioned glasshouses, 'growing-rooms' and cabinets for experimental purposes, the growth, development and time of maturity of vegetable plants can be predicted with complete accuracy. Obviously this is not a practical solution for the outdoor vegetable gardener, but it does show that the more we can minimize adverse effects of the weather the earlier and more predictable the maturity of our crops will be.

The main problem to overcome, both in the early spring and for extending the season in the autumn, is that of low temperatures which reduce growth and may even kill plants if they are at sensitive stages of growth. Drought conditions or exposed areas are more easily remedied by watering or providing shelter.

The adverse effects of low temperature on crops can be minimized in several ways: directly, by covering the seeds or plants with cloches, polytunnels, various mulches, or even with newspapers, for different lengths of time; or, indirectly, by raising plants in greenhouses or frames before planting them out into the open later in the season when the effects of cold spells are not so severe.

Glass cloches of the traditional 'bell', 'barn', or 'tent' type have been used for many years to produce early or late crops of vegetables by providing a warmer environment with protection from wind, storms, and frost. In recent years new materials have tended to replace glass in the traditional cloche, and tunnels made of clear thin polythene supported by wire hoops are a more recent cheap alternative method of protecting crops. Both soil and air temperatures are warmer under cloches and tunnels because the loss of radiant heat from the soil is reduced. If crops such as lettuce are grown throughout their life under such forms of protection they can be ready for cutting up to 3–4 weeks earlier. However crops such as beans, peas, and tomatoes are only started under cloches and tunnels to get earlier germination and plant establishment, which usually results in earlier maturity. Other crops can be protected in the autumn to hasten ripening, or extend the season of production.

Mulches laid over the soil surface can hasten seed germination and early seedling growth by making the soil warmer. Again in recent years traditional materials such as straw, leaves and peat are being replaced by different forms such as paper, paper bonded with polythene, and other forms of polythene sheet. Clear or black polythene is preferred commercially. Rapid developments are taking place commercially on mulches; biodegradable polythene is now available with varying lengths of life, whilst a slitted polythene sheet which is laid down as a mulch is forced up by the growing plants to form a tunnel partially ventilated through the slits or holes in the polythene.

The most important way of modifying the effects of the

weather on plant growth and development is, of course, to raise plants for the first few weeks of their life under good conditions in greenhouses and frames before transplanting them into the garden. The advantages of this method compared with sowing seeds directly in the garden may be summarized as follows: it allows earlier crops to be produced; it enables crops such as sweet corn and tomatoes to be grown more reliably in our short summer season; it provides better conditions for young plants in the early stages of growth which are often critical if good crops are to be obtained; it enables more crops to be grown because the plants occupy the ground for a shorter period of time; and, not the least of the advantages, raising plants under better conditions usually results in more plants being raised from a given quantity of seed. Nearly all of the brassicas are better transplanted into the garden as well as salad crops such as lettuce, bulb onions, and leeks, and the plants can be raised in different types of pots, peat or soil blocks, tubes, or boxes. Plants grown individually in containers or blocks establish themselves after transplanting much quicker than those bare-root transplants which have had to be separated from each other before planting; there is, therefore, less check to growth and earlier crops are obtained from them. In general the younger the plants are transplanted the quicker they become established and the better are the resulting crops, provided they have been hardened off and provided also that the soil and weather conditions in the garden are reasonable. This subject of transplanting and plant raising has been dealt with in detail in Chapter 2.

### Use other cultural methods

All of the common cultural practices used in the garden will affect the way a crop grows and the time it is ready to harvest. However, there are specific cultural methods which can help to produce earlier or later crops of some of our common vegetables, as a few examples will show.

Early crops of broad beans, cauliflower, and salad and bulb onions can be regularly obtained, but not guaranteed, by making autumn sowings of certain varieties which will usually overwinter in an average year without too many losses. The plants have to reach a certain size by late autumn otherwise they will not survive the winter weather and therefore the sowing time for these crops is critical. Detailed information will be found later in this chapter under each crop.

With crops such as parsnip and parsley which are sown directly into soil in the early spring, and take several weeks before seed germination and the seedling emerges, pre-germination of the seed by sowing under optimum conditions in sandwich boxes indoors (see Chapter 2) before fluid-sowing in the garden in March, can give 2–3 weeks earlier seedling emergence and much earlier crops.

With certain crops, 'stopping' of the plant by pinching-out the growing point will encourage earlier development of the upper 'buttons' of Brussels sprouts, of pods on beans, and fruit on tomatoes, whilst removing the leaves shading the fruit trusses of tomatoes will hasten the ripening of the fruit if the weather is warm and sunny.

In a somewhat similar way the use of transplants in brassica crops such as cauliflower provides a means of regulating the supply of mature cauliflower curds. If, from one sowing in an outdoor seedbed, a few plants are lifted at weekly intervals from, say, 4–9 weeks old from sowing, a succession of mature heads can be produced for the kitchen, the older transplants maturing later than those planted earlier.

Some of the more recently developed systems of crop production have considerably modified the maturity characteristics and season of production of vegetables. For example, overwintered crops of bulb onions have been grown for many decades in this country, but with the varieties used even the earliest crops were not obtained until late July. With the introduction of the winter-hardy, intermediate day-length, bolting-resistant Japanese varieties, mature bulbs can be lifted at the end of May, six weeks earlier than even set-raised crops (see Chapter 12, p. 380). A very different example is the 'new' leaf lettuce, so called because the plants are grown so closely spaced that they do not produce a heart. The leaves are ready for harvest much earlier than the conventionally grown hearted crop and the equivalent of four or five normal-hearted lettuce per week from mid-May to mid-October can be obtained from as little as 4–5 square metres (5–6 square yards) of garden using a single variety.

On the other hand, when plants of certain varieties of cauliflower are grown closely spaced they produce small curds or 'mini-cauliflowers' which tend to mature all together and are ideal for home-freezing. The maturity time of these varieties, when grown in this way, is predictable throughout the season from July until October to within three or four days and so, if required, a daily supply of mini-cauliflowers can be reliably planned (see Fig. 8.3).

## The role of storage to extend the season of supply

Having done all that can be done to produce vegetables fresh from the garden for as long as possible, we are still able to extend the season of supply to a greater or lesser extent by various methods of storage. These range from the simple, such as putting lettuce heads into plastic bags before placing them in a refrigerator or other cool place to keep for a few hours or days, to the equally straightforward but rather more time-consuming methods used to prepare crops such as onions and beetroot for storing up to 6–8 months. The various alternative methods which can be adopted for the major vegetable crops are described in Chapter 9.

## Planning for individual crops

The following suggested schemes for planning continuity of supply should only be regarded as guidelines, for each family will have its own preferences and each garden will have its own microclimate resulting from the combined influences of location, aspect, soil, shelter and rainfall. Furthermore, sowing and planting dates must necessarily vary in different parts of the country, and common sense will dictate when adjustments will have to be made. Nevertheless, they will provide a basis on which to develop your own system for planning the timings of each crop. If detailed records are kept in a gardening diary you will find that they will be a great help in perfecting your programme in future years.

## Broad bean

This is usually regarded as a short-season crop but beans can be produced in succession from the end of May until October. The pods must be picked young (before the scar on the bean turns black) if tender beans with the best flavour are wanted. The beans will not 'hold' on the plant without becoming tough, neither can they be stored fresh for any length of time. This means that a succession of crops needs to be grown if the picking period is to last more than 2–3 weeks. Fortunately, this is easily achieved by sowing a number of different varieties, or a single variety, on a number of occasions, as outlined in Table 8.2. The timings of the sowings at 2–3 week intervals are not critical and do not warrant the use of the day-degree method; they will depend more on the suitability of soil conditions for sowing. The results from unprotected sowings in the autumn are not completely predictable.

## French bean

The flavour of the runner bean is usually preferred to that of the French bean if there is a choice, and as a consequence French beans are often grown only for the early crops before runner beans are ready. The very earliest crops to be picked in June are grown throughout in a warm greenhouse. However, by successional sowings at monthly intervals from March or early April to mid-July, French beans can be picked from the garden continuously from late June until October (see Table 8.2). A minimum soil temperature of 10 °C (50 °F) is required before the seed of this crop will germinate. So, for the earliest outdoor crops seed should be sown in pots or blocks and the plants planted out in

**Table 8.2**

**Sowing sequences for broad, French and runner beans**

| Method of growing | Varieties | Harvest period |
|---|---|---|
| **Broad bean** | | |
| *Sequence A* | | |
| (1) Sow outside in autumn late Oct.–Nov. | Aquadulce | early June–July |
| (2) Sow under cloches Jan.–March (or in frames and transplant in April) | Longpod type e.g. Exhibition Longpod | late May–June |
| (3) Sow outdoors at 2–3 week intervals March–May | Longpod followed by Windsor varieties | late June–September |
| *or Sequence B* | | |
| Sow a single variety successionally as above until July. Autumn sowings should be made under cloches | The Sutton (a dwarf variety) | late May–late September |
| **French bean** | | |
| (1a) Sow under glass mid-April, harden off and plant early June | The Prince Tendergreen | late June–July |
| *or* | | |
| (1b) Sow under cloches mid-April and protect until June | The Prince Tendergreen | early July–August |
| (2) Sow outdoors mid-May and mid-June | Glamis Loch Ness Tendergreen | late July–September |
| (3) Sow outdoors mid-July and cover plants with cloches September | The Prince | mid-September–October |

**Table 8.2** (*cont.*)

| Method of growing | Varieties | Harvest period |
|---|---|---|
| **Runner bean** | | |
| (1a) Sow under glass mid-April, harden off and plant early June. Pinch out growing point | Kelvedon Marvel | end June onwards |
| *or* | | |
| (1b) Sow under cloches late April and protect until June | Pickwick | early July onwards |
| (2) Sow outdoors end of May | Achievement<br>Enorma<br>Prizewinner<br>Streamline | early August–October |
| (3) A late sowing in June in mild areas | as (2) | September onwards |

early June after being hardened off. Alternatively, seeds are sown under cloches in March or early April and the plants protected until the risk of frost is passed. Unprotected crops are sown from mid-May until mid-July, but for the latest sowing the plants will need to be covered with cloches when the first frosts are forecast in September or October.

All beans should be picked when young to encourage more to form and to prevent them from becoming tough and stringy. Many of the newer varieties such as Loch Ness and Tendergreen are stringless and pencil-podded, and are excellent for freezing.

### Runner bean

By making two or three sowings, runner beans can be produced from the end of June until the first frosts kill the plants in the autumn. Many gardeners, however, do not try to get very early crops but make just one sowing of a single variety in the open ground in the latter half of May for picking from early August until September or October. Earlier crops can be obtained by mulching with a clear polythene sheet. Experiments have shown that the mulch can raise the soil temperature by 3 °C which has resulted in earlier seedling emergence, flowering, and up to two weeks earlier picking.

Earlier crops can be obtained by sowing dwarf varieties such as Pickwick in late April under cloches or tunnels protecting the plants until mid-June; they will then produce beans in early July. Even earlier crops can be produced by sowing suitable early-flowering varieties into pots of compost in April for raising under glass. These plants must be gradually hardened off before planting out in early June, and the growing points should be pinched out to encourage early flowering and fruiting. It should be remembered that these plants may need to be protected even after planting out if frost is forecast, because runner beans are very susceptible to cold and young plants will be killed by even a slight frost.

Plants from the main sowings will continue to produce flowers over a long period and these will set normally provided all the pods are picked young. Pods should never be allowed to mature on the plants (unless you are saving seed) and a plentiful supply of water should be given to the roots after flowering has started. Experimental work has shown conclusively that syringing of the plants with water does not improve pod-set and is a waste of time.

If as long a picking period as possible is needed, the sowing or planting sequence in Table 8.2 should be followed, making due allowance for the earliness of your own district. The beans cannot be stored fresh for any length of time but can be frozen or salted to extend the season.

### Beetroot

It is not difficult to produce a continuous supply of beetroot from early June until November but the aim should be to get a succession of young tender roots by sequential sowings of globe varieties, the timings of which are not critical. The earliest crops of small beet are obtained from sowing bolting-resistant varieties such as Boltardy or Avonearly under cloches in March; transplanting of beetroot plants is not recommended unless the seedlings are raised in a container or blocks and planted when small. These crops can be followed by sowing the same varieties outside in late March or early April. Later sowings can be made at monthly intervals until July, growing these and other globe varieties or the long-rooted Cheltenham Greentop. For a late autumn crop, Detroit Little Ball is reported to be good for the last sowing in July in mild areas.

To produce beetroot for storage, globe varieties or Cheltenham Greentop are sown in late May or June and lifted in October.

### Broccoli, sprouting

From a single sowing of three or four varieties, sprouting broccoli can be picked from January until May in most years. The single sowing is made in a seedbed outdoors between mid-April and mid-May and the plants are transplanted in June or July. If the young shoots are picked every few days when young and tender the plants will re-sprout and continue to produce for 6–8 weeks. The period of picking can be extended by growing as well as the variety purple-sprouting, early and late selections of it. The later-maturing selections are very hardy and will survive most winters. There are also white sprouting forms for cutting during March and April. The green type, known as calabrese, is discussed on page 267.

### Brussels sprouts

Many new varieties have been introduced in recent years and it is now possible to produce sprouts from August until late March. This crop is a good example of continuity of production being achieved over a six-month period from October to March from a single sowing by a suitable choice of varieties, and five such varieties listed by the NIAB and available for use by gardeners are given in Table 8.3. The single sowing is made between

**Table 8.3**

**Sowing and varietal sequence for Brussels sprouts**

| Method of growing | Varieties | Harvest period |
|---|---|---|
| (1) Sow in cold frames in late Feb. and transplant late April or early May | Peer Gynt* | August–September |
| (2) Sow under cloches or in frames mid-March to mid-April and transplant mid-May to early June | Peer Gynt | September–October |
| | Roger | October–November |
| | Citadel or Widgeon | November–December |
| | Rampart | December–January |
| | Fortress | January–March |

* 'stop' plants for early August picking (see below).

mid-March and mid-April under cloches, in cold frames, or in a sheltered site in the garden, and the plants are transplanted in mid-May to early June at a close spacing of 61 cm. (24 in.) square.

When very early crops are wanted in August and September an early variety such as Peer Gynt is sown under cold glass in late February or early March, and the plants transplanted in late April or early May.

It is possible to obtain continuity from October until early March by growing just one early and one late variety which hold their sprouts on the stem in good condition over a long period of time. Suitable varieties are Mallard or Roger for picking before Christmas and Rampart for later production.

The buttons develop from the base of the stem upwards and are picked over several times when they have reached the required size. The removal of the growing point of the stem, 'stopping', will hasten the growth of the sprouts making them ready for picking earlier than from unstopped plants, but will restrict the length of the picking season. Stopping is best done when the lowest sprouts on the stem are at, or approaching, 12 mm. (½ in.) in size. This practice is only useful for early cropping, for it has little effect if it is done after the beginning of October. Apart from making the sprouts ready earlier, it tends to make all the buttons up the stem more uniform in size which may be an advantage if they are all to be picked at one time for home-freezing.

### Cabbage

By a combination of suitable varieties and sowing dates it is possible to cut cabbages throughout the year. Some of the recently introduced varieties remain in good condition for 2–3 months after they are ready for cutting and this helps to maintain continuity of supply. There are pointed-, round-, and drum-head types, and all are easy to grow. Sowing times and varieties can be conveniently grouped according to the season of production and a summarized continuity programme is given in Table 8.4.

For information on Chinese cabbage see p. 272.

*Spring cabbage.* A single sowing is made in late July or early August directly into the ground in which the plants will mature, or in a seedbed for transplanting in September. The plants are grown closely together in the row if they are for cutting as unhearted greens. The varieties used must be resistant to bolting, and suitable ones for April cutting are Durham Early and Avon Crest. If a wider spacing is used to allow the plants to heart, the varieties Harbinger and Avon Crest mature in May.

*Early summer cabbage.* By sowing into pots or blocks in late February in heat, plants can be transplanted in mid-April and pointed-headed varieties such as Hispi will be ready for cutting in mid-June. Round-headed varieties such as Marner Allfruh mature about a week later, approximately seventy days after transplanting.

*Summer cabbage.* For cutting in late July until September, seed of varieties such as Stonehead and Minicole are sown under cloches or in cold frames from mid- to late March, and the plants put into the garden in late May at a close spacing of 30×30 cm. (12×12 in.) Minicole especially will stand for up to three months after it is ready without serious deterioration.

**Table 8.4**
**Sowing and varietal sequence for all-the-year cabbage production**

| Method of growing | Varieties | Harvest period |
|---|---|---|
| (1) Sow directly into ground late July *or* seedbed and transplant in Sept. | Durham Early, Avon Crest, Offenham selections | March–May |
| (2) Sow in heat in late Feb. in blocks or pots, transplant in mid-April | Hispi<br>Marner Allfruh | May–June |
| (3) Sow in cold frames in late March and transplant late May | Hispi, Marner Allfruh, Stonehead, and Minicole (in order of maturity) | July–September |
| (4) Sow outside early May and transplant June | Hawke | September–November |
| (5) Sow outside late April and transplant early June | Hidena<br>Jupiter | November–December |
| (6) Sow outside mid-May and transplant end June | Tundra, Celtic | December–February |

*Autumn cabbage.* When sown in early May and transplanted in mid-June, varieties such as Hawke will mature in September and will stand up to two months after the heads are mature. For November–December cutting varieties of the winter white type such as Hidena or Jupiter are sown outside in late April. This type can be harvested for storage in November.

*Winter cabbage.* For December to February cutting, varieties such as Celtic and Tundra which mature in succession are sown outside in mid-May and transplanted at the end of June.

When the ground is not immediately required for other crops

the cabbage stumps can be cross-cut with a knife after harvesting to encourage a second crop of small heads to grow.

### Calabrese (or green-sprouting broccoli)

Heads of this increasingly popular vegetable can be obtained from July until October by the use of a number of varieties and sowings. In general the best spears are produced on plants which have been sown where they will mature, but plants can be raised in a seedbed if care is taken to minimize the check to growth after transplanting.

The earliest sowings can be made in late March or early April with an early-maturing variety such as Green Comet. Further sowings can be made at 3–4 week intervals until early June using a single variety such as Green Comet, Mercedes, or Corvet. All four of these varieties can also be sown together as they mature in succession from a single sowing over a period of several weeks. The terminal spear should be cut before the flower buds start to break open; the smaller lateral spears will then develop and will help to provide a succession of pickings until the first frosts.

### Carrots

Carrots can be pulled from the end of May until November and, indeed, throughout the winter if the rows are protected from frost. To produce roots over this long period, a minimum of three sowings is required using different varieties. For the earliest crops a sowing of an early variety such as a selection of Amsterdam Forcing or Early Nantes is made in cold frames or under cloches in January to late February, and the largest of the young roots can be selectively pulled from mid-May until July. A sowing should then be made in the open in April of an Amsterdam type such as Amstel, or one of the selections of Chantenay Red-Cored to produce roots from August until November. For late crops maturing in November and December, and for storage, an Autumn King type such as Vita Longa can be sown in May. The roots of this type are somewhat more frost-hardy than those of the Chantenay type. However, both can be stored if they are protected against frost.

Many gardeners, however, prefer to sow frequently to ensure a constant succession of young plants. To achieve this, sowings of the varieties mentioned can be made at 3–4 week intervals until mid-July. If cloches are available, a final sowing can be made in August and the plants covered in September or October in order to produce young roots in November and December. For the later sowings an early-maturing variety such as Early Nantes should be grown.

## Cauliflower

Except for the mid-winter period cauliflowers can be cut throughout the year in most parts of the country, and sowing times and varieties can be conveniently grouped according to the season of production. A summarized continuity programme is given in Table 8.5.

*Early summer.* For cutting in June and July varieties such as Alpha-Paloma and Montano are sown in cold frames in the first week of October for transplanting as early as conditions will allow in March. Slightly earlier maturity will be obtained if the plants are raised in peat blocks or pots. They will be closely followed by plants raised in a seedbed and transplanted at the same time. An alternative method, if a heated glasshouse is available, is to sow the same varieties in mid-January, the plants being hardened off before planting in March or early April.

*Late summer.* For harvesting mid-July to mid-August a sowing should be made in March under cold glass, the plants being transplanted in the middle of May.

*Early autumn.* Plants from a late April or early May sowing and transplanted in mid-June will be ready for cutting in late August and September.

*Late autumn.* Sown in mid-May and transplanted in late June or early July, varieties of the Australian and Flora Blanca types will

**Table 8.5**
**Sowing and varietal sequence for cauliflowers**

| Method of growing | Varieties | Harvest period |
|---|---|---|
| (1*a*) Sow in cold frame early Oct. and transplant March *or* (1*b*) Sow in heat mid-Jan., harden off and transplant in March | Montano, Alpha-Paloma, White Summer, Dominant (in order of maturity) | mid-June to mid-July |
| (2) Sow under cold glass in March and transplant | Nevada<br>Dok Elgon | mid-July to mid-August |
| (3) Sow in late April and transplant mid-June | Nevada<br>Dok Elgon | late August and September |
| (4) Sow in mid-May and transplant early July | Wallaby<br>Canberra<br>Barrier Reef | September–October<br>October<br>October–November |
| (5) Sow early May and transplant late July (for SW coastal regions only) | Roscoffs | late December |
| (6) Sow in late May and transplant late July (regions other than SW) | Asmer Snowcap March, Walcheren<br>Winter-Armado April, Walcheren<br>Winter-Markanta, Walcheren<br>Winter-Birchington, Vilna | March<br>April<br>late April<br>late April–May<br>late May–June |

mature from September to November if the late autumn weather is not too severe.

*Winter.* Varieties of the Roscoff type can be grown for the November to April heading period *only* in mild coastal areas of the South West. They should not be grown elsewhere. One sowing is made outdoors in early May and transplanting is done in late July.

*Late winter–spring.* For areas other than the South West, varieties of the Walcheren-Winter type can be sown in late May or early June and the plants transplanted in July. Different varieties will mature from March to early June (see Table 8.5).

## Mini-Cauliflower

Mini-cauliflower curds are high quality, complete, mature curds deliberately induced to be small (4–9 cm. (1½–3½ in.) in diameter) by growing certain varieties at very close spacing. Early summer varieties of the Alpha, Danish and Snowball types have given excellent results when grown at spacings of 15×15 cm. (6×6 in.) in a square arrangement (to reduce the edge effect where the plants on the outside, with more space, grow much larger). Either a single or a number of varieties will be ready for cutting in a very predictable time under this form of production and continuity can be obtained by making successional sowings. As the time taken to reach maturity varies with the seasonal trend in temperature, this factor must be taken into account if continuous production throughout the summer is planned. This is illustrated in Fig. 8.3 which can be used as a guide to predict the approximate time of cutting mini-cauliflowers using the variety Alpha sown on different dates. With this variety the earliest crops can be cut in the first week of July and continuity can be achieved with sufficient sowings until October. Plants from each sowing will mature very uniformly, and so several sowings will be needed to maintain supplies over any length of time.

Because of their size, mini-cauliflowers are excellent for freezing whole.

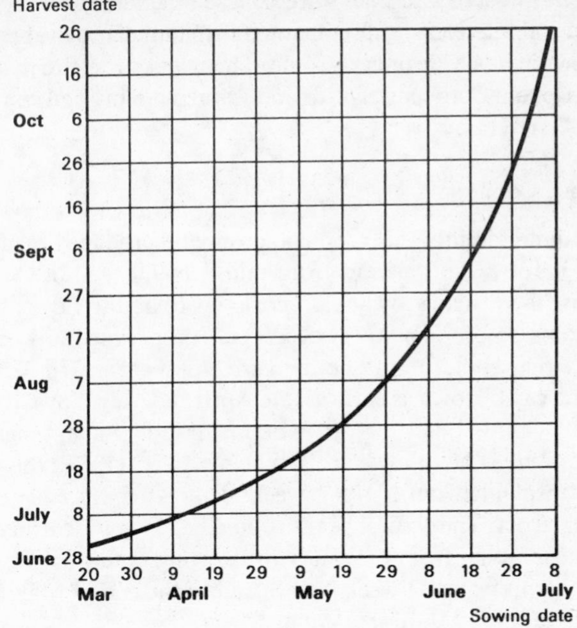


Fig. 8.3. Guide for sowing and harvesting dates for mini-cauliflower.

## Celery

Self-blanching varieties of celery such as Celebrity or Lathom Self-Blanching are grown for use from mid-July until October. The seed is sown in March or early April on the surface of compost under heated glass. After pricking-off into trays, pots or blocks the plants are hardened off and transplanted from early May to early June. If heated glass is not available, cloches can be used for raising plants which are transplanted in early June, but they will mature later than those raised in heat. Celery of the American Green type can also be grown in the same way.

To supply the period from October until February the trench types must be grown. White, pink and red varieties are available, for example, Giant White, Giant Pink, and Giant Red, the latter being the most hardy. Plants are raised in the same way as for the self-blanching celery, before being transplanted into the prepared trenches in late May or early June. The celery sticks are ready for digging from October onwards and will remain in good condition for 2–3 months.

### Chinese Cabbage

Until quite recently this crop could only be produced reliably in the UK for a short period from mid-September until October, because the varieties available were likely to bolt to flower if seed was sown before June. However, recent experimental work has shown that some of the newer varieties such as Tip Top and Kasumi can be sown as early as late April and May. Sown directly into blocks or pots in a greenhouse or polytunnel where the temperature is not allowed to fall below 10 °C (50 °F) the plants are transplanted outside 2–3 weeks later after they have been hardened off. The earliest heads should be ready for cutting from the end of June from the late April sowing, and if sowings are made in this way at 2-week intervals until the end of May, heads will be produced until late August.

Sowings can be made outside *in situ* from mid-June until mid-August and heads will be ready from September onwards. It is advisable to sow very small areas at 10-day intervals because the plants quickly bolt after they are ready for cutting. Two suitable varieties for this season of production are Jade Pagoda and Mei Quing Choi which take from 9 to 12 weeks to reach maturity, depending on the weather conditions.

The heads of Chinese cabbage will keep for several weeks in a refrigerator, but they are not frost-tolerant like normal cabbage.

### Leek

This crop, which can survive even the coldest of winters, is grown mainly for use from November until March and April. However, crops can be produced as early as September if required by sowing an early variety such as King Richard, either in heat under glass in February, or under cloches or in a cold frame in February if weather conditions permit. These plants should be transplanted in April or early May.

Maincrop sowings are made outdoors in March, or under cold glass if soil conditions are not fit, and transplanting should be done by June. Varieties for November to March maturity include the newer ones such as Autumn Mammoth-Argenta and old favourites such as The Lyon for late autumn production. For use from Christmas to March or April, Musselburgh is still one of the hardiest of leeks, while newer varieties such as Swiss Giant–Albinstar stand well until the late spring. For very late lifting in April and May Blauwgroene Winter–Alaska is one of several newer varieties which are suitable.

The largest transplants are normally ready for harvesting first, so if the transplants are planted in order of size along the rows the mature leeks can be lifted from one end of the row or bed, keeping the later-maturing plants in a tidy and small area.

### Lettuce

It is difficult to achieve continuity of production of hearted lettuce from spring to autumn without having gluts and temporary shortages. A number of successional sowings must be made as varieties do not differ sufficiently in their cutting time to help maintain continuity. Gluts occur when two sowings are ready at the same time or when too much seed has been sown, shortages occur when sowings have not been made sufficiently frequently or when the emergence of seedlings from a sowing has been delayed because of drought or high soil temperatures (see p. 246).

To minimize these disruptive effects on continuity every effort should be made to get the seedlings of each sowing to emerge quickly and reliably, and to time the successional sowings to allow for the prevailing weather conditions. To ensure quick emergence of this crop, water the bottom of the seed drill *before* sowing, and if the weather is hot, shade the soil and sow in the early afternoon. Alternatively, the seed can be pre-germinated and fluid-sown. Plants can also be raised in peat blocks or in pots and transplanted. All of these different techniques have been described in Chapter 2.

Although a lot of experimental work has been done to improve the timings of sowings for commercial lettuce production, a simple system is recommended for the garden: make sowings in succession when seedlings of the previous sowing have just emerged, take precautions to reduce high soil temperature effects, and do not sow too much seed at any one time. This method will allow for the effects of prevailing weather and soil conditions on germination and emergence of the seedlings which are major causes of gluts and shortages. Sowing at fixed time intervals such as 7–10 days does not allow for the vagaries of the weather and causes the problems of over- and under-supply.

The earliest crops are produced in late May and early June from plants raised under glass and transplanted at the end of March or early April under cloches or into the open ground. Continuity is then maintained throughout the summer and early autumn by sowing at intervals from March to July as described above. Among varieties suitable for successional sowing over this period are Avondefiance and Dolly (butterhead type), Little Gem and Lobjoits (cos), and Avoncrisp and Saladin (crisphead). A general indication of the harvest dates of butterhead varieties from different sowing dates is given in Fig. 8.4. In sheltered positions or when cloches are available, sowings are made in late August of varieties such as Valdor or Winter Density which will be ready in late May. Plants from a further sowing made under cloches or cold frames in October are transplanted in February or March under cold glass for early May cutting. The sowing programme is summarized in Table 8.6.

### Leaf lettuce

If lettuce *hearts* are not necessarily wanted throughout the summer, growing unhearted plants should be tried because it is very easy to get a continuous supply of lettuce leaves. The term 'leaf lettuce' is generally used to describe lettuce of the Salad Bowl type where the leaves can be picked as required, but a supply of

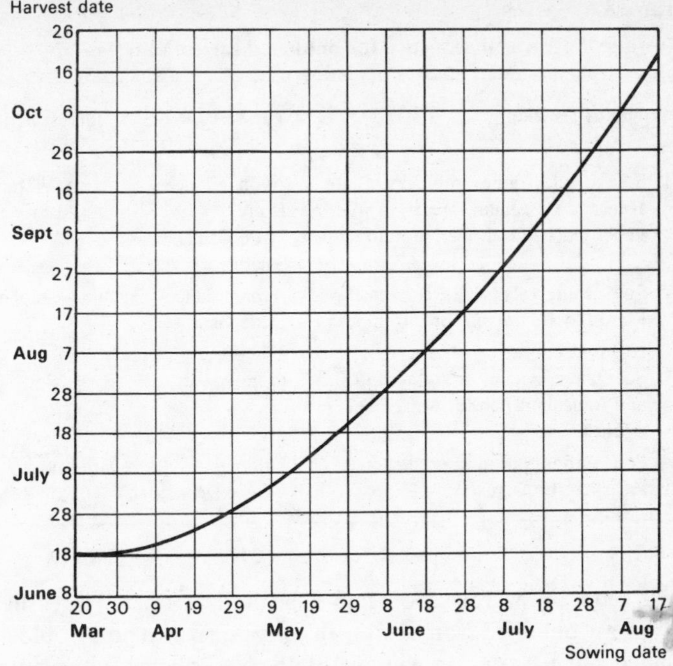


Fig. 8.4. Guide for sowing and harvesting dates for hearted butterhead lettuce. Crisphead varieties will be up to three weeks later maturing.

leaves can be obtained from many cos varieties by growing them at very close spacing so that they cannot produce hearts.

The equivalent of four or five normal-hearted lettuce per week from May to mid-October can be obtained from sowing an area of less than one square yard on each of ten dates. After cutting, the stumps will regrow to produce a second crop of leaves. Full details of sowing dates and of this system of growing lettuce leaves have been given in Chapter 1.

## Marrows and courgettes

Marrow plants produce a succession of fruit provided they are picked regularly, and only two sowings are needed to supply

**Table 8.6**

**Sowing and varietal sequence for outdoor hearted lettuce**

| Method of growing | Varieties | Harvest period |
|---|---|---|
| (1) Sow in cold frames in blocks in late Feb. and transplant in early April under cloches and open ground | Avondefiance<br>Dolly<br>Little Gem<br>Saladin | late May-June |
| (2) Sow at intervals (see text) from March to July *in situ* or into blocks and transplant | Avondefiance<br>Little Gem<br>Saladin | June–October |
| (3) Sow under cloches or frames in Oct. and transplant Feb. or March under cloches | Premier | early May |
| (4) Sow outdoors in mild or sheltered areas in late August | Valdor<br>Winter Density | late May |

courgettes or marrows from mid-June until October. The earliest crops are obtained from sowing in early April into pots or blocks under cold glass or on a windowsill, the plants being transplanted under cloches in late April or early May after hardening off. A second sowing is made from mid- to late April for planting in early June. The bush types produce fruit 2–3 weeks earlier than the trailing type and should be used for early crops. For courgette production, where the fruit are picked small and immature, varieties such as Ambassador and Early Gem are suitable.

## Onions

With the recent introduction of the early maturing, intermediate day-length varieties (see Chapter 12) it is now possible for the gardener to produce bulb onions from early June to October and to have them available throughout the year with storage. The crop can be produced from seed sown directly in the garden, from transplants, or from sets (see Table 8.7).

The earliest crops to mature from late May onwards are grown

**Table 8.7**

**Sowing and varietal sequence for bulb onion continuity**

| Method of growing | Varieties | Harvest period |
|---|---|---|
| (1) Sow outside in August | Express Yellow O-X<br>Imai Early Yellow<br>Senshyu Semi-Globe Yellow | early June<br>mid–late June<br>late June–July |
| (2) Sow in heat in Jan., harden off and plant April | Rijnsburger-Wijbo | August |
| (3) Plant sets in late March or April | Stuttgart Giant<br>Sturon | August |
| (4) Sow outside in March or early April | Hygro<br>Rijnsburger-Balstora | September–October |

over winter from sowings made in August. For this form of *early* production only the varieties of Japanese origin must be grown, and to obtain a succession of mature onions the following are suggested: Express Yellow O-X (harvest in early June), Imai Early Yellow (mid–late June) and Senshyu Semi-Globe Yellow (late June–July). The sowing date in August is of critical importance, for if sown too early for the district, the plants will grow too large before the winter and may bolt in the spring; if sown too late, the plants may not survive the winter or will only produce small bulbs. In Scotland sowing should be done in the first week of August; in the north the second week; in the Midlands and East Anglia the third week; and in the south the fourth week of August. The aim should be to get the seedlings above ground within 7–10 days, so water the drill before sowing if the soil is dry.

The introduction of this early form of production has reduced the need in most areas to raise transplants from sowing in heat in January, and after hardening off, transplanting in late March or early April. This transplanting method should still be used when growing bulbs for exhibition purposes. It can also be used when the soil is heavy or poorly drained, for under these conditions plants will not overwinter satisfactorily. Recently, experimental work has shown that up to five plants can be raised in a 4.3 cm. square (1¾ in.) peat block. They are not separated but are planted out all together. The advantages of this system are a saving in block costs, much higher yields and about 2 weeks earlier maturity than crops sown directly outside.

Mature bulbs can be produced in August from planting onion sets of varieties such as Stuttgart Giant or Sturon in late March or early April. If small-sized or heat-treated sets (see Chapter 12) are used, this method is very reliable and convenient but the temptation to plant the sets in February or early March should be resisted for the plants may bolt.

For harvesting in August, September and October, the main crop should be sown outside in March or early April as soon as soil conditions are fit. Out of many recently introduced varieties Rijnsburger – Adina, Rijnsburger – Wijbo, Hygro, and Rijnsburger – Balstora mature in that order; the last two varieties are recommended for their storage qualities.

### Onions spring or salad

Special varieties of onions such as White Lisbon and White Lisbon-Winter-Hardy are grown closely together, and with successional sowing can be pulled from April until the autumn. The earliest crops in April are grown from sowings made in the open ground from mid-August to early September, and pulling will be possible from these sowings until June. The varieties are very hardy and will survive most winters provided they are grown on well-drained soil. The crop can be advanced by protecting with cloches for all, or the latter part, of the winter.

For a supply of salad onions from June onwards the same varieties should be sown under cloches in late February or early March followed by successional sowings in the open ground at fortnightly intervals until June. The timing of these sowings is not critical because with close spacing the plants when ready will hold for several weeks.

If overwintered bulb onions are sown thicker than required as an insurance against winter losses, thinnings from this crop can also be used for salad purposes from January to April.

### Parsley

Parsley can be picked throughout the year if two sowings are made, one in March and a second in June or July for early spring use. Plants from this latter crop can be covered with cloches from December onwards to encourage earlier leaf growth in the spring. Because the seeds can take many weeks to germinate in the soil there are considerable advantages from pre-germinating the seeds indoors. They are then either fluid-sown directly into the garden soil, which can save several weeks, or pricked off into blocks and subsequently transplanted. Recommended varieties are Bravour, Moss Curled, and Curlina.

### Parsnip

Because this crop is very hardy and the roots store well in the soil without deterioration over the winter period, a single sowing made any time between late February and May will provide roots from October until March. Very early crops of medium-sized roots can be produced in August or September by pre-germinating the seed and fluid-sowing as soon as soil conditions permit. For early production the plants should be widely spaced (20 plants per square metre) so that they do not compete with each other and fast growth should be encouraged by every possible means. Suitable varieties are Avonresister and White Gem.

### Peas

With a combination of sowings and different varieties, peas can be picked from the end of May until late autumn. The earliest crops are produced from sowings made in October or November on well-drained soils in mild areas or, in the north, with cloche protection from December. Round-seeded, hardy varieties are used such as Feltham First or Meteor which mature from late May onwards. To follow, the same round-seeded varieties can be sown under cloches in February if soil and weather conditions permit. It is a waste of time, seed and effort to sow these early varieties under cold, wet conditions for they will not germinate, but only rot even when the seed has been dressed with fungicide.

The sweeter, wrinkle-seeded varieties can be sown from late March until late May giving a succession of crops until August. If four varieties which differ in their time of maturity are sown together, continuity is reliably obtained over a short period and fewer sowing dates are needed. For example, if short lengths of row of the following four dwarf maincrop varieties are sown on the same date their combined picking periods would last 2–3 weeks because they mature in succession: Hurst Beagle, Hurst Canice, Victory Freezer, and Hurst Greenshaft. Therefore a sowing of these varieties every three weeks will provide a succession of crops until August. These newer, dwarf varieties tend to produce most of their pods together on the plants and so do not provide the same long period of picking often found with the older, taller, indeterminate varieties. The timing of the sowings is therefore more important and the keeping of detailed records of sowing and picking dates and daily temperatures will be of great help in planning a sowing programme for your site in future years.

In June or July depending on the district, sowings can be made of a variety such as Senator for picking in September, and even into October with the use of cloches.

### Potatoes

Potatoes can be lifted from late May until late autumn by the traditional practice of growing both early and maincrop varieties. In mild areas, or with some form of protection such as cloches or low polythene tunnels, 'new' potatoes can be lifted in late May, and if a warm greenhouse is available earlies can be forced to provide new potatoes in April or even earlier.

'Chitting' or sprouting of the seed potatoes before planting is essential for early varieties and will enable lifting to be 2–3 weeks

**Table 8.8**

**Sowing and varietal sequence for peas**

| Method of growing | Varieties | Harvest period |
|---|---|---|
| (1) Sow outside in mild areas or under cloches in Oct. or Nov. | Feltham First<br>Meteor | late May–June |
| (2) As (1) in February or early March | Feltham First<br>Meteor | early to late June |
| (3) Sow outside in succession from March to late May (see text) | Hurst Beagle<br>Hurst Canice<br>Victory Freezer<br>Hurst Greenshaft | late June–August |
| (4) Sow outside in June | Senator | September |

earlier, while chitting of maincrop varieties will result in heavier yields if lifted in late summer (see Chapter 12, p. 394).

For the earliest crops the chitted seed tubers are planted in mid- to late March, the shoots being protected from frosts during the early stages of growth by earthing-up. All varieties should only be planted when soil conditions are fit and when the soil temperature at a depth of 10 cm. (4 in.) exceeds 6 °C (43 °F) on more than three consecutive days. For a speculative crop to harvest in December, tubers lifted from an early variety can be replanted in late July and covered with cloches or a tunnel in September. Varietal and planting date suggestions for traditional methods of providing a continuous succession of potatoes are summarized in Table 8.9.

However, recent research has suggested an alternative way of producing both early and late crops using a single variety. These can supply potatoes from late May until the autumn. This is achieved by manipulating the 'physiological age' of the seed tubers, as reflected in sprout development, by means of the temperature regime they experience before planting. The concept of physiological age is described in Chapter 12 (p. 394). An

**Table 8.9**

**Planting and varietal sequence for potatoes**

| Method of growing | Varieties | Harvest period |
|---|---|---|
| (1) Plant early varieties outside in mild areas or under cloches mid-March | Maris Bard<br>Arran Pilot<br>Pentland Javelin | late May–June |
| (2) Plant early varieties early April | as (1) | late June–early July |
| (3) Plant second early varieties mid-April | Estima<br>Marfona | July–August |
| (4) Plant maincrop varieties late April–early May | Desiree<br>King Edward<br>Maris Piper<br>Pentland Squire | September–October |
| (5) Plant an early variety late July and protect in September | Arran Pilot<br>Foremost | December |

example of the method with the early maincrop variety Desiree is as follows:-

In order to produce 'physiologically old' seed tubers at planting it is important to obtain seed tubers in late autumn or early winter before they break dormancy. The tubers should be stored apical-end uppermost in daylight at a temperature of about 10 °C (50 °F) until just before planting, when the temperature may be reduced to 'harden' the tubers and minimize any temperature shock at planting. This will give an early crop. In contrast, a late-maturing crop can be grown from 'physiologically young' tubers which are produced by keeping tubers cool, less than 4 °C (40 °F) but above freezing, until planting.

## Radish

Radishes are one of the quickest and easiest crops to grow and to maintain a supply from May to October. The seed germinates well and it is all too easy to sow too much each time; a short length of row at fortnightly intervals will give good continuity. The earliest sowings of forcing varieties such as Saxa and Saxerre are made in cold frames or under cloches in February and March to pull in May. In the open, successional sowings of varieties such as Cherry Belle and French Breakfast can be made from March until September. Another method is to sow seed of mixed varieties which mature at different times; fewer sowings are then needed. The plants should be pulled young, otherwise the roots can become tough and hot to the taste. This is another reason why small quantities of seed should be sown at frequent intervals. Late sowings can again be protected by cloches.

The large-rooted, winter radish should be sown in July or early August and are thinned to 20 cm. (8 in.) apart. They are quite hardy and can be left in the ground for lifting as required throughout the winter although as a precaution they should be covered with straw during severe weather. Alternatively, the roots can be lifted and stored in November. Suitable varieties available are China Rose, Black Spanish Round and Mino Early.

### Spinach

This crop can be obtained virtually throughout the year. In a similar way to radish, spinach needs to be sown little and often from March until July to provide a succession of young leaves from May until October. The earliest sowings are made under cloches at the end of February if the soil has warmed up, and in the open from March onwards at 2–3 week intervals until July using varieties such as Longstanding Round and Sigmaleaf. The largest fully-grown leaves are taken frequently so that they do not get tough.

For winter production from October until May, winter spinach varieties such as Greenmarket or Sigmaleaf are sown on two or three occasions in August and September on a well-drained site. Best results are obtained if the plants are protected by cloches from October throughout the winter period.

## Swede

A single sowing of this crop in May will provide roots from late August until March direct from the ground, for the plants are extremely hardy. Because of possible problems with mildew the sowings are made in early May in the north of the country and late May or even early June in the Midlands and the south. A suitable variety is Marian.

## Sweet corn

For best results this crop requires a warm, sunny, sheltered site because it does not start to grow until the temperature rises above 10 °C (50 °F) and it is also susceptible to frost damage. Except in the southern part of the country where the seed may be sown directly into the soil in mid-May, it is best to raise young plants in blocks or pots and transplant after the risk of frost has passed.

Seed can be pre-germinated from mid-April onwards and the chitted seed carefully transferred to pots or blocks of compost. Three to four weeks are then needed at a temperature of 10 to 13 °C (50 to 55 °F) to grow the plant to a size ready for transplanting. Early crops can be planted under the protection of cloches or low tunnels in mid-May if the soil has been previously covered. These can be followed by plantings in the open ground in June after the risk of frost is over, or be prepared to protect from frost. The use of clear polythene mulch will advance the maturity of this crop by up to a month. The earliest crops of varieties such as Earliking are ready for picking in late July or August depending on the season. Later varieties such as Sundance and Sweet 77 will mature in September. The cobs should be picked when they are 'milky', before they become over-mature.

## Tomatoes, outdoors

Tomatoes, like sweet corn, are easily killed by frost and need a warm, sunny position if they are to do well outside. The newer bush or dwarf varieties are more tolerant of cold conditions than the older, staked varieties and have become more popular for they can be grown successfully even in Scotland.

The normal method of growing the staked plants out of doors is to sow the seeds under glass or on a window-sill in March or early April in a temperature of 16–18 °C (60–65 °F). The seedlings are pricked off into blocks or pots, and after hardening off are planted outside in early June or when the risk of frost has passed. If cloches or tunnels are available the plants may be transplanted in mid-May provided the soil has been covered and warmed up beforehand. When the plants reach the glass or polythene they are uncovered and staked. A suitable variety is Alicante, which will mature from late July onwards.

Plants raised in this way can also be transplanted into large containers or growbags and placed on paths, terraces or patios, or against a south-facing wall. With these staked varieties the plants should be 'stopped' after four trusses, or in early August. Picking can be continued until the first frosts. The remaining green fruits should be brought inside by mid-September for ripening.

Plants of the bush varieties may be raised and planted in a similar way to that described but are not normally staked or pruned of their side-shoots. An alternative method is to sow pre-germinated seeds thinly in a single row under tunnels or cloches in mid-April. The seedlings should emerge 7–14 days later and if sown thinly no thinning of the plants will be required. The protection can be removed in June. In southern England pre-germinated seeds can be fluid-sown directly into the open ground in late April sowing two or three seeds every 30 cm. (12 in.) along the rows. With both methods using pre-germinated seed there is a risk of damage from late spring frosts, but experience has shown that the risk is low in southern counties. Even if frosts do occur, growth is not severely impaired provided the night temperature does not fall below −2 °C (28 °F). Suitable bush or dwarf varieties are Sleaford Abundance and Alfresco and, depending on the season, ripe fruit can be picked from mid-July onwards. Many believe that the flavour of these bush varieties is better than that of the staked varieties.

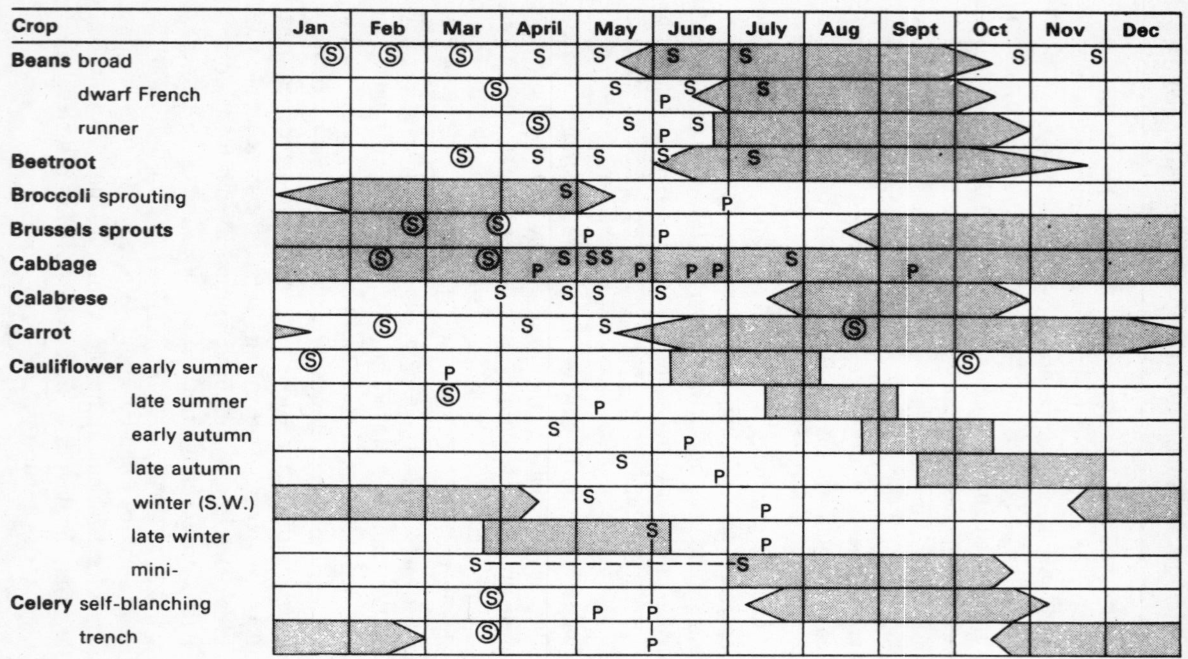
Crop
Jan
Feb
Mar
April
May
June
July
Aug
Sept
Oct
Nov
Dec
**Beans** broad
dwarf French
runner
**Beetroot**
**Broccoli** sprouting
**Brussels sprouts**
**Cabbage**
**Calabrese**
**Carrot**
**Cauliflower** early summer
late summer
early autumn
late autumn
winter (S.W.)
late winter
mini-
**Celery** self-blanching
trench

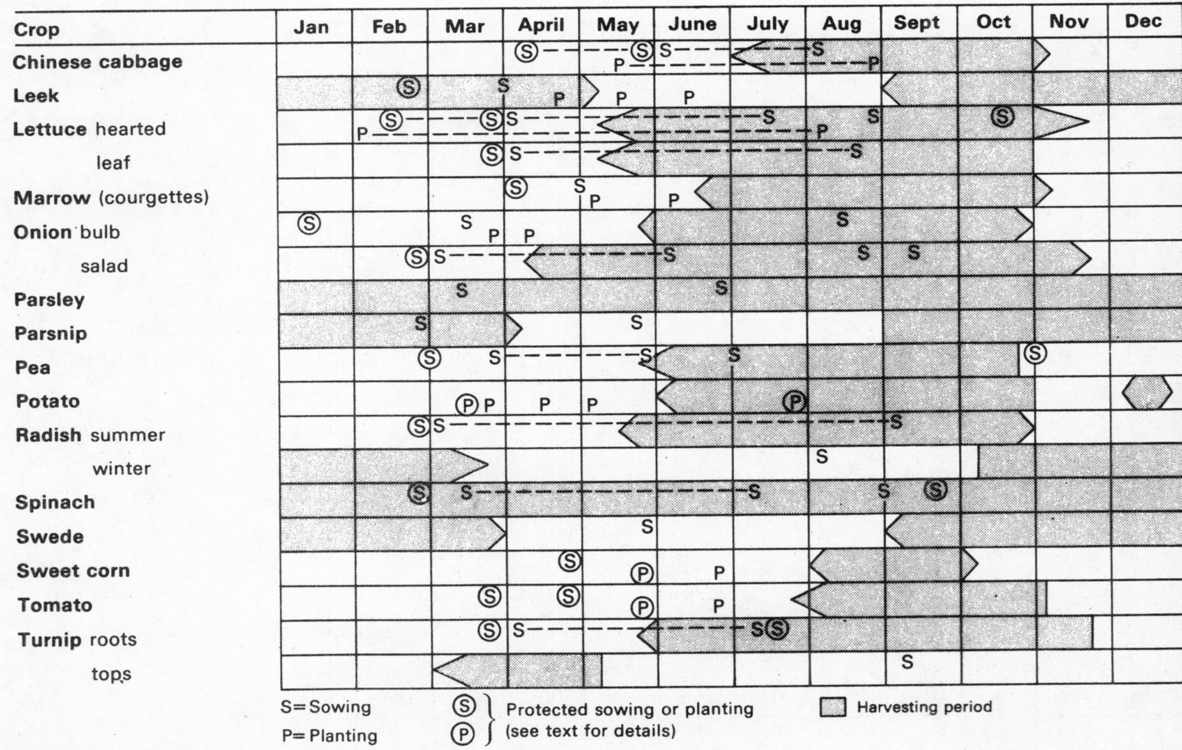


Fig. 8.5. A summary guide to plan crop continuity.

## Turnips

Roots of this crop can be pulled for most of the year from a succession of sowings using varieties suited to the season. The earliest crops are produced in late May or early June from a sowing made under cloches in March of varieties such as Purple Top Milan, Snowball and Sprinter. Successional sowings of the same varieties can be made at 3–4 week intervals until July for pulling in sequence until October.

To provide roots for late autumn and winter, seed of main-crop varieties such as Golden Ball are sown in July and the roots are best lifted and stored in November for use throughout the winter.

The tops of turnips are also grown for cutting as 'spring greens'. These crops are sown in August or September and the tops harvested in March and April but if these plants are protected during the winter earlier pickings of 'tops' can be made.

# 9 Storing vegetables

Vegetables are at their best when they are fresh! They have the best flavour and the highest nutritional content at harvest. Those vegetables which are natural storage organs, such as onions and potatoes, can be as good and fresh for some months when properly stored as described below. The majority of vegetables, however, are not suited to long-term storage, and many such as the leafy vegetables lose crispness and flavour soon after harvest even when they are stored well.

This means that fresh is best and emphasizes a major advantage which the gardener and small operator has, the ability to reduce the time from harvest to the table. Those consumers lucky enough to eat their vegetables within an hour of harvest will know what I mean.

The changes in the nutritional content of vegetables through storage is far from fully investigated, but fortunately for us consumers, the results from case studies are encouraging. These generally show how resilient the constituents of foods, which are important to our diet, are to break down. Proteins, carbohydrates, and vitamins are complex chemicals which change little in today's storage and marketing practices. Their resilience is best demonstrated in relation to cooking, where even boiling in water leaves most of these constituents in a usable form. Other constituents of value are minerals such as calcium, iron and magnesium, the availability of which is unlikely to be changed by storage or cooking. Fats are virtually absent from vegetables. The major changes which the storage of vegetables are likely to make are therefore the loss of flavour and texture.

## Guidelines

Once harvested, vegetables deteriorate, some very rapidly as they are removed from their natural supply of food and water. This means they should be harvested only when there is some good reason for not leaving them in the ground. Fast-growing lettuce and cauliflower, for example, become quickly over-mature and eventually bolt it left uncut and chilled storage is a way of extending the supply of these crops. Similarly, tender vegetables are best harvested and stored before the low night temperatures of late summer cause damage and wastage through 'chilling injury' (see pp. 309–10). However, many root crops, leeks, and most brassicas, can be left in the ground until required as they can stand all but the heaviest frosts. Providing a little frost protection is usually less trouble and is much less wasteful than harvesting and storing these crops. So the first guideline to follow is:

- Harvest and store crops only when they cannot be left in the ground.

Vegetables deteriorate gradually after harvest, using up their in-built supplies of food and water until they become inedible. Because the rate of deterioration is slower at low temperature, many vegetables can be successfully stored in a refrigerator. But each vegetable has its own particular storage requirements and whereas conditions in a refrigerator may suit leafy vegetables, it is not the best place to store tomatoes or potatoes. For this reason the storage requirements of the main groups of vegetables will be discussed separately. In all groups of vegetables it is obviously only possible to get good quality vegetables out of store if they are of good quality when they are put in. In this context good quality means well-formed and undamaged. It follows that three further guidelines should be:

- Harvest carefully and selectively.
- Cool rapidly.
- Store in suitable conditions.

## Store naturally—in the ground

Many brassicas and root crops are ready for harvest by early winter, but the outside temperatures from November to March are generally low enough to restrict further growth and development. At these outdoor temperatures these vegetables do not deteriorate very quickly and they are best 'stored' where they grow, in the ground. This works well for the many vegetables which are reasonably hardy and there are the advantages that we use free, natural refrigeration and also avoid the wastage which commonly develops on tissues damaged at harvest. Successful storage in the ground also depends on good control of pests and diseases. Bad attacks of aphid, carrot fly, and other pests can reduce the quality as well as the yield of vegetables drastically, and where these occur it may be best to harvest, grade and store or deep-freeze the pest-free surplus supplies.

The winter brassicas which are suited to leaving in the ground (see Chapter 8) are not normally given additional protection from the weather, though they may lose some outer layers of leaves because of freezing injury. Vegetables growing at and below ground level, such as carrots, beetroot, swede, turnip and leeks can be given some additional protection from the weather by simply drawing up the earth around them. This and other methods are described in detail later.

## Harvest carefully

Vegetables are made of delicate tissues that are easily damaged when handled at harvest time. Broken tissues exuding sap are an ideal medium for the growth of disease micro-organisms and it is not surprising that the greater the level of damage at harvest the greater the level of wastage that occurs in store. Harvest damage not only wastes edible tissues, it greatly increases the chance of fungal and bacterial infection which can affect the whole vegetable and often adjacent ones in store. Any vegetable that is badly damaged during harvesting is not suitable for storage and should be used up first.

When vegetables are cut or trimmed during harvest the knife used should be cleaned from time to time, as this will reduce the possibility of infection of the wound. The knife should also be sharp enough to make a clean cut, as these wounds dry out and callous over more quickly. Tearing and bruising tissues at harvest should be avoided, as such wounds do not dry out readily. Dropping and banging vegetables together at harvest should be avoided because this causes the breakdown of tissues just under the surface and leads to bruising. Such damage is especially difficult for the plant to repair if the surface is broken and the sap is exposed to infection. The exception is the leaves of root crops which can be removed by twisting off at harvest.

How delicate are vegetable tissues and what happens when they are roughly handled? Three examples are described to illustrate the increasing susceptibility to damage.

## Onion

The onion bulb is a natural storage organ and by the time it is fully grown and dried the edible, fleshy scales of the bulb are surrounded by two or three layers of protective, dried, papery skins. The bulb is then an ideal storage vegetable—a package of dormant, edible tissues, ready-wrapped for storage, and it will remain in a state of rest for many months if properly treated. The length of the storage life can easily be reduced, however, by rough handling. The papery skins protect the bulb from damage and also prevent the fleshy scales from drying out. Even the partial loss, say 20 per cent of the area, of papery skins to reveal the cream-coloured fleshy scale underneath will lead to softening and shrivelling of the bulb after a few months in store. Severe bruising will lead to premature sprouting, but even dropping a bulb as little as 20 cm. (8 in.) onto a hard surface produces a bruise which extends several scales deep into the bulb.

## Carrot

The fleshy tap-root is another storage organ, but one that is not easily harvested without damage. The surface of the root is covered by a very thin skin of dead cells, about half as thick as a human hair. It is specially produced to protect the surface from abrasion by soil particles during growth, but it is also a useful protective barrier during handling. Its usefulness is limited, however, as it is easily scraped off, and during lifting and washing about 20 per cent of the skin of the carrot may be removed. The skin can and does regenerate, but this takes time and is usually accompanied by browning of the surface and the development of bitter off-flavours. It is for these and other reasons that storage in the ground is preferred for this crop.

In addition to skin damage, normal lifting by hand produces serious cuts and abrasions in a proportion of the roots. This type of damage is difficult to repair and frequently never is, as micro-organisms grow readily on the broken tissues. Thus it pays to put on one side carrots damaged in this way for immediate use. Carrot leaves are usually cut short at harvest and the tip of the taproot is also broken. These damaged surfaces also occasionally provide access for rotting organisms.

The choice of cultivar and various cultural practices can also influence the likely damage level at harvest. Cultivars of main-crop carrots, for example from the Chantenay and Autumn King groups, generally have a better developed skin with more layers of cells than the early maturing cultivars, principally from Amsterdam Forcing and Nantes groups. Although the thinner skin of the early cultivars improves their appearance (so that they usually look a brighter orange colour than maincrop cultivars) the thicker skin is useful for protecting the roots if they are lifted for storage. The early-maturing cultivars are fast-growing and produce little cellulose thickening to hold them together. This generally results in a crisper texture than is usual with the late-maturing cultivars. However, this advantage of the earlies turns to disadvantage in wet soil conditions of the autumn and winter, when crisp-textured cultivars often split their roots in the ground or on lifting from the soil. For these conditions the late-maturing Chantenay and Autumn King cultivars are best, especially as some of them have a little built-in frost resistance. Late-maturing carrots for overwintering or for storage are best drilled from mid-May to mid-June in central England, and are mature from mid-October onwards. With any luck these late drillings will miss the first generation of carrot root fly.

### Cauliflower

The extraordinary nature of the cauliflower curd can be appreciated not only on a plate, but also in its fresh state, with a magnifying lens. It is then seen to be extremely delicate, being composed of thousands of unprotected growing points arranged in spiral formations. Unfortunately, these growing points are easily broken by merely touching the curd, and the sap so released is an ideal medium for the growth of micro-organisms. There is no known natural mechanism to repair damage of the curd. Therefore for successful short-term storage avoid anything touching the curd, even water (heavy rain can ruin curds), and trim the outer leaves in such a way that they can be folded over to protect the curd. The cut stem surface is unlikely to rot whilst being stored provided the cut is clean and able to dry out. Cauliflowers cannot be successfully stored for more than two to three weeks because of the peculiar nature of the curd and the difficulty of handling it without damage and preventing fungal and bacterial invasion of the tissues.

The above examples show a typical range of susceptibilities to damage shown by vegetables. Particular care should be taken when harvesting vegetables that are not natural storage organs as these have the least well-developed systems for repairing damage. The benefits of storing vegetables are greater if wastage levels are low, and good storage begins with careful harvesting and the selection of good produce.

## Cool rapidly after harvest

Because vegetables deteriorate rapidly at high temperatures the sooner they can be moved into cool conditions after harvest, the better. As a general guide, the rate of deterioration of plant tissue will be halved for each 10 °C (18 °F) fall in temperature, and so vegetables will respire less and will store much longer if their temperature at harvest can be reduced. Those vegetables which are growing rapidly at harvest in high temperatures in the summer, are likely to benefit most by cooling, providing it is done soon after harvesting.

The benefits of cooling differ from vegetable to vegetable. For example, the rapid growth of lettuce and cauliflower can be effectively stopped by cooling. Similarly, the undesirable conversion of sugars to starch in peas and sweet corn can be greatly reduced by lowering the temperature. Even vegetables which deteriorate slowly over a period of months such as turnips, swede, and beetroot benefit from low temperature storage as this slows down the rate of cellulose thickening which makes them tough to eat.

The expected storage life of vegetables can be calculated by knowing the maximum storage life under ideal conditions (see Tables 9.1, 9.2, and 9.3) and the storage temperature actually available. This effect of temperature can be demonstrated by considering the storage life of a summer lettuce. It can be stored for up to 14 days in a cold refrigerator, so in round terms it uses 1 of its 14 units of food reserves a day at 0 °C (32 °F). As domestic refrigerators commonly run at about 4 °C (40 °F) it will use 2 units a day and so it can be kept for 7 days. At 10 °C (50 °F) it will use 3 units a day, so will store for up to 5 days in a cold cupboard or larder at this temperature. At 20 °C (68 °F) it will use 9 units a day, so will last less than 2 days at room temperature. These figures summarize in a simplified form the results of actual experiments, and the principles of the system work well for most vegetables.

We should only reduce the temperature of vegetables to that of the freezing-point of water 0 °C (32 °F). At temperatures below this, ice crystals can cause irreversible damage to plant tissues, killing the cells. Most vegetables can be cooled to this temperature safely for the heat generated by the plant's respiration prevents it from freezing. It is the ideal temperature to store brassicas, lettuce, and other leafy vegetables, and for most root crops, although gardeners often have to compromise and use warmer temperatures that happen to be available. However, vegetables of sub-tropical origin such as potatoes, tomatoes, cucumber, most beans, and sweet peppers show adverse effects of temperatures well above 0 °C (32 °F), known as 'chilling injury' and we will return to this topic later in the chapter. Deep freezing at −15 to −20 °C (+5 to −5 °F) is a different way of preserving, rather than of storing, vegetables. This temperature level not only kills all the cells but is low enough to suspend virtually all deterioration. This ensures that vitamins, proteins and other unstable food substances are preserved. Micro-organisms that can survive are inactive at this low temperature.

Domestic refrigerators normally run at 2 to 4 °C (35 to 40 °F) and hence there is little danger of freezing vegetables. A very useful storage life can be obtained for many vegetables under such conditions provided they are cooled rapidly after harvest, and it can be worth getting a second-hand refrigerator for this purpose. A bulk of vegetables is best cooled by leaving some gaps between them for the heat to escape, and cooling is therefore most effective if the produce is unwrapped. However, the atmosphere in a refrigerator is fairly dry because moisture present in the air freezes-out on the cooling coil. As a result vegetables and especially leafy vegetables wilt rapidly in a refrigerator. This is avoided by wrapping them in polythene once they are cool.

Whenever possible it is preferable to harvest vegetables in the cooler part of the day (usually very early morning) and once harvested, they should be placed in a cool place such as a cellar or in the shade of a tree. If refrigeration is not available vegetables can be cooled several degrees by the evaporative cooling of water. Water removes heat from its surroundings when it evaporates, so leafy vegetables with a large surface area such as lettuce and cabbage can be kept cool quite effectively if sprayed with water once or twice a day. This will not work if the water cannot evaporate, as when vegetables are placed in a closed polythene bag. Cooling in closed polythene bags will give rise to condensation in the bags which will mark and spoil cauliflower curds and delicate leaf tissue over a period of days.

## Storage conditions for the main groups of vegetables

Not all vegetables want the same storage conditions, and both the temperature and the humidity of the air in which they are stored should, ideally, be controlled if the best results are to be obtained. The importance of *temperature* has already been described.

### Humidity

The water content of most vegetables is very high (90 per cent in carrots and 95 per cent in lettuce) and, until harvesting, is maintained by water being continually absorbed from the soil. Once harvested, however, the plant is removed from its natural water supply, and begins to lose water in the form of vapour to the surrounding air. If this is allowed to go on for any length of time vegetables will wilt and they only have to lose as little as 5 per cent of their weight, to become limp and unattractive. Produce that has deteriorated because of stressful conditions such as cause wilting (or chilling injury or high temperature injury) is much more likely to succumb to fungal and bacterial invasion than when it was freshly harvested. It is therefore very much in our own interests to harvest and handle produce as carefully as possible, and to store it as near to the conditions given in the tables below as we can. The rate of water loss from any given vegetable depends to a large extent on the water-vapour content, that is the humidity, of the air surrounding it. Of course vegetables with lots of thin leaves, like lettuce, lose water far more quickly than compact vegetables, like swedes. But just like washing on a clothes line, vegetables will dry out quicker when the humidity is low – on a good drying day – than when it is high.

As vegetables have a high water content, most of them will store for longer in conditions of high humidity.

Even when the optimum humidity for storing a particular vegetable is known, actually attaining it, and maintaining it, is difficult because air holds much more water vapour at high than at low temperatures. This means that every time air warms up its humidity falls, and vice versa. Humidity is often quoted as per cent relative humidity, which expresses the water-vapour content as a percentage relative to the maximum possible, at that temperature. When air of high humidity is cooled, its humidity rises further until the point is reached when there is too much water vapour for the air to hold. At this point the air is said to be saturated with water vapour (or is at its dewpoint) and its relative humidity is 100 per cent. If cooling continues, then water vapour turns to liquid water, and this is frequently seen on the cooling surface as condensation. We see examples of this in everyday life as condensation inside windows of houses in cold weather, and as dew on the ground. It can also be seen inside polythene bags of vegetables cooling in a refrigerator.

The reverse happens when the temperature rises; for example air saturated at a low temperature (say 4 °C (40 °F)) will only have sufficient water to achieve 50 per cent relative humidity at 10 °C (50 °F), and only 10 per cent at room temperature. Such changes have a dramatic effect on harvested vegetables which are brought into a house temperature of, for example, 18 °C (65 °F) from an outside temperature of 10 °C (50 °F); under such circumstances they are liable to wilt rapidly. This example also shows that temperature and humidity must be considered together and if one wishes to store vegetables at high humidity, the simplest way to do this is to keep the temperature low and make sure that there is some free water in the container with the vegetables.

An unheated shed is a good place to store vegetables during the cooler months but vegetables will also wilt there over a period of days (cabbages) or weeks (swede and beetroot) unless they are stored at a suitable humidity. The temperature and humidity requirements for the main groups of vegetables are given below. At the beginning of each section, and in the tables, the ideal storage conditions to obtain the maximum storage life are described. These are given so that readers can see what conditions to aim for, and what storage life can then be achieved.

It is realized that most gardeners will have to compromise especially as far as temperature is concerned, because they must use whatever facilities are available. Humidity requirements are only given as approximate guides since it is clear that humidity will vary greatly as the temperature changes and furthermore, few people have instruments to measure it. Thus the highest possible humidity, often quoted as 95 per cent plus, is indicated as 'highest possible' in the tables, and is usually achieved by placing in polythene bags, or by using a mist spray. Humidities around the 90 per cent level are indicated as 'high', and can be obtained by leaving bags and containers open to allow some circulation of air, or by using porous paper sacks or boxes of sand in which to store the vegetables. The lower level of humidity required for onion bulbs is best obtained by allowing a very free circulation of dry air.

## Leafy vegetables

Leafy crops such as brassicas, celery, lettuce, spinach, and watercress should be stored ideally at 0 °C (32 °F) at the highest obtainable humidity. If possible leave crops such as Brussels sprouts, cabbage, celery and leeks in the ground. Other leafy crops such as lettuce and cauliflower, however, will have to be cut otherwise they will rapidly over-mature and quality will be lost.

Vegetables in this group are not natural storage organs and with the exception of slow-growing cultivars of cabbage, generally have very limited food reserves. In addition, many in this group are growing quickly at the time of harvest, possibly at high summer temperatures and for all these reasons it is especially important to cool them rapidly after harvest to reduce the rate of deterioration. Once these vegetables are cooled the water content is best conserved by wrapping in polythene.

The attractive green colour of chlorophyll in the green tissues gradually breaks down in store, and turns to yellow, and this shows that the tissues are coming to the end of their useful life. The old, outer leaves of cabbage and lettuce turn yellow before the young inner leaves, as the plant withdraws nutrients and water from them in order to prolong the life of the central shoot. Rapid cooling and storing at high humidity will delay the deterioration of the leafy tissue.

It is useful to remember that ethylene is a gas produced in

**Table 9.1**

**Storage conditions for leafy vegetables**

| | **Ideal storage conditions** | | | **Number of days of likely storage life at low ambient temperatures 4–10°C (40–50°F) in winter** |
|---|---|---|---|---|
| | **Temperature and humidity** | **Freezing point °C (°F)** | **Likely maximum storage life (days)** | |
| **Asparagus** | All of this | −0.5° | 14 | |
| **Broccoli, sprouting** | group | −0.5° (31°) | 10–14 | 5 |
| **Brussels sprouts** | require 0°C | −1° (30°) | 14 | 7 |
| **Cabbage, spring** | (32°F) and | −1° | 7 | |
| Dutch white | highest | −1° | 120 | 60 |
| Chinese | possible | | 60 | |
| **Calabrese** | humidity | | 3 | |
| **Cauliflower** | | −1° | 20 | 4 |
| **Celery** | | −0.5° | 60 | 15 |
| **Kale** | | −0.5° | 14–20 | 7 |
| **Leek** | | −1° | 60 | 15 |
| **Lettuce** | | −0.5° | 14 | |
| **Onion, salad** | | −1° | 14–20 | 5 |
| **Parsley** | | −1° | 30 | 7 |
| **Peas (in pod)** | | −1° | 14 | |
| **Spinach** | | −0.5° | 14 | |
| **Watercress** | | −0.5° | 4 | 1 |

minute amounts by ripening fruits and acts as a ripening regulator. It also accelerates the senescence of green vegetables with which it comes into contact. These two groups of produce must therefore not be stored near to each other in a confined space. A bag of apples, or pears or tomatoes, for example, could produce enough ethylene gas to affect adversely leafy vegetables if stored for several weeks in a refrigerator. However, ethylene would not build up to active concentrations in a well-ventilated shed.

### Root crops

To keep in good condition, carrots, parsnips, beetroots, swedes and turnips require low temperature and the highest possible humidity. For these crops storage can often be avoided simply by leaving the roots in the ground until required for the kitchen (see Fig. 9.1). In this way really fresh carrots and parsnips can be lifted throughout the winter and well into the spring.

Our common root crops are natural storage organs, accumulating sufficient food in the first season of growth to enable them to flower early in the second season. Crops grown for winter supplies should be sown early enough for them to mature by late autumn, but late enough to ensure that they do not mature too early, as unwanted late growth can lead to oversize roots and the undesirable toughening of existing tissues. It is best to sow as late as recommended for any particular cultivar (for guidance see Chapter 8). Slow growth will continue during the winter until the plants are harvested, so they should be grown at a sufficiently high plant population to minimize the risk of oversize roots.

*Freezing injury*. The storage roots of our common root vegetables can withstand slight frosts (see Table 9.2) because the small amounts of ice formed are located harmlessly in between the cells of the outer tissues. The effects can be seen as small spaces or cracks in the tissues when the ice has thawed. The heat of respiration, which is difficult and expensive to get rid of in summer crops is, in this instance, valuable in keeping the tissues from freezing. However, when the storage roots are subjected to temperature lower than −3 °C (26 °F), the amount of ice formed is too great

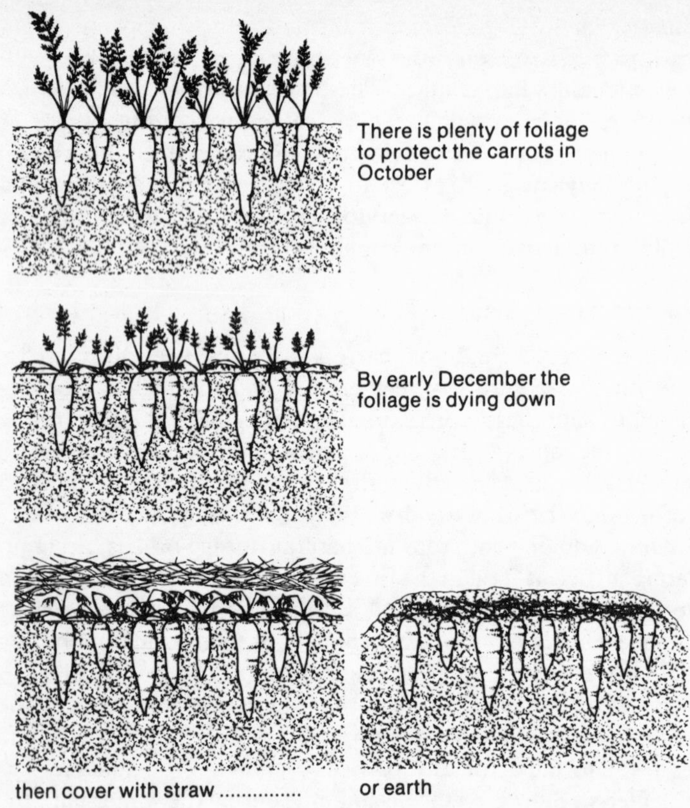


Fig. 9.1. Covering carrots for the winter.

to be contained within the root. Large masses are formed which break through the root surface and cells may be destroyed by ice forming in them. Rotting of the roots may follow as fungi and bacteria invade the cracks and the useful life of the vegetable will be shortened. Carrot cultivars of the Chantenay and Autumn King types are less susceptible to freezing than those of Amsterdam Forcing and Nantes types, a point to be considered when choosing cultivars for overwintering.

**Table 9.2**

**Storage conditions for 'topped' root crops**

| | Ideal storage conditions | | | Number of days of likely storage life if harvested and stored at low ambient temperature 4–10°C (40–50°F) in winter |
|---|---|---|---|---|
| | Temperature and humidity | Freezing point | Likely maximum storage life (days) | |
| **Beetroot** | 4°C (40°F) highest possible humidity | −1°C (30°F) | 120–200 | 120 |
| **Carrot** | 0°C (32°F) | −1°C | 60–150 | 90 |
| **Parsnip** | highest | (30°F) | 150 | 60 |
| **Swede** | possible | | 120 | 60 |
| **Turnip** | humidity | | 150 | 60 |

*Frost protection.* There are many cultivars of carrots in the Chantenay and Autumn King groups, and late parsnips, which grow very slowly during the winter and are ideal for complete overwintering. The carrot leaves form a canopy over the roots and help to protect them from damaging frosts. However, neither the leaves nor the roots can withstand a succession of heavy frosts (below −5 °C (23 °F)) and by early December a large proportion of the leaves blacken and offer little protection to the roots. At this time additional protection must be given, but it is unwise to cover crops before early December as the extra insulation will tend to retain heat in the soil, and the crop is more likely to continue growth. It is a good idea to apply slug bait before covering.

The object of good insulation is to trap air but the material loses its effect if it becomes wet and matted. Suitable materials are loose straw, leaves, sand, sandy or peaty earth, peat, or polythene sheeting. Wheat straw is one of the best materials to use as it is not easily compacted over winter, is not easily blown away and is easily gathered and disposed of. Any remaining fragments can be dug in. An average bale will cover about 6 square metres (60 square feet) to a depth of 15 cm. (6 in.) or more, and this is usually sufficient to prevent carrot roots from freezing.

Parsnips are hardier and can survive most winters with very little extra protection; a light covering of the crowns with earth is usually adequate. Parsnips respond to low temperatures by converting some of their starch to sugar, which makes them taste sweeter. At least 20 cm. (8 in.) of straw is needed for beetroot, swede and turnip, as the edible parts are partly above the ground.

The success of overwintering root crops in the ground can also be affected by the location and the type of soil. A sheltered spot is preferable to an exposed one, and a well-drained soil is essential as long periods of waterlogged conditions can lead to many disorders. Furthermore, a freely draining soil has better insulating properties than a waterlogged one. Gardeners with heavy soil would find it worthwhile to prepare a special area for overwintering carrots by adding large quantities of sand or peat (or both). A raised bed will help drainage in the winter and poorly drained areas should be improved by digging a channel to take the excess water away.

*Loss of quality.* The quality of beetroots, swedes, and turnips tends to deteriorate more than that of carrots and parsnips when left in the ground, possibly because they are more exposed, being at or above soil level. It is normal to harvest these at some stage of the winter in all but the most sheltered districts. Common quality defects are excessive growth of the shoot or root, splitting, and the development of rough inedible tissue on the exposed surface of the root. Frequently the roots will become more fibrous in texture because of the deposition of cellulose thickening as this is part of the natural ageing process as the plant prepares for flowering. This deterioration in quality can be minimized by lifting and storing indoors.

*Harvesting and storage.* Once lifted any remaining leaves act as wicks drawing moisture out of the root, so they are best removed by twisting them off. This simple method is adequate, as broken leaf-bases usually drop off after a few weeks, leaving a neat, protective scar. Twisting off the leaves of beetroot is much better than cutting, as the sap may be lost through the cut tissues for some days. Damage to the crown of these root crops at harvest must be avoided as the terminal shoot is vital to the well-being of the plant, for without it the root becomes moribund and will eventually die and decay.

Root crops should be stored so that there is some circulation of air. Undamaged roots can be roughly size-graded to facilitate packing and stored in wooden boxes (slatted wooden crates are ideal). The roots should be laid down in layers with enough sand between the layers to cover them. The sand separates the roots, reducing the chance of the spread of disease, and allows the movement of air and moisture into and out of the roots. Simpler storage methods, such as putting them in polythene bags, usually result in more waste from rotting because of the root-to-root contact. Clamps are not now generally recommended for root crops because they take a lot of time to construct and generally give poorer results than crops stored in the ground. The possible exception is beetroot, which will store reasonably well in polythene sacks and, for large quantities, in clamps.

The clamp should be made on level ground by piling up beetroot so that the triangular cross-section of the clamp measures about 75 – 100 cm. (30 – 40 in.) across the base and in height. The roots are covered with a 15 cm. (6 in.) layer of straw, and this is followed by a 15 cm. layer of soil put in position in December, when the roots are cool. Beetroot stored in this way will keep until March or April.

Root crops grown in well-drained soil and lifted in dry conditions are usually clean, and need not be washed before being stored. Washing means extra handling and is likely to increase root damage and is therefore undesirable. If, however, roots are lifted from a heavy soil, perhaps in wet conditions so that little of the surface of the roots is visible, it is worth washing them to remove excess soil, which may carry a number of pests and diseases. If high levels of pest attack are suspected, washing will enable damaged roots to be detected and removed before they are stored.

### Potatoes

Main crop potatoes are mature when the leaves die down naturally, and the tubers should be harvested before there is any risk of frost damage. They are best harvested in dry conditions so as to obtain the tubers as clean as possible. Once any damaged tubers have been removed for using up first, sound potatoes should be put into double-thickness paper sacks (obtainable from horticultural suppliers) which are then tied at the neck. Potatoes harvested under wet conditions should be surface-dried before storing. These paper sacks allow surplus moisture to escape and the moisture content of the air around the tubers will equilibrate at a suitable level. Paper sacks exclude low levels of light from the tubers. This is important because light stimulates the formation of poisonous alkaloids in the surface tissues as they turn green. This green tissue must be removed before cooking. Jute and hessian sacks are also suitable provided light is not allowed to reach the tubers. Polythene sacks are not suitable for storage as the humidity will rise and stimulate the development of sprouting as well as some disorders and diseases.

There is no hurry to reduce the temperature of the potatoes to below 10 °C (50 °F) after harvest. Indeed, temperatures between 10 and 15 °C (50 and 60 °F) are beneficial for a few weeks, as the development of a layer of protective corky tissue on the skin and the healing of any minor wounds are stimulated at these temperatures. It is, of course, normal to store potatoes at prevailing (ambient) temperatures in a cool, frost-free place. Large quantities of potatoes may warrant the construction of a field clamp, using the same method as described for beetroot, but omitting the layer of straw. Storage for lengthy periods below 4 °C (40 °F) encourages the undesirable sweetening of the tubers, which is detectable after cooking. This is particularly noticeable with potatoes for chipping or roasting as the sugars formed at low temperatures caramelize on cooking and this results in very dark chips or roast potatoes which can be somewhat bitter. Low temperature effects can be avoided by giving extra insulation, such as layers of newspapers, when the weather is very frosty. Wooden boards under the sacks will insulate the potatoes from below.

The rate of water loss from potatoes is surprisingly low in paper sacks but this will increase as sprouts appear on the tubers in the spring. The sprouts act as wicks drawing moisture out of the tubers and will make the potatoes spongy in time. Sprouting is also accompanied by sweetening of the tuber as food reserves are mobilized in readiness for regrowth. A few extra weeks storage life can be obtained if the sprouts are rubbed off.

### Onions

Ideal conditions for storing onion bulbs are a combination of low temperature (0 °C (32 °F)) and low humidity but these conditions are difficult and expensive to provide and many months of storage life can be obtained at the low, ambient temperatures normally found in an unheated building. The storage procedure for bulbs grown from sets or from seed is similar except that bulbs from sets are harvested 2–3 weeks earlier and have a shorter storage life.

*Harvesting and drying*. Complete drying-off of the leaves to give a well-sealed neck is essential for successful storage. In early September the leaves fall over and die down indicating that the bulb has matured. At this time sprouting-inhibitors produced in the leaves are translocated to the bulb, and for this reason leaves must be left intact and dried on the bulb. When the leaves have fallen over in the majority of the plants, or in any case by mid-September, the plants should be lifted to encourage drying-off. If the weather is good the bulbs can be dried-off in the garden, laid out in rows, for a week or so before moving them under cover to complete drying. Drying is complete when all the green tissue and papery skins around the bulbs are 'rustling' dry. The roots which are fleshy at lifting time should also have withered. In a cool season, a proportion of the plants will develop extra leaves and have a thick, fleshy neck. These plants will not die down and store well, so should be used up as soon as possible. Drying is encouraged by warm, airy conditions and the bulbs should always be laid out to dry under cover to complete drying. The staging of an empty greenhouse is ideal for this purpose. Any warm place can be used to assist drying, but temperatures over 27 °C (80 °F) should be avoided because of the increased risk of splitting the skins which are necessary for successful long-term storage. The higher the temperature the darker the colour of the skin becomes. This looks attractive but does not improve storage performance!

Contact of the bulbs with wet soil or moisture during drying causes staining of the skins. Thus, extended outdoor drying (with a strong possibility of rain or dew) often results in heavily stained skins, whereas bulbs removed and dried under cover should be virtually unblemished. However, staining does not affect the eating quality of the bulbs.

*Storage.* Onion bulbs must be stored under cover with a good circulation of air. Slatted-trays containing not more than two layers of bulbs are ideal for this purpose. Alternatively, the bulbs can be put into nets or made into 'ropes' for hanging in a draughty place, for there is no danger of desiccating them by overventilation. A good circulation of air will remove moisture produced continuously by respiration and will keep the skins 'rustling' dry. In well-dried bulbs the pale, shiny tips of new roots can be found, with a little searching, in a circle around the old withered roots. The new roots should remain about the size of a pinhead (1 mm.) until January when new growth may begin. Any premature growth of the new roots before this is a warning that dormancy has been disturbed and that sprouting could be on the way. If water droplets come into contact with the base of the bulb for more than a few days, new root growth will occur any time after the bulbs are lifted. This may happen if drying outside was poor because of prolonged rain, or if bulbs are put into polythene bags so that condensation builds up. It can be seen that it is essential to keep water away from onions in store.

Until late December the shoot inside the bulb should remain white, but in January it begins to turn yellow as the process of sprouting develops. New root growth also coincides with the development of the shoot. The time taken for the emergence of the sprout from the bulb depends on the storage temperature—the lower the temperature, the better. There is little danger of damaging the bulbs by frost as they have a low freezing-point, for they even recover from being frozen at about –3 °C (26 °F) with little apparent damage. If they do freeze it is best to leave them undisturbed to thaw slowly when the ambient temperature rises. Over 50 per cent of the bulbs will start to sprout from mid-March to the end of April. Storage can be prolonged after this time in a refrigerator which can provide the ideal conditions of low temperature and low humidity. Bulbs should be placed in a net in order to benefit fully from the conditions. If onions are to be stored in a refrigerator, they must be placed there before mid-January or before yellowing of the internal sprout starts. If, despite all your efforts, sprouting occurs prematurely, there is the minor consolation that the sprouts are quite edible but the bulbs should be used up quickly.

Bulbs from the overwintered crop are not usually stored for any length of time. However, they can be dried and stored at ambient temperatures in the same way as the main crop, but with bulbs harvested in June and July, 50 per cent will have sprouted by December.

### Vegetables susceptible to 'chilling injury'

The ancestors of certain beans, cucumbers, marrow, pumpkin and other cucurbits, sweet peppers, and tomatoes all came from subtropical areas of Central and South America. Consequently the plants, including the fruit, are poorly adapted to temperatures below about 10 °C (50 °F) (see Table 9.3) although the seed can survive such temperatures. At temperatures below 10 °C (50 °F) these fruits develop pitting of the surface, loss of flavour and texture, and sometimes internal discolouration. If chilling persists for long enough, internal tissues become very soft and have a

**Table 9.3**

**Storage conditions for vegetables susceptible to chilling injury**

| | **Storage conditions** | | |
|---|---|---|---|
| | **Temperature and humidity** | **Freezing-point** | **Likely maximum storage life (days)** |
| **Beans, French and Runner** | All require 5–7°C | All freeze at −1°C | 8 |
| **Cucumber and Courgette** | (41–45°F) and high humidity | (30°F) | 14 |
| **Marrow and Pumpkin** | | | 60 |
| **Sweet Pepper** | | | 21 |

water-soaked appearance, and their breakdown is completed by spoilage organisms.

The effects of chilling injury are cumulative; a short period at 1 °C (34 °F) is as bad as a longer period at 4 °C (40 °F). Tomatoes and cucumbers kept for a week in a refrigerator at about 4 °C (40 °F) will be irreparably damaged and will be of poor flavour and texture. Furthermore, cool nights in August and September can initiate chilling injury in the garden even before harvest. These fruits and vegetables are best stored in a cool cupboard or room, partly but not completely wrapped, to allow some circulation of air. If they are to be kept for only a few days refrigeration is acceptable as chilling injury symptoms will not have time to develop, though the flavour will probably suffer.

With potatoes and beetroot chilling injury results in an increase in decay and loss of quality at temperatures near to freezing-point.

In conclusion, much can be done to extend the season of supply of many vegetables by simple methods of storage. Neither expensive equipment nor complicated techniques are required to prolong the availability of your own vegetables for weeks or months.

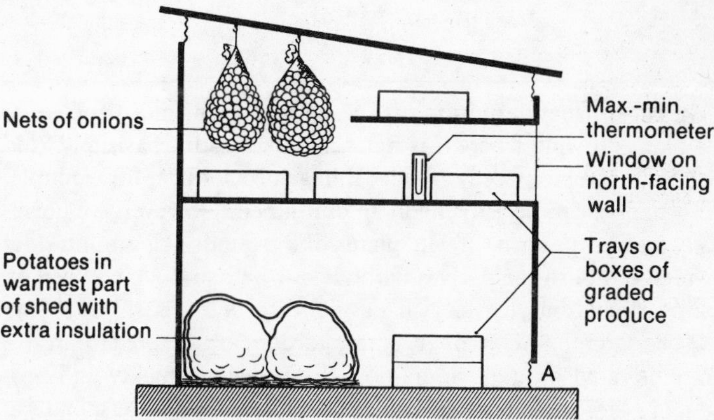


Fig. 9.2. Cross section of a garden shed adapted for the storage of produce. Air circulates in the shed, entering through fresh-air vent A and leaving via small gaps between eaves.

# 10 Weeds and weed control

The most usual definition of a weed is 'a plant out of place' or 'a plant growing where it is not wanted'. On this basis any kind of plant can be a weed, even a cabbage or a lettuce, for example, if it happens to be growing in an onion bed. However, we normally reserve the term for wild plants like groundsel or ground elder which establish themselves without our help and which keep on appearing from year to year despite efforts to get rid of them.

The common weeds of vegetable gardens are adapted to survive in cultivated ground. Some do it by growing quickly and producing large numbers of seeds. Not all the seeds germinate at once; many remain alive but dormant in the soil, germinating and giving rise to seedlings only when the ground is disturbed at some future time. Others survive by forming persistent roots or stems, often deep in the soil, in which food is stored and from which new shoots can arise in later years. These strategies ensure that weeds are always there, ready to take advantage of any opportunity to grow and multiply.

Agriculture has been described as 'a controversy with weeds', and this is no less true of vegetable gardening. On the principle that it is a wise approach to know the enemy, in this chapter we shall look at some of the characteristics of weeds as well as the methods that can be used to keep on top of them.

## Why are weeds harmful?

The purpose in having a vegetable plot is to grow good vegetables, preferably with a minimum of effort, and if weeds make it more difficult to achieve this, then their presence must be considered undesirable. Weeds interfere with crop production both directly and indirectly. Their main direct effect is to reduce crop growth and yield by preventing the crop from using resources that would otherwise be available to it. Indirectly, they can affect the crop by harbouring pests and diseases or they can simply get in the way and make it more difficult to harvest the produce. In order to avoid these effects something has to be done, and this involves time and energy. If there are only a very few weeds they may present no immediate problem, but left untouched they will certainly multiply and become an increasing nuisance in the future.

## Direct effects

It goes without saying that if we grow vegetables on weed-infested ground and take no steps at all to deal with the weeds, the crops will be unable to realize their full potential. This is primarily because of competition. The weeds will take up water and mineral nutrients from the soil so that less are available for the crop, and they may grow above it and prevent the sunlight from reaching it. How serious these effects are depends on various factors.

Some crops are better able to resist competition from weeds than others. A lot depends on the size of the seedling, how quickly it grows and how soon the crop covers the ground. Onions are one of the crops most susceptible to competition. Germination and early growth are slow and the leaves of the young plants are slender and upright, so that quick-growing broad-leaved weeds have a distinct advantage. Broad bean, on the other hand, produces a large seedling so that the advantage is with the crop. If weeds are allowed to remain right through the season in a crop of onions grown from seed, almost the entire crop will be lost; with broad beans, the effects will be much less pronounced and may only be severe if there is a shortage of water in the soil at the time when the pods are filling out. Transplanted crops, especially those in soil blocks or planted out from pots, also have an advantage over weeds germinating from seed.

Weeds themselves differ in competitive ability, although this can vary with the circumstances and the time of year. On the whole it is the tall-growing, vigorous weeds like fat-hen which have the most pronounced effects; seedlings of fat-hen which appear in late summer, however, only form small plants, although these still produce plenty of seeds. Chickweed, generally a low-growing plant, may not present much of a problem in a tall crop during summer, but plants which have overwintered grow rapidly on a fertile soil in early spring and can completely smother crops like salad onions and spring cabbage.

The fact that weeds are present in a crop does not necessarily mean that competition is actually taking place. During the early stages of growth, when both crop and weeds are still small seedlings, each can obtain all the resources needed to grow without interfering with any of the others. As the seedlings increase in size, however, their root systems explore greater volumes of soil and when the supply of nutrients or water is no longer great enough to meet the needs of all of them, competition begins. The weeds must be removed before this happens, otherwise there will be detrimental effects on crop growth.

It is not easy to pinpoint the time at which competition begins, since it depends on several factors. It will occur sooner, for example, when the temperatures are high and rapid growth is taking place than it will in very early spring when things are happening slowly. It is also influenced by the kinds of weeds present and by how many of them there are, as well as by which crop it is. If there are only very few weeds, no more than one or two per square metre, they may have no detectable effect on the crop even if they are left until harvest, but the more weeds there are the shorter the period before competition starts. Experiments with several different spring-sown vegetable crops and naturally-occurring weed populations showed that weeds and crop can co-exist without interference for about three weeks after the crop has come up. This is a reasonable figure to take as a guide.

Once competition does begin, the effects can be quite startling. In some research with onions, the weeds were carefully removed from separate plots at different times during the growth of the crop and the plots were then kept clean. It was found that after competition had started, the final yield of bulbs was being reduced at a rate equivalent to almost 4 per cent per day. So that by delaying weeding for another fortnight, the yield was cut to less than half that produced on ground kept clean all the time. In these experiments there were many more weeds per unit area than there were crop plants, which is what usually happens, and they also grew more rapidly than the crop. By early June the weight of weeds per unit area was more than twenty times that of the crop, and the weeds had already taken from the soil about half the nitrogen and a third of the potash which had been applied in the base fertilizer dressing.

Another reason why onions are particularly susceptible to weed competition is because they only produce a limited number of leaves before they start to bulb (see p. 378). So if the weeds are removed, there is little recovery from the ill effects that may already have occurred. Other crops, like red beet for example, keep on producing new leaves and have much better powers of recovery after weeding, even when this has been delayed. Once a crop has become successfully established and has formed a good leaf canopy, any further weed seedlings that appear are usually suppressed; the crop has the advantage and the weeds are unable to compete effectively. Seeds of many weeds need light for germination, and there is evidence that the presence of a leaf canopy can actually prevent germination. This is because the quality of the light filtering through green leaves is altered in such a way that it tends to promote rather than overcome dormancy in seeds present at or very close to the soil surface.

So far we have been considering the effects of weeds developing from seeds, stimulated to germinate by the soil disturbance involved in preparing the seedbed for the crop. Weed shoots which come from perennials with persistent underground root systems have the advantage of being able to use the stored food and can grow very quickly. Although they may not compete with the crop directly while it is still in an early stage of growth, since the root systems will be at different levels in the soil, they can soon overtop the crop and shade it. There is evidence for some kinds of perennial weeds that substances produced by either the living or decaying parts of the plants can be released into the soil and may inhibit the growth of other plants—a phenomenon called allelopathy. In practice, however, it is difficult to assess these effects and to distinguish them from straightforward competition for limited resources.

### Indirect effects

The fact that weeds serve as hosts for many of the pests and diseases that attack crops is often quoted as a reason why they should be eliminated from the vegetable garden. It is perfectly true that they do harbour a wide range of organisms including insects, fungi, viruses and plant parasitic eelworms, and that these may be able to multiply either on the weeds or within their tissues. The question is whether this really matters from the practical point of view.

So far as insect pests are concerned, the evidence suggests that weeds probably do not play a very important role in the vegetable garden. Although aphids, for example, may be found infesting particular weeds, they are not necessarily the same species or strains that attack the crops. Tests with the common cruciferous weeds, such as shepherd's purse, have shown that they do not act as hosts for the larvae of the cabbage root fly. One exception was found to be wild radish, but this is not usually a weed of established vegetable gardens. It is true that some pests, for example cutworms, may first attack weeds and then move onto crops, but in general it seems that the importance of weeds as hosts for insect pests of vegetables on a garden scale has been over-emphasized. Crop residues, on the other hand, may be of much greater significance. Carrots left in the ground over winter can certainly increase the risk of serious carrot-fly attack in the following year.

A similar conclusion applies in relation to the nematodes (eelworms) that attack vegetables. The presence of black nightshade would be likely to keep up the numbers of potato-cyst eelworm while onion-stem eelworm can carry over on a number of common annual weeds, but there is little evidence to show that weeds on the vegetable plot are of any importance in this respect.

Again, with the fungi that cause diseases in vegetables, weeds probably do not play any important role. Fungi exist in different strains, and those found on weeds may not be the same ones that attack the crops. The 'bridging' effect of having crops of a particular kind present throughout the year is probably a more significant factor. The organism which causes clubroot of brassicas can survive in the living and dead roots of weeds in the same plant family, and in this instance, their presence can be detrimental in reducing the benefits of crop rotation.

In contrast, the role of weeds in providing a reservoir and source of infection for viruses which cause diseases in vegetables has been underestimated, partly because the infected weed plants often show no symptoms themselves. Overwintering weeds such as chickweed and groundsel frequently carry cucumber mosaic virus which may then be transmitted by aphids to a range of crops, including marrows and tomatoes. Chickweed, which shows no symptoms, is especially significant as a source of infection because it has been shown that this particular virus can persist in the seeds produced by an infected chickweed plant. These can then give rise to more infected chickweed plants at some later time. Beet western yellows virus has become increasingly troublesome in lettuce in recent years, causing characteristic yellowing of the outer leaves as the plants develop. This virus also occurs in common weeds like shepherd's purse, groundsel and hairy bittercress, and if these are not destroyed in winter they serve as a bridge and provide a source of infection for lettuce grown in spring. Shepherd's purse and most other cruciferous weeds carry cauliflower mosaic virus, and there are others which could be cited. There are, therefore, good reasons for ensuring that the vegetable garden is cleaned up at some stage during late autumn or winter in order to prevent carry-over of viruses as far as possible. Weeds, however, are not the only sources of infection; many ornamental plants grown in flower borders serve as hosts from which vegetables can acquire viruses transmitted by aphids. This is true of delphiniums, for example, while wallflowers provide an effective bridge whereby turnip mosaic virus can be carried over the winter period.

There are some other indirect effects of weeds which can be very important in commercial vegetable production. When crops are harvested mechanically the mere presence of weed vegetation, even at a level such that there is no competition with the crop, can slow down the operation and make it much more costly. Berries and seed heads can contaminate the harvested crop and make it unacceptable for processing. So it is hardly surprising that the commercial vegetable grower has to maintain a high standard of weed control. Even in the garden twining weeds like field bindweed or black bindweed can make it difficult to pick a crop, while the presence of annual nettle makes the harvesting of one's own produce unpleasant. The presence of weed vegetation may also tend to promote the spread of fungal diseases by impeding airflow and maintaining a moist atmosphere close to the crop.

## Annual weeds

These are weeds which develop from seeds and which grow, flower, set seed, and die all within a year or less. Even among annuals there are differences in the time taken to complete the life-cycle. The frequent cultivations associated with growing a rotation of vegetables in a garden tend to discourage those which have a relatively long life-cycle, and such common cornfield weeds as charlock and wild radish are usually not a problem in gardens. The ones that flourish are those which take only a short time to reach maturity and produce more seeds again. Chickweed, groundsel, shepherd's purse, annual meadow grass, and field speedwell are among those which are universally present in vegetable gardens, and some of them can often complete two and sometimes more generations within the year.

### Growth habits

Annual weeds exhibit great variety in growth form. Some of them, like fat-hen and annual nettle, are erect plants which grow straight upwards. If they have plenty of space they branch out sideways as well and become very large; if they are crowded they just produce single stems. Annual nettle starts to shed seeds while the plant is still small – little more than four weeks after the seedling has emerged – and it goes on seeding right through the season until the winter frosts. Fat-hen, however, sheds all its seeds at more or less the same time at the end of the summer.

Quite a few of the common weeds, such as chickweed, knotgrass, and the speedwells, have a prostrate, creeping habit. They branch extensively and spread over the ground, forming a mat. These weeds tend to produce seeds throughout most of their life; ripe seeds are shed from the capsules formed at the base of the branches while more flowers continue to be formed at the tips. Yet other annual weeds, among them shepherd's purse, hairy bittercress, and the mayweeds, begin by forming a flat whorl or rosette of leaves and then later on the flowering stem develops from the centre of the rosette. These weeds usually produce all their seeds at much the same time, but how long they remain in the rosette stage depends on the time of year at which they germinate. Plants appearing in spring and early summer go up to flower quickly, whereas if they emerge in late summer or autumn they may stay as rosettes through the winter and not flower until the following spring. Such a pattern of behaviour approaches that of biennial weeds. These usually germinate in spring and the plants remain in the vegetative stage during the first season while they build up food reserves; flowering and seeding then take place in the following year. Biennials are common in hedgerows and waste places but again because of the frequent cultivations, they are not usually a problem in a vegetable garden. Two which do sometimes occur are spear thistle and white campion.

Many common annual weeds of gardens are perfectly frost-hardy and can continue to make some growth even at low temperatures, while some of them like the speedwells and red deadnettle can be found in flower in winter. Others normally die off during winter and then fresh seedlings come up in spring; black nightshade is one which is killed by the first severe frost. There are also differences in the tolerance of weeds to drought. Annual meadow grass and chickweed, with their fibrous root systems, are among the first to be killed as the soil dries out whereas the deeper-rooting fat-hen and black nightshade are able to keep going for much longer in dry summers like that of 1976.

## Seed survival

As already mentioned, one of the important characteristics of annual weeds is that they produce large numbers of seeds. The numbers may be very large indeed; a single big plant of fat-hen, for example, may produce 70,000 seeds. However, the average numbers per plant are much less, because there are usually a lot of small plants present. In fact another important feature of annual weeds is their ability to produce seeds even when the plant size is very much reduced through lack of resources. Tiny plants of annual meadow grass growing on an ash path, for example, may still have one or two seeds each even though they are scarcely visible. It is the small plants which are so easily overlooked.

Measurements of the numbers of seeds shed on to the soil where crops have been allowed to become weedy show that there can quite easily be 54,000 per square metre (5,000 per square foot). Many of these, of course, would probably be eaten by birds, and others may germinate immediately if the soil is moist. It is common to see a dense carpet of seedlings beneath a big plant of annual nettle, for example, and large numbers of seedlings of groundsel and smooth sowthistle often appear in late summer wherever plants of these weeds have been allowed to mature. Even with weeds like these, not all the seeds will find suitable conditions for rapid germination and some will become incorporated into the soil. Moreover, seeds of many weeds have a built-in dormancy mechanism which prevents immediate germination or restricts it to only a small proportion of the total number. Seeds of fat-hen and knotgrass are unable to germinate when they are shed from the parent plant in summer or autumn, and will not do so until they have experienced a period of exposure to low temperatures during winter.

As a result, there is almost invariably a sizeable 'seed bank' in the soil made up of seeds which are alive but dormant. Studies of soil samples taken from fields cropped commercially with vegetables have shown that it is quite common to find 10,000 living seeds per square metre (900 per square foot) in the top 15 cm. (6 in.) of soil. In very weedy fields as many as 75,000 per square metre (7,000 per square foot) have been recorded. There are no similar figures for the numbers of weed seeds present in garden soils, but the situation is probably very much the same.

The action of disturbing the soil to produce a seedbed causes some of the seeds present in the soil to germinate, and a flush of seedlings appears unless it happens to be too cold or too dry. It is still not known precisely why soil disturbance has this effect. It used to be thought that it was largely a question of aeration of the soil, but it now seems that exposure of the seeds to light is probably a major factor. However, not all the seeds will be affected; some will retain their physiological dormancy while others may not encounter the right conditions at the time so that they too remain dormant for the present. Recent research has shown that the proportion of seeds in the soil which gives rise to seedlings after any one cultivation is only small. Even under favourable conditions, in spring, say, when the soil is moist, probably no more than one-twentieth of the total store of seeds will germinate so that the weeds which actually appear in a crop represent only the tip of the iceberg.

Besides the seeds which make it to the surface and establish as seedlings, other will be stimulated to germinate but will die because they use up their food reserves before the seedling shoot gets there. Moreover, other seeds present in the soil will die without ever germinating. So that provided no fresh seeds are allowed to come in, the seed bank will tend to decrease naturally. Research has been carried out to determine how quickly this takes place, and the results have proved both interesting and useful. It was found that with a soil which was carrying vegetable crops and which was frequently cultivated, about half the seeds were lost from one cause or another during the year. This means that if no fresh seeding were allowed, the seed bank would be halved each year and would reach a level of 1 per cent of its initial size after seven years. So the old saying 'one year's seeding, seven years' weeding' is perhaps not far from the truth.

There is really no way of speeding up the process and getting the seed bank to decline more rapidly. Cultivating the soil more frequently than is necessary to grow the crops properly will not have very much additional effect. One hope for the future is that a chemical might be discovered which could be applied to the soil and which would stimulate all the seeds to germinate at once so that they could be killed. Certainly there are growth-regulator chemicals which on a laboratory scale are very effective in bringing about germination of dormant seeds of particular kinds of weeds. One problem is that not all seeds respond to any one chemical, and at present this approach has not met with much success in practical terms. The opposite approach would be not to try to make the seeds germinate, but to kill them while they are still dormant. Several of the soil partial sterilant (fumigant) chemicals used in commercial vegetable production, primarily for disease or eelworm control, do have this effect, and the benefit they give in terms of weed control is a useful bonus for the grower. For the gardener, however, the important thing is to prevent the weeds that do come up from reaching maturity and adding their quota of fresh seeds to those already in the soil as a result of seeding in previous years. If this can be done, the seed bank will progressively decline through natural causes, and life will become that much easier.

The question 'how long do weed seeds live?' is one which is often asked but has no simple answer. For one thing, there are differences between species; seeds of groundsel, for example, are relatively short-lived compared with those of fat-hen and many other species. However, there are some general principles. Survival will be shortest when the seeds are close to the soil surface; here they are exposed to light and to the greatest fluctuations in temperature, both factors which promote germination. If the seeds are initially distributed throughout the topsoil, say, to a spade's depth, then regular cultivation will keep bringing seeds near the surface and give them maximum opportunity to germinate. If the soil remains undisturbed, the life of the seeds is prolonged, and this is especially true of seeds which lie some distance below the surface. When buried deeply, seeds of various weeds, among them chickweed, have been shown to survive for forty years or more, and there is evidence that in a few species a proportion of the seeds can remain alive for much longer than that.

## Time of emergence

In general, the greatest emergence of weed seedlings takes place either in spring as the soil warms up, or in late summer/early autumn. In winter the temperature is too low for germination of some seeds to begin, and in any case all growth processes are slowed down during the cold weather. During the height of summer it may be too hot for germination of certain species, but more commonly it is lack of soil moisture which prevents germination at this time. As already emphasized, seeds freshly shed from the parent plants may germinate immediately. It is possible, however, to give some indication of when seeds present in the soil are most likely to produce seedlings, and this is done in Fig. 10.1 for twelve annual weeds.

Quite a number of the commonest weeds are able to germinate over a wide range of temperatures, like the first five species in Fig. 10.1. They are able to take advantage of any opportunity to produce seedlings, and the seedlings can survive no matter when they emerge. This obviously contributes to their success as weeds in vegetable gardens. Others, like fat-hen and annual nettle, have their peak period of emergence in spring but few seedlings appear after early autumn. Black nightshade is one of the species with a restricted period of emergence, not starting until early May and stopping again in September. This means that seedlings often appear after the first flush of spring weeds has been dealt with, and they can easily be overlooked.

Some weeds have specialized means of restricting the period of emergence so that seedlings only appear at times when there is a chance of being able to complete the life-cycle. Research has shown that seeds of knotgrass need exposure to low temperatures

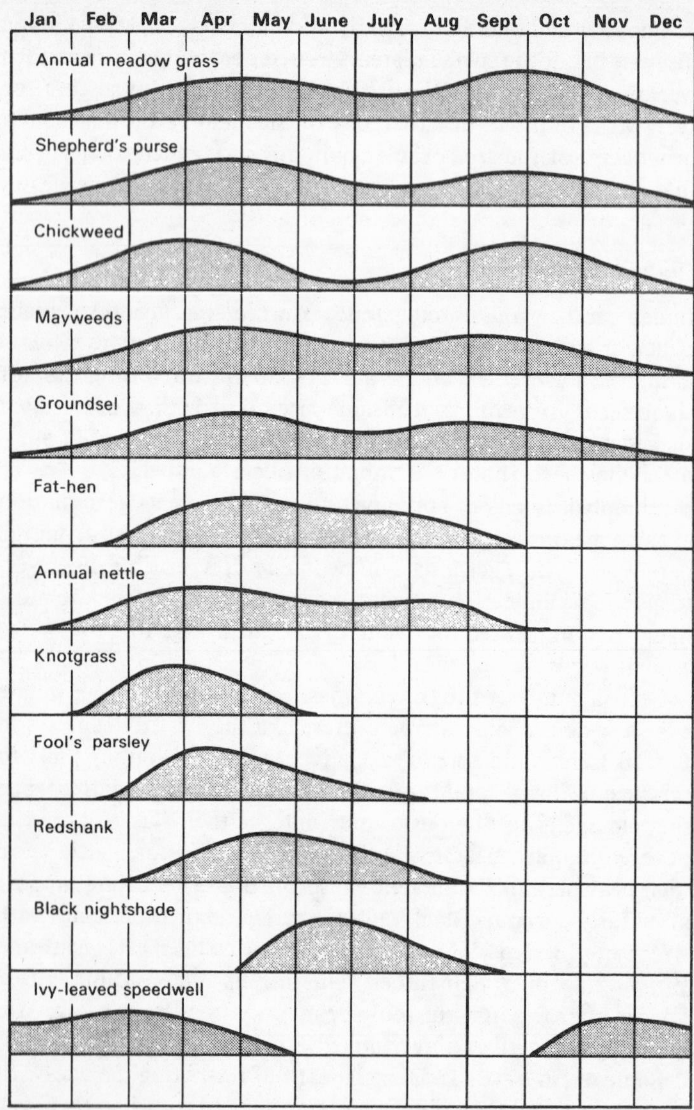


Fig. 10.1. Times of year at which seedlings of twelve annual weeds are most likely to appear following cultivation.

in order to overcome dormancy, and emergence then begins in early spring (Fig. 10.1) High temperatures at the end of May then reimpose dormancy and cause germination to stop, so that the seeds still present in the soil require a further exposure to winter cold before they again become capable of germinating. Ivy-leaved speedwell behaves in the opposite way. It is the high temperatures of summer which overcome the dormancy, and seedling emergence does not begin until October. Seeds of this weed germinate when the temperature is fairly low and seedling emergence continues during winter and spring. During this time dormancy increases in those seeds which remain in the soil, and this is again overcome during summer. With these weeds, therefore, there is a definite seasonal pattern of seedling emergence, and the time of their appearance can be predicted with some confidence.

## Mechanical control

Vegetable crops are, for a variety of good reasons, normally grown in rows and it is necessary to deal with weeds growing both between and within the rows. The possibilities for doing this by physical means come down to four: the weeds can be cut off, pulled up, smothered or burned off. Where there is no crop, digging is an additional option.

*Hoeing*. This is the traditional, and very effective, method of removing annual weeds growing between the crop rows. The usual tool employed is the Dutch hoe, an angled blade on the end of a long handle. This blade is moved back and forth parallel to the soil surface but just beneath it, so that the weed seedlings are cut off below ground level. It is important to keep the blade sharp so that it cuts cleanly and also to keep the depth of working shallow. Hoeing too deeply serves no useful purpose, and indeed is counter-productive since it brings more weed seeds to the surface where they can germinate and also leads to losses of soil moisture. It is also likely to cause damage to the root systems of the crop seedlings. The best time to hoe is when most of the seedling weeds have emerged and the crop rows are clearly visible. Hoeing earlier than this means that it will soon have to be repeated since a lot of the weeds will still be germinating beneath the surface; moreover, there is a risk of cutting into the crop row. Delaying too long, on the other hand, may allow the weeds to begin to compete with the crop. They will also be more difficult to cut through, and may quite easily root again if it rains. Ideally, hoeing is best done in a dry, sunny period but while there is still moisture just below the surface. The blade then flows easily through the soil and accurate working is possible because it does not bounce off dry clods and dislodge crop seedlings, while the weeds that are hoed off quickly die.

Besides the traditional pattern of Dutch hoe, there are nowadays various hoes of improved design, often with a double-acting blade. In larger gardens a wheeled hoe, equipped with L-shaped blades which can be set for different row distances, can be very useful in speeding up the work. With a friable soil and straight rows, very accurate working is possible. Motorized tools can also be used, either with blades or with tines that spin out the weed seedlings. The other common type of hand hoe, the draw hoe, is really not very suitable for removing seedling weeds from between rows of crops. Because it is used with a chopping action, it is easy to dig into the soil too deeply and bring up fresh seeds. It is also easy to leave some weeds undamaged, and because, unlike the Dutch hoe, its use involves walking forwards over the hoed ground, weeds not actually cut through can be trodden into the soil and may root again. Its main use in weed control is to deal with any larger weeds that survive until a later stage.

Hoeing is basically a quick and effective method of destroying annual weeds. There is no advantage in doing it more often than is essential to achieve this purpose; too-frequent hoeing may not only be unnecessary, but it can have detrimental effects as well (see p. 368).

*Hand pulling*. Hoeing is obviously a lot quicker than grasping each weed seedling individually and pulling it out. So it is an advantage to hoe as close as possible to the crop rows without causing any damage, and this is greatly helped by careful sowing in straight rows. Even so, there will be some weeds that appear actually within the rows among the crop seedlings, which must be removed by hand. Again, there is an optimum time for doing this. If done too early the weeds are difficult to get hold of and they are sometimes difficult to distinguish from the crop seedlings. Moreover, the process will probably have to be repeated very soon because more weed seedlings will have emerged. If weeding is left too late, competition with the crop may already have begun and it is also very likely that in pulling up the weeds the crop plants will also be disturbed. Weeds in the seedling stage, when they have still got only two true leaves, are usually easy to remove but it becomes more difficult as their root systems develop. There are some weeds, like fumitory, which are easy to pull up without disturbing the soil even when they are fully grown. Others, such as black nightshade, develop a forked root system which anchors the plant firmly and makes it very resistant to pulling; the stem can easily break off, leaving the plant to regenerate from branches produced at the base. Others again, such as chickweed and annual meadow grass, produce a dense system of fibrous roots and tend to pull up with a mass of soil which can easily bring crop plants with it. Weeds like these root again very readily if they are left lying on the soil in moist conditions.

*Mulching*. Most annual weeds of gardens have small seeds which contain limited reserves of food and it is only those germinating within 2.5 or 5 cm. (1 or 2 in.) of the surface that have sufficient reserves to enable the shoot to reach it. If the ground is covered with a mulch, an additional layer of something which keeps out the light, then the seedlings will not survive. Mulches can be applied between the crop rows and around transplanted crops and have the additional advantage of conserving soil moisture, especially if applied after rainfall or watering. The best organic materials include peat and various kinds of compost, such as weed-free garden compost or spent mushroom compost. Other materials which can be used include straw and grass mowings, though these have some disadvantages. Straw often contains weed seeds and there are usually some cereal grains which quickly germinate. Grass mowings may have a lot of seeds of annual meadow grass, which is a weed very common in lawns. It is, of course, important not to use mowings from a lawn recently treated with a selective herbicide since this could lead to crop damage. There is also a possibility that mulches of this kind can provide shelter for pests such as slugs. A great virtue of organic mulches is that when they have served their purpose they become incorporated in the soil and enrich it, though the nitrogen required in the humus-forming process may need to be replaced. Maintenance of a surface layer of compost is an essential feature of the 'no-digging' approach to vegetable growing (see pp. 364–5). From the point of view of minimizing weed problems this system has the advantage that fresh weed seeds are not constantly brought up from lower down in the soil. Any seedlings that do appear in the surface layer can readily be dealt with because of its friable nature.

An alternative to organic mulches is to use strips of black polythene, laid on the ground and anchored at the edges with soil. Transplants, like brassicas, can be planted through holes made in the plastic. Large seeds of crops like sweet corn can also be dibbled in through holes, and potatoes can be grown in this way. Black plastic does not have the same advantage as clear plastic in raising the soil temperature but it does conserve soil moisture and unlike clear plastic, it keeps the weeds down. Some suitable arrangement, such as slits in the furrows, is needed to let the water through to the soil. The disadvantages are the initial cost, the fact that the plastic has to be removed eventually, and the fact that to many people the appearance of plastic-covered soil is aesthetically unpleasing. On small areas, old carpet can be used as an alternative to black plastic and has the advantage that it does not need to be anchored since its own weight will keep it in place. It is advisable to put down slug pellets before laying the strips of carpet.

As already mentioned, a flush of weed seedlings starts to appear in spring as the soil warms up. It is possible to speed up this process by covering the ground with clear polythene in early spring so as to raise the soil temperature. When it is time to sow, the polythene is removed and the weeds pulled out or killed either by very shallow hoeing or by treating with paraquat/diquat.

Provided soil disturbance is kept to a minimum, this technique can greatly reduce the numbers of weed seedlings that subsequently appear in the crop.

*Flame-weeding.* There are various proprietary flame guns available which can be used to burn off weeds from areas of uncropped ground. Some types can also be used for inter-row weeding among crops, although great care is needed to ensure that the crop is not damaged as well. Since the soil is not disturbed there is no stimulation of fresh germination, and dormant seeds which are on the soil surface or very close to it will be killed.

*Digging.* This is obviously not applicable to ground which is carrying growing crops. However, in parts of the garden from which crops have been cleared in autumn it is the traditional method of starting the preparation for next year's cropping. Annual weeds which are dug in are effectively killed, although burial must be complete; if any parts of creeping or tufted weeds remain above ground they can go on growing through the winter. Undoubtedly the spade is the best tool for the purpose except on heavy soils where it may be easier to use a flat-tined digging fork. To most people, there is something very satisfying in the contemplation of a piece of skilfully dug soil. If, however, there are seeds present on the weeds that are dug in it may be a question of postponing the problem: burial is the best way to ensure survival of weed seeds.

## Chemical control

In the smaller vegetable gardens at any rate, the traditional methods of hoeing and hand pulling are still the mainstay of weed control. Where vegetables are grown commercially on large areas, of course, this is nowadays not feasible and growers rely to a large extent on selective herbicides for controlling weeds. These are chemicals which are applied either to the soil or over the crop after it has come up and which, for various reasons, act selectively to kill the weeds without harming the crop. The development of these techniques over the last thirty years has been a considerable success story, and without them it is difficult to see how vegetables could still be produced economically. To use them successfully requires a lot of care and know-how. Individual herbicides can only be used on particular crops, the application rate has to be carefully controlled, and such factors as the type of soil, the exact stage of crop growth and the weather conditions have to be taken into account. It is not surprising, therefore, that these techniques do not translate readily to a garden scale.

Nevertheless, there are a few herbicides which are available on the retail market and which can be helpful in the vegetable plot. It is most important to read the labels carefully before use, and to use them *only* on those crops for which they are recommended. The following paragraphs are intended to indicate the possibilities; they are *not* a substitute for the manufacturers' directions, which must always be followed.

*Paraquat/diquat.* This is available as a soluble solid formulation. It is not a selective herbicide and will kill the green tissues of both crops and weeds if it comes into contact with them. It acts rapidly, especially in warm weather, and even if rain falls shortly after application its effectiveness is not reduced. Once it reaches the soil it is inactivated, so that it cannot harm the roots of crop plants.

Paraquat/diquat has two main uses in the vegetable plot. First, it can be applied between crop rows using a dribble bar attached to a plastic watering can. Great care is needed in doing this, because if any of the solution splashes onto the crop plants they will certainly be injured and perhaps killed. Used in this way it serves as a 'chemical hoe'. The advantage over hoeing is that because the soil is not disturbed, few fresh weed seeds are caused to germinate and the effect therefore lasts longer. The second use is for killing weeds that have appeared on ground which is not actually being cropped at the time. On parts of the garden from which crops have been cleared in early autumn large numbers of seedling weeds often appear, and these will produce quantities of seeds before the time arrives for digging. This can be prevented by applying paraquat/diquat, either with a dribble bar or through a rose on a can. Shoots of any perennial weeds present will be killed but paraquat/diquat will have no effect on the underground parts, so the benefit is only temporary so far as these weeds are concerned. It can also be very useful for treating weeds that appear on ground which has been prepared some time before it is actually required for sowing or planting. Seeds can be sown immediately after application and plants put in after twenty-four hours. Besides being a lot quicker than cultivation in these circumstances, there are other advantages. The main flush of weed seedlings that follows soil disturbance is avoided, and if the soil is moved as little as possible during sowing or planting out, only a few more weeds may appear. Avoiding cultivation also helps to conserve soil moisture.

*Propachlor.* This is a selective, soil-acting herbicide – a 'weed preventer' – which kills annual weeds as they germinate over a period of six to eight weeks after application. It is available in the form of granules which are shaken lightly and evenly over the soil straight from the container so as to achieve the recommended rate. This herbicide can be used on cabbage, cauliflowers, Brussels sprouts, broccoli, curly kale, swedes, onions and leeks. On sown crops, best results are obtained by applying immediately after sowing; on transplanted crops and onion sets it should be applied within two days after planting out. Propachlor does not kill weeds that are already established so the soil must be clean to start with, and the surface of the seedbed should also be smooth and free from clods. Like other soil-acting herbicides it needs moisture in order to work and should be applied to moist soil, although application under very wet and cold conditions should be avoided. It is important not to disturb the soil in any way after application, otherwise effectiveness will be reduced. Propachlor controls most of the annual weeds that occur frequently in vegetable plots, including annual meadow grass, groundsel, shepherd's purse, chickweed and speedwells. Application can be repeated after six weeks or so in order to prolong the effect, first removing by hand any weeds that have survived the initial treatment.

*Simazine.* This is another soil-acting herbicide which is applied to the soil surface through a sprayer, dribble bar or fine rose and which persists for a period of months, killing weeds as they germinate. However, most vegetables are susceptible to simazine and there are only three for which it is recommended. For sweet corn it is applied within a week after sowing and firming the seedbed. The ground is then left undisturbed. It is advised that no other crop should follow within seven months. In established asparagus beds, simazine can be very useful for keeping down annual weeds throughout the growing season. To do this, the beds are cleaned up in spring, simazine applied according to directions before the spears begin to emerge, and the soil is then left undisturbed. Rhubarb usually controls weeds effectively by itself because of the dense leaf canopy which it provides. Simazine can be used if necessary, however, provided the crop has been established for at least a year. It can be applied in autumn or in early spring. Care is needed to ensure that the proprietary product contains only simazine; those sold for total weed control on paths and which contain other chemicals as well are not safe for use on crops.

## Perennial weeds

These are weeds which always persist for more than a year, and often do so for many years. The two unfavourable periods which all plants have to contend with are winter, with its sometimes severe cold, and summer with the possibility of drought. Annual weeds make sure of the continued survival of the species during extreme conditions by maintaining reserves of seeds in the soil which can give rise to new plants when conditions become favourable again. Those perennials which are not frost-hardy have underground storage organs, so that even though the above-ground shoots die down in winter, new ones can develop as soon as the soil warms up in spring. Many of them are also deep rooted, and can draw water from below so that they are able to thrive during dry summers when other plants are at a disadvantage.

Some perennial weeds spread entirely by vegetative means and either produce no seeds at all, like slender speedwell, or do so only occasionally, like hedge bindweed. Others produce seeds in considerable numbers each year, and may rely on them for colonizing new areas. Perennial weeds in general are discouraged by the cultivations normally involved in growing vegetables, and many of them are not a problem in the vegetable garden. This is true of daisy and ribwort plantain, for example, which are common weeds of lawns. However, there are some exceptions to this rule and it is these which are a particular nuisance among vegetable crops.

From the practical point of view of controlling them and minimizing their effects there are three characteristics of perennial weeds which are especially relevant: first, whether they spread by vegetative means, and if so how; second, whether the perennating parts of the plant which persist from year to year are above the ground, in the surface soil, or deep down in the soil; and third, whether or not they produce seeds.

### Weeds with tap-roots

These produce a large, simple or branched, vertical storage root, bearing one or more rosettes of leaves at its crown from which the flowering stems arise. Common examples are dandelion and the curled and broad-leaved docks. There is no natural vegetative spread, but in a garden, regeneration from roots cut up by cultivations can occur. Both produce numerous seeds which enable them to spread. Those of docks are very persistent in the soil, more so than those of dandelion, though even these can remain dormant for several years in cultivated soil. Another tap-rooted weed often found on the sites of old gardens or allotments is horse-radish. The roots have considerable powers of regeneration and this plant is difficult to control by cultivation; however, it does not usually produce any seeds in this country.

### Creeping weeds

These include the most troublesome perennial weeds of gardens. They produce extensive systems of creeping stems or roots which enable them to spread rapidly and colonize large areas. In some weeds the creeping stems are in the form of stolons or runners above the ground. Plantlets are borne at intervals and these become rooted like strawberries and eventually become detached from the parent. In others, the creeping stems are below the ground and are called rhizomes. They bear small scale-like leaves with dormant buds, and these can be stimulated into growth by fragmentation of the rhizome during cultivation. Finally, there are the weeds in which there is an underground system of horizontal and vertical roots, which can penetrate to considerable depths. These can produce new buds at any position along their length and are often brittle, so that cultivation can easily result in new plants while the old ones regenerate from the deep roots.

### Characteristics of some common creeping weeds

*Creeping buttercup.* Has above-ground creeping stems or runners which bear new plantlets. Some leaves remain green through winter. Also spreads by seeds.

*Slender speedwell.* Originally introduced as a rock-garden plant; has bright blue flowers. Now a common lawn weed and can spread into cropped ground. Stems spread on the soil surface and root at the leaf joints. Does not produce seeds.

*Couch.* The commonest perennial grass weed. Has branched underground rhizomes with dormant buds usually only shallow, within a spade's depth. Shoots remain green in winter. Produces seeds, but main spread in gardens is by fragmentation of rhizomes during cultivation.

*Black bent.* Perennial grass like couch. Has branched underground rhizomes with dormant buds, usually only shallow. Shoots remain green in winter. Feathery flowering heads produce large numbers of very small seeds which readily germinate.

*Stinging nettle.* Has branched, yellow roots and horizontal rhizomes just below the soil surface. Short shoots remain green in winter. Produces quantities of seeds which can persist in the soil.

*Ground elder.* Very common garden weed. Has spreading system of underground rhizomes with dormant buds, usually shallow. Shoots die down in winter. Sometimes produces seeds, but main spread is vegetative by pieces of rhizome.

*Colt's-foot.* Has spreading system of underground rhizomes, often deep in the soil, with dormant buds and shoots bearing clusters of buds. Yellow flowers appear first in spring, followed by large leaves which die down in winter. Produces many seeds. These are dispersed by wind and can germinate immediately if they fall on moist soil, but they do not persist.

*Creeping thistle.* One of the commonest perennials. Has underground system of brittle, horizontal storage roots from which shoots arise; also deeply penetrating vertical roots. Shoots die down in winter. Patches of plants usually all male or all female; seeds sometimes produced, but not important as a means of spread in gardens.

*Perennial sowthistle.* Has underground system of brittle, horizontal storage roots from which shoots arise; also deeply-penetrating vertical roots. Shoots die down in winter. Tall stems with yellow flowers produce seeds which are dispersed by wind.

*Field bindweed.* Very common and persistent weed. Has underground system of deep-penetrating roots from which clusters of shoots arise. Branched shoots initially lie flat on ground, then twine up crops. Produces many pink and white flowers, but seeds not usually important as a means of spread in gardens.

*Hedge bindweed.* Often invades from hedges or fences; very persistent. Has underground system of branched rhizomes with dormant buds, often deep in the soil. The twining shoots die down in winter. Flowers white, larger than those of field bindweed, but rarely produces seeds.

*Field horsetail.* One of the most troublesome and persistent weeds where it occurs. Has underground system of horizontal rhizomes, with vertical penetration deep in the soil. Also has tubers. Not a flowering plant; pinkish-brown fertile stems with spore-bearing cones appear in spring. Followed by erect, spiky green vegetative shoots which die down in winter.

### Mechanical control

Tap-rooted weeds are comparatively easy to deal with. By inserting a garden fork at one side and levering, while at the same time grasping the crown of foliage and pulling, they can usually be removed completely. Docks do not regenerate even if the root breaks, provided that the upper 10 cm. (4 in.) or so is removed. Even the thinner parts of dandelion roots, however, will form new buds if they are allowed to remain, so that it is important to get out as much of the root as possible. Horse-radish also will regenerate from any parts of the root left behind. Weeds like creeping buttercup in which the creeping stems are above ground are quite easy to get rid of, although it means that every plantlet must be dug out, and vigilance is needed to ensure that they do not establish again from the seeds which are probably present in the soil.

Those weeds which have underground systems of creeping rhizomes or roots are a much more difficult proposition. When the rhizomes are near to the surface, as they are in couch, digging out is feasible on ground used for growing annual crops. It is much better to use a fork than a spade for this purpose, since the latter tends to cut the rhizomes into short lengths. These are more difficult to remove, and any left behind will simply sprout again and soon form new plants. An alternative is to try to break up the rhizomes into pieces deliberately, by rotary cultivation for example. This causes a lot of the dormant buds to sprout and the process is then repeated several times as soon as new growth appears. The danger with this is that unless done very thoroughly, the problem can be made worse rather than better. Another alternative for couch is to bury the rhizomes, but it is essential to ensure that all of them are put down to a depth of at least 15 cm. (6 in.).

Digging out is not a practical method of coping with those weeds which penetrate more deeply into the soil. Although the shallower roots and the vertical shoots which develop from them can be removed in this way, there are certain to be thick storage roots much further down than a spade's depth. So that while digging may bring about temporary relief, it is not a permanent solution, and it does of course require considerable time and effort.

In theory, hoeing conscientiously carried out and continued over a period of several years will weaken the plants and gradually eliminate them. Food reserves in the storage organs are used up in sending shoots to the surface and if these are hoed off before they have had time to reverse the process and replenish the reserves, then the weed ought to get weaker. Attacking a weed like creeping thistle just before it flowers, when the food reserves are at their lowest, might also seem sensible. In practice, however, hoeing is not a good way of getting rid of perennial weeds like this; it takes a long time, and some shoots are inevitably missed. It is a common complaint that even assiduous hoeing for many years has failed to make any real impression on an infestation of field bindweed or field horsetail.

There is one weed, oxalis, which is greatly encouraged by hoeing. Fortunately it is not very common, but is extremely serious where it does occur in gardens. The plant does not creep, but produces large numbers of small bulbs (bulbils) which are only loosely attached to the parent. Hoeing, or indeed any soil disturbance, only tends to dislodge them and cause new plants to appear over a wider area. The important thing is to recognize it as soon as it appears in the garden, to remove it carefully together with the soil round it, and then burn it.

Other physical methods of control which can be used against annual weeds are of no avail against those perennials with underground root or rhizome systems. Mulching is not effective, and this is not surprising when it is remembered that shoots of field bindweed can come through an asphalt pavement. Flame-weeding too, like hoeing, has only a temporary effect.

## Chemical control

It is in the control of troublesome perennial weeds that chemicals can be especially valuable in the vegetable garden. To get at these weeds through the roots would require high rates of chemical which would be quite out of the question on ground needed for growing vegetables. Fortunately, however, there are herbicides which are described as being 'translocated', that is moved from place to place within the plant. When applied to the weed foliage, they are taken into the leaves and then move down the stem into the underground parts. Not only are the shoots which are actually treated ultimately killed, but an appreciable part of the below-ground rhizomes or roots will be affected and will be unable to send up more shoots in the future. This is the great advantage of these herbicides; they are actively transported by the plant with the food materials being manufactured in the leaves down to the parts that otherwise cannot be reached. It follows from this that there are two basic requirements for using these herbicides effectively. First, sufficient foliage must be present at the time of treatment to retain an adequate amount of the chemical. Second, the leaves must be manufacturing food and exporting it from the shoots down into the storage organs. So the golden rule is to treat the weeds when they have well-developed shoots with plenty of foliage and are actively growing.

Translocated herbicides for the control of perennial weeds are not selective in vegetables; if any solution gets onto the crop foliage damage will occur. There are two ways, therefore, in which they can be used. The first involves treating the weeds at a time when no crop is present in that particular area. If the plot is fairly heavily infested, early-maturing crops can be harvested and the weed vegetation left behind. This section of the garden can then be treated and after waiting long enough for the herbicide to take effect, late sowings or plantings can be made. Normal crop rotation will allow other sections to be treated in the following year, so that eventually control is achieved over the whole plot without interrupting the cropping schedule. If, on the other hand, there are only scattered shoots or patches of perennial weeds, spot treatment would be the appropriate technique. This involves treating the shoots individually, and if this is done with care, even shoots growing among the crops can be successfully dealt with. Run-off of liquid from the weeds must be avoided; apart from the risk of crop damage, any herbicide solution that falls on the soil is simply wasted.

As with the chemical control of annual weeds, the manufacturers' directions should always be closely followed, not only in relation to the strength of the solution and method of application but also for safe handling and storage of herbicides. The following paragraphs are intended to indicate the possibilities there are at present for chemical control of perennial weeds in the vegetable garden.

*2,4-D.* This is a component of various proprietary products sold mainly for the selective control of broad-leaved weeds in lawns. It is usually combined with other 'growth-regulator' or 'hormone' herbicides, such as mecoprop or dicamba, and products are available in the form of 'guns' or solid sticks for treating individual weeds. In the vegetable garden these can be used for spot-treating shoots of perennial weeds, provided this use is specified on the label. 2,4-D is very effective against creeping thistle, dandelion and field bindweed but has no effect on grass weeds and only limited activity against some of the worst weeds such as ground elder and field horsetail.

*Dalapon.* This herbicide is effective against grasses, and its particular virtue is in the control of couch. Dalapon can be used in established asparagus beds, applying either in spring before the spears emerge if the couch is present and growing actively, or as a spot treatment to the weed foliage in summer when the asparagus fern has fully developed. Contact with the fern should be avoided. It can also be used in rhubarb, applied in autumn or early spring when the crop is dormant but the grass is still growing, avoiding contact with the rhubarb crowns.

*Glyphosate.* This herbicide has proved particularly useful to the gardener for two reasons. First, when used correctly and with a knowledge of the conditions under which it will perform best, it is a very effective chemical. Second, it is active against many of the problem weeds which up to now have been difficult to deal with. When used on a part of the garden which is not being cropped, it can be applied with a dribble bar, through a fine rose on a watering-can, or with a garden sprayer. Best results are usually obtained with a sprayer because more of the solution is retained on the weed foliage, but great care is needed to avoid any drift of spray droplets onto adjacent crops. As already emphasized, the weeds should have plenty of foliage and be growing vigorously. It is also important that the foliage should be dry at the time of application and that there is no rain for six hours in order to give time for the chemical to be absorbed into the plants. Glyphosate acts slowly, and it may be several weeks before the weeds look as though they are really dying. The ground should preferably not be cultivated for at least a week, so that the herbicide has time to be translocated downwards in the shoots to the roots or rhizomes. Any glyphosate which reaches the soil is inactivated almost immediately however, and if necessary crops can safely be sown or planted the day after application.

Some weeds, like couch, are normally killed completely by a single treatment. Others, such as field bindweed and field horsetail which have very extensive underground systems and relatively little foliage require more than one treatment. Spot treatment of individual weed shoots growing among crops is a useful method of following up a glyphosate treatment or preventing perennial weeds from becoming a more serious problem. The solution can be painted on, taking care to avoid all contact with the crop. Spot treatment has now become much easier with the advent of a brush-on gel formulation of glyphosate produced especially for the purpose.

## Living with weeds

Weeds are survivors, well equipped to cope with life in a disturbed habitat and able to take advantage of any opportunity there is to establish themselves and multiply. There is no question of getting rid of all the weeds completely; it is a matter of control, of so organizing things that they do not get out of hand. There are two phases to this. The first is a short-term one of bringing a new or a very neglected garden into a state where it is possible to grow vegetables without serious difficulty. The second is the unending struggle to keep it that way.

## New gardens

It is likely that there will be a mixed vegetation of various grass and broad-leaved perennial weeds, and that the soil will contain large numbers of living seeds of both annual and some perennial weeds. It is easier to make a determined attack on the perennials right at the start than it is later on once cropping has begun. How this is tackled depends partly on the kinds of weeds that are present, and partly on how urgent it is to start cropping. Possible approaches include:

*Digging*. Laborious; although annual weeds and couch can be usefully buried, not effective against deep-rooted perennials which will have to be dealt with later. Digging can be made easier by treating with paraquat/diquat to kill the vegetation which can then be skimmed off before starting.

*Rotary cultivation*. Quick, but tends to propagate perennial weeds by chopping up roots and rhizomes. Best if done several times at intervals of a few weeks. Not effective against deep-rooted perennials.

*Treatment with dalapon*. Useful when it is mainly grass weeds that are present. Sowing or planting can take place after six to eight weeks.

*Treatment with glyphosate*. Very effective way of dealing with both grassy and broad-leaved perennials; also kills annual weeds. Best to apply when perennials are well grown and approaching the bud stage. Sowing or planting preferably should be delayed for three to four weeks to allow the herbicide to exert its full effect, but can be done sooner.

*Treatment with ammonium sulphamate.* Best applied to well-grown vegetation during a dry spell. Corrosive to metals, so plastic sprayer or watering-can needed. Kills a wide range of annual and perennial weeds, but not some deep-rooted ones like field bindweed. Sowing or planting can begin after eight weeks, or twelve weeks if it stays very dry.

*Treatment with sodium chlorate.* Effective total herbicide, killing all kinds of weeds. Best to use a product with a fire depressant in it. Vegetation, wood and clothing sprayed with sodium chlorate become highly inflammable when dry, so great care is needed in handling and application. It is very soluble and can move both sideways and downwards in the soil, so it must not be applied where it could reach the roots of trees or other plants growing nearby. Sowing or planting has to be delayed for up to twelve months after treatment.

Whatever approach is adopted, there will probably be some perennials which escape or are not completely killed, so that in the following years a campaign of spot treatment is necessary.

## Established gardens

Since the development of translocated herbicides, and of glyphosate in particular, it has become much easier to contain perennial weeds than ever before. By diligent spot treatment, which is after all a very easy operation, it should be possible to eradicate these weeds. There will, of course, be new introductions; creeping weeds will invade from hedges or the base of fences, or from the gardens of less horticulturally inclined neighbours. Couch invading in this way is easy to deal with by making a vertical cut with a spade and then forking out the rhizomes. Shoots of deep-rooting perennials can be spot-treated with 2,4-D or glyphosate. Seeds of some common weeds, particularly dandelion and willowherbs, can be carried on the wind from some distance away so that there is a need to recognize perennials developing from seeds and to deal with them before they become established. Hoeing is only effective at the seedling stage; once beyond this, the young plants need careful forking-out. Asparagus beds offer a very favourable habitat for perennial weeds to establish from seeds brought in by the wind or dispersed by birds. If they are allowed to flourish, the useful life of the beds will be shortened, so that they need special attention.

Normal vegetable-growing practices are unlikely to introduce either seeds or root fragments of perennial weeds from elsewhere, although farmyard manure which has been stacked may well contain seeds of nettles. It is very easy, however, to introduce couch and ground elder into a garden in clumps of herbaceous plants, and once established, these weeds can readily spread into the vegetable plot. Introduction of the bulbous oxalis in this way is particularly to be avoided.

By judicious use of herbicides and a degree of vigilance it is possible to eradicate perennial weeds or at least ensure that they do not interfere with cropping. Unfortunately this is not true in respect of annual weeds. Prevention of seeding is the aim, and if this is achieved there is no doubt that the seed bank in the soil can be reduced to a low level. In practice, though, it is very difficult to get it down below a level of about 540 living seeds per square metre (50 per square foot). It only takes a few weed plants to escape and reach maturity for the natural losses to be replaced; a few more, and there may be ten times as many seeds in the soil at the end of the season as there were at the start.

Most of the weed seeds to be found in the soil are produced by plants which have seeded on the spot. In a new garden there may be all kinds of weeds, depending to a large extent on what type of soil it is, what the land has previously been used for, and whereabouts in the country it is situated. The weeds growing on a light, well-drained sandy soil are likely to be very different from those of heavy clay soils, and there are differences in the kinds of plants to be expected in the north and west, for example, compared with the south-east. However, a survey of seeds present in the soil of fields which had been cropped commercially with vegetables for many years showed that there was a similarity in the weeds irrespective of location and soil type. Chickweed, annual meadow grass, annual nettle, groundsel, shepherd's purse, fat-hen, and field speedwell were among the weeds most often recorded, and together these seven species accounted for 70 per cent of all the seeds found. As vegetable cropping proceeds, therefore, the character of the weed vegetation will change, and it is these species which are likely to feature increasingly as the main annual weeds.

Seeds of annual weeds can, of course, be introduced into gardens in various ways. Groundsel and the annual sowthistles have seeds which are readily carried by the wind, while those of black nightshade are carried from place to place by birds which feed on the berries. Manure stacks on farms often become clothed with annual weeds, and the traditional well-rotted manure may contain many seeds of plants such as red goosefoot. The little cruciferous weed hairy bittercress has explosive seed pods which scatter the ripe seeds for some distance, and in recent years this species has entered many a garden with containerized ornamental plants. The actual numbers of seeds brought in by these various agencies are likely to be very small in relation to the considerable quantities present in the soil. However, if they happen to be of species not already found in the garden they could, when once established, add to the existing weed problem.

Accepting that annual weeds are always going to be a nuisance to some extent, the question is how to keep them under control most easily. The one word which goes furthest towards answering this is 'timeliness'. Jobs done at the right time when conditions are most favourable give the maximum benefit with least effort. No matter whether it is hoeing, digging or the use of a herbicide, there is a best time in the particular circumstances; timeliness involves recognizing it and making the appropriate response.

Besides this, it is important to try to avoid making more difficulties than are absolutely necessary. If crops are sown in straight rows at a distance apart which is suitable for hoeing this helps to cut down the time needed for hand-weeding. Crop spatial arrangements which will obviously need a lot of hand-weeding are better avoided unless there is a suitable soil-applied herbicide available or the amount of hand-weeding is considered acceptable. The technique of covering the seed drill with compost (see p. 368) to improve crop emergence has the advantage of reducing the need for hand-weeding.

## Virtues of weeds

In this chapter the main argument has been that weeds are, for various reasons, undesirable in the vegetable garden and that they should either be eradicated or at least kept down to the lowest feasible level. Perhaps it is appropriate to conclude by considering briefly some of the virtues of weeds, about which whole books have been written.

Our climate is such that bare ground which arises through natural processes like landslip or erosion quickly becomes colonized by plants. These plants cover the surface, their roots bind it; they extract mineral nutrients from the rocks and fix carbon from the carbon dioxide of the atmosphere; and when they die, their organic and mineral content passes onto and into the soil and enriches it. In this way fertility is built up. Weeds in a garden have the same effect; the difference is that here it is crops that we are trying to grow. Even in a vegetable garden, however, weeds are not necessarily 'plants out of place' all the time, and it seems sensible that we should take what advantage we can of the benefits they can confer.

On ground which is temporarily free from crops, the presence of weeds may be doing no harm so long as something is done about them before they reach the stage of seeding. So they could be left as long as possible before either being dug in, if digging is needed for other reasons, or killed with paraquat/diquat. It is true that their nutrient value may be only small in relation to what is needed to grow a crop but there is some benefit to the soil. Weeds which are removed from among crops can be composted so that both the mineral and organic contents are re-cycled. Even in a compost heap which heats up properly not all weed seeds will be killed, but in any case the weeds should be removed before they begin to produce seeds. It is usually advised that perennial weeds should not be added to the compost heap but should be burned instead. This seems a pity; even the rhizomes of couch and roots of thistles will rot down to a large extent, and any living parts that remain can easily be picked out and put on the next heap when the ripe compost is being dug out.

# 11 Managing your soil

Vegetables can be grown on a wide range of soils, but to obtain first-class crops careful attention must be given to the fertility and physical condition of the soil. Most gardeners are aware that fertility can be adjusted by appropriate applications of inorganic fertilizers or organic manures but do not always appreciate the basic importance of soil structure. It is the purpose of this chapter to provide a better understanding of the physical conditions required for successful crop growth and to discuss how they might be obtained by suitable soil management.

The knowledgeable gardener will be quick to point out that plants can be grown without soil by using peat-filled growing bags, various granular materials or even by bathing the roots in a continuous flow of nutrient solution. While these modern techniques can eliminate many of the structural problems associated with soils, they are expensive and costly on anything but a small scale, and do not eliminate the need for careful attention to nutritional and environmental requirements. For the extensive production of vegetables, the convenience of soil will ensure its continued importance in the foreseeable future.

What then does a plant require from soil in addition to the obvious needs of support and anchorage? Soil must contain the nutrients required for crop growth, act as a reservoir for water and allow the free passage of air. To utilize these reserves the plant needs a healthy, vigorous root system and this is only attained if the soil is free of pests and diseases and is easily penetrated by young growing roots. The importance of an actively growing root system cannot be overemphasized. Roots are important not only as a means of absorbing water and nutrients but also for the manufacture of some of the growth-regulating hormones essential for the proper development of the plant.

Before considering how to manage the soil, we should take stock of our raw material and see what it consists of and how it varies from soil to soil.

## The nature of soil

Basically, soil consists of a mixture of mineral particles varying widely in size but which are arbitrarily divided into three size ranges; sand, silt and clay in order of decreasing size. The term *texture* is used to describe the different proportions of these particles and should not be confused with *structure* which refers to the way in which the individual particles clump together. With practice, soils of different texture can be recognized by the feel of a moist sample kneaded between the fingers. Sand particles are gritty, silt is smooth and silky, while clay is sticky. If no one size of particle predominates then the soil is a loam. The proportions of sand, silt and clay in some representative soils are shown in Table 11.1. Gardeners often describe sand and silt soils as being 'light', meaning they are loose and easy to cultivate, whereas clay soils, being sticky, are called 'heavy'.

Soil particles are irregular in shape and do not pack tightly together but are separated by spaces or 'pores'. Surprisingly, these occupy between 40–60 per cent of the soil volume. If the soil is

**Table 11.1**

**Approximate percentage composition of some representative soils**

| Soil type | Sand | Silt | Clay |
|---|---|---|---|
| Sandy loam | 65 | 25 | 10 |
| Loam | 40 | 40 | 20 |
| Silt loam | 20 | 65 | 15 |
| Silt clay loam | 10 | 55 | 35 |
| Clay | 20 | 20 | 60 |

mainly sand, the pores will be large and free-draining, but if it is mainly clay then they are small and slow to drain. Most soils, however, consist of particles of a range of different sizes, and consequently the pores vary from small to large. Furthermore, soils do not usually consist of individual particles but are bound together to form aggregates or 'crumbs'; in other words they are structured. Thus, instead of having only small pores, a fine-textured soil will have small pores within the crumbs and large pores between them. This network of variable-sized pores is the basis of a well-structured soil and is most important to plant growth. The large pores empty quickly after rain and allow air to enter, while the small ones retain water which may later be taken up by plants. The large pores are also important for root penetration. Research has shown that roots do not readily enter pores unless the pores are of the same or larger diameter than themselves. Crops with fat roots like peas and beans are therefore more susceptible to soil compaction than those like cabbage and turnips with thin roots.

Soil is not simply a collection of mineral particles but also contains between 1 and 5 per cent organic matter (over 25 per cent for peaty soils). This is composed of the dead and decaying remains of plants and animals and is the food source of innumerable living micro-organisms. As fresh organic matter is decomposed by bacterial and fungal attack there is a gradual release of plant nutrients until finally a residue of dark-coloured material remains, called humus. Humus has an important role to play in soil structure since it binds the soil particles together and helps to stabilize the aggregates.

## How can poor soil structure be recognized and what are its causes?

As we have seen, good soil structure is of great importance to crop growth. Before considering how to maintain or improve structure, however, it is essential to assess the physical nature of your own soil. This can best be achieved by direct examination of the soil profile since not all defects are visible on the surface of the soil.

Dig a hole or trench to a depth of 45 cm. (18 in.), if soil depth will permit, and examine the exposed face. If a network of visible pores and cracks is apparent throughout the profile, all is well since air and roots will be able to penetrate easily and excess water will readily drain away. If, on the contrary, the soil is tightly packed together and plant roots are confined to a few cracks or earthworm channels instead of appearing throughout the mass of the soil, then plant growth will almost certainly be restricted.

Compact soil can often be detected as a resistance when digging or may be revealed by a layer of wet soil occurring above the level of compaction because of reduced drainage. Compact soil is frequently found as a distinct layer or 'hard pan' at the boundary of the topsoil and subsoil. In severe cases, roots will be confined to the topsoil and will be seen spreading horizontally above the hard pan. Taproots of carrots and parsnips will be stunted, or kinked (Fig. 11.1).

Poor structure is often a consequence of soil texture. Light sandy or silt soils with low clay or organic matter contents have nothing to bind them together. Heavy rain will cause them to settle or 'slump' to a density which will restrict root growth. Frequently slumping is confined to the soil surface. Rain falling on a fine seedbed washes small particles from the soil aggregates into the pores between them. On drying, this surface will set hard to produce a crust or 'cap' which is sufficient to restrict or even completely prevent seedling emergence.

Hard pans occur naturally on some soils, particularly old heathland soils, where fine soil particles and iron compounds wash down the profile and are deposited at a depth of about 30 cm. (12 in.) to form a hard impenetrable layer. More frequently, however, hard pans are man-made, as a result of working or travelling on wet soil with heavy machinery. This is a major problem for commercial vegetable growers who, because of market dictates, often have to cultivate and sow or harvest crops when soil conditions are less than ideal. Fortunately, severe hard pans are unlikely to arise in the garden although they may

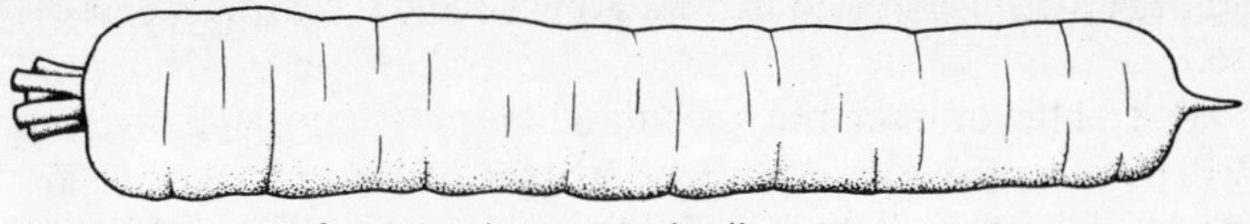

Well-grown roots from good structured soil

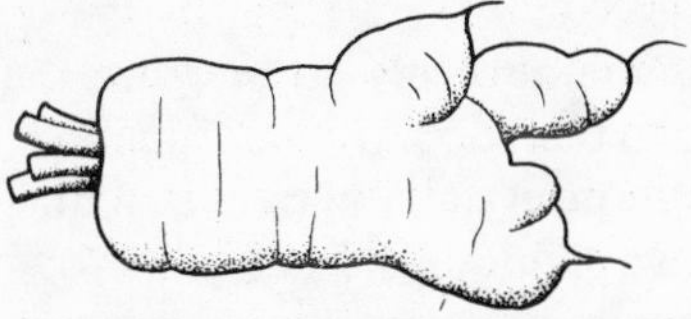

Stunted roots from compact or waterlogged soil

Fig. 11.1. Carrot roots (Amsterdam Forcing type) affected by soil compaction at 7.5 cm. (3 in.) depth. A typical result of preparing a seedbed when the soil is too wet.

survive from previous agricultural use of the land or have been created during house-building. It is important to bear in mind, however, that soil structure is very weak when the soil is wet and compaction can result simply from walking on or trying to cultivate wet soil.

It was noted earlier that the organic matter content of a soil generally falls between 1 and 5 per cent. The exact content depends on a balance between the quantities of fresh organic material added to the soil and the losses due to decomposition. Some crops produce far greater residues than others. In particular, grass returns much larger amounts of organic matter to the soil in the form of root residues than most other crops. The organic matter content of a soil under grass is therefore high and soil structure is generally good. If the soil is then cropped with vegetables, the organic matter content will decline rapidly over the first three or four years, then level off until a new equilibrium is reached. This rapid decline will be due mainly to the lower return of root residues and to the removal of crops. It is often assumed that regular cultivation, by aerating the soil thereby encouraging microbial activity, would also increase the rate of organic matter decomposition but this has not been borne out by experiment. Whether a reduction in organic matter will be detrimental to soil structure depends to a large extent on the type of soil. Chalk and limestone soils are naturally well-structured and are not sensitive to organic matter levels. Other soils, particularly sands and silts, will become increasingly susceptible to slumping while clays will become more difficult to cultivate and will tend to dry into hard clods.

There is no practical way for the gardener to measure the organic matter content of his soil. In fact, even if it were possible, soil scientists would not be able to specify a minimum desirable level because of the considerable variation in effect from soil to soil. Instead, the prudent gardener must always be on the look-out for tell-tale signs of deterioration in structure. Are seedbeds becoming difficult to prepare? Does the soil no longer drain quickly after rain? Do crops wilt readily in short dry spells? Are yields poor despite correct feeding and the absence of pests and diseases? These are the danger signals. Early remedial action or a change in soil management may prevent later crop failure.

## How can texture and structure be improved?

### Drainage

Good drainage is vital to successful soil management. We have already seen that wet soils are more liable to structural damage, but waterlogging also has a direct effect on plant growth. A soil which becomes completely saturated, so that even the large pores and cracks are full of water, contains no free oxygen. Roots will be unable to 'breath' and are killed or seriously damaged and become more susceptible to attack by soil pests and diseases.

Improvements to drainage depend very much on the cause of the problem (Fig. 11.2). Where soil inspection has revealed a hard pan or a layer of unrotted organic matter, a deeper cultivation than normal is all that is required. If the trouble is compaction in the topsoil the remedy is thorough loosening by digging or

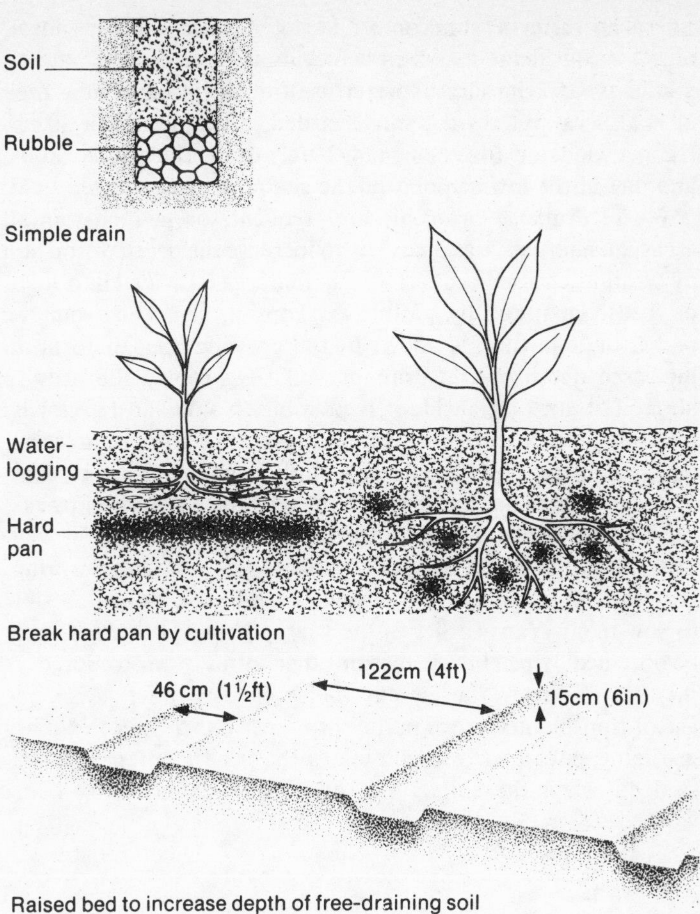


Fig. 11.2. Improving soil drainage.

forking, followed by the regular addition of organic manures to help keep the soil open.

The most difficult drainage problem to overcome is an impermeable clay subsoil. Regular additions of organic materials mixed well into the subsoil will gradually increase the depth of workable soil. The farmers' solution of laying drains, although ideal, requires considerable skill in achieving the correct spacing and gradients, and the surplus water must be disposed of in a ditch or soak-away pit. In the small garden, a simple trench 30 cm. (12 in.) wide and 61–91 cm. (24–36 in.) deep, filled with rubble and dug at the lowest point of the site may be adequate.

Where drainage problems are frequent, or in high rainfall areas, an alternative approach is to increase the depth of top-soil by creating a 'raised bed'. The vegetable area is divided into strips or 'beds' separated by pathways. Topsoil, removed from the paths, or imported, is added to the growing area to form an increased depth of free-draining soil. By keeping the beds to about 120 cm. (4 ft.) wide it is possible to sow and harvest by reaching in from the pathways. In this way the cropped areas are never compacted by trampling. A similar system is used by commercial growers but in their case the pathways are wheel tracks, the beds being spanned by a tractor.

A wet soil is a cold soil and is slow to warm up in the spring. By improving drainage or by using raised beds it will be possible to sow many crops earlier in the year. Additional benefits may be obtained by placing cloches or other forms of protection over the area to be sown a few days before it is required. Also, the use of transplanted crops in the spring permits greater flexibility in timing since their use eliminates the need to prepare a fine seedbed when the soil is wet and easily damaged by being worked.

## Altering texture

Gardeners often wonder if it is possible to improve a sandy soil by adding clay. Many years ago this was a common agricultural practice and was referred to as 'marling'. It is now believed that the benefits of marling were due mainly to the lime content of the clays used rather than to any marked change in soil texture. Some simple calculations will show the impracticality of altering texture in this way.

Suppose you have a sandy-loam soil containing 67 per cent

sand, 23 per cent silt and 10 per cent clay. The soil in a plot 8.2 × 2.7 metres (9 × 3 yards) to a depth of 30 cm. (12 in.) would weigh about 10 tons (or tonnes). An addition of 1 ton of clay, if it could be thoroughly mixed in, would raise the clay percentage to 18 per cent. The soil would still be predominantly sandy! Similar calculations may be made for the addition of sand to clay soils.

Small improvements in the water retention of coarse-textured soils can be made by adding ashes, but this practice is not recommended since many ashes, particularly those of industrial origin, may contain toxic materials.

If it is accepted that texture cannot easily be altered, we must learn to manage the soil we have and to channel our efforts into improving its structure.

## Organic manures

Many gardeners rely on bulky organic manures such as compost or farmyard manure to maintain or increase the organic matter content of their soils and thereby preserve or improve structure and workability. Research has shown, however, that the amounts generally applied are often insufficient to have the desired effects. To increase the level of organic matter in a soil requires the *annual* addition of manure at a rate of at least 5.4 kg. per square metre (10 lb. per square yard). As soon as you stop applying manure the organic matter level will again start falling towards a new equilibrium. We must ask ourselves, is it practical to apply such large amounts regularly and are the benefits worthwhile? Bear in mind too that the root residues of a well-grown vegetable crop will to a large extent help to maintain structure. Beneath each square metre of a turnip crop is 24 km. (12½ miles per square yard) of root!

Studies which have attempted to answer these questions are complicated by the fact that most organic manures contain appreciable amounts of plant nutrients. To test whether they have an advantage over inorganic fertilizers requires careful balancing of the nutrients applied. This is easier said than done, but the results of carefully conducted experiments show that yields on some organically treated soils are slightly higher than on those soils receiving inorganic fertilizers alone. To some extent this is due to differences in the distribution and availability of nutrients in the soil; manures generally are ploughed or dug in to a greater depth than fertilizers, which are applied during seedbed preparation. Some of the additional benefit, however, is attributable to improvements in the physical condition of the soil. In particular, regular, heavy applications of well-rotted manures will increase water retention of coarse-textured soils, while more fibrous material will help to keep clay soils open and improve their workability. To achieve these effects, it is preferable for the manure to be mixed throughout the topsoil. Applying it as a layer at the bottom of a trench, as is often suggested, should be avoided since this can reduce aeration, cause waterlogging, and restrict root growth, and does not maximize the effect on physical conditions.

If supplies of organic manures are limited, do not spread them thinly but apply them at high rates to those crops which are known to be most responsive such as leeks and runner beans. This is one consideration in planning crop rotations and is examined towards the end of the chapter.

*Farmyard manure.* Farmyard manure, or FYM as it is often referred to, is perhaps the most widely available soil amendment but can be expensive to obtain in urban areas. It consists of animal dung and urine, usually from cattle, together with straw or other animal bedding, which has been stored and rotted. Its value to the soil is largely due to its nutrient content but this can vary widely depending on how the manure has been made and stored. Nitrogen and potassium, and to a lesser extent phosphate, are washed from the manure heap if it is exposed to rain, and much of the original nitrogen can be released to the air as ammonia or nitrogen gases during decomposition. Obviously, the gardener has no control over the production of FYM but its variable nature emphasizes the need for occasional soil analysis using a proprietary soil test kit so that any nutrient deficiency can be made up with additional fertilizer.

To reduce the loss of nutrients caused by winter rainfall, well-rotted FYM is best incorporated in the soil in late winter or early spring. Manure with a high proportion of unrotted straw can cause a temporary deficiency of nitrogen as it breaks down because of a rapid increase in micro-organism activity and the 'locking-up' of nitrogen as microbial protein. Strawy manure is best, therefore, applied in late autumn. If incorporation just before sowing time is unavoidable, extra fertilizer nitrogen should be used to help overcome any temporary nitrogen deficiency.

FYM, together with most other organic manures, should not be applied at the same time as lime because chemical reactions will waste nitrogen which is released as ammonia gas.

*Garden compost.* Well-made compost is a good substitute for FYM and can contain slightly more plant nutrients. In some gardening books compost-making is treated almost as an art since although the scientific principles involved are well known it is often difficult to provide the conditions necessary to produce a good humus-like material.

Composting involves the partial decomposition of vegetable matter by micro-organisms and requires air, moisture, and heat. How these conditions can be met are dealt with in great detail in the gardening literature and will not be repeated here. However, it is appropriate to consider some of the problems which arise in attempting to produce good compost on a scale suited to the small garden. Temperatures of about 66 °C (150 °F) are necessary throughout the compost heap in order to ensure rapid decomposition of the material and to kill unwanted weed seeds, pests, and fungal spores. Inevitably, the temperature of a heap will be greatest in the centre, reducing towards the sides and top. This problem will be much worse with a small heap because of the high ratio of surface area to volume. Enclosure in a purpose-made compost bin to retain heat will help overcome this problem, but ideally it should be emptied occasionally and the heap turned in order to introduce air. In situations where compostable material is only available in small quantities and over a period of time, high temperatures are rarely attained and the compost will inevitably be very variable in quality. In conclusion, the main difficulty in using compost is in producing it in the large amounts needed to give a worthwhile improvement in soil structure.

*Peat.* Peat is a good source of organic matter and is particularly effective at opening up clay soils, where its effects last longer than those obtained with FYM. However, it is low in plant nutrients, and when used at high rates can make the soil acid. It is also expensive and hence is not usually practicable unless a cheap local supply is available. There is also growing public concern that commercial peat extraction is unnecessarily destructive to a scarce wildlife habitat. Use of alternatives, such as coir, a by-product of the coconut-processing industry, should be considered.

*Other organic manures.* A number of alternative organic manures may be available to the gardener. Their value should be judged on cost and on their content of plant nutrients but some of them have drawbacks and require care in their use.

Straw and sawdust are both readily available but low in nutrients and can cause temporary nitrogen deficiency unless composted before being added to the soil. Sawdust from timber treated with wood preservatives should be avoided.

Sewage sludge and municipal compost are available in some areas and can be cheap. However, some samples, especially from industrial areas, contain high levels of toxic metals which can accumulate in acid soils and could be taken up by plants if regular, heavy dressings are used. Permissible levels of metal contaminants are controlled by regional codes of practice and anyone considering using these materials should contact their local Water Company or Municipal Authority for advice.

Poultry manure is often available cheaply but can be smelly and unpleasant to handle. It has the advantage of being rich in nitrogen and phosphate but unless mixed with straw or sawdust will have no effect on soil structure. Fresh droppings may release ammonia in amounts harmful to young plants, unless composted or added to the soil at least a month before sowing.

Spent mushroom compost is a well-rotted manure with about the same nutrient content as FYM. However, some samples contain lime and these should not be used regularly on neutral or alkaline soils since excess lime can cause deficiency of some minor elements.

Organic fertilizers such as hoof and horn, meat and bone meal, and dried blood are used only for their nutrient value and have no value in improving soil structure.

*Green manuring.* A green manure crop is one grown specifically for incorporating into the soil. It is usually dug in when about 25 cm. (10 in.) high or, alternatively, pulled and composted prior to adding to the soil. This is a time-honoured practice which is recommended in many gardening books as a means of improving soil structure. It seems unlikely, however, that green manuring will increase the organic matter content of the soil to any great extent, particularly if only used infrequently. As an example, a soil with an initial organic matter content of 2 per cent will contain about 6 kg. of organic material per square metre (13 lb. per square yard) to a depth of 20 cm. (8 in.). If we dig in an average green manure crop yielding about 0.25 kg. of *dry matter* per square metre (0.5 lb. per square yard) and assume one-third remains after decomposition, we have increased the organic matter reserves by only 0.08 kg. per square metre (0.17 lb. per square yard). If this amount were added annually it would take 36 years to increase the soil organic matter content from 2 to 3 per cent!

However, experiments have demonstrated yield increases in crops following green manuring. This has been attributed to the release of plant nutrients, particularly nitrogen, which occurs as the green manure decomposes. The increase in yield will be greatest if no nitrogen fertilizer is applied to the succeeding crop but will decline with increasing levels of applied fertilizer. Nevertheless, in some years, yields can be improved more by green manure than by nitrogen fertilizer applied as a seedbed dressing. This may be due to soil structure effects but more likely to a more gradual release of nitrogen during the season. It would appear therefore that green manuring could lessen the dependence on fertilizer nitrogen which many gardeners would consider a worthwhile achievement.

There are also other benefits to be obtained from green manuring. When a crop is harvested its residues biologically degrade and nitrates are released. This is particularly prevalent in autumn when the soil is still warm. A green manure crop sown at this time will mop up the highly soluble nitrates which otherwise would be washed through the soil by the winter rains thereby causing a potential pollution problem. A leafy cover will also protect the soil surface from the pounding effect of winter rain which can readily damage soil structure, especially on light soils. The presence of a crop over winter will tend to keep the soil slightly drier so that cultivation and cropping can start earlier in the spring.

It is often claimed that deep-rooted green manure crops benefit succeeding crops by recycling nutrients which have been extracted from the subsoil. This seems unlikely. Most vegetables have roots which penetrate much deeper into the soil than gardeners generally realize. Research has shown that the roots of many vegetables growing in a free-draining soil will reach a depth of at least 1.2 m. (4 ft.) by the time the crop is harvested.

A successful plant for green manuring needs to establish quickly after sowing, grow rapidly in the remaining season and be frost-hardy if overwintered. Care also needs to be taken to prevent the carry-over of soil-borne pests and diseases. Mustard and rape belong to the cabbage family and should not be grown on ground infected with club-root. Since the main benefit from using green manure is its influence on nitrogen supply, it is often recommended that leguminous crops, such as tares and clovers, which have the ability to extract nitrogen from the air, are grown. However, while such crops often have a higher nitrogen content than, say, ryegrass, they are less winter-hardy and tend to have a lower bulk so that the amount of nitrogen added to the soil is not always highest. Grazing rye is commonly used as a green manure crop as it can be sown as late as October and is winter-hardy. It may be sown broadcast at 34 g. per square metre (1 oz. per square yard) or in rows about 23 cm. (9 in.) apart.

### Liming and soil structure

Lime is essential to soil fertility both to provide a plant nutrient (calcium) and for correcting acidity, and these aspects have been fully discussed in Chapter 3. It is widely believed that liming is also beneficial in stabilizing the structure of non-calcareous clay soils and reducing their stickiness, but the experimental evidence for this is not conclusive. Nevertheless, liming, by promoting crop growth and encouraging earthworm and micro-organism activity, will have indirect effects on soil structure, first, through the binding action of a vigorous root system and second, by improved breakdown of organic matter to humus.

Old gardening books often recommended gypsum (calcium sulphate) as a soil conditioner but apart from its well-known use in reclaiming soils which have been flooded by sea water, its effects on normal soils are likely to be negligible.

## Cultivations

Cultivation is perhaps the most effective and immediate way of producing soil conditions favourable to crop establishment and growth. Yet the trend in agriculture over the last decade has been towards a reduction in cultivations. This has prompted many gardeners to question whether the cultivations traditionally associated with the vegetable garden, particularly deep digging and regular hoeing, are entirely necessary. Before answering this question, we will consider why cultivations are normally carried out and examine the background to this recent trend.

Traditionally, cultivations have served two main purposes, to remove weeds and to produce a suitable tilth for plant growth. Obtaining a tilth invariably involves two stages, an initial ploughing, or digging, aimed at inverting the topsoil to bury weeds, followed by a number of secondary cultivations to create a seedbed. In recent years the development of effective herbicides has given the grower the option of controlling weeds without resorting to the plough or spade. This allows a reduction or even elimination of secondary cultivations with a greater reliance placed on the natural processes of structure formation. Unfortunately, systems of reduced cultivation are not without problems. Many soils, particularly sands and silts with a low organic matter content, gradually settle and become compacted when uncultivated to such an extent that root growth may be restricted. This is not so critical for crops with a long growing season such as winter cereals, but for short-season vegetable crops rapid root extension, as we shall see later, can be important. Nevertheless, experiments have shown that many vegetables can be grown successfully with reduced cultivations on well-drained soils, providing that care is taken not to damage soil structure at harvest since there are no opportunities for remedial cultivations. Although this is an important consideration for the commercial grower, in the garden, with hand-harvesting, the problem should not arise. However, the gardener is seldom likely to benefit from the main advantage of reduced cultivation systems, which is speed of operation and which enables the farmer to sow large areas rapidly whenever soil conditions are ideal.

Before considering whether reduced cultivations have a part to play in managing soil in the garden, let us examine the various cultivation methods and cultural techniques available to the gardener.

## Single digging

Digging is the main cultivation in the garden and aims to invert the topsoil so as to provide a surface free of weeds and crop debris ready for the preparation of a seedbed. Digging also breaks up the soil to produce an open structure through which water and air can enter and in which roots can grow and proliferate. It is also used as a means of incorporating lime and bulky manures.

Single digging involves working the soil to a depth of about 25 cm. (10 in.) using either a spade or a fork. The choice is one of personal preference but a fork is often easier to use on heavy or stony soils. As a general guide soil should only be worked if it is dry enough not to stick to your boots. This means that heavy soils are best dug in early autumn, before they have been wetted by winter rains.

The soil should not be worked initially to a fine tilth since it will recompact during the winter and lie wet in the spring causing delays in early sowings or plantings. Instead, it should be roughly levelled and left as fist-sized clods. This will allow rain to penetrate and the clods will gradually weather and break down under the action of alternate freezing and thawing to form a 'frost-mould'. If larger clods are left, there is a danger that when the soil is worked in the spring the frost-mould will disappear into the cracks and voids. This would create a patchwork of weathered and unweathered soil which is difficult to work down to an even seedbed. If digging is unavoidably delayed until the spring, clods should be broken down as digging proceeds.

Some gardeners may possess or be contemplating buying a mechanical cultivator. They are most useful for seedbed preparation rather than as a substitute for digging since they tend to pulverize the soil and create a fine tilth. If they are used regularly for all cultivations there is a danger of the tines creating a hard pan at the normal depth of working.

### Double digging

This consists of working the soil to a depth of about 50 cm. (20 in.) and involves first opening a trench to the depth of a spade and then forking the exposed subsoil, care being taken to avoid mixing top- and subsoil. This laborious process was a matter of routine in the vegetable garden at the turn of the century but today's gardener may ask if the effort and time involved are worthwhile, in view of the trend towards reduced cultivations. But it should be realized that high yields will only be obtained consistently if root growth is not impeded by subsoil compaction. Therefore, if soil inspection has revealed a hard pan, deep cultivation is essential.

Recent research has shown benefits of deep cultivation on well-drained soils which are not visually compact and in which roots normally penetrate to at least 90 cm. (36 in.). These benefits are sometimes spectacular. In one experiment the yield of broad bean pods was increased by 95 per cent. While this was exceptional, yield of a range of vegetables has generally been increased by 10 to 30 per cent. Records show that these results are due mainly to improvements in water supply. Plants take up water from the soil through their roots. By loosening the soil we enable the roots to penetrate deeper more rapidly. In the event of a dry spell, the water reserves in the subsoil are immediately available for uptake. This means that the effects of double digging will be small in wet years or if regular watering is practised, since in those circumstances there will be no shortage of water in the topsoil. Double digging can therefore be regarded as an insurance against drought and the ban then imposed on the use of garden hosepipes.

Double digging need not be carried out annually, for although the soil gradually resettles, the effects on yield in one series of experiments persisted for at least four years. Stabilizing the loosened subsoil by incorporating bulky organic manures would probably extend this period, and would also increase its fertility. This is particularly valuable in dry weather since plant roots can only absorb nutrients which are in solution in the soil water. As the topsoil dries out, the nutrients it contains become progressively less available. However, if there are roots and nutrients at depth then uptake can continue from the moist subsoil.

## 'No-digging'

The 'no-digging' system, strongly advocated by some gardeners, is similar to the reduced cultivation technique of the farmer in that it relies on natural processes of structure formation. It differs in that earthworms are actively encouraged by annually covering the soil surface with a layer or 'mulch' of organic manure to a depth of 2.5–5.0 cm. (1–2 in.) Under these condition the earthworm population flourishes and by dragging the organic material into their burrows they gradually build up the fertility and structure of the topsoil without the necessity of digging. The earthworms which are most useful for this task are the large burrowing species and not the small, red manure-worms or brandlings found in the compost heap. Gardeners should be cautious of so-called 'commercial' earthworms sometimes offered for sale as soil improvers. They are invariably surface-dwelling species which live in high organic matter situations and do not survive for long in normal soil.

Providing that the large amounts of organic manure required – 0.05 m.$^3$ per square metre (1½ cubic feet per square yard) – are obtainable, mulching as a technique has much to commend it. By protecting the soil surface from the drying effects of sun and wind, a mulch will reduce the amount of water lost from the soil by evaporation. Consequently, the soil beneath the mulch will remain moist, stimulating micro-organism activity and improving nutrient uptake. A mulch will also protect the soil surface from the destructive effects of heavy rain, and have an insulating effect which will keep the soil cooler during the day and warmer at night. A further benefit, providing the soil is free of perennial weeds and the mulch material is weed-seed free, is that mulching will help suppress weed growth and will thus reduce the need for hoeing.

Many of the benefits obtainable by mulching with organic materials can also be achieved by using a clear or black polythene mulch but, of course, the latter do not contribute to soil structure or fertility and may not be aesthetically desirable in the garden.

'No-dig' systems, whether based on mulching or simply on reduced cultivations are unlikely to be successful on all soils unless structural defects can first be remedied by careful cultivations and by incorporating bulky manures. Those soils where the surface layers are weakly structured and prone to slumping, or those with poorly drained subsoils are those least likely to be suitable.

### Seedbed preparation

The preparation of a seedbed is the most important cultivation carried out in the vegetable garden. Failure to produce a 'good' seedbed will result in poor seed germination or seedling establishment and, inevitably, lower yields. In spite of its obvious importance, little research has been directed towards defining the ideal tilth for each crop since in practice it would be difficult to produce a specified tilth given the wide range of soil and weather conditions encountered. Nevertheless, we know enough of the requirements for germination and establishment for us to give reliable guidelines to the soil conditions desirable. Let us start by considering these requirements and then how they might be met.

For a seed to germinate it requires warmth, air and water. A dry seed placed in contact with moist soil will immediately begin to absorb water. If the seed is viable, air is present, and the soil sufficiently warm, then the seed's food reserves are mobilized and growth begins. Germination culminates in the outer seed-coat rupturing as the young root thrusts downwards and the shoot upwards. The young seedling is now at a critical stage. Rapid root growth is essential if the uptake of water and nutrients is to be adequate once the seed reserves are exhausted. Already we can appreciate what is required from the seedbed. First, the seed must be in good contact with the moisture in the soil if the initial water uptake is to be rapid. This is easier to achieve if the tilth is fine rather than cloddy. Second, the soil below the seed must be uncompacted if root growth is to be rapid, and it should contain a readily available supply of nutrients. Finally, the soil above the seed should be loose enough for the delicate shoot to emerge unhindered and begin photosynthesizing (Fig. 11.3).

If the soil has been dug in the autumn and a good frost mould exists, then a seedbed can be readily prepared as the soil dries in the spring, simply by a light raking. Heavy soils which have been dug in the spring or light soils which have compacted over winter will require more work on them. Loosen the soil to about 10 cm. (4 in.) either by forking or better still, because there is less risk of bringing up wet soil, by using a tined cultivator. Seedbed preparations should only be attempted when the soil is dry enough for clods to crumble easily. This may mean a few days delay to allow the soil to dry, but you will be rewarded by better crop growth than if the soil was worked wet and became compacted below the depth of sowing. Drying can always be hastened by covering the

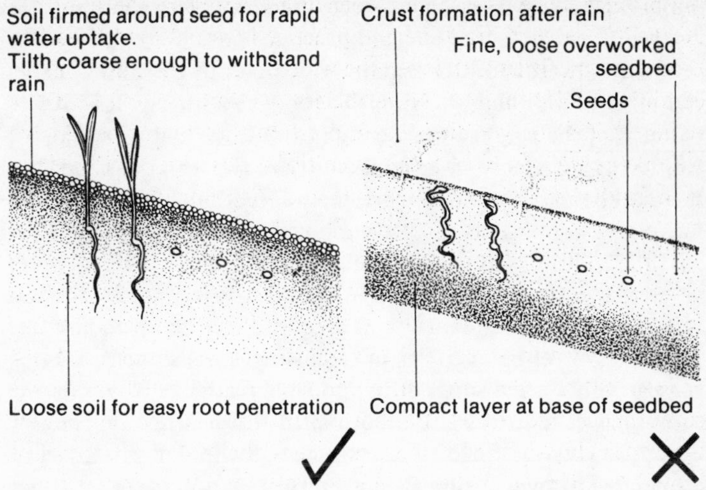


Fig. 11.3. Seedbed preparation.

soil with a cloche for a few days before the seedbed is required. If the soil is too dry to produce a good tilth, watering the area a day or two before final preparation will help the clods to break down.

If the soil has been dug in the spring it may be necessary, particularly on light sands and peats, to firm the soil, preferably by rolling rather than treading. This reduces the risk of surface drying during germination and ensures that the roots come into contact with the water held in the soil pores. In most circumstances treading or rolling is unnecessary and should never be attempted on wet soil.

It is common practice for gardeners to apply and work in fertilizers in the final stages of seedbed preparation. This procedure requires care, however, since too high a concentration of nitrogen or potassium fertilizer can inhibit seedling emergence by scorching young roots, especially if the soil should dry out. This problem can be overcome by watering or applying only part (up to one-third) of the fertilizer prior to sowing with the remainder applied as a top-dressing between the rows after the crop has emerged.

The final seedbed preparation is carried out by raking, experience suggesting that the aim is to produce a tilth with about 70 per cent of the aggregates ranging in size from that of a grain of rice to that of a pea. In general, the finer the tilth the better but it would be undesirable to work the soil too much since it would be very susceptible to surface capping if heavy rain occurred.

If the soil is dry at the time of sowing it is preferable to water to ensure sufficient wetting of the soil rather than to rely on rainfall. Light rain can easily wet the soil to seed depth and initiate germination yet be insufficient to ensure establishment, leaving the partially wetted seeds at risk to fungal attack. If you decide to water it is best to wet the bottom of the drill line thoroughly before sowing and then to cover the seed with dry soil to act as a mulch. This will ensure fast, even germination and emergence under the most adverse conditions.

Providing the soil surface is not excessively wet, carefully firm the drill line with the front of a rake after covering in order to push the seeds into contact with the surrounding soil, especially if the tilth is at all coarse. If subsequent rain causes cap formation, water frequently, with a rose on the watering can, to keep the surface soft. It is a good idea, if the soil is prone to capping, to cover the seeds with a material such as potting compost, vermiculite or perlite which is stable enough not to cap even after heavy rainfall.

### Inter-row cultivation

Hoeing is a quick and effective way of killing annual weeds which otherwise would compete with the growing crop for water, nutrients and light. Contrary to popular belief, frequent hoeing to maintain a loose surface tilth or 'dust mulch' has a negligible effect on water loss from the soil. This is primarily because the greatest water loss occurs when the soil is too wet for hoeing. In any case, well aggregated soils dry rapidly at the surface and are in effect self-mulching. Excessive hoeing can be harmful, by damaging crop roots, bringing wet soil to the surface, and producing a loose surface unstable to rainfall. It is therefore preferable to reduce hoeing to a minimum. Hoe only if weeds are present and keep as shallow as possible.

Many gardeners regard potatoes as a 'cleaning crop', the conventional widely spaced rows allowing control of perennial weeds by hoeing and by the subsequent cultivations involved in earthing-up. Current commercial practice, with the introduction of effective herbicides, is to control weeds by spraying and to reduce the number of inter-row cultivations to the minimum. Perhaps it is no coincidence that potato yields have increased markedly since this change in practice; gardeners could profitably adopt the same procedure. Potatoes can be successfully grown 'on-the-flat', without earthing-up, and this method is useful for no-diggers where the minimum of soil disturbance is desirable to avoid destruction of the natural structure which has developed. Try planting small tubers weighing about 56 g. (2 oz.), 10 cm. (4 in.) deep at a spacing of 40 × 45 cm. (16 × 18 in.).

## A soil management system for the garden

In addition to nutritional fertility, soil management is, essentially, concerned with the manipulation of soil structure. The aim of good management is to produce and maintain a stable structure to a good depth, which is free from any defects that would inhibit seed germination and seedling emergence or prevent the free exploitation of the soil by roots. The management problems associated with sands, silts, clays and loams are quite different from each other so that strict adherence to any one system for all soils is fraught with difficulties. Nevertheless, an extension of the bed system, briefly discussed already in connection with drainage, can be recommended and adapted to suit personal circumstances and inclinations.

The main purpose of a bed system is to avoid compaction of the soil by unnecessary trampling. If this system is combined with deep loosening, we have the basis for a system of wide

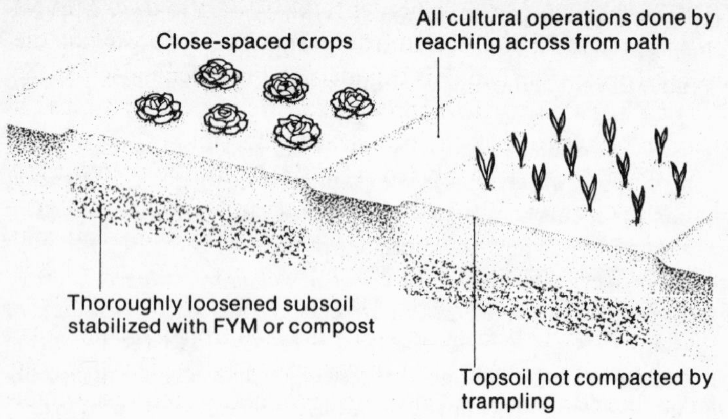


Fig. 11.4. Deep-bed system.

applicability referred to by some gardeners as the 'deep-bed' method (Fig. 11.4). The method begins with double digging to remove any subsoil compaction and to create a structure favourable to free drainage, aeration and root penetration. If available, organic manures should be incorporated at this stage to help preserve the loose structure, improve water retention, encourage soil fauna and increase fertility. Do this operation thoroughly and it will be unnecessary to repeat it for several years, especially if the structure initially created by cultivation is stablilized by subsequent root residues and biological activity.

Keep the pathways as narrow as possible to avoid wasting ground, 30–35 cm. (12–14 in.) is about right or 45 cm. (18 in.) if you wish to use a wheelbarrow. It is not essential to form a raised bed. Although this has advantages in high rainfall areas and makes reaching into the centre of the bed easier, in dry areas it may lead to an exaggerated loss of water by evaporation from the exposed sides. Even in the latter areas, however, it may be advantageous to have one raised bed which could be used for early sowings, by virtue of its better drainage and earlier warming-up in the spring. If you are really keen, sloping the bed 5–10° towards the south will help raise soil temperature.

It is important to remember with this system that *all* cultural operations should be executed from the paths. *Never* walk on the cropped area. If difficulty is experienced in stretching across the bed use a wide board to spread your weight evenly or use a wooden bridge to span the bed clear of the soil.

Since the crop can be tended from the paths, the need for the widely spaced rows formerly required for access is unnecessary. Instead, the crop can be grown at a higher density than usual, and with an even pattern of plant arrangement full use can be made of available land (see Chapter 1).

This enables the same yield to be produced from a smaller area, or alternatively a higher yield from the same area. The crop also makes better use of sunlight, nutrients and water, since these resources are no longer wasted between the rows. Closely spaced plants will also cover the ground quickly and smother many annual weeds, thereby reducing the need for hoeing.

After harvesting the crop, give careful thought to the next operation. If the topsoil has not slumped and is free of weeds and crop debris, digging is superfluous and reduced cultivation methods can be adopted.

## Crop rotation

If some crops are grown year after year on the same patch of ground, yields tend to decrease, even if adequate nutrients are supplied. The reasons for this vary from crop to crop but in most cases can be attributed to an increase of a specific pest or disease in the soil. Since some of these are difficult to eradicate once they are established, it is normally suggested that the same crop, or group of closely related crops, should not be grown repeatedly on the same site. This is good gardening practice, but it does require careful planning if one susceptible crop is not to follow another.

Most gardening books recommend a crop rotation plan which, in addition to disease considerations, is based on nutritional and liming requirements. An example of one rotation frequently suggested is shown below:

**Typical 3-year rotation**

| **Add organic manure** | **Add fertilizer and lime** | **Add fertilizer** |
|---|---|---|
| Group A. Other crops | Group B. Brassicas | Group C. Root crops |
| Pea | Cabbage | Carrot |
| Bean | Cauliflower | Parsnip |
| Onion | Brussels sprout | Beetroot |
| Leek | Broccoli | Potato |
| Lettuce | Swede | Tomato |
| Celery | Turnip | |

**Group sequence**

| 1st year ABC | 2nd year BCA | 3rd year CAB |
|---|---|---|

The adoption of this type of plan is an effective way of reducing pest and disease problems. However, good soil management may require a more flexible approach to manuring than is commonly suggested. Applying organic manures one year in three is unlikely to increase soil organic matter appreciably. Yet more frequent applications are not suggested because it is widely believed that organic manures will cause root crops such as carrot and parsnip to grow forked or misshapen. This is not borne out by experiment. Additions of 5.4 kg. per square metre (10 lb. per square yard) of *well-rotted* FYM had no effect on the root shape of carrots. In fact, many root crops are very responsive to organic manures and it might well be used to advantage at their stage in the rotation.

Apart from this minor criticism of most plans, crop rotation can be regarded as a valuable aid to soil management. It encourages an orderly sequence of cropping so that as one crop or group of crops is harvested the land they occupied can be immediately prepared for the next. In this way, the need for digging is often reduced. For example, overwintered brassicas can follow early peas with little soil preparation beyond hoeing off any weeds and raking in fertilizer or lime if required. Similarly, ground from which early potatoes have been lifted can easily be levelled for autumn-sown onions or overwintered broad beans.

## Conclusions

Good soil conditions are the basis for the production of high yields of good quality vegetables. Fortunately, even the most unproductive soils can be made to flourish, given time and skilful management. Conversely, bad management can ruin a potentially good soil.

As a guide to good soil management, always observe the following points:

- Ensure that the soil is free-draining. Good drainage is vital to good structure.
- Check acidity and lime if necessary.
- Eliminate compaction by thorough cultivation. Ideally double dig the vegetable plot at least once, even if you are working towards a no-dig system.
- Maintain or improve organic matter levels by using bulky organic manures whenever available. However, do not expect vast improvements unless large quantities are applied regularly.
- Return crop remains to the soil via the compost heap.
- Do not cultivate or walk on soil which is very wet.
- Always do the minimum cultivation necessary to achieve the desired effect. Do not overwork a seedbed as it will exacerbate capping problems.
- Do not hoe unless weeds are present and then keep as shallow as possible.
- Rotate your crops to reduce the chance of a build-up of soil-borne pests and diseases.

# 12 How vegetables grow and develop

We expect vegetable plants to change as they grow and so provide the part we eat in its familiar form. The pea seedling grows but as it does so it changes and develops flower buds which grow into flowers which, in turn, develop into pods which then grow and are harvested. The stimuli causing the changes in the patterns of growth, which is what development is, can be internal or external. Internal stimuli arise within the plant itself as it grows, whereas external stimuli are changes in the environment in which the crop grows which, in turn, affect the workings of the plant. Important external changes which we will see govern development can be in such factors as the temperature or the length of the light period encountered each day. Knowing how these external and internal stimuli can affect the development of different vegetable crops enables the gardener to use their effects to maximum advantage. If we grow cauliflowers at a spacing of 15 cm. × 15 cm. (6 in. × 6 in.) we restrict the *growth* of the individual plants but development proceeds more normally, and small curds, minicauliflowers (see p. 270), are produced, each being a one-person portion and suitable for freezing whole. In producing minicauliflower, we have altered the normal relationship between growth and development to get what we wanted.

Normally we are most concerned with not allowing growth and development to get out of step. Bolting is one of the consequences of things being out of step. But as we will see with the onion and the cauliflower, we can sometimes obtain useful control by manipulating the relationship between growth and development. First of all we will discuss growth, the basic process which enables us to harvest the sun's energy in a form we can use to provide us with the food energy we need.

## Growth

All green plants use the process of photosynthesis to fix the sun's energy, making it into the substance and structure of the plant. In the early stages of the growth of seedlings, the rate at which this takes place and the way in which it occurs is similar to compound interest accumulating in a savings bank. The rate of interest is termed the 'relative growth rate' and, of course, the actual amount of interest depends upon the amount invested and the rate of interest.

In the savings bank, interest is usually quoted as some percentage per annum. If it is 10 per cent we know that £110 will earn £10 in a year and that if this is reinvested, which is what plants do, it will earn 10 per cent of £110 = £11 in the second year. Crop physiologists who study growth express interest rate slightly differently and would say that 10 per cent interest was £0.1 per pound per annum. Interest in banks can be paid monthly or even daily on the amount deposited, but in plant growth it is paid instantly so that the interest is immediately put to work to earn more growth. Further, the period of investment is often short, as when a crop of, say, radishes is mature in only a few weeks. So, relative growth rates are quoted as increases in weight, per unit weight, per day. A common rate is 0.1 g. per g. per day or a 10 per cent interest rate in only a day.

Temperature is one of the main factors limiting the growth of vegetables in the open. The relative growth rate of plants roughly doubles for every 10 °C (50 °F) increase in the temperature within the range normally encountered. If you are a pessimist it is equally true to say that it is halved for every 10 °C drop in temperature. The effects of this are striking.

If we take the relative growth rate as being 0.1 g. per g. per day, a plant weighing 10 g. (about ⅓ oz.) will weigh 11 g. after one day, 12.1 g. after 2 days, and 19.5 g. after a week. If the relative growth rate is doubled by increasing the temperature by 10 °C the original 10 g. becomes 12 g. after one day, 14.4 g. after 2 days and 35.8 g. after a week. So although we have only doubled the relative growth rate the warmer plants would be 84 per cent heavier than the cooler plants after only a week, and would have increased in weight by 25.8 g. as compared with 9.5 g. The value of cloches or frames to increase the temperature is obvious, but another feature of compound interest is that you earn more by having more in the bank.

For example, a 30 g. seedling at low temperature will, at the relative growth rate we are assuming, increase its weight by three times that of a 10 g. seedling, so in a week the increase will be 28.5 g. This is more growth than our 10 g. seedling made in a week at a 10 °C higher temperature. It illustrates the value of using transplants, which may only have the same relative growth rate as seeds sown directly, but because they will be bigger at the time of transplanting will earn more interest. Indeed, the bigger seeds from within a packet will similarly show advantages over the smaller seeds just because the bigger seeds have 'more in the bank' to start with. However, these simple rules of growth only apply to seedlings well spaced from each other. In older plants or in younger ones crowded together, other factors soon begin to limit and reduce the relative growth rate.

The reduction in relative growth rate as plants grow is to some extent predetermined just as we stop growing as we get older. However, part of it comes about as a result of more of the daily energy captured from the sun being used to maintain the older lower leaves which become shaded by the younger ones as the plant grows. Similarly, leaves of neighbouring plants can cast shade, and this competition for light reduces relative growth rate. As we shall see, changes in development can also reduce the growth rate by diverting the products of photosynthesis into parts such as bulbs and roots which are not earning their keep by photosynthesizing.

Widely spaced leafy crops which are harvested at a relatively early stage of what could be their full life-cycle are those which maintain the highest relative growth rates for longest. Lettuce is a good example of such a crop and as such it is amongst the most responsive to temperature. However, we have been considering here the unbridled growth of plants. In the garden all kinds of factors operate to limit growth rates. Two of them we have already identified, namely, low temperature and shading. Vegetable gardening is largely about removing as many of these factors limiting growth as we can. Thus we explained in earlier chapters how to control the pattern of plant arrangement to reduce the competition between plants and how to use fertilizers and water to get maximum growth rates. Chapter 10 makes it clear how important weed control is in allowing us to achieve the maximum growth of crop plants. This growth is channelled by development into different organs at different times, and by understanding the factors which control development we can manipulate vegetables to get more edible produce from our gardens.

## Development

The mature plant ready for harvest is not simply a bigger version of the seedling. If it is a pea or bean it has developed flowers and fruit during its growth. If it is a lettuce or a cabbage it has developed cupped leaves giving us the familiar hearting—or it may not have done, in that it could have bolted to flower without hearting. What causes this skipping of a stage in the normal development? Can we do anything about it and, if so, what can we do? We can answer these questions for most vegetable crops but the amount of detail available varies. As a prime example of a crop where gardeners can control growth mechanisms, we look first at onions.

### Onions

The bulb we eat is the storage organ which gets this biennial plant through to its second year of growth in which it normally flowers and seeds. But let us start with the normal crop grown from seed sown in the spring, using varieties which are now usually of the

Rijnsburger type. The emergence of the seedling though the soil and its growth are initially slow because the temperatures are low. As the days get warmer the growth rate of the seedlings increases and more leaves are formed. However, as the days get warmer, so also does the length of the light period each day; this not only acts to increase the growth we get but it also induces developmental changes.

It must be explained that it is not the length of the day that is important but rather the length of the night. In nature, the two go hand-in-hand, long days giving us short nights, but scientists have shown that they can, for example, obtain a long-day effect by interrupting a long night by a short period of low intensity light from ordinary electric light bulbs. In spite of this, scientists continue to talk of long-day and short-day effects, and here we are concerned with the effect of long days on our onion seedlings.

With the spring-sown bulb onions grown in Britain, a day-length of 16 hours stop the production of ordinary leaves and instead the fleshy scale-leaves which make up the bulb are formed. Once the plant has been programmed in this way, it is irreversibly committed to bulbing and to ripening. If only a small amount of green leaf per plant has been produced before bulbing begins then the onion bulb is bound to be small. A small amount of foliage can only produce a small bulb. It follows that getting the maximum amount of foliage before the long days cause the switch to bulbing is of great importance if good yields are to be obtained. One way to do this would be to increase the temperature early in the growth by protecting the seedlings under cloches, or transplants could be raised in mild heat to give bigger plants earlier. Most commercial onion growers rely on early sowing but amateurs often favour using onion sets.

*Onion sets* are very small onion bulbs which are stored and planted the following year and it follows from what has been said that they are produced by late sowing. In Britain, seeds are sown in about the third week in May, only a month before the day-length reaches its maximum. Bulbing therefore takes place with very little leaf on each plant, so small bulbs are formed. Because we know they are only going to be small they are sown very thickly, much as one would sow seed in a seed-box to raise young plants. Indeed, the amateur can often raise enough sets for his own use in one or two seed-boxes; this has the advantage that they can be put in a frame or glasshouse to assist their ripening.

The ripened set, just like the larger bulb grown in the garden, is at first dormant. Unfortunately, dormancy is readily broken, otherwise it would be easy to store both sets and bulbs. The factor which most commonly breaks dormancy early in the bulb's life is water. Ripe bulbs or ripe sets left out in the rain will soon begin to sprout. However, if they are kept dry, temperature is the major factor controlling dormancy of bulbs. Dormancy is preserved at both high (about 21 °C, 70 °F) and low (about 0 °C, 32 °F) temperatures and is broken at intermediate temperatures, particularly those around 10 °C (50 °F). Once dormancy is broken, any reasonable temperature will induce sprouting and sprouted bulbs soon deteriorate.

Because the onion is a biennial plant, if we planted large bulbs that we had stored, we would get flowering plants the following year. This is how the seedsman raises seed. But with sets we do not want flowers, for we have grown the set to give us a start in the race to produce plenty of leaf before the days lengthen and induce bulbing. Sets do often give at least a proportion of flowering plants and their yield is lost. How can this be avoided?

The low temperatures of winter start a developmental response in the stored bulbs causing them to form flower buds inside the bulb. Fortunately, small bulbs are too 'young' to indulge in this change to flowering. They are often spoken of as being in the juvenile phase and not having reached puberty. They are not large enough for sexual reproduction even though they receive a stimulus that would provoke bigger bulbs to form flowers. Varieties used for sets generally have a slightly bigger bulb size at puberty than ordinary varieties but it is unwise to use sets larger than 15 mm. (0.6 in.) in diameter unless they have been 'heat-treated'.

Heat-treatment prevents flower formation in bulbs which would otherwise be susceptible, by denying them the cold stimulus they would need. The sets must be stored throughout the winter at 25–30 °C (87–98 °F), temperatures usually only found in the home in airing cupboards. Because of exposure to low temperatures in transit and in the shops, it is usually safest, and more economical, to buy small sets. The alternative way of getting a good start is to sow seeds in the autumn.

*Autumn-sown onions* fall into two groups. With traditional long-day varieties, autumn sowing in protected conditions is used to produce transplants for putting out in the spring. The bulbs produced in this way are larger but very little earlier than those from spring-sown seeds because the plants have to wait for the long-day (16 hour) stimulus before bulbing can start. With the newer, intermediate-day-length varieties, which we introduced largely from Japan, the seed can be sown in the open where the crop is to be grown and no transplanting needs to be done. Very early crops in June can be obtained from some of these varieties, because they can *start* to bulb when the days are 12 hours long—at the end of March. From a developmental point of view the problem with both groups is the same—to avoid bolting.

We have already seen that bulbs bigger than 15 mm. (0.6 in.) in diameter will form flower buds in response to low temperatures. Onion plants also behave similarly in that small plants will not respond to the stimulus of the low winter temperatures and so do not flower in the following year. In raising plants under protection, either by autumn sowing or very early sowing (January in Britain), they can be protected from the low temperatures that would trigger off flowering. But in the open we have to rely on not getting the plants too big by avoiding sowing too early. The problem is that if sowings are made too late the plants may be too small to survive the rigours of winter.

For this reason very precise sowing dates have been determined by experiment for autumn sowing the Japanese type of onion in different parts of Britain. In the south of England the last week in August was found to be reliable, whereas in the Midlands sowing should be made in mid-August, and in the north and Scotland in the first week of August. It follows that you should not just sow but you should also water, if necessary, to get rapid germination and the plants started at the right time.

Because autumn sowing gives us a long if somewhat cold period for leaf growth, we can get good yields from varieties that bulb in days much shorter than the traditional varieties grown in Britain. The earliest varieties will start to bulb when the day is only 12 hours long and so will give ripe bulbs in early June. Varieties bulbing in 13 to 14 hours are also available giving later ripening but also higher yields. Unfortunately, most of these Japanese types do not keep well so they should be grown for summer use within a month or two of harvest. One peculiarity of these autumn-sown onions should be noted here and that is that they bolt less if they are kept well supplied with nitrogen fertilizers during the winter months. At present we do not understand why this should be so but experiments have shown it to be most important in reducing bolting.

If you enter for shows you may want to save your own seed from a prized bulb. Generally, this is not a wise move as saving seed from one or only a few plants could weaken the strain, but you could try growing from 'pips'.

*Pips* are small bulblets which sometimes form naturally between the flower stalks of the globular flower heads of onions and leeks. Pot leek growers, those who grow mammoth leeks for show, particularly in the north-east of England, nearly always grow their prize specimens from such pips treating them like onion sets. You can induce the formation of pips in the flower head of onions and leeks by shaving off the flower buds with a razor blade just before they open. Be sure to leave the flower stalks, and in due course you will find the little bulblets forming. They ripen like the true bulbs on an onion.

Having looked at onions in detail, we can now use them as a basis for understanding the development of other vegetables as it affects us as vegetable gardeners.

### What causes plants to bolt?

'Running to flower' when there should not be any flowers is referred to by gardeners as 'bolting' and sometimes the plants will

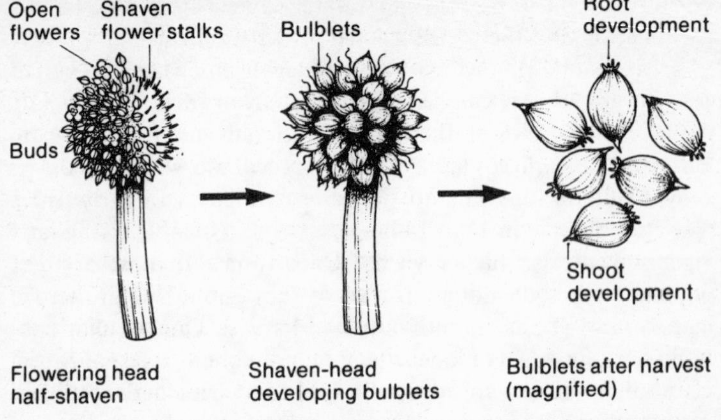


Fig.12.1. The flower heads of onions and leeks can be made to produce bulblets ('pips') by cutting off the buds just before they open. The bulblets are about 6 mm. (¼ in.) long and can be planted like sets.

be said to have 'shot'. Because bolting stops root swelling and tends to make what is there rather woody, it can be very annoying to find all the beetroot going up to flower just when it looked as though the roots were reaching a harvestable size.

Many vegetables, like the onion described above, are biennials. This strictly means that they require a cold stimulus to start the formation of flower buds but they are not sensitive in this way to cold when they are seedlings or young plants. The onion we have already described is therefore a classical biennial. There are also vegetables which behave similarly but are classed rather as winter annuals in that even the seed that has taken up water but has not yet started to grow is receptive to low temperatures as a stimulus for flower initiation.

Nature is never quite as tidy as scientists would like it to be so we find that there are examples of intermediate groups between true winter annuals and true biennials. Turnips are winter annuals in that their seed can be 'vernalized' by being put in the cold in an imbibed state. (This is not to be confused with 'stratification' which involves exactly the same treatment but is done to overcome dormancy in seeds, often of trees and shrubs, and does not induce flowering.) Celery appears to be a transitional type in that very young plants are receptive to cold but are not as receptive as older plants. However, before we consider the responses of different vegetables let us see if we can define more precisely the temperature conditions required to initiate flowering.

Generally, the best temperatures for *vernalization*, the cold effect on flowering, are within a degree or so of 4 °C (39 °F). At lower temperatures processes get slowed down too much, and at temperatures above about 12 ° to 14 °C (54 ° to 58 °F) there is usually no stimulus to flower. Indeed, provided higher temperatures occur soon after vernalizing temperatures, the vernalization effect of the lower temperatures is often cancelled out. Thus cold nights followed by warm days tend not to count in clocking-up the stimulus to flower in biennials or winter annuals. But if the days are also cool, the plants are set along the path to flowering. As a very rough guide it takes only about six weeks at low temperatures to induce the initiation of flowers, but you may not see the effect until several weeks later. Usually we *see* bolting in early summer but the cause was invariably the cold in early spring. We have already dealt with onions so now let us consider other crops more specifically.

### Bolting in root crops

*Turnips.* We have already noted that the seed of this crop is sensitive to cold so they rate as one of the most vulnerable crops; the only answer is to delay sowing or raise early crops under the protection of cloches or frames where the temperature will be higher than in the open.

*Beetroot* is the next most sensitive root crop where the usual recommendation is to delay sowing into late spring. The imbibed seeds are not sensitive to cold but the young plants are sensitive. Incidentally, we are unable to show that transplanting red beet encouraged bolting although a lot of gardeners seem to consider that it does. Could the explanation be that they tend to transplant the biggest seedlings which are more sensitive to low temperature than smaller plants? You will probably have noticed that only some of the plants from an early sowing bolt. The ones that do not could be younger in that they have come up later and hence have clocked up less cold stimulus. However, it is equally likely that the non-bolters were inherently more resistant to bolting. In beetroot these genetic differences in the tendency to bolt have been exploited by breeders and at least two varieties are on the market, Avonearly and Boltardy, which can be sown in early spring with much reduced chances of bolting.

*Radishes* readily run to seed in the long days of summer. This is because it is an annual that only requires long days to make it flower. Seedsmen have selected types suitable for sowing at the different seasons of the year, and it is important to use varieties appropriate to their season. The summer varieties will form edible radishes before 'bolting' provided they are well nourished and watered. In poor conditions they will bolt without forming proper radishes first.

*Carrots* of the modern varieties rarely bolt as a result of early sowing but they will frequently do so if autumn sowing is attempted. As far as is known, the young plant with one true leaf is the minimum size that can be vernalized.

*Parsnips* have not been studied in detail but they seem even less likely to bolt than carrots. The same cannot be said for celery and celeriac which belong to the same family.

### Bolting in leaf crops

*Celery and celeriac* are very sensitive to cold and become much more so as the seedlings increase in size. Practical experience suggests that maximum sensitivity occurs at about the plant size usually aimed at for transplants. There is a grave danger with these crops that keenness to slow down rather advanced seedlings by hardening them off can lead to a high proportion of bolting plants a little later. If you really must slow down some transplants try clipping them with scissors to about 8 cm. (3 in.) high and do not put them outside until it is warm. The clipping will give you sturdy plants which, in experiments with celery, have transplanted better.

*Cabbages and Brussels sprouts* are quite big seedlings before they respond to low temperatures. Like onions, they have a clear-cut 'puberty' in that no amount of cold applied to young plants will cause them to bolt. Generally, puberty coincides with the top of the stems becoming about as thick as a pencil.

It is very unusual for bolting to be a problem in Brussels sprouts, summer cabbage, or winter cabbage, although the latter will obviously run to seed in the spring. The major problems are usually encountered with spring cabbage, which is a crop which is always bound to be on a razor's edge as far as bolting is concerned.

As with overwintered onions, already discussed, an important step in controlling bolting in spring cabbage is to choose the correct sowing date. About 20 July is right in the Midlands of England with sowing being a week earlier in the north and a week later in the south. Plant breeders have done a great deal to reduce the risks of bolting and our variety, Avon Crest, is particularly resistant to bolting and can be left until later in the spring to form good hearts if required. If you see signs that your spring cabbage crop is going to bolt, then the best thing you can do is to eat it quickly and make a note to sow a little later next year.

It is useful to realize that mild autumns and winters are the worst conditions for bolting in both spring cabbage and autumn-sown onions. The mildness allows growth which advances the plants on their path to puberty and even mild winters are cold enough for good vernalization – indeed they can be better in this respect than really cold weather. So do not be tempted to put cloches too early over spring cabbage, cover them only when the spring weather begins to arrive.

*Chinese cabbage* is becoming increasingly popular, but the main problem with its culture under British conditions is the tendency to bolt. Germinating seed and plants are triggered by temperatures below about 10 °C (50 °F) to form flower buds and our long days of early summer enhance this effect of low temperature. Some varieties, notably some of the varieties from Japan, are less prone to bolting than others but even with such varieties it is unwise to plant transplants raised at temperatures above 7 °C (45 °F) before mid-May, or to make sowings out-of-doors before mid-June.

*Lettuce* varieties usually grown in the open will only bolt after hearting. They are responding to the long days of summer in doing this and when the days are longest and warmest there is often only a matter of days between a heart being mature and it beginning to grow out into a flower stalk. The varieties adapted for growing under glass in the winter are different in that they will bolt without hearting if grown in long days. So do not be tempted to use one of these winter glasshouse types for your summer crop.

*Spinach* is known to scientists as one of the most sensitive plants to long days. Only one long day of 13 hours duration will induce some varieties to flower, the male and female flowers being on separate plants. Thus, the best seasons for the production of spinach are in the shorter days of the autumn, winter and spring, although some protection is usually needed for crops during the coldest periods. These crops in short days will produce leaves over a long period and can be relied on to give several harvests. For summer use, a succession of sowings has to be made as each sowing will usually only give one picking before bolting stops leaf production.

*Spinach beet* sometimes also called 'Silver Beet' or 'Perpetual Spinach', is a form of beetroot which has been bred for its spinach-like leaves. It only bolts in similar conditions to beetroot and hence can provide a good source of summer spinach without fear of bolting, provided it is not sown so early that it receives the cold stimulus it needs for flowering.

## Flowering

Up to now we have been dealing with vegetables that most gardeners never want to see in flower. We have seen how to control it and so reduce its devastating effects on yield. Now we turn to those vegetables that we do wish to see flower or, in the case of the first group, to form flower buds.

*Cauliflower, calabrese, and broccoli.* The cauliflower curd, the part we eat, is really a mass of partially developed flower buds. This is more obvious in sprouting broccoli and calabrese. Low temperature is still the stimulus for bud formation in all this group and, like cabbages and onions, puberty has to be reached before the plants are sensitive, in this developmental way, to cold. The temperature responses of calabrese and broccoli are similar to cauliflower, which shows an enormous diversity between types in the temperatures to which they respond.

The winter cauliflower types need the lowest temperatures for the longest time to start flower formation and this prevents them producing curds in the autumn. On the other hand, some varieties of summer cauliflower can form curds when the temperatures are as high as 21 °C (70 °F). So as a group, cauliflower and its relatives do not obey the temperature rules given for root crops, cabbage and Brussels sprouts, and onions.

Sometimes quite young cauliflower plants will form curds which are very small (about 5 cm. (2 in.) in diameter). These are edible but they are, of course, disappointing as compared with the full-sized curds expected. It is usually only the earliest cauliflower varieties that suffer from this fault which is known as 'buttoning'. These varieties produce relatively few leaves before they form a curd and if for any reason these leaves are smaller than they should be, the plants cannot produce large curds, only 'buttons'. The main factors causing the leaves to be smaller than normal can be summarized as ones which produce a check to normal growth. Any such check seems to predispose plants of these early varieties to buttoning. A period of low temperatures, a shortage of water, exposure to wind and a shortage of nutrients are all factors which have been associated with buttoning.

With the summer and later groups of cauliflowers the best quality and head size have been obtained by transplanting no later than five to six weeks after sowing. These relatively young transplants give crops that are more uniform in their maturity and higher yielding than crops from older transplants.

Experiments at Wellesbourne have shown that cold treatment of cauliflower transplants can also improve the uniformity of maturity of crops. The treatment 'saturates' the cold requirement of all the plants making sure that any natural variability in their cold requirement is swamped. It can be done in a domestic refrigerator by putting the transplants into a polythene bag and placing them in the refrigerator in a position where they will not freeze. Usually, the compartment recommended for the storage of salad vegetables is satisfactory. They will not take harm for up to 21 days but usually 14 days is sufficient to ensure the desired effect is obtained.

It is unusual for the gardener to want all his plants from one sowing to mature within a short period, although if the intention is to deep-freeze florets for later use this can be convenient. For fresh consumption a good spread of harvesting from one sowing is what is needed. This can be achieved by transplanting some plants from the seedbed when they are five to six weeks old and storing others in the refrigerator, as described, for planting at weekly intervals over the next three weeks.

Cold-stored plants should not be transplanted when it is hot and sunny. It is best to try to choose a cool, dull day, but if this is impossible shade the transplants and sprinkle them with water for the first few days.

*Peas and beans* all flower without any environmental stimulus. They are inherently programmed to flower and are mostly true annuals in that, having flowered and produced seed, they then die. The exception is the runner bean which is a true perennial, although it is usually treated as an annual because its fleshy roots, which can survive from year to year, are usually killed by frosts. If you lift them in the early autumn and store them like dahlia tubers in moist sand or peat in a frost-free place, then you can plant them in late spring and stand a good chance of an earlier crop.

If you do decide to try this, be careful to save only the roots of healthy plants. You run the risk of accumulating diseases over the years if you continue to use this method of propagation.

To return to flowering, the most usual complaint of gardeners about peas and beans is not that they are short of flowers, but rather that many of the flowers fail to produce pods. In general, this failure of many flowers to set is entirely natural as once the plant has set some seed it concentrates its resources on those pods to ensure the survival of the species. The extent of the pod-load that a plant will stand depends very much on the plant's size. For example, when commercial varieties of peas are grown at close spacings, say, 60 per square metre (6 per square foot) the individual plants are small and each will only bear 3–5 pods that contribute to yield. Indeed, flowering stops once this number of pods has been set. A wider spacings, say, 20 per square metre (2 per square foot), the individual plants are larger, so that one will and can bear more pods. This is unlikely to be enough to keep the yield per unit area comparable to that obtained at the close spacing, but it would be more per plant, probably 6–10, and you would notice that the flowering period went on for longer. The same holds true for French beans, but with broad beans and runner beans there are complications.

The peas and French bean flowers pollinate themselves, whereas the broad beans and runner beans need insects to pollinate them. Thus, if there are no insects about to do the job, flowers of broad and runner beans will drop off even though the pod-load is not restricting them. Fortunately, they keep producing more flowers under these circumstances and sooner or later pod-set is obtained.

Experiments have clearly shown that syringing runner bean flowers with water does nothing to promote their setting pods. Warm weather that promotes plenty of insect activity is the only thing that will ensure the set of those first runner bean flowers. Thereafter, the most important factor which will help to give continuity of cropping is regular, frequent and thorough picking. If you see any pods that you missed when picking earlier and that have, as a result, got so big and tough as to be inedible, pick them off and throw them away. If you leave them on the plant it will only cause the flower buds or very young pods to drop off. Of course, poor growing conditions and, in particular, conditions that are too dry, will also cause the plant to carry a much reduced pod-load. So it is important that the roots are kept moist and proper attention has been paid to the nutritional needs of the crop. If this is done and you pick thoroughly and frequently, you should get good crops and a long picking period.

Recently, seedsmen have re-introduced white- and pink-flowered varieties of runner beans which are claimed to set pods more readily than the scarlet-flowered types. We have no evidence that would support this view.

*Tomatoes* never fail to produce flowers but sometimes the flowers on the first truss fail to open because the plant is growing so fast that they are bypassed and abort. More commonly, the flowers, particularly on the earliest trusses of outdoor crops, may fail to set. This is most likely to be because it has been too cold for the pollen to grow and fertilize the flower. The best temperature for the pollination of tomatoes is about 25 °C (77 °F), while at temperatures of about 5 °C (41 °F) pollination ceases. It is important to appreciate that we are talking here of the growth of the pollen needed to fertilize the flower. The transfer of pollen can sometimes cause problems in the still atmosphere of a glasshouse and shaking the plants to assist transfer is sensible. However, in the open, pollen transfer is not limited but low temperatures, particularly at night, can and do limit early fruit-set. Some newer, outdoor, bush varieties of tomato have been bred to have pollen which will be effective at temperatures as low as 6 °C (43 °F).

It is possible, however, to substitute for the pollen by spraying the open flowers with hormones. These stimulate the growth of the fruit even at temperatures too low for pollen to work, but the fruits will be seedless. It is important to follow the directions on dilution and application with great accuracy as hormones are likely to produce odd results if care is not taken. Properly used, they are entirely reliable and can be very helpful in giving you earlier tomatoes.

*Marrows, courgettes, cucumbers, ridge-cucumbers, and gherkins* all flower readily but have separate male and female flowers. Naturally, only the female flowers bear fruit. In all this group there is a tendency for the proportion of female flowers to increase as the days get longer. Gardeners often get frustrated by finding that the first flowers on their marrows are all male but this is only a manifestation of the lingering effect of the shorter days of early summer and very quickly female flowers are formed.

Marrows are the only ones in this group that may need some help with pollination. Pick off the male flowers when they are fully open, strip off the petals and thrust the pointed mass of anthers into the centre of the female flower. You can leave it there or pollinate more than one female flower with it by repeating the operation. Only pollination will ensure the growth of the marrow. Female flowers are easily recognized in all this group by the minifruit immediately behind the petals. The males have no such small fruits.

The only other problem is to ensure that frame-type or glasshouse-type cucumbers do not get pollinated. With most of the modern varieties this is no problem as they have been bred to produce only female flowers. If you choose to use one of the old varieties that produces male flowers you should remove them before they open so that insects do not get a chance to pollinate for you. It seems strange to be preventing pollination, but pollinated cucumber flowers tend to give flask-shaped fruits which are often bitter to eat and, of course, have seeds in them. The fruit has been bred to develop without pollination into the cucumber we know and enjoy.

It is sometimes recommended to pinch out the growing tip of young cucumber plants to induce branching. The plant then spreads out better to fill a square frame. This leads us now to consider what we are doing when we nip out growing points.

## Apical dominance and controlling growth

Although it is easy to nip off the growing tip of a shoot the consequences of doing so are complex and have been much studied by scientists.

Apical dominance is the scientific term for the control that the primary growing tip of a shoot exerts over the growth of the lateral buds. Those buds nearest the growing tip are dominated by it and do not grow. Such buds are, of course, the younger ones so it does not seem too unexpected that they do not immediately produce shoots. It also seems reasonable to suppose that the growing tip of the shoot takes priority for the supply of materials for growth.

As usual, there is some truth in these common-sense deductions but they are far from the whole story. Scientists have long ago shown that small amounts of a chemical substance called auxin is produced at the tip of growing shoots and in passing down the shoot it stops the leaf buds growing. As it passes down the shoot it becomes diluted and eventually is no longer effective, so the lower leaf buds can grow out and produce shoots.

Thus, if we want to make leaf buds grow and we know that the growing tip of the shoot is preventing them, we can nip out the growing tip and remove its dominance. It follows that we only need to remove the smallest tip which actually contains the growing point. We can leave all the young leaves as these do not exert any influence other than being useful in producing wanted components for growth.

Plants differ in the degree of apical dominance they exhibit. Any plant that produces a single stem with no branches, like a sunflower, has strong apical dominance. We see weak apical dominance in plants that are typically bushy in habit like sprouting broccoli. Onions have been bred for strong apical dominance in that usually one plant gives us only one bulb; occasionally a plant produces two or three bulbs within an outer casing which looks like one bulb. This is because some of the buds, which are present at the base of each scale, have grown and, in turn, produced a bulb. The dominance of the main growing point has been upset in some way, often by damage, to allow this to happen. However, in shallots we see a multiple sprouting from planted bulbs in contrast to the single sprouting we usually get from onion sets. In the shallot the lack of apical dominance in the bulb after storage is contrasted with the normal onion-like apical dominance seen in each daughter shallot as it grows. This serves to show us how finely tuned these systems have become as a result of hundreds of years of selection.

*Brussels sprouts* are above all other vegetable crops in exhibiting apical dominance on a grand scale. The leaf buds, the sprouts themselves, are large and important to us as the part we eat. We know the bottom sprouts will be ready to harvest first and now we recognize that one reason for this is that they are furthest away from the main growing point of the plant. If we want the upper sprouts to grow faster we can encourage this by removing the growing tip of the main stem. This is often done commercially to enable all the sprouts on a plant to be harvested at one time, so reducing harvesting costs and, in particular, making it possible to mechanize harvesting. Normally in the garden the cut-and-come-again progression of sprout growth on each plant is a blessing as it gives continuity of supply. But where, say, pigeons are troublesome in the winter there is a lot to be said for harvesting all the sprouts early and keeping the supply going by deep freezing.

If you remove the growing tip when the bottom sprouts are about the size of your little finger nail you will find that in due course you will have all the sprouts on the plant ready for a single harvest. This 'stopping', as it is termed, must be done at the right stage of growth as defined above, and before 1 October. If you leave it after that there is not enough good growing weather to get the effect required.

## Keeping growth in step with development

Scientists have found it convenient to recognize that the age measured in normal time, or the size of a plant, is not sufficient to describe it fully, so in addition they refer to its 'physiological age'. This is often a term used rather loosely, so it can mean different things depending on its context. Generally, though, plants are regarded as being of the same physiological age when they are at the same stage of development. Puberty (see p. 379) is an age-point on the time-scale of physiological age, as is flowering and seed ripening. There is one popular vegetable crop where the manipulation of physiological age is important to the gardener. This crop is the potato.

*Potatoes* are grown from seed tubers and it is their physiological age which has marked effects on yield and earliness. In brief, the 'younger' the seed tubers the lower is the early yield and if they are very young even final maincrop yield may be reduced. 'Middle-aged' seed tubers give the best maincrop yields and physiologically 'old' seed tubers the best early yield (Chapter 8, pp. 281–2). But how do we manipulate 'age' when the seed tubers are all bought at the shop and all planted within a month or so of each other?

All seed tubers are dormant when harvested and remain so for periods that vary with variety and the year and site of their growth. Once dormancy is over sprouts begin to appear as very tiny specks around the 'eyes' of the seed tuber. The warmer the conditions after dormancy has ended the quicker the sprouts will begin to grow, and it has been found that the length of the longest sprout, *when sprouting has taken place in daylight*, is a good measure of physiological age. Sprouting in daylight is most important since if kept in the dark the sprouts elongate excessively, are very fragile and their length is less representative of their 'age'. At temperatures below 4 °C (39 °F) sprout growth stops in most varieties, so such low temperatures can be used to keep seed 'young'.

Any temperature above 4 °C (39 °F) causes growth of the sprouts and experiments have shown that the length of the longest sprout is directly related to the number of day-degrees above 4 °C. This concept of day-degree is also discussed in Chapter 8 (p. 250) but quite simply a day at 8 °C is a day at 4 degrees above the lowest temperature for growth and counts as 4 day-degrees. Thus, a day at 6 °C (2 day-degrees), followed by a day at 10 °C (6 day-degrees) followed by a day at 4 °C (0 day-degrees) would give a total of 8 day-degrees.

With the old variety Home Guard harvested on 15 June, the highest yields were obtained with 'old' seed that had encountered about 1,000 day-degrees since harvest and had sprouts 80 mm. long. These yields were about 30 per cent more than those obtained from exactly similar seed tubers which had only encountered 100 day-degrees and had sprouts about 5 mm. long. By 30 June when another harvest was taken, the yields from 'old' and 'young' seed tubers were similar but 'middle-aged' seed tubers, which had encountered about 500 day-degrees and had sprouts 40 mm. (1½ in.) long at planting, were giving yields 27 per cent higher than either the 'younger' or 'older' seed.

Later still, on 18 July, the 'middle-aged' seed was still the best but now the 'younger' seed was only 13 per cent lower yielding. However, the 'oldest' seed was poorer yielding giving 17 per cent less than the 'middle-aged' seed. The plants from the old seed stopped growth and died down first and this is why they became the lowest yielding.

These results have been quoted in some detail as this whole subject is still in its infancy and it is slightly dangerous to assume that the same is true of all modern varieties and other crops in other places. However, the broad effects of advanced physiological age are becoming clear and can be listed as:

- earlier emergence after planting
- earlier commencement of tuber formation
- fewer tubers developing per plant
- smaller final plant size and a slower growth of the tubers
- an increased susceptibility to drought
- more nitrogen fertilizer needed to get maximum yield
- earlier die-down of the tops

These points are mostly self-evident summaries of behaviour that was exemplified by the results quoted with Home Guard. The high early yield from 'old' seed tubers is because they start to develop tubers earlier and concentrate their resources on relatively few tubers. However, late yield is poorer from old tubers because they are fewer, individually grow more slowly, and the plant dies sooner. The susceptibility to drought appears to be associated with a less extensive root system.

The preliminary indications with the maincrop variety Desiree are that an 'age' of 1,000 day-degrees is about the optimum for maximum yield at the end of the season.

Seed can start to 'age' before you buy it, so for maximum control of physiological age you should aim to purchase your seed as early as possible. If you can see the sprouts beginning to grow as tiny greenish white dots around the eyes, then you can be sure that the dormancy has finished and that 'age' is beginning to be clocked up. Remember that the guidance given on sprout length for Home Guard is for the length of the longest sprout when it has grown with enough light to prevent it elongating unduly.

Gardening is essentially the practical control of growth and development of cherished plants by manipulating their environment. The more you know about the factors affecting growth and development, the more successful you should be.

# Index